The Passion of
CLAUDE McKAY

Selected Poetry and
Prose, 1912-1948

Edited with an Introduction and Notes by
WAYNE F. COOPER

SCHOCKEN BOOKS · NEW YORK

To E. W. C.

Acknowledgments

This book was completed because of the active cooperation of many individuals and groups. I would particularly like to thank Claude McKay's daughter, Mrs. Hope McKay Virtue, and her agent, Mr. Carl Cowl, whose permission and patient moral support made this book possible in the first instance. I would also like to thank Mr. James Ivy, who made available to me the Claude McKay letters to him which appear in this volume; my thanks also to Dr. Herbert Aptheker, the executor of the W. E. B. Du Bois Papers, who furnished me with the McKay letter to Du Bois which is printed for the first time in this volume.

Before his death in 1969, Max Eastman generously loaned me his correspondence with Claude McKay and provided indispensable encouragement in the early stages of this work. Eastman remained to the end McKay's staunch friend and supporter, and I am grateful to Mrs. Max Eastman for her permission to print the two letters from Max Eastman to McKay included in Chapter 2. The Eastman Papers, including his correspondence with Claude McKay, are now housed in the Indiana University Library at Bloomington.

I would next like to thank the following publishers and journals for permission to include in this volume the poems, excerpts, and articles by Claude McKay listed below: Twayne Publishers, Inc. for permission to reprint from the *Selected Poems of Claude McKay* (New York, 1953), "The Tropics in New York," "Flame Heart," "My Mother," "The Plateau," "Adolescence," "Africa," "Outcast," "Enslaved," "In Bondage," "The Lynching," "To the White Fiends," "The White House," "Baptism," "If We Must Die," "The White City," "America," "Like a Strong Tree," "St. Isaac's Church, Petrograd," as well as the excerpt from "Tiger"; Harcourt Brace Jovanovich, Inc. for permission to reprint "Another White Friend," from Claude McKay, *A Long Way from Home,* Harvest Book edition (New York, 1970), and "The Business of Numbers," from Claude McKay, *Harlem: Negro Metropolis,* Harvest Book edition (New York, 1970); *Crisis* for permission to reprint "Soviet Russia and the Negro"; the *New Leader* for permission to reprint "Communism and the Negro," "On the League of American Writers," "Anti-

Semitism and the Negro," "A Reply to Ted Poston," "Nazism vs. Democracy," "Out of the War Years," and "North Africa and the Spanish Civil War"; the *Jewish Frontier* for permission to reprint "For Group Survival"; the *Nation* for permission to reprint "Harlem Runs Wild," "Labor Steps out in Harlem," and "North African Triangle"; *Opportunity* for permission to reprint "Race and Color in East Asia"; the *New York Amsterdam News* for permission to reprint "Negro Extinction or Survival," "On Adam Clayton Powell, Jr.," and "The Negro in the Future of American Democracy"; the W.C.C. Publishing Co. for permission to reprint from the *New York Herald-Tribune* "A Negro Writer to His Critics."

This book necessitated research at a succession of libraries, all of which provided exceptionally good service. These included the Tulane and Xavier University libraries in New Orleans, where my research first began; the Yale University Library, American Literature Collection, where the Claude McKay Papers form part of the James Weldon Johnson Memorial Collection of Negro Arts and Letters; the New York Public Library, which includes the Schomburg Collection of Negro Literature and History; and the Howard University Library in Washington, D.C. The Harvard University Library kindly furnished me with copies of the manuscript poems and letters of Claude McKay in their William Stanley Braithwaite Papers, and the U.S. Department of Labor Library twice made available to me Sylvia Pankhurst's radical weekly, the *Workers' Dreadnought*. Finally, I must add a word of personal thanks to Dr. Donald Gallup, the Curator of the American Literature Collection at Yale, and to his assistant, Mrs. Ann Whelpley; to Mrs. Jean Blackwell Hutson and Mr. Ernest Kaiser at the Schomburg Collection; and to Miss Dorothy Porter at the Howard University Library.

In addition I must acknowledge the help of a number of other individuals whose knowledge, encouragement, and criticism enabled me to complete this book. My thanks go first to Dr. Robert C. Reinders, now of Nottingham University in England. His high standards of scholarship and unassuming respect for all his students first enabled me to begin my research. I would also like to thank Frances Witlin of Brooklyn, New York. Her tactful but always honest criticisms helped me over numerous rough spots. Other persons who provided assistance and encouragement at crucial periods include Herbert Hill, Ben Waknin, and Glen Carrington —all of New York City; Selma Burke of New Hope and Pittsburgh, Pennsylvania; Kenneth Payne of London, England; and last but not least Daniel Moreau and Mrs. William Aspenwall Bradley of Paris, France.

Space does not permit the inclusion here of all who helped in innumerable ways toward the completion of this book. In conclusion, however, I owe a special acknowledgment to my parents and to my wife, Eleanor, who endured far beyond the call of duty.

In a work of this sort, of course, the final responsibility for any errors, distortions, or omissions lies with the editor and with him alone.

Throughout the text spelling, punctuation, and usage have occasionally been altered for the sake of consistency and for the reader's benefit.

W. C.

Contents

Illustration Section follows page 42.

I. THE RADICAL ESTRANGEMENT, 1912–1925

II. THE EXPATRIATE YEARS, 1923–1934

All my life I have been a troubadour
wanderer, nourishing myself mainly on the
poetry of existence. And all I offer here
is the distilled poetry of my experience.

—Claude McKay in *A Long Way from Home*

Introduction

This volume brings together for the first time a comprehensive selection of poetry and prose by Claude McKay, the pioneering Jamaican-American writer. Although best known as a leader in the Negro Renaissance of the 1920s, McKay's life actually encompassed a much greater period, spanning the six decades between 1889 and 1948. His work reflects to an unusual degree the action and passion of his times.

As a Jamaican schoolboy at the end of Victoria's reign, as a West Indian immigrant to the United States, as a radical during the First World War, as an expatriate in Europe and North Africa throughout most of the 1920s, and as a prophetic champion of the black masses in the United States during the 1930s and 1940s— McKay transcends any one decade or movement. In fact, his literary significance can be understood only within the full context of his life and career.

McKay was necessarily preoccupied with the place of the Negro in the modern world. Western civilization left him no other choice. His very preoccupation, however, made imperative a larger effort on his part to comprehend and relate to the great social and political forces of his age. McKay sought a viable identity as a black man; he also tried to understand the various ways blacks as a whole could best participate in the larger human community. Such an endeavor did not take place within a historical vacuum. Nor was it of brief duration. The selections in this anthology, therefore, go well beyond the concerns of any one race or decade. The poems, articles, letters, and stories contained herein bespeak a spiritual odyssey toward the very uncertain present we know today.

As much as any single man, McKay led the revolt during the Negro Renaissance period against the restraints that had traditionally been imposed upon black writers in the United States. In contrast to the innocuous plantation dialect of Paul Laurence Dunbar at the turn of the century, McKay's militant verse after World War I breathed anger, alienation, and rebellion into American Negro poetry. And later, in *Home to Harlem* (1928), he created a raw novel of black lower-class life that flew in the face of the older, more genteel portraits of Negro existence in the fiction of Dunbar, Charles Chesnutt, and W. E. B. Du Bois.[1]

Although a seminal figure in the development of modern black literary themes, McKay has received little critical attention or public recognition. The reasons for this neglect are no doubt many and complex, but to a large extent he has simply shared the fate of most black writers who matured in the 1920s. For McKay, as well as for other notables of the Negro Renaissance—Jean Toomer, Countee Cullen, Rudolph Fisher, and Wallace Thurman, to name a few—the Wall Street crash of 1929 destroyed the economic props that had supported their earlier development. At the same time, it swept away the unique social circumstances that in the 1920s had encouraged the development of a group of self-conscious but relatively individualistic and undogmatic black literati. The Great Depression hit America's black communities especially hard and disrupted a decade of promising cultural growth marked by an intense preoccupation with the Negro's folk heritage. In the 1930s, Negro writers generally turned outward and considered their own situation in relation to the larger problems that beset society. Moreover, those whites who had responded so enthusiastically to jazz, Harlem, and the Negro vogue in the Roaring Twenties, quickly moved on to more pressing economic concerns shared by everyone in the 1930s. As a result, the New Negro, who had sprung so abruptly out of America's postwar ferment, just as suddenly faded before the new social and political militancy of the literary left during the Depression years. To many critics, and to some of the Renaissance figures themselves, their earlier efforts appeared in retrospect to have been only part of another insubstantial fad from a decade of frenzied self-delusion.[2]

After 1940 the writers of the Negro Renaissance sank even further into the shadows of critical memory. In that year Richard Wright produced *Native Son;* thereafter, Wright's overwhelming stature dominated the critical imagination of blacks and whites alike and threw the pioneering achievements of the Negro Renaissance into deep eclipse. Wright's pre-eminence in the black literary scene has ever since tended to discourage any thorough examination of those black writers who matured earlier in the century. Many critics still recognize no serious black literary achievements before him.[3]

The present collection should help to correct such shortsighted views by demonstrating the relevance of Claude McKay to contemporary developments in black American literature. His life and work represent, after all, a continuous chain of creative development stretching from the time of Booker T. Washington forward toward the Black Power movement of the late 1960s.

The youngest son of a prosperous black peasant farmer, Festus Claudius McKay was born September 15, 1889, on the family farm in the hills of Clarendon Parish in south central Jamaica. His parents, Thomas Francis and Ann Elizabeth Edwards McKay, were pillars in the local Baptist church and were respected as leaders in their isolated rural community of Sunny Ville. Although scarcely a generation removed from slavery, they succeeded through hard work in pushing their children into Jamaica's newly emerging black middle class.[4]

Claude spent his grammar school years with an older brother, Uriah Theophilus McKay, who at the turn of the century was teaching school in a small town near Montego Bay. It was under "U'Theo's" tutelage that Claude received his early education. After completing grammar school, he was for awhile apprenticed to a wheelwright and cabinetmaker in Brown's Town, St. Ann's Parish; but after his mother's death in 1910, he went to Kingston, where he joined the island's constabulary. He had grown into a sensitive and handsome young man of medium height and build, "whose eyebrows arched high up and never came down, and his finely modeled features wore in consequence a fixed expression of ironical and rather mischievous scepticism." [5]

McKay left home to escape his father's inhibiting religious fundamentalism and to establish a life of his own. Like U'Theo before him, he had rejected his father's Christian fundamentalism and considered himself a freethinker and Darwinian evolutionist. Although McKay respected his father, he was never able to accept his narrow, Old Testament severity of character. He instead identified most completely with his mother. "My mother," he wrote, "didn't care very much about what people did and why and how they did it. She only wanted to help them if they were in trouble. . . . She loved all people. It was a rich warm love." [6]

Although already a rebel where religion was concerned, McKay's general stock of ideas in 1910 seems to have been rather conventional. "The direction of our schooling," he once wrote, "was of course English, and it was so successful that we really believed we were little black Britons."

McKay's experience as a "constab" tried to the breaking point such insular complacency. As an idealistic recruit fresh from the country, he was revolted by the brutality and corruption that constantly imposed itself upon him as a seemingly normal part of the policeman's lot. He also disliked with equal intensity the unending discipline of a semimilitary life and the policeman's preoccupation with "making cases." Above all, McKay resented the class distinctions he found in Kingston. He was especially resentful of the scorn exhibited by the urban whites and mulattoes toward peasants newly arrived from the country, and he was appalled to learn that as a constable he was viewed with distrust by his fellow blacks, who considered all policeman allies of the upper classes. In his early Jamaican poetry, McKay responded to these experiences by reaffirming his black peasant origins and expressing a desire to return to the tranquil countryside of his youth. His reaffirmation, however, was imbued with a disillusionment and pessimism that could not be cured by a simple retreat to the countryside.[7]

McKay had begun to write poems in childhood, and as an adolescent he had composed many verses in stilted, self-conscious imitation of the English models set before him as a child of British colonialism. In Brown's Town, however, he had chanced to meet an English student of the Jamaican dialect, Walter Jekyll, who pointed out to him the beauty of his native dialect and urged him as a talented black to write in the vernacular. After some hesitation, McKay agreed and under Jekyll's guidance and patronage, he produced his first literary works.[8]

In 1912, at the age of twenty-three, he authored two volumes of dialect poetry, *Songs of Jamaica* and *Constab Ballads.*[9] These early works revealed his strong lyric gift and his keen sensitivity to the good and evil in man and nature. They also betrayed his youthful naiveté and provincialism.

In his excellent study *Les poètes nègres des Etats-Unis,* Jean Wagner emphasizes the realism of McKay's Jamaican portraits, and he favorably contrasts McKay's dialect verse with Paul Laurence Dunbar's in the United States. Of the two Wagner concludes McKay's was more purely and authentically of the people, "for whom it was written." [10] Wagner can be faulted, however, for failing to make clear the deep ambivalence in the youthful poet's work. For while he was stoutly affirming loyalty to his fellow blacks in Jamaica, McKay was also wistfully yearning in his dialect poems for another spiritual homeland, England. Both of his dialect volumes contain many poems that reflect a naive infatuation with all things British, an infatuation that McKay undoubtedly shared with most educated Jamaicans during this period. He expressed it most directly and simply in the poem "Old England":

> I've a longin' in me dept's of heart dat I can
> conquer not,
> 'Tis a wish dat I've been havin' from since I could
> form a t'o't,
> Just to view de homeland England, in de streets
> of London walk,
> An' to see de famous sights dem 'bouten which
> dere's so much talk,
> An' to watch de fact'ry chimneys pourin' smoke up
> to de sky,
> An' to see de matches-children, dat I hear 'bout
> passin' by.

He concludes his imaginative tour with trips to famous national landmarks, climaxed by a visit to "de lone spot where in peaceful solitude/ rests de body of our Missis Queen, Victoria de Good." [11] The poem ends with his satisfied return to Jamaica.

As an educated youth of black peasant origins, McKay thus displayed to a painful degree the psychological ambivalence inculcated among West Indians under British colonialism. Both the strength and weakness of his dialect poetry flowed from this attempt to embrace his black Jamaican origins, while simultaneously clinging to Britain as a spiritual homeland. He was not an Englishman and could not become one; yet custom and education mandated his adherence to British imperialistic values and traditions. He consequently demonstrated in his dialect poetry what Paul Bohannan has described as the "working misunderstanding," which typifies relations between colonized and colonizer the world over.[12] *Songs of Jamaica* and *Constab Ballads* were nevertheless pioneering attempts by a black West Indian to portray realistically the life of his people. At the very least, they remain invaluable historical documents, richly illustrative of Jamaican psychology and social values prior to World War I. In addition, a familiarity with these early works is indispensable to a full appreciation of McKay's subsequent development.

For despite his youthful obeisance to British colonialism, McKay had grown to manhood in a society whose population was overwhelmingly black and largely free from the overt white oppression which constricted the lives of black Americans in the United States during this same period. A remembrance of this black, rural environment, strong upon its own foundations, would always sustain him during the restless wanderings of his later years.

Finally, one can see even in McKay's early Jamaican development a propensity for rebellion that foreshadowed the direction his career would take in the United States and Europe. In a short preface to *Constab Ballads,* he summed up his personality in a disarmingly candid self-analysis:

> Let me confess it at once. I had not in me the stuff that goes to making a good constable; for I am so constituted that imagination outruns discretion, and it is my misfortune to have a most improper sympathy with wrongdoers. I, therefore, never "made cases," but turning like Nelson, a blind eye to what it was my manifest duty to see, tried to make peace which seemed to me better.
>
> Moreover, I am by temperament unadaptive; by which I mean that it is not in me to conform cheerfully to uncongenial usages. We blacks are all somewhat impatient of discipline and to the natural impatience of my race there was added in my particular case, a peculiar sensitiveness which made certain forms of discipline irksome, and a fierce hatred of injustice. Not that I ever openly rebelled, but the rebellion was in my heart, and it was fomented by the inevitable rubs of daily life—trifles to most of my comrades, but to me calamities and tragedies. To relieve my feelings, I wrote poems, and into them I poured my heart in its various moods.[13]

To the conservative, ultra-British Jamaican elite, white and black, McKay's verse seemed a novel, but harmless departure from the prevalent classical norms. Most found it entertaining but discounted its seriousness.[14] Nevertheless, *Songs of Jamaica* and *Constab Ballads* were well received, and McKay gained a certain notoriety. In recognition of his accomplishment, the Jamaican Institute of Kingston awarded him a gold medal. He was the first black to have been so honored by the Institute.

For his part, McKay returned to his father's farm, determined somehow to find a place among his rural kinsmen. He did not expect to earn his way as a poet. He chose instead to devote his energies to the advancement of Jamaican agriculture. To prepare for this task, he decided to attend Booker T. Washington's famed Tuskegee Institute in Alabama. The next major phase of his career thus began with his arrival in the United States. The same year his dialect poetry appeared he left Jamaica to study agronomy at Tuskegee.

Nothing in his Jamaican experience had prepared McKay for the vicious realities of American race relations. In British Jamaica, racism had over time and by slow degrees blended into a class consciousness that assigned whites and near whites to the top of the social scale; but by extending civil liberties to everyone, the black masses were also left with the hope that they too could advance to higher social positions through education and hard work. Many black Jamaicans in McKay's childhood did own their own land, and they were more often burdened by rural poverty and isolation than by any keen sense of racial oppression, no matter how prominently such oppression may have figured in the larger scheme.[15] In 1912 such was not the case for Negroes in the United States.

There the status of the Negro had reached its lowest level since the Civil War. By legal and illegal means, the Reconstruction Amendments guaranteeing him full citizenship had been largely circumvented, especially in the South, and the Negro had once again been pushed by the combined forces of law and popular prejudice into a permanently inferior color caste. The white majority who towered over him was by turns benevolently paternalistic and viciously repressive. In such a system, the Negro was at best an object of pity, and at worst, a creature of contempt.

McKay reacted to this state of affairs with incredulity and anger, although nearly six years passed before he finally channeled his anger into a decisive rebellion against the social system which supported such injustices.

After six months in Alabama, he transferred to the less oppressive surroundings of Kansas State College, in Manhattan, Kansas, where he remained for two years. There he moved uneasily among a small, midwestern black elite, who cautiously maintained their precarious status amid an intermittently hostile white majority. Relief from this sterile environment came in 1914, when McKay received "a few thousand dollars" from "an English admirer" of his Jamaican dialect verse.[16] With this windfall McKay left Kansas and went to New York City, where he invested his capital in a small restaurant. While establishing himself as a restaurateur, he asked a childhood sweetheart, Eulalie Imelda Edwards, to join him in New York. She accepted his proposal, and they were married on July 30, 1914.

As it turned out, his marriage and business lasted only a few months, primarily, it would seem, because New York had awakened in him new interests and sensations, which proved inimical to domesticity. The city's size, energy, and variety all nourished his restless spirit of adventure; above all, he found in Harlem a refuge among his own people.

Before too long, "high living" and "bad business" had swallowed all his money. His marriage was next to go. "My wife," McKay wrote in 1918, "wearied of the life in six months and returned to Jamaica." After her return, she gave birth to their only child, Ruth Hope, whom Claude was destined never to see.[17]

McKay had reached a turning point. Even in Jamaica his adherence to the conventions of middle-class respectability had been tenuous and fraught with fundamental dissatisfactions. Now, with the end of his marriage, there was nothing to hold him to conventional ambitions, and he decided to pursue seriously a writing career. His original intention—to return to Jamaica and teach agronomy—had ended with his move to New York.

For the next five years, he held a series of odd jobs in and around New York and began once again to write poetry. In his new American verse, McKay dropped the use of dialect altogether and began to write in standard English. His absorption in the traditions of English poetry had been evident in his dialect verse, and he now reverted to traditional sonnet and short lyric forms, reminiscent of the Elizabethans and English Romantics. In an age of stylistic experiment and innovation, he thus clung devotedly to those conventional forms most revered by the educated elite of nineteenth-century Jamaica. Through these older forms, however, he conveyed a startlingly bitter, and essentially modern, message of despair, alienation, and rebellion.

While McKay was returning to the conservative poetic style of his youth, he was, ironically, moving far to the left politically. When he finally embraced socialism at the end of World War I, it was with the poet's intuitive logic and with an enthusiasm akin to religious zeal:

My ear is tuned unto new voices shrieking
Their jarring notes of life-exalting strife;
My soul soars singing, with flame-forces seeking
The grandest purpose, noblest path of life;
Where scarlet pennants blaze like tongues of fire
There—where high passion swells—is my heart's desire.[18]

World War I and the Russian Revolution precipitated this fervid commitment, but the grounds for such acceptance had been long in the making. All his life McKay had witnessed the practical effects of market economics on the lives of ordinary people. As the son of a farmer, he had learned early how the laws of economic colonialism, operating in the international marketplace, affected agricultural prices, and hence the lives of Jamaican peasants. Later in Kingston he had become involved in a labor dispute over an increase in the city's streetcar fares. Identifying with the protesters, he had contributed to their cause a remarkable poem, whose theme anticipated the practices of Gandhi in India and Martin Luther King, Jr., in the United States (see p. 116). Even as he sought a place in Jamaica's conservative social structure, he had displayed a tense impatience that threatened open rebellion.

By the time McKay left Jamaica, he had acquired a general understanding of socialist doctrines. In fact, *Songs of Jamaica* had been dedicated to the Fabian Socialist Sir Sydney Olivier, who in 1912 was serving as the island's governor. McKay himself, however, never actively espoused the socialist cause until after 1918.

The sustained shock of American racism gradually broke McKay's attachment to the political status quo, and once in New York, he swung to the left. An expanded racial loyalty accompanied his growing radicalism. As variously a stevedore, porter, houseman, and finally as a dining-car waiter on the Pennsylvania Railroad during World War I, McKay came to know, appreciate, and identify with the transient black workers of America's industrial northeast, just as he had previously identified with the newly arrived black peasantry in urban Kingston.

In Jamaica he had sought a place within the framework of British imperialism; as a black man, he had attempted to reconcile himself to the Social Darwinist ideas then prevalent, which assigned the black race to the bottom of mankind's "natural" ladder of progress. By such pseudoscientific rationalization, the white man absolved himself from any responsibility for the Negro's impoverishment. If blacks wished to advance, they must prove their worth, as Booker T. Washington was attempting to do at Tuskegee.[19] The stark oppressiveness of American race relations finally revealed to McKay the hypocrisy of such ideas and enabled him to perceive the exploitive nature of world capitalism. Finally, and most decisively,

World War I destroyed for him, as it did for many other colonials, all illusions concerning European invincibility. When the Russian Revolution occurred, therefore, McKay was ready to accept Bolshevism as a first step toward the eventual restructuring of world society. For McKay it was imperative that blacks everywhere should be ready to participate in the coming revolution: "Africa! long ages sleeping, O my motherland,/ awake!" [20]

In New York McKay eagerly read the many radical and bohemian literary journals that flourished there. From the first, he sought publication in them. When he finally emerged upon the American literary scene, it was in company with the celebrated literati of Greenwich Village, which by World War I had become the center of New York's cultural avant-garde. In 1917, Waldo Frank and James Oppenheim accepted for *Seven Arts Magazine* two of his sonnets, "The Harlem Dancer" and "Invocation." [21] A year later he was discovered by Frank Harris and brought to public notice again in *Pearson's Magazine*.

During his first years in New York, McKay was especially attracted to the *Masses,* that uninhibited journal of revolutionary politics and art edited by Max Eastman, John Reed, and Floyd Dell. "I liked," he later recalled, "its slogans, its make-up, and above all, its cartoons."

> There was a difference, a freshness in its social information. And I felt a special interest in its sympathetic and iconoclastic items about the Negro. . . . There was one issue particularly which carried a powerful bloody brutal cover drawing by Robert Minor. The drawing was of Negroes tortured on crosses deep down in Georgia. I bought the magazine and tore the cover off, but it haunted me for a long time. There were other drawings of Negroes by an artist named Stuart Davis. I thought they were the most superbly sympathetic drawings of Negroes done by an American. And to me they have never been surpassed.[22]

McKay submitted several poems to the *Masses,* but it was not until after the magazine was suppressed by the Federal government in 1917 for its militant opposition to the war, and then resurrected as the *Liberator,* that he was finally published in it.

In 1919 he met the magazine's chief editor, Max Eastman, who was impressed by McKay and his poetry. Despite obvious differences in their backgrounds, the two had much in common and soon became friends. Eastman's parents had been Congregationalist ministers in upstate New York, but like McKay he had rejected his parents' religion. At the time of their meeting, both men placed great faith in science as an alternative to religion and both believed socialism was "an experiment that ought to be tried." Where politics were concerned, however, neither was blindly dogmatic. Under Eastman's leadership, the *Masses* and the *Liberator* printed a wide spectrum of left-wing opinion, ranging from expressions of "Wobbly" anarchism to "progressive" bourgeois reformism. Both Eastman and McKay generally shared the same ideas regarding the arts, especially poetry. Neither was a stylistic innovator. Both adhered stubbornly to classical forms in composing their own verse, but McKay was in fact more inclined than Eastman to tolerate such innovators as T. S. Eliot and e. e. cummings. Finally, both men sought great freedom in their personal lives. In July 1919, McKay wrote to Eastman: "I was glad to see how you live—so unaffectedly free—not striving to be like the masses like some radicals, but just yourself. I *love* your life—more than your poetry, more than your personality." [23]

In short, although McKay usually accepted Eastman's criticism concerning his poetry and sometimes looked upon the older man as a sort of father confessor, their meeting was from the first essentially one of equals. And as their friendship grew and ripened, it remained on the basis of mutual respect for one another's ideas and personalities. Because of Eastman's greater fame, there arose a tendency in later years for many to regard McKay as merely his ideological protégé. Such was never the case, as the selections in this volume make clear.

As a result of his meeting with Eastman, McKay quickly gained acceptance as a member of the *Liberator* circle in Greenwich Village. Eventually, as a member of the magazine's editorial staff, he would encounter an impressive roster of American writers and artists. The successor to the *Masses,* the *Liberator* attracted many of the nation's best, including men and women as diverse as William Gropper, Adolph Dehn, Edmund Wilson, John Dos Passos, John Reed, Elinor Wylie, Jo Davidson, Carl Sandburg, and Helen Keller.[24]

In 1919 Eastman and his staff were eagerly praising the young Communist government of Russia, violently denouncing the repressive postwar hysteria at home, and writing stories and poems that ranged from fighting proletarian propaganda to tender pieces on home and mother. Few magazines, then or now, could match the

Liberator in enthusiasm. "On the surface," Daniel Aaron has written, "the *Liberator* reflected the aimless, pointless life of the Village." Yet, after World War I it displayed a "toughness and militancy in its social attitudes" that belied its Bohemian character.[25]

Into such an atmosphere McKay fitted well. Eastman described him then as a very black, handsome, high-spirited young man "whose attitude toward life is like Shelley's, free and yet strenuously idealistic. . . ." [26] Another old radical, Joseph Freeman, also remembered in his autobiography McKay's charm, wit, and passion.[27]

If McKay was sometimes given to gaiety, he had good reason in the summer of 1919 to exhibit a greater seriousness, as well as toughness. Nineteen-hundred nineteen was the year of the Great Red Scare, one desperate phase in the national effort to return to prewar normalcy. For Negroes, whose large wartime migrations to the urban North threatened the nation's racial status quo, the year turned into a nightmare of bloody riots and violent death. From June until January there occurred no less than twenty-five riots in major urban centers throughout the country. The Chicago riot of July was the worst. When it was over, authorities counted thirty-eight Negroes and whites dead, over 520 injured and over a thousand families homeless.[28] Like all Negroes, McKay felt the emotional effects of such battles.

In the July 1919 *Liberator* he responded to these events with a two-page spread of sonnets, whose revolutionary ardor won him instant recognition among Negro Americans. Above all, blacks responded enthusiastically to his poem "If We Must Die," accepting it as an eloquent expression of every black man's feeling of desperation and defiance before white mobs (see p. 124). The poem was widely reprinted in the nation's black press, and McKay was at once acknowledged to be an important new poet by black Americans.

Before his new public could further acquaint themselves with this bold newcomer, however, he abruptly left the United States. In the fall of 1919, only a few months after his first *Liberator* appearance, McKay seized a passing chance to visit Great Britain. Two English admirers of his poetry, who were passing through New York from the Orient on their way to Spain, invited him along. Because they offered to pay all expenses, he agreed to accept a passage across the Atlantic, but alone and only as far as England and the Low Countries.[29]

As it turned out, McKay remained in London for more than a year. While there he advanced his literary career in two ways. First, he established a friendship with the critic and editor C. K. Ogden, who in the summer of 1920 published a generous sampling of his poetry in the prestigious *Cambridge Magazine.* Later in the year, he also arranged for the publication of McKay's first slim volume of new verse, *Spring in New Hampshire.* Ogden even persuaded his friend and fellow critic I. A. Richards to write a brief preface to the pamphlet-sized book. "The poems here selected may, in the opinion of not a few who have seen them in periodical form, claim a place beside the best work that the present generation is producing in this country." [30] But forty-six years later Richards said: "I never met McKay and I haven't read his poetry since." [31]

In England McKay continued his involvement in radical politics and acquired valuable journalistic experience by working in London with Sylvia Pankhurst on her small communist weekly, the *Workers' Dreadnought.* A famous suffragette, Sylvia Pankhurst had become a militant socialist during World War I. As one of the most vocal members of Britain's small, newly emerging Communist party, she was stoutly championing the Soviet cause when McKay met her. He had no illusions about Pankhurst's miniscule influence on the British left, but he admired her energy and zeal. He also found in her an uncompromising defender of dark-skinned colonials against the day-to-day injustices of British and European imperialism. [32]

As a member of the *Dreadnought* staff throughout most of 1920, McKay performed various editorial duties and contributed a number of articles, book reviews, and poems to its pages. In contrast to the poems which appeared in the *Cambridge Magazine,* his *Dreadnought* verses were for the most part proletarian doggerel of the worst sort. Most read as if they had been written on the back of envelopes twenty minutes before press time. For this reason, perhaps, some appeared under the pseudonym Hugh Hope, and only one was ever reprinted in his published volumes.

In a real sense McKay completed in London the political self-education he had begun in the United States. At the International Club in East Road Shoreditch, he heard a wide range of British and European left-wing speakers and was impelled for the first time to read the works of Karl Marx. [33] On the more personal side, he experienced during his stay an extreme disillusionment with England and Englishmen in general.

As a young man in Jamaica he had embraced British culture as his own and had idolized its great men of letters. Once in the United States, of course, he had acquired a broader, soberer view of the world. But he had, nevertheless, gone to England with some of his old schoolboy enthusiasm still intact. After all, as a "black Briton," was he not at last going home? Once among the English, however, McKay quickly discovered that the kinship he felt for them was not reciprocated. On the contrary, he found all classes and shades of political opinion imbued with frank, scarcely conscious assumptions of racial superiority, as well as with an amazing ignorance of the psychological effects European imperialist rule had had upon the colonized peoples of the world.

McKay was especially critical of the British left's obtuseness regarding racial and colonial matters, and he voiced doubts about their ability to seize the opportunities afforded international Communism by the spread of nationalist movements in Ireland, India and elsewhere in the colonial world (on this point, see pp. 57ff.). As a consequence, when McKay returned to New York early in 1921, he was not only thoroughly disenchanted with England but also more critical of socialist politicians and their politics.[34]

After his return McKay resumed his association with the *Liberator,* and in April 1921, he joined its editorial staff. For the next fifteen months, he participated directly in its monthly production and contributed a steady stream of poems and articles to its pages. During this period the *Liberator*'s circulation at times reached 60,-000; in terms of both its readership and list of contributors, it was the leading journal of revolutionary politics and art in the United States.[35]

In joining the *Liberator* and espousing the Bolshevik cause, McKay placed himself outside the mainstream of American Negro protest, which since 1909 had been best represented by the National Association for the Advancement of Colored People. Through vigorous moral suasion and unremitting legal action, the NAACP hoped eventually to win for all Negroes full citizenship under the American Constitution.

Although he had become a member of Greenwich Village's radical bohemia, McKay was at the same time ideologically linked to a small but talented group of black socialists who emerged in Harlem toward the end of World War I. Of these, A. Philip Randolph and Chandler Owen became the best known and most widely respected; along with W. A. Domingo, they edited the *Messenger,* which was the first and most influential Negro socialist monthly in the country. Other prominent black radicals of the period included Cyril Briggs, the editor of the *Crusader* and the founder of the semisecret African Blood Brotherhood; William Bridges, editor of the *Challenge;* and McKay's personal friend, Hubert H. Harrison, editor of the short-lived *New Negro*. All these men acknowledged at one time or another the importance of race protest and agitation and their intellectual debt to such older leaders as Frederick Douglass, William Monroe Trotter, and W. E. B. Du Bois. But they harshly criticized the NAACP for neglecting the economic aspects of the Negro problem. They maintained that the achievement of "full citizenship" in a capitalistic society would be meaningless as long as Negroes remained an economically oppressed group.[36]

A number of these early Harlem socialists, including McKay, sought to influence Marcus Garvey's back-to-Africa nationalist movement during its early development at the end of World War I. In 1920, for example, Harrison helped edit Garvey's weekly paper, the *Negro World;* Briggs sought to join forces with Garvey but was spurned; McKay had announced his support of Garvey's movement while in England and had sent the *Negro World* a series of articles about a Negro soldiers-and-sailors club he frequented in London.[37]

After joining the *Liberator* editorial staff in 1921, McKay arranged for several "black reds" from Harlem to meet with him in the *Liberator* office to discuss, among other things, the possibility of making the Garvey movement more class-conscious. Nothing positive came of such efforts. Marcus Garvey himself remained the main obstacle to any implementation of McKay's ideas. Garvey adamantly opposed socialism and felt that "the fundamental issue of life [is] the appeal of race to race . . . of clan to clan . . . of tribe to tribe, of observing the rule that self-preservation was the first law of nature."[38] (For McKay's contemporary observations concerning Garvey and his Universal Negro Improvement Association, see pp. 53, 65–69.)

It was also during 1921 and 1922 that McKay first became acquainted with the more solidly established Negro intelligentsia of New York, many of whom were officials in the NAACP. Some were themselves writers and were anxious to meet the dashing young Jamaican who was making such a name for himself in Greenwich Village. The NAACP group included W. E. B. Du Bois, for many years the editor of the *Crisis,* the Association's official journal; James Weldon Johnson, field secretary (later executive secretary) for the

NAACP; the young Walter White, pale and blue-eyed, who made a name for himself as a special NAACP investigator covering lynchings in the deep South; and Jessie Fauset, the literary editor of the *Crisis*.

These individuals showed great respect for McKay, but only one, the cosmopolitan Johnson, ever became a truly close friend. The rest, while applauding his poetry, remained wary of his militant radicalism.

Although McKay became acquainted with both radical and reformist elements in New York's black population during this period, his success with a predominantly white journal in Greenwich Village placed him in a social category apart from either group. As a result, he established no firm and lasting place for himself among the black reformists, on the one hand, or with Harlem's radical elements, on the other. Accordingly, McKay suffered from a personal and social isolation within the black American community that would grow more acute with time.[39]

This is not to say that he did not identify with American blacks during these years. On the contrary, he felt naturally allied with those black workingmen and women with whom he had labored from 1914 until 1919. And it was these people, the common blacks of America's urban ghettoes, who would later occupy the central place in his novels and short stories during the late 1920s and early 1930s.

As a *Liberator* editor in 1921 and 1922, he had two principal concerns. From a political point of view, he sought to alert white radicals to the importance of blacks as necessary allies in any successful radical movement in the United States (see p. 73). At the same time, he wished to awaken blacks themselves to the new possibilities for social change that flowed from World War I, the Russian Revolution, and the resurgence of suppressed nationalities in Europe and Asia. McKay's second major concern during this period was with his poetry. As a poet, he conveyed a deeply personal but no less significant social message. Through his sonnets and other short lyrics, which appeared regularly in the pages of the *Liberator,* he spelled out with clarity and precision the bitter anger and profound alienation he experienced as a black man in a white-dominated society. Although couched in the highly personal terms of the lyric poet, his was an alienation clearly shared in varying degrees by all blacks as an inevitable condition of their existence within the American racial caste system.

Upon returning to the United States from England, McKay had

once again faced the bitter truth that outside Greenwich Village and a few progressive circles, there was no welcome for a Negro in America. At a time, therefore, when he was achieving his greatest success as a poet and probably had more white than black friends, he was also writing some of his most bitter "race" poems.[40] His contributions to the *Liberator* during this period make it clear that his primary concern was the well-being of his race, not theoretical Marxism. Communism was to be a means to an end, and that end was full freedom for the black man.

In the spring of 1922, McKay's reputation as a poet was greatly enhanced by the publication of his fourth volume of verse, *Harlem Shadows.* By far his most important book of poetry, it contained all the best poems he had written since his first arrival in the United States in 1912.

There were seventy poems in *Harlem Shadows,* and thematically they could be about equally divided into three categories—nostalgic poems concerning Jamaica and nature, love poems, and poems bearing on racial themes. Almost all the poems in his previous book, *Spring in New Hampshire,* were included in *Harlem Shadows.*

With the appearance of *Harlem Shadows,* McKay was immediately acclaimed the best Negro poet since Paul Laurence Dunbar. The *New York Times* noted that McKay's efforts marked a clean break with the dialect tradition of Dunbar. It also noted McKay's preference for "the more conservative verse forms" and speculated that he was perhaps attempting to portray the spirit of the modern Negro "in a high and lofty manner." The reviewer concluded by stating that although "certain portions unravel into mere sentiment," McKay had by and large succeeded in his purpose.[41]

The most searching review was Robert Littel's in the *New Republic.* Littel considered McKay "a real poet, though by no means a great one. . . . A hospitality to echoes of poetry he has read has time and again obscured a direct sense of life and made rarer those lines of singular intensity which express . . . [his] naked force of character." Littel nevertheless praised McKay where he thought praise was due, and he was especially impressed by his protest poetry. In the same review he also surveyed James Weldon Johnson's *Book of American Negro Poetry* and wrote:

> If McKay and the other poets don't stir me unusually when they travel over the poetic roads so many others have traveled . . . they make me sit up and take notice when they write about their race

and ours. They strike hard and pierce deep. It is not merely poetic emotion they express, but something fierce and constant, and icy cold, and white hot.[42]

Negro reviewers were generally less reserved in their assessment of McKay's poetry. Walter White, for instance, called McKay "without doubt the most talented and versatile of the new school of imaginative, emotional Negro poets." He ended his review by boldly asserting that "Mr. McKay is not a great Negro poet—he is a great poet." [43] James Weldon Johnson in the *New York Age* reaffirmed White's contention:

> Mr. McKay is a real poet and a great poet. . . . No Negro has sung more beautifully of his race than McKay and no poet has ever equalled the power with which he expresses the bitterness that so often rises in the heart of the race. . . . The race ought to be proud of a poet capable of voicing it so fully. Such a voice is not found every day. . . . What he has achieved in this little volume sheds honor upon the whole race.[44]

With *Harlem Shadows* McKay became in effect the pacesetter for a new generation of black American poets and novelists, who, as the Twenties progressed, would move significantly beyond the genteel tradition of previous generations in their exploration of the black American experience. By the time Alain Locke formally introduced the "New Negro" in his famous anthology of 1925, McKay himself would already be embarked on a new career as an expatriate novelist.[45]

McKay's role as a *Liberator* editor ended not long after the publication of *Harlem Shadows*. Earlier, in November 1921, Max Eastman had resigned as chief editor in order to devote himself to creative writing. The *Liberator* was a co-operative endeavor, controlled and managed by the writers and artists on its staff, and upon Eastman's recommendation they agreed that McKay and Michael Gold should together be appointed as his successors. Accordingly, with the January 1922 issue McKay and Gold assumed their new roles as co-editors of the magazine. It proved to be an unhappy harnessing of two strong, but opposing personalities.

Michael Gold, whose real name was Irwin Granich, was a young American Jew who had grown up in the slums of New York's lower East Side. In both his manners and his writings he always emphasized his proletarian background. "He affected dirty shirts," Joseph Freeman remembered, "a big, black uncleaned Stetson with the brim of a sombrero; smoked stinking, twisted Italian three-cent cigars, and spat frequently and vigorously on the floor—whether that floor was covered by an expensive carpet in a rich aesthetic's studio or on the bare wooden floor of [his] . . . small office." [46]

From the start he and McKay found working together difficult. McKay had little of Gold's proletarian air and could at times affect a haughty, British-West Indian aristocratic manner that irritated both Gold and another *Liberator* staff member, the artist Robert Minor. In *A Long Way From Home,* McKay recalled that Minor had once remarked that "he could not visualize me as a Negro. . . . He thought of a Negro as of a rugged tree in the forest. Perhaps Minor had had Negro playmates like that in Texas and he could not imagine any other type." [47]

The most serious differences between Gold and McKay were ultimately ideological. As McKay explained in his autobiography, Gold was "still intellectually battling up from the depths of proletarian starvation and misery."

> Gold's idea of the *Liberator* was that it should become a popular proletarian magazine, printing doggerels from lumberjacks and stevedores and true relevations from chambermaids. I contended that while it was most excellent to get [such] material, it should be good stuff that could compare with any other writing.[48]

Gold had found his salvation in Marxist ideology and wanted to use the *Liberator* to advance his new faith. McKay, on the other hand, was not so willing to submerge art in the class struggle. In alluding to McKay's position in the conflict, Joseph Freeman later stated that "Claude McKay's warm, sensuous . . . heart swam in thoughtlessness; he was aggressively antirational on the principle that art comes exclusively from the emotions and that he was primarily an artist." [49] Daniel Aaron has stated that the McKay–Gold dispute only symbolized the larger struggle that finally killed the *Liberator*. "The dispute represented the still unsettled war between art and revolution, between the free, undisciplined writer and the disciplined party member." [50] In this regard, it is significant that McKay drifted away from his communist associates in the 1920s while Gold and Robert Minor became loyal party members.

Despite their differences, the content and form of the *Liberator* seems to have been little affected by their joint editorship. This was perhaps because neither ever had complete control of the magazine. Floyd Dell and Eastman continued to send in articles and editorials regularly, and the general temper of the magazine continued in the tone set by them in earlier years. But it was apparent to all concerned that Gold and McKay could not work together. For his part, McKay did not wish to push matters to a crisis and imperil the *Liberator*'s existence. In June 1922, therefore, he resigned as coeditor.

Although McKay later stressed personal differences with Gold as his immediate reason for leaving, his articles and letters from the period reveal that he also harbored a more general dissatisfaction with the magazine's approach to the race problem. With both the *Workers' Dreadnought* in London and the *Liberator* in New York he found a rare personal camaraderie, but in general with neither the British nor American left did he find the foresight regarding racial matters that he thought essential if radicals were to win the black masses to their cause. On the contrary, he found that far too many communists and socialists were themselves still afflicted with the racist phobias common to the age and that, when it suited their purpose, they did not hesitate to voice them.

McKay actually functioned on two levels as a *Liberator* editor. On one level he was simply an artist among equals and was accepted as such. There was always room for disagreements and arguments at staff meetings, and the *Liberator* reflected the wide diversity of opinions current among its editors and writers. It was in this highly individualistic atmosphere that McKay debated with Gold and others about the relationship between art and revolution. On a strictly racial level, however, McKay was disadvantaged in such a free-wheeling atmosphere. As the magazine's solitary black man, he brought to it a perspective on the racial question that the other staff members could share only up to a point. For McKay, the revolutionary's handling of the racial problem was necessarily of decisive importance, while to the other *Liberator* editors it was only one important problem among many. Because of their other preoccupations and also because their readership was overwhelmingly white (and extremely flighty where race was concerned), the white staff members never wished to devote as much space to racial matters as McKay thought they should. McKay recognized the futility of demanding more space than his fellow editors could give, but he did point out that since Negroes constituted ten percent of the nation's population it would not be unfair to devote at least that amount of space in the *Liberator* to their problems. Even this seemed to some a proposal which, if carried out, would jeopardize the magazine's appeal to its white readers. In short, McKay's position as a black man vitally concerned with pushing forward a black-radical perspective on a predominantly white journal created for him problems that figured prominently among the underlying reasons he finally left the *Liberator*. These racial considerations eventually became the subject of a heated correspondence with a surprised Max Eastman months after both had left the magazine (see pp. 78–90).

After McKay left the *Liberator* staff in June, he decided upon a journey to Russia to see for himself "the grand experiment" in progress there. He had grown weary of the never-ending race consciousness that was part of Negro life in America. In *A Long Way from Home,* he related how the unexpected reappearance of his wife, whom he had not seen in more than seven years, forced all other plans aside and sealed his determination to leave the United States. As he recalled, he wished to "escape from the pit of sex and poverty, from domestic death, from the cul-de-sac of self-pity, from the hot syncopated fascination of Harlem, from the suffocating ghetto of color-consciousness." [51]

McKay went to Russia as a poet committed to the professed aims of the Russian Revolution—he had no formal connections with the newly emerging American Communist party, nor did he have any official invitation from the Soviet government. Friends helped finance his trip. At the suggestion of James Weldon Johnson, McKay sent autographed copies of *Home to Harlem* to "a select list of persons connected with the NAACP" and asked for a five-dollar donation. In addition, Max Eastman's sister, Crystal, appealed to friends of the *Liberator* on McKay's behalf. Between his Negro and white admirers—liberals, radicals, and bohemians—enough money was raised to get him to Germany, where he secured permission from the Soviets to enter Russia.[52]

McKay arrived in Moscow early in November 1922, just before the convening of the Fourth Congress of the Third Communist International (the Comintern). The Comintern had been founded in 1919 and was, of course, dominated by the new Bolshevik government of Russia. The Fourth Congress started November 5, 1922, and lasted a month. McKay wanted to attend the Congress as an observer, but his right even to be in Russia, much less attend the Congress, was challenged by the American Communist delegation.

The American Communist party had brought to Moscow for final settlement the bitterly disputed problem of whether they should maintain or abolish their illegal, underground apparatus, which actually served no real purpose except to satisfy an older, European revolutionary tradition. A majority of the American delegates at the Fourth Congress favored a continuation of the underground party. Upon arriving in Moscow, McKay was ignorant of the deep cleavage within the delegation over this issue. When asked by Rose Pastor Stokes, one of the defenders of the illegal party, what he thought about the matter, McKay stated there was really no need for an underground party in the United States. By thus inadvertently lining up with the minority delegates headed by James P. Cannon, McKay incurred the wrath of the majority. Although Cannon's faction finally won the Comintern's support, the majority view prevailed before the Congress got under way, and McKay later maintained they had actually had him thrown out of the Lux Hotel where they were staying. For a while he feared the Soviet government would expel him from Russia.

After considerable uncertainty and tension, McKay finally won the right to attend the Congress as "a special delegate." His success seems to have resulted from support given by two unexpected sources. The first was the people in the streets. His color and unmistakable Negroid features made him an object of curiosity, and popular with Moscow crowds. His second was Sen Katayama, the Japanese Communist who had lived for years in the United States. In his younger days. Katayama had attended Fisk University; unlike most Russian and American Communists, he was thoroughly familiar with the American Negro problem. In 1922, he was a Comintern official and a great favorite with Russian Communists. He listened to McKay's explanation of his dilemma and interceded on his behalf.[53]

Besides McKay, there was present as an American party delegate another Negro, Otto Huiswoud. Together, Huiswoud and McKay were the first Negroes to discuss the American race problem before the Third International. It is worth noting that both were immigrants to the United States, Huiswood being a native of Dutch Guiana.

Although in his autobiography McKay denied that he addressed the Fourth Congress, both he and Huiswoud spoke on the American Negro and his relation to International Communism. McKay in particular spoke briefly but forcefully of the racial prejudices he had found among American Communists, and he reiterated that white radicals must rid themselves of such prejudices if they wished to influence the black masses. Theodore Draper has pointed out that McKay's accusation of race prejudice among party members was "the first of many such complaints" to be voiced by blacks through the years.[54] His speech, which had been buried for fifty years, has been exhumed from the pages of the *International Press Correspondence* and included in its entirety in this volume (see p. 91).

The combined presence of Huiswoud and McKay perhaps had some influence on the proceedings of the Congress. For the first time, a Negro Commission was created. It consisted of Huiswood and a few other party members. The Commission's "Resolutions on the Negro Question," formally adopted by the Fourth Congress, represented the Comintern's "first real effort to state its position" on the Negro problem. The resolutions noted the unrest that had developed among many American Negroes and black colonials as a result of World War I. It then stated that "the history of the Negro in America fits him for an important role in the liberation struggle of the entire African race." There followed a brief survey of the Negro's struggle against American oppression, which took special note of the "post-war industrialization of the Negro in the North and the spirit of revolt engendered by post-war persecutions and brutalities." The document concluded by reminding Negroes that their struggle was primarily a struggle against capitalist imperialism. It then outlined steps by which Communists could more effectively secure the Negro's support in the proletarian struggle for freedom.[55]

"The Fourth Congress," Draper has written, "opened a period of Communist policy for the American Negro in which the international and especially the African aspect predominated."[56] McKay's role in developing this policy was minimal at best and was certainly no greater than Huiswoud's. Their presence, however, probably added a measure of reality to the deliberations and encouraged more than a hollow gesture. In effect, they were representative of several immigrant black radicals in the United States who, after World War I, contributed substantially to left-wing Negro thought. In general they derived part of their radical inspiration from a black nationalist impulse that had its origin in their colonial, as well as their American, experience. In this respect, the official policy of the Comintern after 1922 seems to have been most applicable to West Indians who were simultaneously much more nationalistic, class-conscious, and international-minded than were native American Negroes, who by and large continued to cling tenaciously to the hope of justice under the American Constitution.

If West Indian radicals influenced to some degree Comintern thoughts concerning the American Negro, there were certainly other, equally important factors that determined its emphasis on the international aspects of the Negro problem. In the first place, Marxist–Leninist theory concerning the relationship between capitalism and imperialism would seem to impel such emphasis. In addition, the response of urban Negroes in the North to Garvey's Universal Negro Improvement Association perhaps provided the Comintern with some hope of eventually winning Negroes to the Communist brand of "universal improvement."

After the conclusion of the Fourth Congress in December 1922, McKay remained in Russia for six more months. During those six months, he became something of a celebrity:

> Never in my life did I feel prouder of being an African, a black, and no mistake about it. . . . From Moscow to Petrograd and from Petrograd to Moscow I went triumphantly from surprise to surprise, extravagantly feted on every side. . . . I was like a black ikon in the flesh. The famine had ended, the NEP [New Economic Policy] was flourishing, the people were simply happy. I was the first Negro to arrive in Russia since the revolution, and perhaps I was generally regarded as an omen of good luck! Yes, that was exactly what it was. I was like a black ikon.[57]

McKay met Trotsky and other important political figures (Lenin was gravely ill at the time). He also met and spoke before many major poets, writers, and other Soviet dignitaries. In addition, he wrote poems and articles for the Russian press, for which he was handsomely paid. Trotsky sent him on a tour of Soviet military installations, and he was elaborately toasted by the Red Army and Navy.

McKay's visit was brought to a grand climax in Petrograd during the May Day celebration of 1923. "For hours," he later wrote, "I stood with Zinoviev and other Petrograd leaders in the reviewing stand in the Uritsky Square." [58] That night McKay returned to the former palace of the late Grand Duke Alexander where he was staying and tried to sleep, but the colorful throngs continued to march before his eyes. He finally sat down at the Grand Duke's desk and wrote what proved to be his farewell to Russia. In the concluding stanza of "Petrograd: May Day, 1923," McKay caught some of the exultation he felt, not only on that particular day, but throughout his Russian adventure:

> Jerusalem is fading from men's minds,
> And sacred cities holding men in thrall,
> Are crumbling in the new thought of mankind—
> The pagan day, the holy day for all!
> Oh, Petrograd, oh proud triumphant city,
> The gateway to the strange, awakening East,
> Where warrior-workers wrestled without pity
> Against the power of magnate, monarch, priest—
> World Fort of Struggle, hold from day to day
> The flaming standards of the First of May! [59]

Shortly after writing these lines, McKay left for Germany, where he embarked upon an entirely new career as an expatriate novelist.

The Comintern leadership no doubt hoped that the friendly reception given McKay in the Soviet Union would lead to his complete acceptance of Communist party politics. In fact, just the opposite occurred. His Russian journey proved to be only a grand finale to his radical activism. From the beginning of his association with the *Liberator,* McKay stressed his ultimate independence as a writer and poet. He felt a subservience to Communist party discipline would limit his freedom and violate the integrity of his art. It should be remembered, too, that he had gone to Moscow already disillusioned and somewhat bitter with his American comrades over the race question. Thus, despite the overwhelming success of his tour, McKay left the Soviet Union eager to resume what he considered the modern writer's proper function—namely, to record as best he could the truths of his own experience, let the chips fall where they may.

After his return to Germany, however, he did write for *Crisis* magazine a detailed report of his trip, in which he reaffirmed his support of the larger aims of the new Soviet state. But in the same article he also noted the weariness and boredom he had sometimes experienced with Communist politicians and ideologues at the Fourth Congress and the relief he had found among Russia's surviving non-Communist literary intelligentsia (see p. 102).

McKay arrived in Germany from the Soviet Union in June 1923. He was almost thirty-four years old. Although he had four books of poetry to his credit and considerable journalistic experience, he had little money and no settled plans for the future, beyond a firm desire to earn his way as a writer. He did not expect to support himself through poetry alone. In the long run, fiction promised greater financial rewards, and he had long desired to experiment with the more expansive possibilities of the novel.

In his poetry, McKay had rebelled against the spiritual genocide to which white racism condemned blacks. In his prose fiction, he attempted to move beyond rebellion to a positive affirmation of black life at its simplest, most basic folk level.

In his review of *Shuffle Along* in the December 1921 *Liberator,* McKay had already looked forward to the day when Negro artists could burst through "the screen of sneering bigotry put between them and life," and capture "the warmth, color and laughter" of black life. "In Harlem, along Fifth and Lenox Avenues, in Marcus Garvey's Hall with its extravagant paraphernalia, in his churches and cabarets, [the Negro] expresses himself with a zest that is yet to be depicted by a true artist" (see p. 63). With his arrival in Germany, McKay at last decided to accept the challenge implicit in his own thinking and immediately set out to learn the difficult art of prose fiction.

In the fall of 1923, he went to Paris, where he suffered a lengthy period of illness and hospitalization during the winter of 1923–24.[60] From Paris he moved to the more congenial climate of Toulon. There, despite precarious finances, he completed his first novel in the spring of 1925.

This novel, which he called "Color Scheme," was never published, and he eventually destroyed the manuscript. His letters to his friend A. A. Schomburg, the black bibliophile, during this period, however, reveal that in its general tone and spirit it anticipated his later novels. With "Color Scheme" he clearly hoped to break through the inhibitions that had constrained earlier Negro writers. "I make my Negro characters yarn and backbite and fuck like people the world over," he wrote.[61]

Already McKay anticipated that such boldness would upset the more conservative Negro critics at the NAACP, as well as other black middle-class organizations and newspapers. To Schomburg he wrote, "American Negroes have been living their lives behind closed shutters (I mean the better-off ones), not allowing the light in for fear of Cracker insults and mud. For the sake of artistic self-expression the light should be let in" (see p. 142).

McKay spent the summer of 1925 in Brittany, anxiously awaiting news regarding the fate of "Color Scheme." By August 1925, it became clear his novel was not to be published. Broke and disgusted, he returned to the south of France, where he began a series of short stories on various aspects of black life in Harlem.

He also began another novel. Deciding "Color Scheme" had been too frank regarding sexual matters for acceptance in the American market, he retreated (at least for a time) to a safely traditional theme—the problems encountered by a light-skinned Negro who is tempted to "pass" out of black into white society. Fortunately, McKay never finished this project, for in the spring of 1926, Louise Bryant Bullitt, Jack Reed's widow, took the short stories he had written and through intermediaries found for McKay both a publisher in America and a literary agent in Paris. Harper & Brothers accepted his short stories, and upon Mrs. Bullitt's advice, he agreed that William Aspenwall Bradley, the foremost American literary agent in Paris, should act as his representative in all negotiations with them.

One of the short stories McKay sent to Harper's concerned a Negro soldier's return to Harlem after World War I. At Harper's suggestion Bradley urged McKay to save the other stories for later publication and to expand the Negro soldier's return into a novel. McKay agreed and the result was *Home to Harlem,* which he submitted to Harper's in the early summer of 1927, almost four years to the day since his first arrival in Western Europe from the Soviet Union. His long and often difficult apprenticeship as a novelist was over.[62]

When *Home to Harlem* finally appeared in the spring of 1928, it proved an immediate popular and financial success. In part, its success was due to the receptive climate that had been generated for black literature since McKay's departure in 1922. While he was engaged in his solitary labor abroad, a rising chorus of young black writers in the United States had begun their own affirmation of Negro folk life. In 1923 *Cane,* Jean Toomer's lyric novel of rural Georgia, had appeared. Countee Cullen's first volume of poetry, *Color,* was published in 1925. Also in 1925, Alain Locke in his influential anthology *The New Negro* apprised the world that the emerging generation of Negro writers and artists shared a common sense of purpose. The following year, Langston Hughes's first volume of poetry, *The Weary Blues,* provided further proof of the new self-affirmation among Negro writers. The Negro Renaissance had arrived.*

As used by Locke the term "New Negro" referred to more than a rising generation of black writers. The New Negro also included the Negro masses in general and especially the young among them. "For the younger generation," Locke noted, "is vibrant with a new psychology." This new spirit he described as basically a renewal of "self-respect and self-dependence." [63]

The young writers of the Negro Renaissance were buttressed psychologically and socially by an older generation's political and social reawakening. And they were further inspired by the quickening tempo of black American life evident after World War I.

On the larger scene, the Negro Renaissance partook of the general revolt by the white writers of the decade against the gross materialism of America's new industrial society. Surrounded by Babbittry (not to mention a resurgent Ku Klux Klan), Negro writers looked inward and found unexpected strength in their own folk culture. As Robert Bone has written, the Negro Renaissance was essentially "a period of self-discovery, marked by a sudden growth of interest in things Negro." [64]

To some extent, the New Negro's emphasis on the folk was undoubtedly heightened by the sympathetic treatment many white writers accorded Negroes in the Twenties. After World War I, writers as diverse as Gertrude Stein, Eugene O'Neill, Waldo Frank, Sherwood Anderson, Marc Connelly, and Carl Van Vechten thought they saw among blacks a naturally creative spontaneity that had not been completely stifled by the general decadence of modern society. An unexpected reservoir of life was discovered in Eliot's wasteland.

As the Twenties progressed, the Negro and his arts enjoyed a considerable vogue in both the United States and Europe. Art col-

---

* It was also in 1926 that Carl Van Vechten published his novel of Harlem night life, *Nigger Heaven* (New York, Knopf). McKay had heard in 1924 that Van Vechten was writing a novel about Harlem, and he had hoped to complete "Color Scheme" before it appeared. As it turned out, the controversy created by *Nigger Heaven* (which McKay did not see until after he had completed *Home to Harlem*) probably helped prepare the ground for the popular success of McKay's own work.
Carl Van Vechten (1880–1964), music critic, novelist, and photographer, was a friend of many participants in the Negro Renaissance and a consistent supporter of black American artistic endeavor.

lectors sought the best of primitive African sculpture and other arti-
facts. Jazz, of course, became popular everywhere. Negro singers
and musicians found a receptive public, and the Blues entered the
mainstream of American music. In many respects, American Negroes
had in the Twenties a favorable opportunity for an assessment of
their past accomplishments and future potentials.

However, the great emphasis on the primitive and on folk cul-
ture led to some naive delusions. Just as whites had previously
built a stereotype of the happy, simple-minded plantation Negro,
many in the Twenties cast Negroes as unfettered children of nature,
bubbling over with uninhibited sexuality and childlike originality.
To the extent Negro writers accepted such an image, they limited
the depth and richness of their own evaluations of Negro American
life.[65]

Home to Harlem appeared at the height of this new interest in
black culture and quickly reached bestseller status. As McKay had
foreseen, its unblushing depiction of the seamier side of Harlem life
generated a storm of protest in the Negro press. In telling the story
of Jake Brown, the novel's working-class hero, McKay sketched
in a rogue's gallery of Harlem "low-life" characters. Love-starved
"grass widows" and the "sweetmen" who preyed upon them,
pimps and prostitutes, homosexuals and drug addicts, loan sharks
and labor scabs, alcoholics, gamblers, sado-masochists, and corrupt
cops—all were found in *Home to Harlem*. In 1928 the existence of
such types in black communities, though privately acknowledged,
was not publicly advertised in respectable black publications. To
some, McKay's book seemed a betrayal of racial trust and solidarity.

After reading *Home to Harlem,* W. E. B. Du Bois remarked
that he felt distinctly unclean and in need of a bath.[66] And Dewey
Jones, the black critic of the *Chicago Defender,* lamented that "white
people think we are buffoons, thugs and rotters anyway. Why should
we waste so much time trying to prove it? That's what Claude McKay
has done." [67]

Such convictions were probably re-inforced when some white
critics went to the opposite extreme in their acceptance of the book.
For instance, John R. Chamberlain in the *New York Times* exhib-
ited an uncritical enthusiasm that verged on caricature: "[*Home to
Harlem* is] beaten through with rhythm of life that is the jazz
rhythm . . . the real thing in rightness. . . . It is the real stuff, the
lowdown on Harlem, the dope from the inside." [68] A more conserva-
tive critic, Carl Van Doren, noted the episodic structure of the book

and discounted it as a novel, declaring it instead a compilation of Harlem folklore.[69]

The novel was indeed episodic, almost picaresque in form. Its loose construction reflected both McKay's view of Harlem as a vital but chaotically disorganized community and his own unresolved search for meaning and direction in black life.

Home to Harlem relates the story of Jake, a Negro doughboy, and his adventures upon returning to Harlem after World War I. Toward the end of the War, Jake deserts his unit, an all-black labor battalion in Brest, and after a brief stint in London, slips quietly back to New York as a seaman. Once back, he resumes his old role as a casual worker and vagabond lover. Jake is McKay's idealized folk hero, the essentially wholesome natural man, whose existence, if rather aimless, is never marred by pretense, pettiness, or unnecessary bother over problems that do not immediately concern him. Jake does not particularly like the squalor of Harlem but neither does he let it corrupt or embitter him. He takes life as it comes and, without fear or rancor, maintains a steady equilibrium. Despite the anarchy that surrounds him, he entertains a somewhat vague but persistent dream of eventually settling down to a more stable existence.

Contrasted to Jake is Ray, an educated Haitian immigrant, whom Jake meets after his return to America. A highly intelligent and sensitive individual, Ray is impelled toward a writing career, but he has been forced by the American environment into Jake's casual orbit. Ray admires Jake's skill in maneuvering unscathed through the confusion of modern urban existence, and he regrets that his own greater self-awareness makes it unlikely he can ever achieve a similar stability. Nevertheless, Ray looks upon Jake as a model pointing the way to survival. Basically both Ray the intellectual and Jake the worker share the same problems in a world that forces all blacks into a single social category. In *Home to Harlem* McKay thus sought to reconcile two seemingly incongruous viewpoints—a harsh social realism with a romantic celebration of the primitive vitality of black folk, who somehow manage to survive and even to flourish under the most brutal of circumstances.

After completing *Home to Harlem*, McKay almost immediately began his second novel, *Banjo*, which appeared in 1929. This novel grew out of McKay's experiences in Marseille during the fall and winter of 1925. Even more than *Home to Harlem*, *Banjo* is written in a purely picaresque mode. It concerns the adventures of a group of black seamen from the West Indies, Africa, and the United States who have been haphazardly thrown together on the beach in Marseille. The novel's chief character, Lincoln Agrippa Daley, or Banjo as he is called, is a more roguish version of Jake Brown. Like Jake, Banjo chances upon Ray, the wandering Haitian intellectual, and a friendship develops which McKay uses once again to present two contrasting but complementary versions of black reality. As in *Home to Harlem,* the characters exist amid the bawdy residue of commerce and industry, this time in the Vieux Port section, "the Ditch," of Marseille. Confined in "the Ditch" are the city's prostitutes, pimps, gangsters, and other marginal types, including beached seamen of every nationality.

Among this melange, Banjo moves with a sure confidence gained from years of living solely by his superior wit and intuition. Though not deliberately vicious, he is nevertheless something of a rogue. At the novel's conclusion, he signs on a ship bound for America and draws a large advance against his salary. When the time comes to sail, however, he announces to Ray that he will instead abscond with his advance to another part of Europe. Banjo justifies his action by maintaining that blacks such as himself "kain't afford to choose [between right and wrong], because we ain't born and growed up like the choosing people. All we can do is grab our chance every time it comes our way." [70] Upon reflection Ray concurs and agrees to accompany Banjo: "He had associated too closely with the beach boys not to realize that their loose, instinctive way of living was more deeply related to his own self-preservation than all the principles or social morality lessons . . . of the civilized machine." [71]

In both *Home to Harlem* and *Banjo,* McKay identified with the earthbound realism and forthright candor of his black folk heroes, and he placed himself in opposition to the mechanically regimented "progress" of Western industrialism. In this regard McKay was very close in spirit to D. H. Lawrence, the modern writer whom he admired above all others.* He also made plain his belief that within

---

* On March 18, 1930, McKay wrote W. A. Bradley his agent that "it was very sad to hear of D. H. Lawrence's death. Although I never met him, it was like losing a close friend." In *A Long Way from Home,* McKay wrote, "I thought D. H. Lawrence was more modern than James Joyce. In . . . Lawrence I found confusion—all of the ferment and turmoil, the hesitation and hate and alarm, the sexual inquietude and the incertitude of this age, and the psychic and romantic groping for a way out. . . . Some of my friends thought I showed a preference for D. H. Lawrence because he was something of a social rebel. But it was impossible for me seriously to think

the Negro group racial salvation did not lie in the hands of either black intellectuals or the black bourgeoisie:

> At college in America and among the Negro intelligentsia . . . [Ray] had never experienced any of the simple, natural warmth of a people believing in themselves, such as he had felt among the rugged poor and socially backward blacks of his island home. . . . Only when he got down among the black and brown working boys and girls of the country did he find something of that raw unconscious and the-devil-with-them pride in being Negro that was his own natural birthright. . . . Among them was never any of the hopeless, enervating talk of the chances of "passing white" and the spector of the Future that were the common topics of the colored intelligentsia. Close association with the Jakes and Banjoes had been like participating in a common primitive birthright. . . . He loved their natural gusto for living down the past and lifting their kinky heads out of the hot, suffocating ashes, the shadow, the terror of real sorrow to go on gaily grinning in the present. . . . Ray had felt buttressed by the boys with a rough strength and sureness that gave him spiritual passion and pride to be his human self in an inhumanly alien world. . . . From these boys he could learn how to live—how to exist as a black boy in a white world and rid his conscience of the used-up hussy of white morality. He could not scrap his intellectual life and be entirely like them. He did not want or feel any urge to "go back" that way. . . . But a black man, even though educated, was in closer biological kinship to the swell of primitive earth life. And maybe his apparent failing under the organization of the modern world was the real strength that preserved him from becoming the thing that was the common white creature of it. . . . The more Ray mixed in the rude anarchy of the lives of the black boys . . . and came to a realization of how close-linked he was to them in spirit, the more he felt that they represented more than he or the cultured minority the irrepressible exuberance and legendary vitality of the black race. And the thought kept him wondering how that race would fare under the ever tightening mechanical organization of modern life.[72]

Despite the general condemnation such sentiments elicited from the Negro press, some influential blacks defended McKay. James Weldon Johnson consistently supported him, though even he felt

---

of Lawrence as a social thinker after having studied the social thinking of creative writers like Ruskin, W. Morris, Tolstoy, and Shaw. . . . What I loved was the Lawrentian language, which to me is the ripest and most voluptuous expression of English since Shakespeare" (pp. 247–48).

that McKay had unfairly disparaged the black middle class.[73] The youthful Langston Hughes had no such reservations. He wrote McKay that *Home to Harlem* was "undoubtedly . . . the finest thing 'we've' yet done. . . . Your novel ought to give a second youth to the Negro Vogue." [74] Whatever misgivings Johnson and other officials in the NAACP had regarding his novels, they probably played a key role in the Harmon Foundation's decision to bestow upon McKay its annual achievement award for 1928, a cash prize of four hundred dollars, which of course McKay gratefully accepted. (He had earlier expressed disdain for such prizes. See p. 141.)

Banjo sold fewer copies than *Home to Harlem,* but it still proved a financial success. For the first time, McKay found he could live off his royalties. After 1928 he resided only for brief periods in France and traveled extensively in Germany, Spain, and North Africa. He quickly developed a preference for the peoples and cultures of Spain and Morocco. In 1931 he finally settled in Tangiers, where he remained until his return to the United States in 1934.

McKay's frequent travels sometimes hampered but never halted his creative productivity for long. After completing *Banjo,* he lived for awhile in Spain and there began work on another novel, "Romance in Marseille," which he completed in 1930. It was based in part on the true story of a young West African McKay first met while living among the beach boys in Marseille during the winter of 1925–26.[75] This unfortunate young man had stowed away on a ship bound for America. He had been discovered at sea and thrown into an ice-cold brig, where his feet became so frostbitten that upon arrival in New York they had had to be amputated. While recuperating, a New York lawyer filed a damage suit on his behalf against the shipping company responsible for his neglect. As a result, the African won a large settlement, acquired artificial limbs, and returned to Marseille in comparative affluence. The remainder of the novel is McKay's imaginative account of the amputee's disastrous affair with a racially mixed Arabic prostitute in Marseille.

As it turned out, "Romance in Marseille" was never published. After its completion, McKay decided it needed revision, but he was tired and felt he could not face the task. Since his contract called for three novels and a volume of short stories, he prevailed upon Harper's to publish his short stories instead. Besides the earlier Harlem stories (first written in 1926–27), he added several new ones on Jamaican topics written during 1930–31. And in 1932 there duly appeared *Gingertown.*

With *Gingertown* McKay hoped to prove to his critics the range and depth of his interests. To Max Eastman he wrote, "I want to have the short stories published because they will show that I am a writer of many moods and open the way for any book on any theme I may choose to write instead of my being taken solely as a writer of picaresque stories." [76]

There are twelve stories in *Gingertown*. Three—"Brownskin Blues," "Highball," and "Mattie and Her Sweetman"—deal with the practical effects of obsessive color consciousness, which plagued many within the Harlem community. In "Truant," he shows how the frustrations engendered by a lack of career opportunities in a racist society cause one black man to desert his family. Another Harlem story, "Near-White," describes the anguish of a young woman who is tempted to pass over the color line. And in "The Prince of Puerto Rico," he relates the sadly ridiculous end of a handsome young Puerto Rican barber in Harlem, who unwittingly allows himself to be caught *in flagrante delicto* by an enraged husband. One story, entitled "Nigger Lover," is set in a Mediterranean port resembling Marseille, while the action in "The Little Sheik" takes place in Morocco.

By far the most refreshing new material in *Gingertown* are the four stories which deal with Jamaican themes—"The Agricultural Show," "Crazy Mary," "When I Pounded the Pavement," and "The Strange Burial of Sue." These are all written in a gently nostalgic vein that contrasts sharply with the grim realism of his Harlem stories. In style and theme, they anticipate McKay's last novel, *Banana Bottom*.

McKay had begun it after finishing the last of his stories, and it appeared in 1933, only one year after *Gingertown*. Unlike *Home to Harlem* and *Banjo, Banana Bottom* is a carefully plotted story of a young Jamaican woman's return home after completing her education in England. In relating the story of her successful readjustment to Jamaican country life, McKay succeeds in painting a richly nostalgic portrait of the Jamaica he had known as a boy at the turn of the century. At the same time, he carries forward to a successful resolution the themes he had elaborated in his earlier novels.

After her return, Bita Plant, the novel's heroine, finds she must choose between a life rooted in native folkways and the more rigidly structured life mapped for her by the missionaries who had been responsible for her education. Bita rejects the artificiality of a dying missionary tradition and instead successfully reintegrates herself into the simple but robust folk life from which she had come. In its unity of style and theme, as well as in the richness of its detail, *Banana Bottom* represents the high point of McKay's career as a novelist. With its publication, he confidently expected another critical and financial success. Despite *Gingertown*'s complete financial failure a year earlier, the full consequences of the Great Depression had been slow to reach McKay in his Moroccan retreat. He was shocked, therefore, when *Banana Bottom* also failed and left him in debt to a publisher no longer willing to advance him money for another book.[77]

Left penniless in Tangiers, McKay appealed for aid to friends in the United States. They responded with money for a return voyage, and McKay arrived in New York on February 2, 1934. He had been away almost twelve years.

Throughout his stay abroad, McKay had looked upon the United States as his adopted home, but he had consistently delayed his return, partly because he feared he would be denied re-entry. Technically, he was still a British subject, and more important, he had a radical past. These considerations made McKay hesitant in applying for a return visa, but they were not the major reasons for his twelve-year exile. Like many black artists before and after him who lived abroad, McKay dreaded to face once again the harsh conditions imposed upon Negroes by American racism. One impelling reason for his trip to Russia, which had started him on his long expatriation, had been a desire to "escape from . . . the suffocating ghetto of color consciousness." After his return in 1934 he wrote:

> But oh! I was reluctant coming back,
> I felt like one expelled from heaven to hell,
> To the arena packed of black-and-white,
> America's heart-breaking spectacle.[78]

At the same time, McKay looked forward to contributing in some substantial way to black American life. But the United States in 1934 was in many ways worse off than when he had left it in the fall of 1922. Upon returning, he found a wrecked economy, almost universal black poverty, and little sense of unity among those black writers and intellectuals he had hoped to work with in the years ahead. On the political left he also found extreme disarray, as Stalinists and Trotskyites, anticommunist socialists, and anarchists all warred with one another for the workingman's soul.

McKay's private misfortune soon equalled the public misfortunes that surrounded him. Publishers were no longer interested in black authors. Eugene Saxton, who had handled his work at Harper's, bluntly informed McKay that his popularity had been part of a passing fad. The Negro Renaissance was over. There was no longer a market for his work. If this were not enough, McKay shortly discovered there were no jobs at all available for him, even unskilled ones, and he was soon forced by extreme poverty into a city-operated camp for destitute men in upstate New York. (This experience is vividly described in the series of letters to Max Eastman beginning on p. 203).

With the assistance of Eastman and the young black sculptress Selma Burke, McKay soon escaped Camp Greycourt and returned to New York City. As the author of eight volumes of poetry and fiction, he had naturally resented Saxton's curt dismissal of his literary prospects. With the continued support of Miss Burke and Eastman, toward the end of 1935 he was able to begin work on his autobiography. He soon received a further boost by gaining regular employment with the newly established Federal Writers' Project. Along with a handful of other authors in New York City, he was allowed to continue his creative work at home. As a result, his autobiography, *A Long Way from Home,* appeared in 1937.[79]

By and large, it is a pleasantly unpretentious account of his experiences in New York, London, Russia, Europe, and North Africa. It contains interesting descriptions of the many individuals he had met during his travels, including such famous personalities as Frank Harris, Charlie Chaplin, George Bernard Shaw, H. G. Wells, Paul Robeson, and Henri Cartier-Bresson. Those chapters devoted to his work on the *Liberator* and his travels in England and Russia are detailed and especially valuable from a historical point of view.

McKay could not refrain, however, from occasionally bitter attacks upon his critics. These included several black journalists who had condemned his fiction, as well as those American Communists who considered his political independence a form of degenerate bourgeois adventurism. McKay also questions in *A Long Way from Home* the motives of many blacks whom he felt had merely used the Negro Renaissance to advance their social status among whites. In his final chapter McKay offers a general criticism of America's established Negro leaders. He maintains that their single-minded opposition to segregation was detrimental to any effective black community organization and to the development of a positive group spirit among blacks.

Despite McKay's protest that he had never been an enemy of "polite Negro society," he could not have been too surprised when *A Long Way from Home* received generally hostile reviews in the Negro press.[80] In addition, he suffered an unexpected reversal when his new publisher, Lee Furman, went out of business shortly after the book's release. As a result, it received very little promotion and failed to enhance either McKay's reputation or his financial status.

McKay's criticisms in *A Long Way from Home* were only partially indicative of how completely involved he had become in the social and political controversies that dominated the American literary scene in the 1930s. By 1937 his best efforts were going into the occasional articles he managed to sell to such journals and newspapers as the *Nation,* the *New Leader,* and the New York *Amsterdam News.* In these articles he set forth more fully his position regarding the future of social change, both within and without the black community. Broadly speaking, McKay tried to maintain throughout the 1930s and 1940s the independent, left-wing stance he had first adopted as a *Liberator* editor after World War I. In this regard his position was similar to George Orwell's in England. Unlike the younger Orwell, however, his days as a creative writer were drawing to a close. The energy he had previously devoted to poetry and fiction went instead into his polemical articles.

Along with his letters from this period, these wholly neglected articles constitute Part III of the present volume. In a real sense they represent the culmination of his writing career, a summing up of his concerns as a creative writer. As such they form a logical sequel to his earlier preoccupations as a poet and novelist.

McKay's attitude regarding the perennial question of racial segregation versus integration was similar to the position W. E. B. Du Bois had adopted in the late 1920s.[81] Like Du Bois, he opposed the legal separation of the races and the perpetuation of the historical injustices of the American racial caste system. But he argued that Negroes should recognize the difference between forced racial segregation and a natural racial aggregation based upon common cultural interests and concerns, which he believed would continue far beyond any successful resolution of the black struggle for civil rights. In the long run, McKay foresaw that Negroes would eventually have to integrate into American society not only as individuals, but also as an ethnic group. He insisted, therefore, that every possible effort be made to strengthen black community organizations; only by such efforts could blacks as a whole develop the collective strength necessary to make their weight felt as a progressive force within the American nation.

In the field of literature and the arts—his own special domain —McKay rejected outright the notion that black artists should be dependent for their development and growth upon either white patronage or passing social fashions. His effort after his return to found in Harlem a black literary journal is documented in this volume, as is his later attempt to establish a black writer's guild (see pp. 201, 232). In each instance McKay hoped that an independent black forum would result, where black writers and artists could freely explore among themselves their own peculiar problems. Both projects failed.

Despite McKay's protests to the contrary, middle-class Negroes dismissed his insistence on black community development as a form of black nationalism. On the left, those Negroes allied with or sympathetic to the American Communist party were equally offended by McKay's loud protests that blacks could not strategically afford to ally themselves with a party controlled by a foreign government. In short, McKay's views were rejected by those whom he had most hoped to influence.

As the decade progressed, McKay found himself virtually isolated from all sources of power within the Harlem community. He had many friends and acquaintances. These included young artists such as Romare Bearden and Jacob Lawrence, and older writers such as James Weldon Johnson and Countee Cullen, all of whom valued his artistic judgment and accomplishments.[82] But by and large, his volatile temperament and complex ideas were more feared than understood by those best situated to help him gain a secure position within the Harlem community.

As a consequence, his only steady income in the late 1930s came from his employment with the Federal Writers' Project. His work there also proved valuable in another way. The black writers on the Project compiled a vast amount of material relating to the past history and contemporary status of Negroes in New York. Using this material, as well as his own independent research, McKay completed in 1940 his last book, *Harlem: Negro Metropolis*. In it he briefly traces the history of Harlem as a predominantly black community and devotes some space to a description of Harlem businessmen and politicians.[83]

His principle focus, however, is upon the poor quality of Harlem's community life, which he believed resulted largely from the American black's obsessive battle against segregation:

This issue of Segregation is a formidable specter, paralyzing to the progress of the Negro community in every aspect of its life: in politics, in culture, in business and labor. The Negro community is feverishly agitated and divided by it. And in this respect it is unlike any other American community. Negroes realize that they are segregated and thus hate their community. . . . Thus in Negro communities there is a tacit evasion of direct social responsibility that is peculiar to them. The Negro accepts the substance of segregation and remains fixedly frightened by the shadow of it. And every aspect of his life suffers therefrom. . . . Undoubtedly the chaotic defeatish mentality of the Negro community is responsible for the phenomenal increase of supernatural agencies, cults, numbers games, dream books and other mumbo-jumbo, and the maze of abortive movements among the masses.

Even white-collar movements . . . were initiated by the common people. Unlike the Negro intelligentsia ineffectually fretting its soul away over a symbolic gesture, the inarticulate Negro masses realize that they have special community rights.[84]

Predictably, McKay's best chapters deal with the folk movements of Harlem and the charismatic figures who led them. For instance, his long chapters on Father Divine and on Sufi Abdul Hamid and his boycott of Harlem merchants probably remain the best essays ever done on these subjects. His chapter entitled "The Business of Numbers," though shorter, is likewise well written and provides a unique history of that venerable institution, which continues to flourish today as strongly as it did in the 1930s (see p. 264).

The critical response to *Harlem: Negro Metropolis* was largely negative. Black reviewers such as Ted Poston in the *Nation* and *New Leader* and Roi Ottley in the *New York Times* contended the book gave readers a distorted view of Harlem life.[85] They accused McKay of overemphasizing its primitive and exotic side and of adopting a generally anti-intellectual stance in his criticism of the Negro intelligentsia. They also charged he had exaggerated the Communist party's influence in Harlem. His anticommunism, they maintained, actually flowed from personal resentments he had against his former friends. Finally, they asserted that McKay's portrait of Sufi Abdul

Hamid as a sincere (if misguided) labor leader was false. The Sufi was in reality only a petty labor racketeer, who shook down Harlem merchants and spread anti-Semitic propaganda. On the whole, they concluded, it was McKay who was out of touch with the realities of Harlem life, not those whom he had attacked in his book.

Such reviews left McKay bitter and more isolated than ever. He had failed to win the critical acceptance he needed either to make the book a success or to revitalize his career. He consequently found himself at the age of fifty with no position, no money, and no prospects. Whether justified or not, his reputation as a temperamental iconoclast had become a trap from which he could not escape.

To make matters worse, his health, which had bothered him for years, began to break down completely after 1940. He had long suffered from hypertension and he now developed dropsy, an affliction involving the abnormal retention of body fluids and affecting the heart and other vital organs. Ironically, as his health deteriorated his weight increased, and he assumed a rotund, cherubic appearance that masked his true condition.

In the winter of 1941 a friend, the Catholic writer Ellen Terry, found him alone and seriously ill in a Harlem rooming house. She enlisted the aid of Friendship House, a local Catholic social agency run by Catherine de Hueck, a lay worker and White Russian exile. The volunteers at Friendship House provided McKay with a doctor and helped nurse him to a partial recovery. McKay in turn visited Friendship House and established cordial relations with its staff. It was his first step toward a new life within the Catholic church.[86]

He moved to Chicago in the spring of 1944, at the invitation of Bishop Bernard Sheil, one of America's most progressive, reform-minded churchmen (some referred to him as Chicago's "Red Bishop," since he was to be among the first to attack Senator Joseph McCarthy). Under Bishop Sheil's guidance, McKay joined the Catholic church and was baptized October 11, 1944.

For McKay the decision to become a Catholic had not been easy. As a "free-thinker" from childhood, it had meant a complete reversal of his former beliefs. To those who knew him it seemed an astonishing turnabout.[87] To McKay, however, the Church appeared as a last refuge in an increasingly dehumanized world. Unlike many left-wing critics of communism, McKay refused to become an apologist for capitalist imperialism. Although he had become an American citizen in 1940, he felt the United States had learned

nothing from the collapse of European colonialism, and he feared
American world dominance after World War II:

> Europe and Africa and Asia wait
> The·touted New Deal of the New World's hand!
> New systems will be built on race and hate,
> The Eagle and the Dollar will command.
> Oh Lord! My body, and my heart too, break—
> The tiger in his strength his thirst must slake! [88]

Having found no place for himself within the black American
community and having rejected a servile role as a spokesman for
either capitalism or communism, McKay turned to the Church
simply for personal salvation. To Max Eastman he wrote, "I have
had a hard time but I have also had some superb moments and in
spite of my chronic illness I don't want to go sour on humanity,
even after living in this awful land of the U.S.A. I still like to think
of people with wonder and love as I did as a boy in Jamaica and
the Catholic Church with its discipline and traditions and under-
standing of human nature is helping me a lot" (see p. 311).

Despite frequent hospitalization over the next four years, McKay
managed to teach at the Catholic Youth Organization in Chicago
and to compile his *Selected Poems,* which finally appeared posthu-
mously in 1953. On May 22, 1948, he died of heart failure in a
Chicago hospital. After a Roman Catholic service in Chicago, his
body was brought back to Harlem for a final service, and he was
then buried in a local cemetery in Queens.[89]

This collection of poetry and prose presents as a coherent
whole Claude McKay's lifelong struggle to come to terms with
himself, his people, and his world.

WAYNE COOPER

New York City
March 1973

Claude McKay in his Jamaican Constabulary uniform, circa 1911.
(Photo by Cleary.)

In Memoriam:
Booker T. Washington:

I vividly recall the noonday hour
  you walked into the wide and well-filled hall:
We rose and sang, at the conductor's call,
Dunbar's Tuskegee hymn. A splendid tower
Of strength, as would a gardener on the flower
  Nursed tenderly, you gazed upon us all
  Assembled there, a serried, sable wall
Fast mortared by your subtle tact and power.

O how I loved, adored your furrowed face!
  And fondly hoped, before your days were done,
You would look in mine too with paternal grace.
  But vain are hopes + dreams! — gone: you are gone;
Death's hand has torn you from your trusting race,
And O! we feel so utterly alone.

                    Rhonda Hope.
                    (Claude McKay)

Unpublished manuscript poem by Claude McKay in the W. S. Braith-
waite Papers, Harvard University Library. Note the pseudonym
McKay used when he first sent Braithwaite the poem. (Courtesy of
Harvard University Library.)

"I bought the magazine and tore the cover off, but it haunted me for a long time." *(Photo courtesy of the Ben and Beatrice Goldstein Foundation. Artist: Robert Minor.)*

One of the attractions for McKay of the *Masses* and the *Liberator* was their art work, especially the drawings of Negroes by a young artist named Stuart Davis. This one, entitled "The Return of the Soldier," appeared in the *Liberator,* March 1919. *(Photo courtesy of the Ben and Beatrice Goldstein Foundation.)*

Claude McKay and Max Eastman together in Moscow during the Fourth Congress of the Third International, 1922. *(Wide World Photos.)*

McKay addressing the Fourth Congress from the Throne Room in the Kremlin; see page 91. *(Photo from the jacket of* "A Long Way from Home," *1937.)*

КЛОД МАК-КЭЙ

НЕГРЫ В АМЕРИКЕ

ПЕРЕВОД С АНГЛИЙСКОГО
П. ОХРИМЕНКО

My call is the call of battle.
I nourish **active** rebellion.
Walt Whitman

Мой зов — это клич боевой.
Я пламя питаю восстанья.
Уот Уитмэн

ГОСУДАРСТВЕННОЕ ИЗДАТЕЛЬСТВО
МОСКВА... 1923 ... ПЕТРОГРАД

The title page from McKay's Russian book, *Negry v Amerike* ("Negroes in America," Moscow, 1923), never published in an English-language edition. *(Courtesy of the Slavonic Division, The New York Public Library, Astor, Lenox and Tilden Foundations.)*

Claude McKay in the 1920s. This photograph was taken while he was in Paris, probably in 1924 or 1925. *(Photograph by Berenice Abbott.)*

McKay in 1934, shortly after his return to the United States from Tangiers. *(Photograph by Carl Van Vechten courtesy of the Estate of Carl Van Vechten and the Henry W. and Albert A. Berg Collection, The New York Public Library, Astor, Lenox and Tilden Foundations.)*

Claude McKay in 1941 at the beginning of his long illness. *(Photograph by Carl Van Vechten courtesy of the Estate of Carl Van Vechten and Yale University Library.)*

I.

THE RADICAL ESTRANGEMENT 1912–1925

1. Early Articles, 1918-1922

Claude McKay came of age as a writer in the years following World War I. Between 1919 and 1924, he wrote his best poetry. During these same years, he also worked as a radical journalist and produced a small but prophetic body of prose, much of it critical of English and American radicalism. As a writer for the *Workers' Dreadnought* in London during 1920 and as an editor of the *Liberator* in New York from 1921 until the summer of 1922, McKay supported the international communist movement during its formative revival following the Russian Revolution.

Like many writers and artists of the period, he had welcomed the Revolution. At the end of the Great War, other Marxist revolutions had followed in Central Europe. Together they had seemed to augur a new age. If the West could follow the Bolshevik example, capitalism with its cold indifference to the welfare of the masses would be swept away and replaced by a more equitable socialist system. Such expectations animated all shades of left-wing opinion throughout Europe and the United States in 1918 and 1919.

For Claude McKay, revolutionary organization and action seemed clearly preferable to a continuation of the labor and racial strife that marred the American scene after the War. The nation that had vowed in 1917 "to make the world safe for Democracy," wound up in "the Red Summer" of 1919 with an orgy of violence and repression at home. America had thus begun her retreat to "normalcy." And as the revolutions in Central Europe collapsed, hopes for imminent revolution in Western Europe faded. But along with other politically conscious writers on the left, McKay continued to nourish his dreams of revolutionary change and to ponder how they could be realized in the future.

In contrast to the poetry he wrote during this period, McKay's radical journalism has received almost no attention. It remains important, however, for several reasons. As an editor of the *Liberator,* McKay was the only black on a leading journal of revolutionary politics and art at a time when close co-operation between black and white radicals had barely begun. His comments concerning the pitfalls to such co-operation have a continuing relevance.

McKay warned white radicals that unless honestly faced, the racial problem would endanger the success of any American revolutionary movement. He found the white racism that was endemic to the United States and England reflected in their socialist and communist movements, and he did not hesitate to point it out. He repeatedly stressed that a strong black and white workingclass alliance would not be possible until white radicals freed themselves of their racist assumptions. Unless they showed more awareness of the special difficulties Negroes faced because of racism, they would never win black workers to their cause. In the meantime, the capitalist managers of American society would continue to use this primary racial cleavage in the labor force to their own great advantage. McKay did not wish American radicals to duplicate the paternalism and subtle condescension so characteristic of bourgeois philanthropy. Long after he had disassociated himself from communism, his criticism would be echoed by other blacks inside the American Communist party. He also anticipated those black militants in the civil rights movement who directed similar complaints against their white counterparts in the late 1960s.

Like those who popularized the "Black Power" slogans after 1965, McKay recognized that the need for racial pride, greater self-sufficiency, and group unity could not be supplied by white radicals, no matter how great their sympathy and understanding of the race problem. For this reason, McKay, along with certain other black socialists in New York (notably W. A. Domingo and Hubert Harrison), worked with Marcus Garvey's Universal Negro Improvement Association in its early days. Through Garvey's newspaper, the *Negro World,* they hoped to make his movement responsive to international communism, as well as to other revolutionary trends in the colonial world. While in England McKay contributed several articles to the *Negro World.* Garvey, however, grew increasingly hostile to any ideas not his own, and by 1922 McKay had abandoned his movement.

Through his activities with the Garveyites, McKay had tried to reconcile his racial loyalties with his broader hopes for an international proletarian brotherhood. Although Garvey disappointed him, McKay continued to press in other areas for a more uninhibited articulation of black themes and group identity. In several drama reviews published in the *Liberator,* he looked forward to a theater that could freely express the black experience in America. He called upon Negro artists to abandon all restrictive confines—

whether of simple protest, apologetics, or mere imitation of white standards—and give full expression to the indigenous black spirit in America.

McKay was not only black but also a West Indian colonial, and he expressed a realistic appreciation of the role European imperialism had played in sustaining the capitalist system. Furthermore, he clearly foresaw that "movements of national liberation" would be the logical vehicles for the spread of communist ideas throughout the colonial world. In his view, Europe's economic system as well as her political dominance would be rejected when subject peoples freed themselves from colonial rule. He therefore cautioned white radicals against dismissing the Irish and Indian independence movements as simply nationalistic manifestations of no consequence for the future of communist revolutions in Europe and America.

McKay supported the fledgling communist movement after World War I, but as his essays reveal, he never served it as an uncritical mouthpiece. Throughout his communist years, he maintained an independence obviously incompatible with the ideological rigidity that came with the establishment of an American Communist party subservient to Moscow. From 1919 until 1923, McKay moved freely among the most notoriously contentious radicals of England and America as a solitary representative of black radicalism at its best and most sophisticated. His forthright efforts to increase awareness of the difficulties of achieving a genuine black and white working-class alliance necessitated courage. That he approached his lonely task with honesty, passion, wit, and learning is evident in the articles and reviews collected here.

From 1918 through 1924, McKay wrote approximately twenty-two essays, book reviews, and letters that appeared in the *Workers' Dreadnought* (1920), the *Liberator* (1921–1922), and the *Crisis* (1923–1924). The eight included in this chapter were selected because they seem best to reflect McKay's chief preoccupations. They include some of his most provocative essays, a literary form whose relative importance has been sadly neglected in most considerations of Negro American literature. All the pieces which follow are in the chronological order of their original publication.

A NEGRO POET

I am a black man, born in Jamaica, B.W.I., and have been living in America for the last six years. During my first year's residence in America I wrote the following group of poems. It was the first time I had ever come face to face with such manifest, implacable hate of my race, and my feelings were indescribable. I sent them so you may see what my state of mind was at the time. I have written nothing similar to them since and don't think I ever shall again.[1]

The whites at home constitute about 14% of the population only and they generally conform to the standard of English respectability. The few poor ones accept their fate resignedly and live at peace with the natives. The government is tolerant, somewhat benevolent, based on the principle of equal justice to all. I had heard of prejudice in America but never dreamed of it being so intensely bitter; for at home there is also prejudice of the English sort, subtle and dignified, rooted in class distinction—color and race being hardly taken into account.

It was such an atmosphere I left for America to find here strong white men, splendid types, of better physique than any I had ever seen, exhibiting the most primitive animal hatred towards their weaker black brothers. In the South daily murders of a nature most hideous and revolting, in the North silent acquiescence, deep hate half-hidden under a puritan respectability, oft flaming up into an occasional lynching—this ugly raw sore in the body of a great nation. At first I was horrified, my spirit revolted against the ignoble cruelty and blindness of it all. Then I soon found myself hating in return but this feeling couldn't last long for to hate is to be miserable.

Looking about me with bigger and clearer eyes I saw that this cruelty in different ways was going on all over the world. Whites were exploiting and oppressing whites even as they exploited and oppressed the yellows and blacks. And the oppressed, groaning under the lash, evinced the same despicable hate and harshness toward their weaker fellows. I ceased to think of people and things in the mass—why should I fight with mad dogs only to be bitten and probably transformed into a mad dog myself? I turned to the individual soul, the spiritual leaders, for comfort and consolation.

I felt and still feel that one must seek for the noblest and best in the individual life only: each soul must save itself.

And now this great catastrophe [World War I] has come upon the world proving the real hollowness of nationhood, patriotism, racial pride and most of the things which one was taught to respect and reverence.

There is very little to tell of my uneventful career. I was born in the heart of the little island of Jamaica on the 15th of September, 1889. My grandparents were slaves, my parents free-born. My mother was very sweet-natured, fond of books; my father, honest, stern even to harshness, hard working, beginning empty-handed he coaxed a good living from the soil, bought land, and grew to be a comparatively prosperous small settler. A firm believer in education, he tried to give all his eight children the best he could afford.

I was the last child and when I was nine years old my mother sent me to my eldest brother who was a schoolmaster in the northwestern part of the island.[2]

From that time on I became interested in books. The school building, to which was attached the teacher's cottage, was an old slave house, plain, substantial and comfortable. My brother, an amateur journalist, country correspondent for the city papers, was fond of good books and possessed a nice library—all the great English masters and a few translations from the ancients. Not caring very much for play and having plenty of leisure I spent nearly all my time out of school reading. I read whatever pleased my fancy, secretly scribbling in prose and verse at the same time, novels, history, Bible literature, tales in verse like Scott's I read, and nearly all Shakespeare's plays for the absorbing story interest. As yet I couldn't perceive the truths. Now, looking back, I can see that that was a great formative period in my life—a time of perfect freedom to play, read and think as I liked.

I finished elementary school with my brother and helped him to teach while studying further under him. In 1906 I passed an examination for the Government Trade Scholarship and was apprenticed to a wheelwright and cabinet maker. But I couldn't learn a trade.

At this time I began writing verses of Jamaican peasant life in Negro dialect. I met an Englishman [Walter Jekyll] who loved good books and their makers more than anything else. He opened up a new world to my view, introduced me to a greater, deeper literature—to Buddha, Schopenhauer and Goethe, Carlyle and

Browning, Wilde, [Edward] Carpenter,[3] Whitman, Hugo, Verlaine, Baudelaire, Shaw and the different writers of the Rationalist Press —more than I had time to read, but nearly all my spare time I spent listening to his reading choice bits from them, discussing the greatness of their minds, and telling of their lives, which I must confess I sometimes found even more interesting than their works.

Trade proved a failure. I gave it up, joined the Jamaican Constabulary 1910–11, despised it and left. With Mr. Jekyll's help, the Englishman mentioned before, my *Songs of Jamaica* was published at this time.[4] I went home and farmed rather halfheartedly. The government was then encouraging the younger men to acquire a scientific agricultural education so that it could employ them to teach the peasantry modern ways of farming. I came to America in 1912 to study agriculture, went to Tuskegee, but not liking the semi-military, machinelike existence there, I left for the Kansas State College where I stayed two years.

In the summer of 1914 I came to New York with a friend. We opened a little restaurant among our people which also proved a failure because I didn't put all my time and energy into it.[5]

After a while I got married, but my wife wearied of the life in six months and went back to Jamaica. I hated to go back after having failed at nearly everything so I just stayed here and worked desultorily—porter, houseman, janitor, butler, waiter—anything that came handy. The life was different and fascinating and one can do menial work here and feel like a man sometimes, so I don't mind it.

I am a waiter on the railroad now.[6] Here are a few of my poems.

From *Pearson's Magazine* (September, 1918), pp. 275–76.

SOCIALISM AND THE NEGRO

Aside from the autobiographical sketch above, "Socialism and the Negro" seems to have been Claude McKay's first magazine article. It appeared in Sylvia Pankhurst's small London communist weekly, the Workers' Dreadnought. *McKay was in London from the fall of 1919 through 1920.*

Chiefly through the efforts of Dr. [W. E. B.] Du Bois, author of *The Souls of Black Folk,* there came into being in the United States, some ten years ago, the National Association for the Advancement of Colored People. In the main, the organization strove to combat the wide and insidious influence of Booker [T.] Washington who, making light of the social and political status of his race, had put into practice, for its material benefit, the principle of work advocated by the latter-day Carlyle.[7] A group of wealthy and socially and politically influential bourgeois of the North, helped to launch the movement [the NAACP] and became its directing spirit.

In it were men and women representative of the old conservative and Quaker aristocracy of New England and Pennsylvania, and the liberal capitalists. It comprised intellectual and commercial Jews, and its finest spirit was Oswald Garrison Villard, editor of the American *Nation* and grandson of the great Abolitionist, who, vilified and denounced by the hide-bound capitalist press, stands out as the solitary and only consistent representative of the American bourgeoisie, counseling peace and moderation between aggressive Capitalism and its government, and Militant Labor and Socialism, and all the forces of passion struggling in America today.[8] This group, palpably ignorant of the fact that the Negro question is primarily an economic problem, evidently thought it might be solved by admitting Negroes who have won to wealth and intellectual and other attainments into white society on equal terms, and by protesting and pleading to the political and aristocratic South to remove the notorious laws limiting the political and social status of colored folk. So far as I am able to judge, it has done good work on the technically legal and educational side. It developed race-consciousness in the Negro and made him restive; but on the political side it has flirted with different parties and its work is quite ineffective.

Further, it has taken a firm stand against segregation, which is a moot and delicate question. While all Negroes are agreed that the social barriers must be removed, there is much difference in regard to education and some institutions like hospitals and churches. The growing numbers of cultured Negro men and women find it extremely difficult to obtain employment that is in keeping with their education under the capitalist system of government. For one instance, had a scholar like Dr. Du Bois been white he would certainly have secured a chair at Harvard, Yale or Columbia University, for which he is eminently fitted. Many Negroes have obtained a sound education at great sacrifice, only to be forced, upon completion of their studies, into menial or uncongenial toil. In the black belt of

New York City, where there is an estimated population of 100,000 Negroes, the Police Force, hospital, library, and elementary schools —patronized chiefly by colored people—are entirely manned by white staffs. It would be impossible for such conditions to exist under a soviet system of Government.

Just about the beginning of the late War the Socialists and I.W.W. [The Industrial Workers of the World], realizing that the Negro population offered a fertile field for propaganda, began working in earnest among them.[9] With the aid of the *Messenger Magazine,* edited by two ardent, young Negro university men,[10] and the *Liberator,* they have done real constructive work that is now bearing fine fruit. The rank-and-file Negroes of America have been very responsive to the new truths. Some of them have been lured away by the siren call of the American Federation of Labor to enter its ranks. For years this reactionary association held out against Negro membership, but recently the capitalist class, alarmed over the growth of revolutionary thought among the blacks, used its creature, Gompers,[11] to put through a resolution admitting Negroes to membership at the last conference. It has, however, had no effect on the lily-white and inconsequential trade unions of the South.

A splendid result of the revolutionary propaganda work among the blacks was the Conference of the National Brotherhood of Workers of America (entirely Negro) which was held at Washington, D.C., in September of last year.[12] Its platform is as revolutionary in principle as that of the I.W.W. Over a hundred delegates were in attendance and the majority came from the South. As always, the colored workers are ready and willing to meet the white workers halfway in order that they might unite in the fight against capitalism; but, owing to the seeds of hatred that have been sown for long years by the master class among both sections, the whites are still reluctant to take the step that would win the South over to Socialism. The black workers hold the key to the situation, but while they and the whites remain divided the reactionary South need not fear. The great task is to get both groups together. Colored men from the North cannot be sent into the South for propaganda purposes, for they will be lynched. White men from the North will be beaten and, if they don't leave, they will also be lynched. A like fate awaits colored women. But the South is boastful of its spirit of chivalry. It believes that it is the divinely appointed guardian of sacred white womanhood, and it professes to disfranchise, outrage and lynch Negro men and women solely for the protection of white women.

It seems then that the only solution to the problem is to get lovely and refined white women volunteers to carry the message of Socialism to both white and black workers. There are many of them in the movement who should be eager to go. During the period of Reconstruction a goodly number went from New England to educate the freedmen, and, although they were socially ostracized by the Southerners, they stood to their guns. Today they are needed more than ever. The call is louder and the cause is greater. Among the blacks they will be safe, respected and honored. Will they rise to their duty?

Strangely, it is the professional class of Negroes that is chiefly opposed to Socialism, although it is the class that suffers and complains most bitterly. Dr. Du Bois has flirted with the Socialist idea from a narrow, opportunist-racial standpoint; but he is in spirit opposed to it.[13] If our Negro professionals are not blindly ignorant they should realize that there will never be any hope—no sound material place in the economic life of the world—for them until the Negro masses are industrially independent. Many colored doctors, lawyers, journalists, teachers and preachers literally starve and are driven to the wall because the black working class does not earn enough to give them adequate support. Naturally, the white workers will hardly turn from their kind to colored aspirants to the professions, even though the latter should possess exceptional ability. And even when they are capable they are often up against the prejudice of their own people who have been subtly taught by the white ruling class to despise the talented of their race and sneer at their accomplishments.

During the War, Marcus Garvey, a West Indian Negro, went to New York and formed the Universal Negro Improvement Association, and African Communities' League for the redemption of Negro Africa, and the return thither of Negroes in exile. The movement has had an astonishing success. Negroes from all parts of the world, oppressed by the capitalists, despised and denied a fighting chance under the present economic system by white workingmen, have hailed it as the star of hope, the ultimate solution of their history-old troubles. It now numbers over two million active members. The capitalist press which ridiculed it at first now mentions the Association in flattering terms, especially since it successfully floated the Black Star Line Steamship Company. At the beginning the company had much trouble with the local authorities, but it has never been persecuted by the State or Federal Government, for it is non-Social-

istic, of course. Although an international Socialist, I am supporting
the movement, for I believe that, for subject peoples, at least, Na-
tionalism is the open door to Communism. Furthermore, I will try
to bring this great army of awakened workers over to the finer sys-
tem of Socialism. Some English Communists have remarked to me
that they have no real sympathy for the Irish and Indian movement
because it is nationalistic. But, today, the British Empire is the
greatest obstacle to International Socialism, and any of its subjugated
parts succeeding in breaking away from it would be helping the
cause of World Communism. In these pregnant times no people who
are strong enough to throw off an imperial yoke will tamely submit
to a system of local capitalism. The breaking up of the British Em-
pire must either begin at home or abroad; the sooner the strong
blow is struck the better it will be for all Communists. Hence the
English revolutionary workers should not be unduly concerned over
the manner in which the attack should begin. Unless, like some
British intellectuals, they are enamored of the idea of a Socialist (?)
British Empire! Unless they are willing to be provided with cheap
raw materials by the slaves of Asia and Africa for the industries of
their overcrowded cities, while the broad, fertile acres of Great
Britain are held for hunting and other questionable pleasures.

From *Workers' Dreadnought* (January 31, 1920), pp. 1–2.

A BLACK MAN REPLIES

*When Germany violated the Versailles settlement by allowing its
soldiers to enter the demilitarized Ruhr in the spring of 1920,
France retaliated. On April 6, 1920, French troops, including con-
tingents of African colonials, occupied several German towns along
the Rhine. In Britain, most left-wing opinion feared the French
action might topple the shaky Weimar government and pave the
way for a return to power of German reactionaries and extreme
nationalists. Hoping to arouse public opinion against the French,
Britain's leading socialist newspaper, the* Daily Herald, *stirred the
racial fears of its readers by publishing a front page article on April
10, 1920, entitled "Black Scourge in Europe: Sexual Horror Let
Loose by France on Rhine . . . ." Authored by E. D. Morel (1873–*

*1924), a left-liberal champion of blacks in Africa who had earlier
exposed King Leopold's infamous regime in the Congo, the article
touched off international protests against the French action which
Morel nourished for more than a year with further racist charges.
The Herald's editor, George Lansbury (1859–1940), a prominent
socialist and Labour politician, declined to print McKay's letter of
protest, which appeared in the Workers' Dreadnought April 24,
1920. It was the only substantial reply to Morel's allegations from
the British radical press.*[14]

Dear Editor: The following letter, replying to E. D. Morel's article
on the black troops in Germany, was sent to the [London] *Daily
Herald* on April 11th [1920], but apparently the *Herald* refuses a
hearing to the other side, which is quite inarticulate:

The Editor of the *Daily Herald.*

Sir: The odiousness of your article headlined "Black Scourge in
Europe: Sexual Horror Let Loose" is not mitigated by your explana-
tory editorial and note stating that you are not encouraging race
prejudice and that you champion native rights in Africa. If you are
really consistent in thinking that you can do something to help the
white and black peoples to a better understanding of each other,
there is much that you might learn from Liberal and Conservative
organs like the *Nation,* the *New Statesman* and the *Edinburgh Re-
view,* which have treated the problem (exposing the iniquities prac-
ticed upon the natives and showing up the shortcomings of the latter)
in a decent and dignified manner.

Your correspondent, who peddles his books and articles on "the
poor, suffering black," is quite worked up over the African warriors
carrying off prizes of war like the heads and eyes of their victims.
But, verily, trophies of war are trophies of war, whether they are
human works of art like paintings and sculpture, or nature's, like
man's hands and heads. I am quite ignorant of the "well-known
physiological reasons that make the raping of a white woman by a
negro resultful of serious and fatal injury." Any violent act of rape,
whether by white, yellow or black, civilized or savage man, must
entail injury, serious or fatal, especially if the victim be a virgin.
The worst case of rape I ever heard of took place in Kansas City
some eight years ago; the woman was white, the perpetrators three
white men, and the result was well-nigh fatal. In the West Indies
there have been many instances of white soldiers raping colored

women with awful consequences. Your correspondent employs the same methods used by the German propagandists during the War without any real effect. England, France, even America, all used their black troops in the War. Surely the *Daily Herald,* by the light of experience, ought to find a more effective and honest way of combating a grave evil.

Why all this obscene, maniacal outburst about the sex vitality of black men in a proletarian paper? You might say the negro is oversexed; the same statement may be made of the Italians and Jews of the Caucasian race. To say that the black man is "sexually unrestrainable" is palpably false. I, a full-blooded negro, can control my sexual proclivities when I care to, and I am endowed with my full share of the primitive passion. Besides, I know of hundreds of negroes of the Americas and Africa who can do likewise. When white men go among colored races they do not take their women with them; hence the hundreds of mulattos, octoroons and eurasians disowned of the Caucasian race.

During my stay in Europe, I have come in contact with many weak and lascivious persons of both sexes, but I do not argue from my experience that the English race is degenerate. On the other hand, I have known some of the finest and cleanest types of men and women among the Anglo-Saxons.

If the black troops are syphilitic, they have been contaminated by the white world. According to competent white investigators, syphilis is a disease peculiar to white and yellow peoples; where it is known among the blacks it has been carried thither by the whites. Houses of prostitution have always been maintained, officially or otherwise, for soldiers. They were a notorious fact during the late War. I think the key to your exposure may be found in your excerpt from *Clarte,* which states that "German girls of barely marriageable age sell themselves because 20 francs are worth 150 marks, and 50 francs 400 marks." In this intolerable age the great majority of peoples, male and female, in different ways, is more or less given to prostitution. The stopping of French exploitation and use of the North African conscripts (not mercenaries, as your well-informed correspondent insists they are) against the Germans is clearly a matter upon which the French Socialists should take united action. But not as you have done.

I do not protest because I happen to be a negro (I am disgusted when I read in your columns that the white dockers would prohibit their employers using Chinese and Indian labor), I write because I feel that the ultimate result of your propaganda will be further strife and blood-spilling between the whites and the many members of my race, boycotted economically and socially, who have been dumped down on the English docks since the ending of the European War. I have been told in Limehouse by white men, who ought to know, that this summer will see a recrudescence of the outbreaks that occurred last year. The negro-baiting Bourbons of the United States will thank you, and the proletarian underworld of London will certainly gloat over the scoop of the Christian-Socialist-pacifist *Daily Herald.*

Yours etc.,

Claude McKay

HOW BLACK SEES GREEN AND RED

Early in 1921 McKay returned to the United States and in the spring became an associate editor of the Liberator. *"How Black Sees Green and Red" summarizes a significant part of his British experience, his impressions of the Irish revolutionary movement, the Sinn Fein, which was then waging its determined and eventually successful fight for Ireland's independence.*

Last summer I went to a big Sinn Fein demonstration in Trafalgar Square. The place was densely packed, the huge crowd spreading out into the Strand and up to the steps of the National Gallery. I was there selling the *Workers' Dreadnought,* Sylvia Pankhurst's pamphlet, *Rebel Ireland,* and Herman Gorter's *Ireland: The Achilles Heel of England;* I sold out completely. All Ireland was there. As I passed round eagerly in friendly rivalry with other sellers of my group, I remarked aged men and women in frayed, old-fashioned clothes, middle-aged couples, young stalwarts, beautiful girls and little children, all wearing the shamrock or some green symbol. I also wore a green necktie and was greeted from different quarters as "Black Murphy" or "Black Irish." With both hands and my bag full of literature I had to find some time and a way for hearty handshakes and brief chats with Sinn Fein Communists and regular Sinn

Feiners. I caught glimpses also of proud representatives of the Sinn Fein bourgeoisie. For that day at least I was filled with the spirit of Irish nationalism—although I am black!

Members of the bourgeoisie among the Sinn Feiners, like Constance Markiewicz [15] and Erskine Childers,[16] always stress the fact that Ireland is the only "white" nation left under the yoke of foreign imperialism. There are other nations in bondage, but they are not of the breed; they are colored, some are even Negro. It is comforting to think that bourgeois nationalists and patriots of whatever race or nation are all alike in outlook. They chafe under the foreign bit because it prevents them from using to the full their native talent for exploiting their own people. However, a black worker may be sensitive to every injustice felt by a white person. And I, for one, cannot but feel a certain sympathy with these Irish rebels of the bourgeoisie.

But it is with the proletarian revolutionists of the world that my whole spirit revolts. It matters not that I am pitied, even by my white fellow-workers who are conscious of the fact that besides being an economic slave as they, I am what they are not—a social leper, of a race outcast from an outcast class. Theirs is a class, which though circumscribed in its sphere, yet has a freedom of movement —a right to satisfy the simple cravings of the body—which is denied to me. Yet I see no other way of upward struggle for colored peoples, but the way of the working-class movement, ugly and harsh though some of its phases may be. None can be uglier and harsher than the routine existence of the average modern worker. The yearning of the American Negro especially, can only find expression and realization in the class struggle. Therein lies his hope. For the Negro is in a peculiar position in America. In spite of a professional here and a businessman there, the maintenance of an all-white supremacy in the industrial and social life, as well as the governing bodies of the nation, places the entire Negro race alongside the lowest section of the white working class. They are struggling for identical things. They fight along different lines simply because they are not as class-conscious and intelligent as the ruling classes they are fighting. Both need to be awakened. When a Negro is proscribed on account of his color, when the lynching fever seizes the South and begins to break out even in the North, the black race feels and thinks as a unit. But it has no sense of its unity as a class—or as a part, rather, of the American working-class, and so it is powerless. The Negro must acquire class-consciousness. And the white workers must accept him and work with him, whether they object to his color and morals or not. For his presence is to them a menacing reality.

American Negroes hold some sort of a grudge against the Irish. They have asserted that Irishmen have been their bitterest enemies, that the social and economic boycott against Negroes was begun by the Irish in the North during the Civil War and has, in the main, been fostered by them ever since.[17] The Irish groups in America are, indeed, like the Anglo-Saxons, quite lacking in all the qualities that make living among the Latins tolerable for one of a conspicuously alien race. However, I react more to the emotions of the Irish people than to those of any other whites; they are so passionately primitive in their loves and hates. They are quite free of the disease which is known in bourgeois phraseology as Anglo-Saxon hypocrisy. I suffer with the Irish. I think I understand the Irish. My belonging to a subject race entitles me to some understanding of them. And then I was born and reared a peasant; the peasant's passion for the soil possesses me, and it is one of the strongest passions in the Irish revolution.

The English, naturally, do not understand the Irish, and the English will not understand unless they are forced to. Their imperialists will use the military in Ireland to shoot, destroy and loot. Their bourgeoisie will religiously try to make this harmonize with British morality. And their revolutionists—I would almost say that the English revolutionists, anarchists, socialists and communists, understand Ireland less than any other political group. It appears that they would like to link up the Irish national revolution to the English class struggle with the general headquarters in England. And as Sinn Fein does not give lip-service to communism, the English revolutionists are apparently satisfied in thinking that their sympathy lies with the Irish workers, but that they must back the red flag against the green.

And the Irish workers hate the English. It may not sound nice in the ears of an "infantile left" communist to hear that the workers of one country hate the workers of another. It isn't beautiful propaganda. Nevertheless, such a hatred does exist. In the past the Irish revolutionists always regarded the Royal Irish Constabulary as their greatest enemy. Until quite recently its members were recruited chiefly from the Irish workers themselves; but the soldiers of the Irish Republican Army shot down these uniformed men like dogs, and when at last thousands of them deserted to Sinn Fein, either from fear of their fighting countrymen, or by their finer instinct asserting itself, they were received as comrades—hid, fed, clothed and provided with jobs. I saw one of the official Sinn Fein bulletins which called upon the population to give succor to the deserting policemen. They were enemies only while they wore the uniform and carried out the orders of Dublin Castle. Now they are friends, and the British have turned to England and Scotland for recruits. And so all the hatred of the Irish workers is turned against the English. They think, as do all subject peoples with foreign soldiers and their officers lording it over them, that even the exploited English proletariat are their oppressors.

And it is true at least that the English-organized workers merrily ship munitions and men across the Channel for the shooting of their Irish brothers. Last spring, following on a little propaganda and agitation, some London railmen refused to haul munitions that were going to Ireland. They had acted on the orders of Cramp,[18] the strong man of their union. But the railroad directors made threats and appealed to Lloyd George, who grew truculent. J. H. Thomas, the secretary of the Railwaymen's union, intervened and the order was gracefully rescinded. As usual, Thomas found the way out that was satisfactory to the moral conscience of the nation. It was not so much the hauling of munitions, he said, but the making of them that was wrong. The railroad workers should not be asked to shoulder the greatest burden of the workers' fight merely because they hold the key to the situation!

It is not the English alone, but also the anglicized Irish, who persist in misunderstanding Ireland. Liberals and reactionary socialists vie with each other in quoting Bernard Shaw's famous "Ireland Has a Grievance." [19] Shaw was nice enough to let me visit him during my stay in London. He talked lovingly and eloquently of the beauty of medieval cathedrals. I was charmed with his clear, fine language, and his genial manner. Between remarking that Hyndman [20] was typical of the popular idea of God, and asking me why I did not go in for pugilism instead of poetry—the only light thought that he indulged in—he told of a cultured Chinaman who came all the way from China to pay homage to him as the patriarch of English letters. And just imagine what the Chinaman wanted to talk about? Ireland! It was amusingly puzzling to Shaw! Yet it was easy for me to understand why a Chinaman whose country had been exploited, whose culture had been belittled and degraded by aggressive imperial nations, should want to speak to a representative Irishman about Ireland.

Whilst the eyes of the subject peoples of the world are fixed on Ireland, and Sinn Fein stands in embattled defiance against the government of the British Empire; whilst England proclaims martial law in Ireland, letting her Black and Tans run wild through the country, and Irish men and women are giving their lives daily for the idea of freedom, Bernard Shaw dismisses the revolutionary phenomenon as a "grievance." Yet the Irish revolutionists love Shaw. An Irish rebel will say that Shaw is a British socialist who does not understand Ireland. But like Wilde he is an individual Irishman who has conquered England with his plays. There the fierce Irish pride asserts itself. Shaw belongs to Ireland.

I marvel that Shaw's attitude towards his native land should be similar to that of any English bourgeois reformist, but I suppose that anyone who has no faith, no real vision of International Communism, will agree with him. To the internationalist, it seems evident that the dissolution of the British Empire and the ushering in of an era of proletarian states, will give England her proper proportional place in the political affairs of the world.

The greatest tradition of England's glory flourishes, however, in quite unexpected places. Some English communists play with the idea of England becoming the center of International Communism, just as she is the center of International Capitalism. I read recently an article by a prominent English communist on city soviets. It contained a glowing picture of the great slums transformed into beautiful dwellings and splendid suburbs. When one talks to a Welsh revolutionist, a Scotch communist, or an Irish rebel, one hears the yearning hunger of the people for the land in his voice. One sees it in his eyes. When one listens to an earnest Welsh miner, one gets the impression that he is sometimes seized with a desire to destroy the mine in which his life is buried. The English proletarian strikes one as being more matter-of-fact. He likes his factories and cities of convenient makeshifts. And when he talks of controlling and operating the works for the workers, there burns no poetry in his eyes, no passion in his voice. English landlordism and capitalism have effectively and efficiently killed the natural hunger of the proletariat for the land. In England the land issue is raised only by the liberal-radicals, and finds no response in the heart of the proletariat. That is a further reason why England cannot understand the Irish revolution. For my part I love to think of communism liberating millions of city folk to go back to the land.

The English will not let go of Ireland. The militarists are hoping that the Irish people, persecuted beyond endurance, will rise protesting and demonstrating in a helpless and defenseless mass. Then they can be shot down as were the natives of Amritsar in India. But against a background of experience the generals of the Irish Army are cautious. The population is kept under strict discipline. The systematic destruction of native industries by the English army of occupation forces forces them to adopt some communist measures for self-preservation. They are imbibing the atmosphere and learning the art of revolution. I heard from an Irish communist in London that some Indian students had been in Dublin to study that art where it is in practical operation. It is impossible not to feel that the Irish revolution—nationalistic though it is—is an entering wedge directed straight to the heart of British capitalism.

From *Liberator*, vol. 4 (June, 1921), pp. 17, 20–21.

A NEGRO EXTRAVAGANZA

There are shovelfuls of humor and barrels of joy in the Negro Burlesque [21] playing at the Sixty-third Street Music Hall. Despite adverse and pointless criticism, the comedy has survived the summer and should sweep along through this season. A burlesque show is a burlesque with its inevitable commingling of grain and chaff and overdoing of the obvious. And the metropolitan notational critics who have damned *Shuffle Along* for not fulfilling the role of an Italian light opera are as filmy-sighted as the convention-ridden and head-ossified Negro intelligentsia, who censure colored actors for portraying the inimitable comic characteristics of Negro life, because they make white people laugh! Negro artists will be doing a fine service to the world, maybe greater than the combined action of all the white and black radicals yelling revolution together, if by their efforts they can spirit the whites away from lynching and inbred prejudice, to the realm of laughter and syncopated motion. After the ugly post-war riots between white and black in the big English ports, George Lansbury of the *Daily Herald* brought the American Southern Orchestra [22] from the West End of London to sing in Poplar, the very heart of the trouble. And soon all the slums of London, forgetting the riots, were echoing with syncopated songs.

Although so far apart apparently, the ready-to-wear comment of white and black Americans on "Afro-American" artistic endeavor is really very similar. It rises from the same source—colorphobia and antagonism on both sides. The American public is dimly aware of a great storehouse of Negro Art in this country. But with its finer senses blurred by prejudice, it turns to Yankee–Dixie impersonators and Semitic imitators for the presentation of Negro Art. And from these bastard exhibitions the current standards are set. The Negro critics can scarcely perceive and recognize true values through the screen of sneering bigotry put between them and life by the dominant race. So against the worthless standards of the whites, the black intelligentsia, sensitive and pompous, would oppose such solid things as the aristocracy of St. Phillip's Church,[23] the compositions of Coleridge-Taylor [24] and Mr. Harry Burleigh,[25] the painting of Mr. Tanner,[26] the prose of Mr. Du Bois, the critiques of Mr. Braithwaite [27] and the poetry of Mr. James Weldon Johnson, as the only expression of Negro Culture. For such a list would earn the solemn approval of the *New York Times*. Negro art, these critics declare, must be dignified and respectable like the Anglo-Saxon's before it can be good. The Negro must get the warmth, color and laughter out of his blood, else the white man will sneer at him and treat him with contumely. Happily the Negro retains his joy of living in the teeth of such criticism; and in Harlem, along Fifth and Lenox avenues, in Marcus Garvey's Hall with its extravagant paraphernalia, in his churches and cabarets, he expresses himself with a zest that is yet to be depicted by a true artist.

Shuffle Along somewhat conflicts with my international intelligence and entices me to become a patriotic barker for my race. It makes me believe that Negroes are not civilized enough to be vulgar, nor will they ever express themselves through the medium of respectability.

"A cheap imitation of Broadway"—this is what some critics say of it. And it is superficially true. Negroes of America, who by an acquired language and suffering, are closer knit together than all the many tribes of Africa, alien to each other by custom and language, cannot satisfy the desire of the hypercritical whites for the Congo wriggle, the tribal war jig, and the jungle whoop. The chastisement of civilization has sobered and robbed them of these unique manifestations. American Negroes have not the means and leisure to tour Africa for ancestral wonders. And those carping whites who are in a like quandary might well visit Coney Island and the circuses to get acquainted with the stunts of Savagedom. Or they might take a look into themselves. The conventions of *Shuffle Along* are those of Broadway, but the voice is nevertheless indubitably Africa expatriate. It is this basic African element which makes all Negro imitations so delightfully humorous and enjoyable. It is this something that always sent me to see the Lafayette Players at 131st Street and Seventh Avenue in white plays after they had been passed up by Broadway.[28] To me the greatest charm is that the erotic movements are different. And besides, "The Negroes make their eyes talk." Such eyes! So luminously alive!

How deliciously appealing is the mimicry of Miss Florence Mills,[29] the sparkling gold star of the show. She can twist her face in imitation of a thousand primitive West African masks, some patterns of which may be seen at the American Museum of Natural History. Her coo-cooing and pooh-poohing tintinnabulate all over the hall. She is prettiest in her vivid orange frock. She might have been featured more. She is like one of those Southern rarities that used to bowl one over in the cabarets of Philadelphia and Baltimore during the wonderful wet days. Noble Sissle [30] knows his range and canters over it with the ease and grace of an antelope. The Harmony Kings [31] are in the direct line of the Jubilee Singers, whether they give a plantation melody or syncopate a Tyrolese or Hawaiian song.

The show is built on an excellent framework: the lines and measurements just crazy enough to make everything funny. Black Jimtown is like any other town; the business of governing is graft. Sam Peck and Steve Jenkins [32] are uproariously in the game, and also the perfect "Onion" Jeffrey.[33]

But the ensemble is a little disappointing and lacking in harmony. Instead of making up to achieve a uniform near-white complexion the chorus might have made up to accentuate the diversity of shades among "Afro-Americans" and let the white audience in on the secret of the color nomenclature of the Negro world. For, as the whites have their blonde and brunette, so do the blacks have their chocolate, chocolate-to-the-bone, brown, low-brown, teasing-brown, high-brown, yellow, high-yellow and so on. The difference on our side is so much more interesting and funny. It is whispered in some circles that the "Blue-vein" Societies among the Afro-American elite bar the black girls from the stage. But this can hardly be true; for I have rarely seen any social gathering of American Negroes where there were not very dark damsels through whose skin the blue veins could not show! However, there is a dearth of black girls in Negro theatricals whose presence would surely give more distinction and realism to the stage. I believe that the colored actors prefer the lighter-skinned girls. The latter are vivacious, pushing and pretty, but prettiness is always plentiful, while beauty is rare and hard to find. If black men in general favor the lighter women of their race, it is a natural phenomenon beyond criticism. The Negroes of the western world are producing and fostering new types. The deep-rooted animosity of the lily-white and the bombastic mouthings of the "sable-ites" against miscegenation are both but foam on the great, natural, barrier-breaking current of interracial contact. Still, despite this fact, Negro artists ought not to ignore the variety of material at hand.

Review of *Shuffle Along,* a musical review by Noble Sissle and Eubie Blake, from *Liberator,* vol. 4 (December, 1921), pp. 24–26.

GARVEY AS A NEGRO MOSES

"Garveyism" is a well-known word in Negro New York. And it is known among all the Negroes of America, and throughout the world, wherever there are race-conscious Negro groups. But while Garvey is a sort of magic name among the ignorant black masses, the Negro intelligentsia thinks that by his spectacular antics—words big with bombast, colorful robes, Anglo-Saxon titles of nobility (Sir William Ferris, K.C.O.N., for instance, his editor, and Lady Henrietta Vinton Davis, his international organizer), his steamroller-like mass meetings and parades and lamentable business ventures— Garvey has muddied the waters of the Negro movement for freedom and put the race back for many years. But the followers of Marcus Garvey, who are legion and noisy as a tambourine yard party give him the crown of Negro leadership. Garvey, they assert, with his Universal Negro Improvement Association and the Black Star Line, has given the Negro problem a universal advertisement and made it as popular as Negro minstrelsy. Where men like Booker T. Washington, Dr. Du Bois of the National Association for the Advancement of Colored People, and William Monroe Trotter [34] of the Equal Rights League had but little success, Garvey succeeded in bringing the Associated Press to its knees every time he bellowed. And his words were trumpeted round the degenerate pale-face world trembling with fear of the new Negro.

To those who know Jamaica, the homeland of Marcus Garvey, Garveyism inevitably suggests the name of Bedwardism. Bedwardism is the name of a religious sect there, purely native in its emotional and external features and patterned after the Baptists. It is the true religion of thousands of natives, calling themselves Bedwardites. It was founded by an illiterate black giant named Bedward about twenty-five years ago, who claimed medicinal and healing properties for a sandy little hole beside a quiet river that flowed calmly to the sea through the eastern part of Jamaica. In the beginning prophet Bedward was a stock newspaper joke; but when thousands began flocking to hear the gigantic white-robed servant of God at his quarterly baptism, and the police were hard put to handle the crowds, the British Government in Jamaica became irritated. Bedward was warned and threatened and even persecuted a little, but his thousands of followers stood more firmly by him and made him rich with great presents of food, clothing, jewelry and money. So Bedward waxed fat in body and spirit. He began a great building of stone to the God of Bedwardism which he declared could not be finished until the Second Coming of Christ. And in the plentitude of his powers he sat in his large yard under an orange tree, his wife and grown children, all good Bedwardites, around him, and gave out words of wisdom on his religion and upon topical questions to the pilgrims who went daily to worship and to obtain a bottle of water from the holy hole. The most recent news of the prophet was his arrest by the government for causing hundreds of his followers to sell all their possessions and come together at his home in August Town to witness his annunciation; for on a certain day at noon, he had said, he would ascend into heaven upon a crescent moon. The devout sold and gave away all their property and flocked to August Town, and the hour of the certain day came and passed with Bedward waiting in his robes, and days followed and weeks after. Then his flock of sheep, now turned into a hungry, destitute, despairing mob, howled like hyenas and fought each other until the Government interfered.[35]

It may be that the notorious career of Bedward, the prophet, worked unconsciously upon Marcus Garvey's mind and made him work out his plans along similar spectacular lines. But between the mentality of both men there is no comparison. While Bedward was a huge inflated bag of bombast loaded with ignorance and superstition, Garvey's is beyond doubt a very energetic and quick-witted mind, barb-wired by the imperial traditions of nineteenth-century England. His spirit is revolutionary, but his intellect does not understand the significance of modern revolutionary developments. Maybe he chose not to understand; he may have realized that a resolute facing of facts would make puerile his beautiful schemes for the redemption of the continent of Africa.

It is rather strange that Garvey's political ideas should be so curiously bourgeois-obsolete and fantastically utopian. For he is not of the school of Negro leader that has existed solely on the pecuniary crumbs of Republican politics and democratic philanthropy, and who is absolutely incapable of understanding the Negro-proletarian point of view and the philosophy of the working-class movement. On the contrary, Garvey's background is very industrial, for in the West Indies the Negro problem is peculiarly economic, and prejudice is, English-wise, more of class than of race. The flame of revolt must have stirred in Garvey in his early youth when he found the doors to higher education barred against him through economic pressure. For when he became a printer by trade in Kingston he was active in organizing the compositors, and he was the leader of the printers' strike there, ten years ago, during which time he brought out a special propaganda sheet for the strikers. The strike failed and Garvey went to Europe, returning to Jamaica after a few months' stay abroad, to start his Universal Negro Society. He failed at this in Jamaica, where a tropical laziness settles like a warm fog over the island. Coming to New York in 1917, he struck the black belt like a cyclone, and there lay the foundation of the Universal Negro Improvement Association and the Black Star Line.

At that time the World War had opened up a new field for colored workers. There was less race discrimination in the ranks of labor and the factory gates swung open to the Negro worker. There was plenty of money to spare. Garvey began his "Back to Africa" propaganda in the streets of Harlem, and in a few months he had made his organ, the *Negro World,* the best-edited colored weekly in New York. The launching of the Black Star Line project was the grand event of the movement among all Garveyites, and it had an electrifying effect upon all the Negro peoples of the world—even the black intelligentsia. It landed on the front page of the white press and made good copy for the liberal weeklies and the incorruptible monthlies. The *Negro World* circulated 60,000 copies, and a perusal of its correspondence page showed letters breathing an intense love for Africa from the farthest ends of the world. The movement for African redemption had taken definite form in the minds of Western Negroes, and the respectable Negro uplift organizations were shaken up to realize the significance of "Back to Africa." The money for shares of the Black Star Line poured in in hundreds and thousands of dollars, some brilliant Negro leaders were drawn to the organization, and the little Negro press barked at Garvey from every part of the country, questioning his integrity and impugning his motives. And Garvey, Hearst-like, thundered back his threats at the critics through the *Negro World* and was soon involved in a net of law suits.

The most puzzling thing about the "Back to Africa" propaganda is the leader's repudiation of all the fundamentals of the black worker's economic struggle. No intelligent Negro dare deny the almost miraculous effect and the world-wide breadth and sweep of Garvey's propaganda methods. But all those who think broadly on social conditions are amazed at Garvey's ignorance and his intolerance of modern social ideas. To him Queen Victoria and Lincoln are the greatest figures in history because they both freed the slaves, and the Negro race will never reach the heights of greatness until it has produced such types. He talks of Africa as if it were a little island in the Caribbean Sea. Ignoring all geographical and political divisions, he gives his followers the idea that that vast continent of diverse tribes consists of a large homogenous nation of natives struggling for freedom and waiting for the Western Negroes to come and help them drive out the European exploiters. He has never urged Negroes to organize in industrial unions.

He only exhorted them to get money, buy shares in his African steamship line, and join his Universal Association. And thousands of American and West Indian Negroes respond with eagerness.

He denounced the Socialists and Bolshevists for plotting to demoralize the Negro workers and bring them under the control of white labor. And in the same breath he attacked the National Association for the Advancement of Colored People, and its founder, Dr. Du Bois, for including white leaders and members. In the face of his very capable mulatto and octoroon colleagues, he advocated an all-sable nation of Negroes to be governed strictly after the English plan with Marcus Garvey as supreme head.

He organized a Negro Legion and a Negro Red Cross in the heart of Harlem. The Black Star line consisted of two unseaworthy boats and the Negro Factories Corporation was mainly existent on paper. But it seems that Garvey's sole satisfaction in his business venture was the presenting of grandiose visions to his crowd.

Garvey's arrest by the Federal authorities after five years of stupendous vaudeville is a fitting climax.[36] He should feel now an ultimate satisfaction in the fact that he was a universal advertising manager. He was the biggest popularizer of the Negro problem, especially among Negroes, since *Uncle Tom's Cabin*. He attained the sublime. During the last days he waxed more falsely eloquent in his tall talks on the Negro Conquest of Africa, and when the clansmen [37] yelled their approval and clamored for more, in his gorgeous robes, he lifted his hands to the low ceiling in a weird pose, his huge ugly bulk cowing the crowd, and told how the mysteries of African magic had been revealed to him, and how he would use them to put the white man to confusion and drive him out of Africa.

From *Liberator,* vol. 5 (April, 1922), pp. 8–9.

HE WHO GETS SLAPPED

"Wouldn't your dramatic critic like to see *He Who Gets Slapped?*" So, very graciously, wrote the Theater Guild's publicity agent to the *Liberator*. Our sometime dramatic critic, Charles W. Wood,[38] having deserted us for the season, I elected myself dramatic critic by acclamation. It would be pleasant to sit in a free front-row parquet seat along with "The Press," instead of buying a ticket for the second balcony. And as for the other seat—free seats come in pairs—I decided to take along William Gropper,[39] *Liberator* artist of the powerful punch and vindictive line, and master of the grotesque.

So on the appointed night we presented ourselves at the box office of the Fulton. It was with keen pleasure I anticipated seeing this fantastic play of Leonid Andreyev's—*He, The One Who Gets Slapped*. A curious and amusing theme!

The stubs were handed to Gropper and we started towards the orchestra. But the usher, with a look of quizzical amazement on his face, stopped us. Snatching the stubs from Gropper and muttering something about seeing the manager, he left us wondering and

bewildered. In a moment he returned, with the manager. "The—
the wrong date," the manager stammered and, taking the stubs
marked "orchestra," he hurried off to the box office, returning with
others marked "balcony." Suddenly the realization came to me. I
had come here as a dramatic critic, a lover of the theater, and a free
soul. But—I was abruptly reminded—those things did not matter.
The important fact, with which I was suddenly slapped in the face,
was my color. I am a Negro.

He, The One Who Gets Slapped! . . . Gropper and I were
shunted upstairs. I was for refusing to go, but Gropper, quite prop-
erly, urged compromise. So brooding darkly, madly, burnt, seared
and pierced and over-burdened with hellish thoughts, I, with Grop-
per beside me half averting his delicate pale face, his fingers run
through his unkempt mop of black hair, shading his strangely child-
like blue eyes, sat through Leonid Andreyev's play.

Andreyev's masterpiece, they call it. A masterpiece? A cleverly
melodramatic stringing together of buffoonery, serious-comic phi-
losophy, sensational love-hungriness and doll-baby impossibilism,
staged to tickle the mawkish emotions of the bourgeois mob! So I
thought. I sat there, apart, alone, black and shrouded in blackness,
quivering in every fiber, my heart denying itself and hiding from
every gesture of human kindliness, hard in its belief that kindliness
is to be found in no nation or race. I sat inwardly groaning through
what seemed a childish caricature of tragedy. Ah! if the accident of
birth had made Andreyev a Negro, if he had been slapped, kicked,
buffeted, pounded, niggered, ridiculed, sneered at, exquisitely tor-
tured, near-lynched and trampled underfoot by the merry white
horde, and if he still preserved through the terrible agony a sound
body and a mind sensitive and sharp to perceive the qualities of life,
he might have written a real play about Being Slapped. I had come
to see a tragic farce—and I found myself unwillingly the hero of
one. He who got slapped was I. As always in the world-embracing
Anglo-Saxon circus, the intelligence, the sensibilities of the black
clown were slapped without mercy.

Dear Leonid Andreyev, if you had only risen out of your intro-
spective Nihilistic despair to create the clown in the circus of hell,
the clown slapped on every side by the devil's red-hot tongs, yet
growing wiser, stronger and firmer in purposeful determination,
seeking no refuge in suicide, but bearing it out to the bitter end, you
might have touched me. But your veiled message means nothing to

me and mine. In the great prison yard of white civilization in which Negro clowns move and have their being, your play is a baby babbling in the bedlam of the Christian market-place. And a baby has no chance under the cloven hoofs of the traders in the mart. It is marked for destruction even as I am marked; for, to the hard traders I am a mere pickaninny grown up, that has no claim to the privileges of a man. The purpose of the great traders is clear. They have a little place, a groove for their pickaninny. He must not think, hope, aspire, love in his own way, utter himself and delight in the wonderful creative experience of life as other men. For thousands of other pickaninnies who feel their painfully tragic position in the trader's world may be aroused to action.

I cry my woe to the whirling world, but not in despair. For I understand the forces that doom the race into which I was born to lifelong discrimination and servitude. And I know that these forces are not eternal, they can be destroyed and will be destroyed. They are marked for destruction. Mesopotamia, Egypt, Greece, Carthage, Arabia, Babylonia, Tyre, Persia, Rome, Germania! The whole historical pageant of the human race unfolds before me in high consolation.

Big business thrives on color lines and race differences. Its respectable institutions and criminal governments draw strength and power from race hatreds, class distinctions and social insults and discriminations against Negroes. I know the mighty world forces that reach out to control even such organizations as the tiny Theatre Guilds that are doubtless, so far as they can be, radical. So when the representative of the Guild talks over the telephone to the *Liberator*: "So sorry about Mr. McKay, but you will understand why we must give him a balcony seat," I, too, understand her quite perfectly. I know of the cruel competition of the theater business. I know that most of the productions are financial failures. And so, not I would ask any theater or any business, however exquisitely artistic, however moral and aloof from the market, to shoulder the burden of the Negro race.

Poor, painful black face, intruding into the holy places of the whites. How like a specter you haunt the pale devils! Always at their elbow, always darkly peering through the window, giving them no rest, no peace. How they burn up their energies trying to keep you out! How apologetic and uneasy they are, yes, even the best of them, poor devils, when you force an entrance, blackface, facetiously, incorrigibly smiling or disturbingly composed. Shock them out of their complacency, blackface, make them uncomfortable, make them unhappy! Give them no peace, no rest. How can they bear your presence, blackface, great, unappeasable ghost of Western civilization!

Yet for the Negro pilgrim there is sometimes a gleam in the dismal, gloomy wood, A little light that saves the sensitive, swarthy face, bruised and bloody, from constant butting against the lignum-vitae trunks of deep-rooted stress. In the populous Sahara of the whites there are little oases where the black pariahs may quench their thirst. Yes, even in the little section of the Metropolitan theaters. For example, at the *Chauve Souris* we had orchestra seats, but at that time the whole atmosphere, audience and all, was so un-American, so foreign-looking, that it must have made no difference.[40] The patrons seemed so simple and Bolshevik-like—they probably didn't care if I was a Negro. They seemed so different from the philistine art lovers of the Greenwich Village Theater, where I was placed apart in the balcony when the *Liberator* sent me to see Bernard Shaw's *Candida*. And again, at the Princess Theater, when Eugene O'Neill's *Emperor Jones* was being played, I suffered no annoyance—maybe because [Charles] Gilpin, the Negro actor, was the leading man! Could the "non-commercial" Theater Guild venture on a play like the *Emperor Jones* with a Negro as the star? How would it solve the problem of the hundreds of well-off Negroes in New York, interested in the artistic achievements of their race, who would demand orchestra seats? Easily, perhaps, in the traditional one hundred per cent American way of not noticing such a situation. Easily, for judging from the list of plays the Guild has produced, the best talent, for it, is outside of America.

Damn it all! Good-night, plays and players. The prison is vast, there is plenty of space and a little time to sing and dance and laugh and love. There is a little time to dream of the jungle, revel in rare scents and riotous colors, croon a plantation melody, and be a real original Negro in spite of all the Tom Dixon [41] crackers and the subtly sneering fictioneer Stribling's *Birthright* [see pp. 73ff.]. Many a white wretch, baffled and lost in his civilized jungles, is envious of the toiling, easy-living Negro.

Cherish your strength, my strong black brother. Be not dismayed because the struggle is hard and long, O, my warm, wonderful race.

The fight is longer than a span of life; the test is great. Gird your loins, sharpen your tools! Time is on our side. Carry on the organizing and conserving of your forces, my dear brother, grim with determination, for a great purpose—for the Day!

Review of *He Who Gets Slapped* by Leonid Andreyev, from *Liberator,* vol. 5 (May, 1922), pp. 24–25.

BIRTHRIGHT

Some friendly critics think that my attitude towards the social status of the Negro should be more broadly socialistic and less chauvinistically racial as it seems to them. These persons seem to believe that the pretty parlor talk of international brotherhood or the radical shibboleth of "class struggle" is sufficient to cure the Negro cancer along with all the other social ills of modern civilization. Apparently they are content with an intellectual recognition of the Negro's place in the class struggle, meanwhile ignoring the ugly fact that his disabilities as a worker are relatively heavier than those of the white worker.

Being a Negro, I think it is my proud birthright to put the case of the Negro proletarian, to the best of my ability, before the white members of the movement to which I belong. For the problem of the darker races is a rigid test of Radicalism. To some radicals it might seem more terrible to face than the barricades. But this racial question may be eventually the monkey wrench thrown into the machinery of American revolutionary struggle.

The Negro radical wants more than anything else to find in the working-class movement a revolutionary attitude towards Negroes different from the sympathetic interest of bourgeois philanthropists and capitalist politicians. And if this difference is not practically demonstrated, Negro leaders can hardly go to the ignorant black masses and show them why they should organize and work by the standard of the white workers. Karl Marx's economic theories are hard to digest, and Negroes, like many other lazy-minded workers, may find it easier to put their faith in the gospel of that other Jew, Jesus. The Negroes might remain, in the United States of America, a solid army, twelve million strong, a reactionary mass, men, women and children. They might remain a reactionary fact, distrustful of the revolutionary activities of the white working class. They might remain the tool of the ruling class, to be used effectively, as in the past, against radical labor. And in that event the black workers will suffer—the white workers will lose—the ruling class will win.

And so it is not only the birthright of the Negro radical to educate the black worker, but it is also his duty to interpret him to the uninformed white radical who is prone to accept the colorful fiction rather than the stark reality of the Negro's struggle for full social and economic freedom. Where the white radical is quite sharp in detecting every bourgeois trap, however carefully hidden, that is set for the white worker, he very often loses his keen perceptions when he approaches the Negro question, and sometimes falls into the trap. And by his blunder he not only aids the bourgeoisie, but also the ultra-nationalist Negro leaders who, in their insistent appeal to the race prejudice of blacks against whites, declare that no class of white people will ever understand the black race.

And such a point of view is quite justifiable if judged by the silly rot about Negroes in general that sometimes gets printed in the radical press. A typical case is an article called "Outcry Against Black Horror" which appeared in the London *Communist* of April 8th under the endorsement of the editor. With an unconscious sense of the comic the editor of the *Communist* remarks that "it is part of the normal brutality of imperialism to ignore things like those set out herein." But if this communist editor had any real knowledge or judgment or taste or sense of humor he would have recognized the article in question as a patently cheap and vicious sort of bourgeois propaganda—a document that would disgrace the pages of the most flamboyant Northcliffe or Hearst sheet, and only fit for a publication like *John Bull*.[42] By its ugly phrases and false statements—such as "crime against the white race," "In the Wild West when a colored man outrages a white woman he is lynched without ado," "white people being enslaved by black and colored savages" —and its stirring up of the most primitive racial passions, the article violates every principle of Communism and shows the incompetency of the English editor for his job. It is on a par with the unscrupulous propaganda of Viereck's *American Monthly*.[43]

And another example of this well-organized and farflung propaganda is the recent statement in the *Japan Chronicle* (a mouthpiece of the English bourgeoisie, published in Kobe, blowing hot and cold, liberal where the interests of the British governing class are concerned, but intolerant and hostile towards the interests of the Japanese ruling class); it says that Americans, having been forced to resort to stern measures against Negroes because of the blacks' abnormal passion for white women, should be foremost in protesting against the presence of colored troops in Germany.

It happens at this moment to be expedient that the Anglo-Saxon bourgeoisie (which in its slave-holding and colonial rule has followed a set policy of exploiting and degrading the men and women of the colored masses everywhere) should resent the presence of colored troops in Germany; but the reaction of those Anglo-Saxons who make a profession of communism is not quite so clear.

The truth is, as shown by the statistics of the case, the percentage of crime among the colored troops in Germany is remarkably low in comparison with that of white occupational troops in India, the West Indies, Africa and other lands over which imperialism holds sway. And it is very low when set against the natural crimes of any white capitalist army. Lewis Gannett, after an impartial and thorough investigation of the charges against the colored troops in the Rhineland, gave his report in the New York *Nation* of May 25, 1921, and it discredits all the prejudicial and highly colored accounts that have been written about the crimes of the black troops in Germany. Surely it is the bounden duty of the radicals, having regard to the high purpose of their work, to get the proper information on such important subjects. It is their business to reject the stupid bourgeois custom of general indictment of a nation of people on the basis of the practices of an individual or a minority.

From this lowest level of radical absurdity it is pleasing to rise to the higher plane of artistic bourgeois propaganda. *Birthright,* a recent novel by T. S. Stribling, is a powerful plea for the preservation of existing Southern standards. The white man, it says in effect, has his own code of morals, a code which makes for a special kind of culture. The black man possesses another, immutably different. They are two streams that will never meet. This is the main theme of the narrative. The hero of the tale, Peter Siner, is quite incidental to the plot. Siner is a mulatto college graduate of weak character. There is nothing very remarkable about him. He might have been white; there are many such people in the world, persons of good intentions who lack the impulse or means to carry them out.

Mr. Stribling believes in the institution of entailment. The white man of the South holds title to his property and culture, which he transmits to his children. The white town also holds Niggertown in fee. Whitetown does not exert itself to work. It lives a leisurely life on the back of Niggertown. Whitetown has a double standard of sex morals by which its best young blood flows regularly into the rising stream of Niggertown and gives America the finest results of mixed mating in the world. Niggertown itself is very dirty, filthy and immoral. It transgresses all the superficial standards of the moral code by which Whitetown lives. Niggertown, according to the standards of Whitetown, is lazy and unthrifty, yet, by its labors, Niggertown keeps Whitetown clean, respectable and comfortable. Niggertown, like most servants' quarters, is ugly because it gives its best time to making Whitetown beautiful.

Birthright is a lovely and admirable description of life in the sunny South, where only the white bourgeoisie can afford the luxury of laziness. Mr. Stribling is an ardent advocate of this birthright of the white ruling class. All that is necessary to change the beautiful picture is that the Negroes of the South should realize that they are entitled to an equal share of the white birthright which they have created. The Negroes have the potential power to that share. They need only the knowledge in order to use that power rightly.

And Mr. Stribling gives the key to that power. He says: "No white Southerner knows his own village so minutely as does any member of the colored population. The colored villagers see the whites off their guard and just as they are, and that is an attitude in which no one looks his best. The Negroes might be called the black recording angels of the South. If what they know should be shouted aloud in any Southern town, its social life would disintegrate."

Well, for my part, as a lover of humanity and freedom and truth, I say let it disintegrate, and make way for something better and nobler. Let the Black Recording Angel speak out!

Review of *Birthright* by T. S. Stribling, from *Liberator,* vol. 5 (August, 1922), pp. 15–16.

2. The Russian Experience, 1922-1923

McKay's last *Liberator* article appeared in August 1922, two months after he had left the magazine's editorial staff. The review of *Birthright* was his reply to those "friendly critics" on the *Liberator* staff who thought him too "chauvinistically racial" in his social criticisms. It was the closest McKay ever came to quarreling publicly with his co-workers over the racial question. On this point his dissatisfaction with them remained relatively subdued until his journey in the fall of 1922 to Moscow, where he and Max Eastman attended the Fourth Congress of the Third Communist International.

While there he wrote a book about the American race problem, based largely upon his own experiences and impressions. In it McKay for the first time elaborated upon his differences with the *Liberator* staff regarding racial matters; and to the pained astonishment of Max Eastman, he cited these differences as one reason for his resignation as an editor. A Russian-language version of McKay's work appeared in 1923, but his original, English-language manuscript has since disappeared. The Russian work, long out of print and apparently unknown in America, has yet to be translated back into English.*

However, McKay's correspondence with Max Eastman concerning the book has survived and is included here.

Negroes often point out that most whites are completely unaware of the many injuries white racism inflicts upon blacks. McKay was certainly aware of such wounds in a personal way that Eastman could not share. Yet, their friendship remained throughout their lives remarkably steadfast. Each held the other in high regard for reasons transcending race, and both always demonstrated a willingness to forgive the other's indiscretions and verbal blunderings regarding the racial question.

McKay remained in Russia from November 1922 until June

---

* Claude McKay, *Negry v Amerike* ("The Negroes of America"), trans. by P. Okhrimenko (Moscow and Petrograd: Gosizdat, 1923). This book of 135 pages is cited in Clarence Gohdes, ed., *Russian Studies of American Literature: A Bibliography* (Chapel Hill, N.C.: University of North Carolina, 1969), p. 136.

1923. It was an exciting time in the history of the new Soviet state. The Civil War which followed the Revolution in 1917 had ended, and the victorious Bolsheviks had embarked upon an ambitious program of economic recovery and consolidation. The Soviet Union stood ready to welcome friendly visitors.

McKay's stay included a long, triumphant tour of factories, schools, and Soviet naval and army bases in and around Moscow and St. Petersburg. He had also an interview with Leon Trotsky and later submitted to him a memorandum on the American racial problem in relation to revolutionary politics. A summary of McKay's thinking on this subject appeared in the *International Press Correspondence,* November 21, 1922, and is reprinted here for the first time.

Following his departure from Russia, McKay wrote for *Crisis* "Soviet Russia and the Negro," the article which concludes this section. It not only summarizes McKay's Russian experience, but urges black Americans to place their struggle for justice in a new, global context.

AN EASTMAN–McKAY EXCHANGE

[Moscow, Spring 1923]
Dear Claude,

I want to tell you all the reasons why I think your chapter about the *Liberator* is unwise. In the first place you give the public to understand that your withdrawal from the magazine was the direct result of a disagreement about the race question. So far as I am informed the race question had nothing whatever to do with it. I received several letters from members of the board describing and explaining that incident, and none of them that I remember ever mentioned the subject. I myself replied that I agreed in the choice of Mike Gold as a better solitary editor, without even knowing that there *was* a dispute about the race question. The fact is, as I understand it, that you and Mike Gold announced your incompatibility, and compelled the board of editors to choose between you. It was not an easy choice, and the result was fatal,[1] but was a choice made entirely upon the basis of intrinsic fitness for that particular job. For my part when I left New York I should have chosen you, but on the basis of the magazines you each put out, in spite of the superior reliability and delicacy of yours, I was in favor of Mike because his magazine had more "pep."

In the second place, in your discussion of the disagreement which *did exist* about the race question, you distort completely the nature of that disagreement. There was never any disagreement between you and the editors of the *Liberator,* so far as I am aware, about the proper communist policy toward the race question in the United States. In so far as you had at that time worked out the policies which you now advocate, or confided them to us, we were all in complete accord. The disagreement which arose after I left was a disagreement about how to further those policies, along with the others for which the *Liberator* stood, in that particular magazine.

So long as I was there you were influenced either by your friendship for me, or by my insistence on practical thinking, so that no disagreement on this question even arose. You say that in joining the staff you were moved by a desire to further a solution of the Negro problem in the revolution. I refuse to believe that you were moved solely by that consideration, because I know that you are not a more simple person than others; rather you are more complex. But of course you realize that we also were moved by that consideration in inviting you to join. Moreover you and I tacitly agreed, as it seemed to me, about the manner in which your presence there could be made most effective—about the amount of material dealing with the race question which could [with] good effect be introduced—or rather, perhaps, the rate of speed at which it could be introduced. There was never a word of difference between us.

After my departure, however, you seem to have abandoned altogether the habit of practical thinking about this problem. You began to introduce so much material about the race question into your magazine that it was destined to have exactly the opposite effect from the one we desired. That is, instead of correcting the tendency of its readers to dismiss and ignore the Negro problem, it would be dismissed and ignored itself by them as a thing essentially concerned with that problem.

You show how completely you have abandoned the habit of practical thinking, when you lay down the dogma that a revolutionary magazine ought to contain the same proportion of material dealing with the Negro as the proportion of the Negroes to the white population of the United States. Where is your training as a political engineer? Do you live in the age of Lenin or Tom Paine? You have a magazine circulating practically entirely among whites. You have these whites full of peculiar ignorance and intolerance of the Negro and the Negro problem, which you describe in your book as the chief problem of the revolution in America. You as a Negro enter into the staff of that magazine with a view to moving forward a solution of that problem. And your tactical proposal is to throw the Negro and the Negro problem in the faces of those white readers in the same proportion in which Negroes stand to whites in the census of the United States! With that kind of thinking you will never solve any problem. What you will do is to destroy your instrument, and that is all. And what you describe in your chapter as a congenital incapacity of *Liberator* editors to understand the Negro problem, is simply a childlike and altogether proper instinct upon their part to save their magazine.

Your attempt to represent a disagreement about how to run the *Liberator* as a disagreement about the Negro problem, is peculiarly distressing to me, because so far as you interpret the Negro from the standpoint of the class-struggle, there is not a hair's difference between you and me—except of course your more sustained thoughtfulness about it. If you will come down from the heights of your literary hypothesis, and use your memory or your perception, you can not help acknowledging this fact. And if you will look once more in the letter from me which you quote here, you will find a sentence which you omitted because it conflicted with your hypothesis, to the following effect: "I am not writing at any length because I know there is not any difference between us about the principle involved, and this is just to indicate my idea as to the practical way to conduct the magazine."

There is a third reason why I think it is unwise to publish this chapter. And that is that it reveals the fact that you have not yourself an objective and unemotionalized [sic], to say nothing of a "scientific," conception of the Negro problem. You say in the beginning of your chapter that the editors of the *Liberator* were unable, with two exceptions, to see the Negro problem from the point of view of the class-struggle. Toward the end of the chapter you quote a correspondence with one of the editors, in which you denounce him as "indulging in the chimerical fancies of a child," because he insists upon seeing the Negro problem from the point of view of the class-struggle, and that it will disappear with the disappearance of economic classes. In support of your denunciation you make an assertion about the race problem in Russia, which is false, and which anybody having the habit of viewing race problems from the standpoint of the class-struggle would instinctively know was false. You say it was the strong arm of the Bolshevik Government which put a stop to the pogroms. The Commander-in-chief of that strong arm [Leon Trotsky] told me only two weeks ago that there never had been an impulse to a pogrom, even under the czar, which was not instigated by the government. Everybody knows that the pogroms disappeared *automatically* with the establishment of the working-class rule. That this proved to [be] true is one of the convincing triumphs of that "authentic science" which you invoke so lightly at the beginning of your chapter.

I do not say that this would happen in America, although I think it would. I only say that if you are setting out to write a book about the Negro problem, it behooves you to make up your mind forcefully whether you are going to view the Negro problem "from the standpoint of the class-struggle" or not. You can not take two opposite positions with the same lofty and condescending tone of voice in the same chapter.

There is another reason, underlying these, why I think your chapter is unwise. That is that it is quite manifestly dictated in large part by some obscure emotion of resentment. I can not tell what this emotion is, or what the cause of it, because I was not there. But in the first place, you would not publish without asking permission the private correspondence of people toward whom you felt friendly. And in the second place, you would not publish a letter of your own so rather sneeringly scornful as yours to Boardman Robinson,[2] if your motive was to try to create understanding, and not merely to resent the lack of it. That you look down upon the *Liberator* editors first for their failure to view the Negro problem from the standpoint of the class-struggle, and then later for their childishness in so viewing it, is the result, in my opinion, not of a natural cloudy-headedness, but of an underlying desire to look down on the editors of the *Liberator*.

You have at least written a chapter which will irritate, and tend to alienate from you every one of them, and if they have, as you say they have, the "broadest sympathetic, social and artistic understanding of the Negro" of any white group in America, your chapter is a very poor beginning of an effort to extend that understanding.

I've written this letter before coming to see you, because I thought our discussion would be more profitable if you knew my viewpoint, as I know yours, in advance.

[MAX EASTMAN]

Moscow, April 3, 1923

Dear Max:

The chapter which includes my experience with the *Liberator* group shall remain as it is, for in your letter I cannot find any convincing reason for omitting it; but, on the contrary, there is every reason for publishing it, if it will provoke stimulating argument and discussion, such as your letter reveals, on the Negro problem in America.

There are, however, a few knotty points in your exquisitely phrased letter which I have picked out—points insinuatingly questioning my motives and charging me with dishonesty, which I will take up with you in order as they appeared.

You will understand that I do not intend to argue with you about my motives and honesty—to prove or disprove anything, I am only attempting to *enlighten* you.

(1) I had and have no intention of letting the public think I withdrew from the executive editorship of the *Liberator* solely because of a disagreement over the race question. As my letters to you and yours to me will show I was preparing to leave the work of active editorship of the *Liberator* months before I finally gave up the job. But I want to state emphatically, and to let those who are interested in the matter understand, that my colleague on the executive editorship [Michael Gold] made the race story in the June [1922] *Liberator* the basis of his attack on me,[3] and his opinion, your letters and the artist's [Boardman Robinson?], and the discussions of the affair by the *Liberator* group, revealed to me that the group did not have a class-conscious attitude on the problem of the American Negro. I think it is very important that this fact should be published especially if it will make for profitable discussion on the race question. The race matter was merely incidental to my quitting the executive work, but it was most important in that it disclosed the truth that the leading minds of the *Liberator* group did not, to me, have a comprehensive grasp of the Negro's place in the class-struggle.

(2) You write respectively in a single paragraph: "In your discussion of the disagreement which *did exist* about the race question,

you distort completely the nature of that disagreement" (second italics mine) and "There was never any disagreement between you and the editors of the *Liberator,* so far as I am aware about the proper communist policy towards the race question in the United States." I cannot reconcile these sentences. You know very well that you were virtually the boss of the magazine and that you *made* me your assistant and later announced it to the readers and the other editors. But, as is implied in your letter, you never discussed the Negro problem as a policy of the *Liberator* with me. Nor did any of the other editors. The *Liberator* group, therefore, could not be in "complete accord" with me as you write about my policy on the race question, when we never discussed it as a group. In fact as a group we never even discussed the labor movement seriously. My position on the *Liberator* I discussed seriously only with the radical Negro group in New York. As I quite remember, I tried to discuss the Irish and Indian questions with you once or twice with a view of getting articles on them for the magazine, but with little sympathy you said that they were national issues. I never once thought you grasped fully the class struggle significance of national and racial problems, and little instances indexed for me your attitude on the race problem. It was never hostile, always friendly, but never by a long stretch revolutionary.

However, I remember one day when we could not find a decent restaurant to accommodate us both on Sixth Avenue, and we finally had to lunch in a very dirty place, that you remarked, perhaps jestingly, "If I were a Negro I couldn't be anything but a revolutionist!" I don't know why, my dear Max, but the atmosphere of the *Liberator* did not make for serious discussions on any of the real problems of Capitalist Society much less the Negro.

(3) But you write: "You say that in joining the staff you were moved by a desire to further a solution of the Negro problem in the revolution. I refuse to believe that you were moved solely by that consideration, because I know that you are not a more simple person than others; rather you are more complex." You honor and flatter me by stating that I am more complex than others. You ought to know for you are a learned Freudian excelling in your judgment of human nature. However, I have not said anywhere that in accepting the job you gave me on the *Liberator* I was moved *solely* by a desire to further a solution of the Negro problem in the Revolution. I can afford to be frank. My first necessity on returning from Europe in 1921 without any money was to get a job so that I should be

assured of shelter and food. My job on the *Liberator* secured me these. But my attitude was not very different from what it was in 1916 when I applied for a job as a houseman in a hotel in New Hampshire. The manager told me that he could only engage me temporarily because all the other workers (about 25) were white men and women and perhaps they would object to my working with them because I am a Negro. I went into that hotel to work with the full knowledge that I was not merely an ordinary worker, but that I was also a Negro, that I would not be judged on my merits as a worker alone, but on my behavior as a Negro. Up there in that little inn, nestling among the New Hampshire hills, the Negro (as in thousands of other places in America) was on trial not as a worker but as a strange species. And I went into that hotel to work for my bread and bed and also for my race. This situation is forced upon every intelligent Negro in America. In a few weeks I had won over the little hostile minority among the hotel workers; they all made demands on my company. For me to accomplish that, my dear Max, it was necessary to be complex! And I am complex enough to forgive your sneer at my saying that in joining the staff of the *Liberator* I was "moved by a desire to further a solution of the Negro problem in the revolution."

(4) I must repeat that you and I never had any tacit understanding on the race problem as you assert. So you could not have influenced me in any way on the subject. But you controlled the policy of the magazine as chief editor, and the files of the magazine are available to show what you, as chief editorial writer, said about the problem of the Negro in the Revolution. Nothing at all. In the December issue of 1921 you had a serious idea on the Negro of which you made a brilliant joke.[4] You say that I introduced too much race matter during the months of my editorship. You say this would not make the readers think about the Negro problem, they would rather "dismiss" it. Such is your opinion, which gives me a picture of you as a nice opportunist always in search of the safe path and never striking out for the new if there are any signs of danger ahead. I do not think you are a competent judge of my policy. The fact is that I received letters of encouragement and appreciation from working-class leaders and *Liberator* readers as soon as I began printing those articles. The article "He Who Gets Slapped" which appeared in the May *Liberator* [1922] was reprinted in part in the New York *World* and syndicated all over the United States even in some of the Southern States! It had the practical re-

sult of arraying certain members of the Theater Guild against the Management on the issue of racial discrimination.

I still maintain that a revolutionary magazine in advocating the issues of the class struggle in America should handle the Negro problem in the class struggle in proportion to the Negro population and its position in the labor world. And more, I hold to this point of view because the strategic position of Negro labor in the class struggle in America is by far greater and of more importance than the proportion of the 12 millions of blacks to the 100 millions of whites. This obvious truth you would know, had you been in the least acquainted with the way in which the big capitalists have been using Negroes to break the great strikes in the basic industries during the last decade. Furthermore, I am quite willing to lay this debatable point before a jury of internationally class-conscious minds, but I certainly could not accept your opinion only as trustworthy.

Tom Paine was of his time and so is Lenin. To me there is no comparison. During the age of the French Revolution, Paine performed herculean tasks in England, France and America and if you had in your whole body an ounce of the vitality that Paine had in his little finger, you with your wonderful opportunities, would not have missed the chances for great leadership in the class struggle that were yours in America.

(5) Again you deliberately distort the truth when you say that [Boardman] Robinson said the Negro problem "will disappear with the disappearance of the economic classes." Robinson used no such scientific phrase as economic classes, but the poetic phrase "with the triumph of Labor"—meaning the rule of Labor. Hence your paragraph about the Workers' Government of Russia and the Jewish pogroms is ludicrous and untenable. First, because economic classes have not disappeared in Russia. What we have here is a dictatorship of proletarian rule under which the bourgeoisie are disfranchised and shorn of political power precisely as the Negro workers of the South are barred from politics by the white bourgeoisie. I have shown your paragraph about the pogroms to a number of comrades and my translator [P. Ochremenko] and they have all characterized it as phrase-mongering. You write "The commander-in-chief told me only two weeks ago that there never has been an impulse to a pogrom, even under the Czar, which was not instigated by the imperial Government. Everybody knows that the pogroms disappeared *automatically* with the establishment of the working-class rule."

Firstly, I hardly think the War Commissar would have used

that loose word "impulse." On reading your sentence, Comrade Ochremenko who lived in the Ukraine (where there are great masses of Jews) before and through the Revolution, remarked: that the number of Jewish dead from the pogroms since the 1917 Revolution is greater than all that ever occurred under the reign of the Czars. Again the "Imperial" system in Russia ended with the Revolution. Even the advanced bourgeoisie were against that system. All plots against the Soviet Government since then are the machinations of the counter-revolutionary bourgeoisie against the Soviets. These operations involve the instigation of pogroms against Jews, the inciting of the ignorant peasantry to sabotage, uprisings in remote districts against the Communists, exploitation of national differences, etc. The pogroms like the visible activities of the Mensheviks and Social Revolutionaries in Russia have "disappeared *automatically* with the establishment of the working-class rule" because the Communists possess automatic machine guns and military control. If you would get out of your studio to see the strenuous feverish work of the Russian workers in competition against the NEP bourgeoisie, to study the work of the G.P.U. [Gosudarstvennoe Politicheskoe Upravlenie, the state police apparatus], the Department of National Minorities and the numberless political commissars—the Communists alert against the "impulse" to counter-revolutionary tendencies— you would lose your romantic feeling about the Communist Dictatorship and get down to its reality.

You have read only one chapter of my book, but you assert that in it I say that the Negro problem is the chief problem of the Revolution in America. When you come to read my book you will find that I have said no such thing. What I say is that the Negro question is an integral part and one of the chief problems of the class struggle in America, and I stand by that declaration.

If I am possessed of any "obscure emotion of resentment" it is merely that of publishing the truth as it appears to me. If what I write about the *Liberator* will "alienate from me every one of them" it would only show that, like you, they all have a personal rather than a social view of men and affairs. I am unwilling to believe with you that Robert Minor, Charles W. Wood and even Boardman Robinson himself would be of those alienated.

I cannot find in your letters that I have by me the paragraph which you quote and charge that I deliberately left out because it conflicted with my opinion. It may be in one of those left in America, but I don't see where it helps you in any way. It rather puts you in a weak and vacillating position. However, and finally, though I could not leave out the chapter, I am quite willing to publish your letter to me and my answer as an appendix if you want that; if not I cannot promise that if at any time after the publication of my book, a controversy should arise involving you and me, I shall not publish this exchange of letters.

Fraternally yours,
CLAUDE MCKAY

Moscow, April 12, 1923

Dear Claude,

I am astounded that you should think my letter accused you of dishonesty. Nothing could be further from my thoughts, or from what is possible. I accused you of forming an erroneous and unjust hypothesis about the *Liberator,* and in consequence presenting an erroneous and unjust view of the facts.

If you would attack the spirit of the *Liberator,* since you do not like it, you might express your emotion without falsifying the facts. But with a false hypothesis you will inevitably falsify the facts. For instance you speak as though it were not the quantity, but the quality—the vigor and "strikingness"—of what you introduced that was disagreed about. Your article on "He Who Gets Slapped" is one of the best pieces of English prose, as well as one of the most desirable articles from the standpoint of our political and journalistic policy, that we ever printed. It is unjust for you to imply that there is any disagreement about that. Don't you see that it is?

You are at liberty to make any use of my article [letter] that you like. Only I ask you, if you publish it, to publish also this statement, that nothing could be further from my thoughts than a reflection upon your honesty of motive. Your publishing the part of my letter which sustained your view of the facts, when you were not aware of my opposite view, was a perfectly natural thing. Your presenting your withdrawal from the *Liberator* as having to do essentially with the race problem, might be an accident of your engrossment with that problem, or it may be your view of the underlying fact. Certainly there is not the least reason to question your honesty in so presenting it.

As for your assertion that I "sneered" at you upon the question of your motives in joining the *Liberator*—Claude, if you can find a sneer in those words, how can I speak to you without arousing your anger? It happens that I never even dreamed of your having any special economic motive in joining the *Liberator.* Of course you had to earn your living, but God knows nobody earned a sumptuous living out of the *Liberator.* What I wanted to remind you of, is that when you joined the *Liberator* you were like some of the rest of us a poet. You wanted more than anything else free time to write your poetry. You had not yet discovered in yourself—at least so it seems to me—this very solemnly consecrated political soul that now appears, and looks down upon the *Liberator,* discovering what I never knew, that it had a cult of "Playful Work." You can at least permit me to hold this opinion about you without being offended.

You misunderstood the wording of my letter at one point, I meant that if we published too much material about the Negro, our white readers would dismiss the *magazine,* not the material. They would stop buying it and reading it. In other words, what I wanted to do, and the other editors too, was to save the magazine for use, instead of expressing an abstract principle in it and throwing it away. That was the issue between you and the editor of the *Liberator,* and you refuse to touch it.

I think it would be a great mistake to publish this correspondence in your book, if you realize that your coming on the *Liberator* was helpful to the solution of the race problem in the revolution. I think you might see that your having a violent split with it, would be harmful. And for that reason I cannot see why you want to make this difference of opinion both more politically significant, and more personally acrimonious than it was, or is.

My own motive in writing was simply to try to persuade you not to do something that I consider harmful. I failed to persuade you and that ends it for me.

I wonder if I might not still persuade you, however, of the folly of publishing that statement about Russia. If you will read over your letter you will see that you are arguing on my side of the question. You set out to prove that the revolution does not solve the race problem, and in order to prove that you find yourself explaining to me that the revolution is *not yet achieved* in Russia, and that *therefore* the race problem is not solved.

The situation of the Jew in Russia before the revolution is the one thing in the world comparable to the situation of the Negro in the United States. A proletarian revolution has occurred, or is occurring, here. The persecution of Jews has ceased. The two most powerful men in the government at this moment are Jews. The race problem in its basic outlines has disappeared. For you, the leading revolutionary figure in the Negro world, to come out at this moment with a statement that it is "indulging in the chimerical fancies of a child" to imagine that the race problem will be solved by the proletarian revolution (the triumph of labor) is really a tragedy.

MAX

Petrograd, May 18, 1923

Dear Max:

I thought I would send a word to you before leaving here for the South. In your last letter you said something about persuading me from writing the truth (from the Communist point of view). The Communists, and especially the Bolsheviks of Russia, are too strong-minded, clear-headed and convinced of the sure triumph of their ideas, to be afraid of such facts as may not be very favorable to their program at a certain period. Everything depends on the angle from which the facts are presented.

I see that you are confusing a revolutionary overturn with revolutionary constructive work. Do you think any fool could think that with the revolutionary overturn in Russia all class, national and racial differences would disappear as if by magic? Do you think the Communist leaders and the rank and file could by a single stroke change the minds of all the fossil-minded, stereotyped and mannikin wrecks of humanity that have been warped by hundreds of years of bourgeois traditions and education?

I have no more my "solemnly consecrated political soul" today than at the time when I first went to the *Liberator*. I still love to laugh, dance and wine and delight in pleasures. If you had seen me standing on street corners and selling red literature in London 1920–21, you would not make such a funny remark. If you had seen me doing propaganda work among the colored soldiers you would modify your "opinion." [5] And I never missed a single opportunity in enjoying living then as now. Do you think I was playing when twice in 1921 you saw colored men and women at the *Liberator* office discussing political and race problems with me—and you did not like it from fear of the Department of Justice? You have been entirely deceived about me, Max. I suppose it is due to this everlastingly infectious smile of mine.

Best wishes,
CLAUDE

[Petrograd]
May 1923
Dear Max,

I cannot dine with you tonight for I was bound to make two other engagements of a political nature. Sorry, but it is best, I think, for I have not finished my reply to your letter—would not like to talk about the subject before you receive that letter and would detest sitting with you and mouthing empty phrases when the thought uppermost in both our minds could not be discussed.

I shall have the answer sent to you tomorrow and if you don't reply immediately you may not be able to see me again for some time. I may be given traveling orders at any time. Uncertain as to time myself. But you could address me to Amer. Express—Berlin.*

Fraternally,
CLAUDE

THE RACIAL ISSUE IN THE U.S.A.: A SUMMARY

The Negro population of America is estimated at between 12 and 15 millions. About 20% of this number is distributed throughout Northern states; the rest live in the South.

Negro workers of the South may be roughly divided into four sections. In the cities they are (1) stevedores, (2) small factory workers and artisans. In the country they are (3) small farmers and (4) cotton plantation workers. The Southern Negroes are largely unorganized, although of late years there has sprung up some movement for organization among the land workers. The Southern whites are also unorganized except in the old craft and railroad unions.

The Negro today is not loyal to any party. From the end of the Civil War until the period of the [Theodore] Roosevelt Administration he was fairly loyal to the Republican party as the party of Lincoln who emancipated the slaves. But he is now disillusioned; he has many great grievances against "white" America, such as Lynching, Disfranchisement and Serfdom in the South and Social and Industrial Discrimination in the North; but in the main he is only

* The following month McKay was in Berlin and remained there until the fall of 1923. [Ed.]

race-conscious and rebellious, not revolutionary and class-conscious. It may even be said that Negroes are anti-socialistic, except for a goodly number of young colored intellectuals who have been forced back into the masses by competition and suppression. Since, however, America entered the European War, the Negroes have been ripe for revolutionary propaganda. The Garvey, "Back to Africa" movement has swept American Negroes like a storm. Although the mass of them know that they must remain in America, they responded to the emotional appeal as a relief from their sufferings.

But the future of American Negroes whether they become the pawn of the bourgeoisie in its fight against white labor or whether they become class-conscious, depends on the nature of the propaganda that is conducted among them and the tactics adopted towards their special needs. At present the blacks distrust and hate the whites to such an extent that they, the blacks, are very hostile to the radical propaganda of the whites. They are more partial to the humanitarians.

The blacks are hostile to Communism because they regard it as a "white" working-class movement and they consider the white workers their greatest enemy, who draw the color line against them in factory and office and lynch and burn them at the stake for being colored. Only the best and broadest minded Negro leaders who can combine Communist ideas with a deep sympathy for and understanding of the black man's grievances will reach the masses with revolutionary propaganda. There are few such leaders in America today.

"The Racial Question: The Racial Issue in the United States," *International Press Correspondence*, vol. 2 (November 21, 1922), p. 817.

SPEECH TO THE FOURTH CONGRESS OF THE THIRD COMMUNIST INTERNATIONAL, MOSCOW

Comrade McKay: Comrades, I feel that I would rather face a lynching stake in civilized America than try to make a speech before the most intellectual and critical audience in the world. I belong to a race of creators but my public speaking has been so bad that I have been told by my own people that I should never try to make speeches, but stick to writing, and laughing. However, when I heard the Negro question was going to be brought up on the floor of the Congress, I felt it would be an eternal shame if I did not say something on behalf of the members of my race. Especially would I be a disgrace to the American Negroes because, since I published a notorious poem in 1919 ["If We Must Die"], I have been pushed forward as one of the spokesmen of Negro radicalism in America to the detriment of my poetical temperament. I feel that my race is honored by this invitation to one of its members to speak at this Fourth Congress of the Third International. My race on this occasion is honored, not because it is different from the white race and the yellow race, but [because it] is especially a race of toilers, hewers of wood and drawers of water, that belongs to the most oppressed, exploited, and suppressed section of the working class of the world. The Third International stands for the emancipation of all the workers of the world, regardless of race or color, and this stand of the Third International is not merely on paper like the Fifteenth Amendment of the Constitution of the United States of America. It is a real thing.

The Negro race in the economic life of the world today occupies a very peculiar position. In every country where the Whites and Blacks must work together the capitalists have set the one against the other. It would seem at the present day that the international bourgeoisie would use the Negro race as their trump card in their fight against the world revolution. Great Britain has her Negro regiments in the colonies and she has demonstrated what she can do with her Negro soldiers by the use that she made of them during the late War. The revolution in England is very far away because of the highly organized exploitation of the subject peoples of the British Empire. In Europe, we find that France had a Negro army of over 300,000 and that to carry out their policy of imperial domination in Europe the French are going to use their Negro minions.

In America we have the same situation. The Northern bourgeoisie knows how well the Negro soldiers fought for their own emancipation, although illiterate and untrained, during the Civil War. They also remember how well the Negro soldiers fought in the Spanish-American War under Theodore Roosevelt. They know that in the last war over 400,000 Negroes who were mobilized gave a very good account of themselves, and that, besides fighting for the capitalists, they also put up a very good fight for themselves on returning to America when they fought the white mobs in Chicago, St. Louis and Washington.

But more than the fact that the American capitalists are using Negro soldiers in their fight against the interests of labor is the fact that the American capitalists are setting out to mobilize the entire black race of America for the purpose of fighting organized labor. The situation in America today is terrible and fraught with grave dangers. It is much uglier and more terrible than was the condition of the peasants and Jews of Russia under the Tzar. It is so ugly and terrible that very few people in America are willing to face it. The reformist bourgeoisie have been carrying on the battle against discrimination and racial prejudice in America. The Socialists and Communists have fought very shy of it because there is a great element of prejudice among the Socialists and Communists of America. They are not willing to face the Negro question. In associating with the comrades of America I have found demonstrations of prejudice on the various occasions when the White and Black comrades had to get together: and this is the greatest difficulty that the Communists of America have got to overcome—the fact that they first have got to emancipate themselves from the ideas they entertain towards the Negroes before they can be able to reach the Negroes with any kind of radical propaganda. However, regarding the Negroes themselves, I feel that as the subject races of other nations have come to Moscow to learn how to fight against their exploiters, the Negroes will also come to Moscow. In 1918 when the Third International published its Manifesto and included the part referring to the exploited colonies, there were several groups of Negro radicals in America that sent this propaganda out among their people. When in 1920 the American government started to investigate and to suppress radical propaganda among the Negroes, the small radical groups in America retaliated by publishing the fact that the Socialists stood for the emancipation of the Negroes, and that reformist America could do nothing for them. Then, I think, for the first time in American history, the American Negroes found that Karl Marx had been interested in their emancipation and had fought valiantly for it. I shall just read this extract that was taken from Karl Marx's writing at the time of the Civil War:

> When an oligarchy of 300,000 slave holders for the first time in the annals of the world, dared to inscribe "Slavery" on the banner of armed revolt, on the very spot where hardly a century ago, the idea of one great democratic republic had first sprung up, whence the first declaration of the Rights of Man was issued, and the first impulse given to the European revolution of the eighteenth-

century, when on that spot the counter-revolution cynically pro-
claimed property in man to be "the cornerstone of the new edifice"
—then the working class of Europe understood at once that the
slaveholders' rebellion was to sound the tocsin for a general holy
war of property against labor, and that (its) hopes of the future,
even its past conquests were at stake in that tremendous conflict
on the other side of the Atlantic.[6]

Karl Marx who drafted the above resolution is generally known as
the father of Scientific Socialism and also of the epoch-making vol-
ume popularly known as the socialist bible, *Capital*. During the
Civil War he was correspondent of the *New York Tribune*. In the
company of Richard Cobden, Charles Bradlaugh, the atheist, and
John Bright,[7] he toured England making speeches and so roused up
the sentiment of the workers of that country against the Confederacy
that Lord Palmerston, [the] Prime Minister, who was about to recog-
nize the South, had to desist.

As Marx fought against chattel slavery in 1861, so are present-
day socialists, his intellectual descendants, fighting wage slavery.

If the Workers party in America were really a Workers party
that included Negroes it would, for instance, in the South, have to
be illegal, and I would inform the American Comrades that there
is a branch of the Workers party in the South, in Richmond, Vir-
ginia, that is illegal—illegal because it includes colored members.
There we have a very small group of white and colored comrades
working together, and the fact that they have laws in Virginia and
most of the Southern states discriminating against whites and blacks
assembling together means that the Workers party in the South must
be illegal. To get round these laws of Virginia, the comrades have
to meet separately, according to color, and about once a month they
assemble behind closed doors.

This is just an indication of the work that will have to be done
in the South. The work among the Negroes of the South will have
to be carried on by some legal propaganda organized in the North,
because we find at the present time in America that the situation in
the Southern States (where nine million out of ten million of the
Negro population live), is that even the liberal bourgeoisie and the
petty bourgeoisie among the Negroes cannot get their own papers
of a reformist propaganda type into the South on account of the
laws that there discriminate against them.

The fact is that it is really only in the Southern States that
there is any real suppression of opinion. No suppression of opinion

exists in the Northern states in the way it exists in the South. In the Northern states special laws are made for special occasions—as those against Communists and Socialists during the War—but in the South we find laws that have existed for fifty years, under which the Negroes cannot meet to talk about their grievances. The white people who are interested in their cause cannot go and speak to them. If we send white comrades into the South they are generally ordered out by the Southern oligarchy and if they do not leave they are generally whipped, tarred and feathered; and if we send black comrades into the South they generally won't be able to get out again —they will be lynched and burned at the stake.

I hope that as a symbol that the Negroes of the world will not be used by the international bourgeoisie in the final conflicts against the World Revolution, that as a challenge to the international bourgeoisie, who have an understanding of the Negro question, we shall soon see a few Negro soldiers in the finest, bravest, and cleanest fighting forces in the world—the Red Army and Navy of Russia— fighting not only for their own emancipation, but also for the emancipation of all the working class of the whole world.

Reprinted as "Report on the Negro Question," *International Press Correspondence,* vol. 3 (January 5, 1923), pp. 16–17.

SOVIET RUSSIA AND THE NEGRO

I.

The label of propaganda will be affixed to what I say here. I shall not mind; propaganda has now come into its respectable rights and I am proud of being a propagandist. The difference between propaganda and art was impressed on my boyhood mind by a literary mentor,* Milton's poetry and his political prose set side by side as the supreme examples. So too, my teacher—splendid and broadminded though he was, yet unconsciously biased against what he felt was propaganda—thought that that gilt-washed artificiality, *The Picture of Dorian Gray,* would outlive *Arms and the Man* and *John Bull's Other Island.*[8] But inevitably as I grew older I had perforce

* Walter Jekyll (see Introduction, p. 4).

to revise and change my mind about propaganda. I lighted on one of Milton's greatest sonnets that was pure propaganda and a widening horizon revealed that some of the finest spirits of modern literature—Voltaire, Hugo, Heine, Swift, Shelley, Byron, Tolstoy, Ibsen—had carried the taint of propaganda. The broader view did not merely include propaganda literature in my literary outlook; it also swung me away from the childish age of the enjoyment of creative work for pleasurable curiosity to another extreme where I have always sought for the motivating force or propaganda intent that underlies all literature of interest. My birthright, and the historical background of the race that gave it to me, made me very respectful and receptive of propaganda and world events since the year 1914 have proved that it is no mean science of convincing information.

American Negroes are not as yet deeply permeated with the mass movement spirit and so fail to realize the importance of organized propaganda. It was Marcus Garvey's greatest contribution to the Negro movement; his pioneer work in that field is a feat that the men of broader understanding and sounder ideas who will follow him must continue. It was not until I first came to Europe in 1919 that I came to a full realization and understanding of the effectiveness of the insidious propaganda in general that is maintained against the Negro race. And it was not by the occasional affront of the minority of civilized fiends—mainly those Europeans who had been abroad, engaged in the business of robbing colored peoples in their native land—that I gained my knowledge, but rather through the questions about the Negro that were put to me by genuinely sympathetic and cultured persons.

The average Europeans who read the newspapers, the popular books and journals, and go to see the average play and a Mary Pickford movie, are very dense about the problem of the Negro; and they are the most important section of the general public that the Negro propagandists would reach. For them the tragedy of the American Negro ended with *Uncle Tom's Cabin* and Emancipation. And since then they have been aware only of the comedy—the Negro minstrel and vaudevillian, the boxer, the black mammy and butler of the cinematograph, the caricatures of the romances and the lynched savage who has violated a beautiful white girl.

A very few ask if Booker T. Washington is doing well or if the "Black Star Line" is running; perhaps some one less discreet than sagacious will wonder how colored men can hanker so much after white women in face of the lynching penalty. Misinformation, indifference and levity sum up the attitude of Western Europe towards the Negro. There is the superior but very fractional intellectual minority that knows better, but whose influence on public opinion is infinitesimal, and so it may be comparatively easy for white American propagandists—whose interests behoove them to misrepresent the Negro—to turn the general indifference into hostile antagonism if American Negroes who have the intellectual guardianship of racial interests do not organize effectively, and on a world scale, to combat their white exploiters and traducers.

The World War has fundamentally altered the status of Negroes in Europe. It brought thousands of them from America and the British and French colonies to participate in the struggle against the Central Powers. Since then serious clashes have come about in England between the blacks that later settled down in the seaport towns and the natives. France has brought in her black troops to do police duty in the occupied districts in Germany. The color of these troops, and their customs too, are different and strange and the nature of their work would natually make their presence irritating and unbearable to the inhabitants, whose previous knowledge of Negroes has been based, perhaps, on their prowess as cannibals. And besides, the presence of these troops provides rare food for the chauvinists of a once proud and overbearing race, now beaten down and drinking the dirtiest dregs of humiliation under the bayonets of the victor.

However splendid the gesture of Republican France towards colored people, her use of black troops in Germany to further her imperial purpose should meet with nothing less than condemnation from the advanced section of Negroes. The propaganda that Negroes need to put over in Germany is not black troops with bayonets in that unhappy country. As conscript-slave soldiers of Imperial France they can in no wise help the movement of Negroes nor gain the sympathy of the broad-visioned international white groups whose international opponents are also the intransigent enemies of Negro progress. In considering the situation of the black troops in Germany, intelligent Negroes should compare it with that of the white troops in India, San Domingo and Haiti. What might not the Haitian propagandists have done with the marines if they had been black instead of white Americans! [9] The world upheaval having brought the three greatest European nations—England, France and Germany—into closer relationship with Negroes, colored Americans should seize the opportunity to promote finer interracial understanding. As white Americans in Europe are taking advantage of the situation to intensify their propaganda against the blacks, so must Negroes meet that with a strong counter-movement. Negroes should realize that the supremacy of American capital today proportionately increases American influence in the politics and social life of the world. Every American official abroad, every smug tourist, is a protagonist of dollar culture and a propagandist against the Negro. Besides brandishing the Rooseveltian stick in the face of the lesser New World natives, America holds an economic club over the heads of all the great European nations, excepting Russia, and so those bold individuals in Western Europe who formerly sneered at dollar culture may yet find it necessary and worthwhile to be discreetly silent. As American influence increases in the world, and especially in Europe, through the extension of American capital, the more necessary it becomes for all struggling minorities of the United States to organize extensively for the worldwide propagation of their grievances. Such propaganda efforts, besides strengthening the cause at home, will certainly enlist the sympathy and help of those foreign groups that are carrying on a life-and-death struggle to escape the octuple arms of American business interests. And the Negro, as the most suppressed and persecuted minority, should use this period of ferment in international affairs to lift his cause out of his national obscurity and force it forward as a prime international issue.

Though Western Europe can be reported as being quite ignorant and apathetic of the Negro in world affairs, there is one great nation with an arm in Europe that is thinking intelligently on the Negro as it does about all international problems. When the Russian workers overturned their infamous government in 1917, one of the first acts of the new Premier, Lenin, was a proclamation greeting all the oppressed peoples throughout the world, exhorting them to organize and unite against the common international oppressor—Private Capitalism. Later on in Moscow, Lenin himself grappled with the question of the American Negroes and spoke on the subject before the Second Congress of the Third International. He consulted with John Reed, the American journalist, and dwelt on the urgent necessity of propaganda and organizational work among the Negroes of the South.[10] The subject was not allowed to drop. When Sen Katayama of Japan, the veteran revolutionist, went from the United States to Russia in 1921 he placed the American Negro problem first upon his full agenda. And ever since he has been working unceasingly and unselfishly to promote the cause of the exploited American Negro among the Soviet councils of Russia.[11]

With the mammoth country securely under their control, and

despite the great energy and thought that are being poured into the revival of the national industry, the vanguard of the Russian workers and the national minorities, now set free from imperial oppression, are thinking seriously about the fate of the oppressed classes, the suppressed national and racial minorities in the rest of Europe, Asia, Africa and America. They feel themselves kin in spirit to these people. They want to help make them free. And not the least of the oppressed that fill the thoughts of the new Russia are the Negroes of America and Africa. If we look back two decades to recall how the Czarist persecution of the Russian Jews agitated Democratic America, we will get some idea of the mind of Liberated Russia towards the Negroes of America. The Russian people are reading the terrible history of their own recent past in the tragic position of the American Negro today. Indeed, the Southern States can well serve the purpose of showing what has happened in Russia. For if the exploited poor whites of the South could ever transform themselves into making common cause with the persecuted and plundered Negroes, overcome the oppressive oligarchy—the political crackers and robber landlords—and deprive it of all political privileges, the situation would be very similar to that of Soviet Russia today.

In Moscow I met an old Jewish revolutionist who had done time in Siberia, now young again and filled with the spirit of the triumphant Revolution. We talked about American affairs and touched naturally on the subject of the Negro. I told him of the difficulties of the problem, that the best of the liberal white elements were also working for a better status for the Negro, and he remarked: "When the democratic bourgeoisie of the United States were execrating Czardom for the Jewish pogroms they were meting out to your people a treatment more savage and barbarous than the Jews ever experienced in the old Russia. America," he said religiously, "had to make some sort of expiatory gesture for her sins. There is no surfeited bourgeoisie here in Russia to make a hobby of ugly social problems, but the Russian workers, who have won through the ordeal of persecution and revolution, extend the hand of international brotherhood to all the suppressed Negro millions of America."

I met with this spirit of sympathetic appreciation and response prevailing in all circles in Moscow and Petrograd. I never guessed what was awaiting me in Russia. I had left America in September of 1922 determined to get there, to see into the new revolutionary life of the people and report on it. I was not a little dismayed when, congenitally averse to notoriety as I am, I found that on stepping upon Russian soil I forthwith became a notorious character. And strangely enough there was nothing unpleasant about my being swept into the surge of revolutionary Russia. For better or for worse every person in Russia is vitally affected by the revolution. No one but a soulless body can live there without being stirred to the depths by it.

I reached Russia in November—the month of the Fourth Congress of the Communist International and the Fifth Anniversary of the Russian Revolution. The whole revolutionary nation was mobilized to honor the occasion, Petrograd was magnificent in red flags and streamers. Red flags fluttered against the snow from all the great granite buildings. Railroad trains, street cars, factories, stores, hotels, schools—all wore decorations. It was a festive month of celebration in which I, as a member of the Negro race, was a very active participant. I was received as though the people had been apprised of, and were prepared for, my coming. When Max Eastman and I tried to bore our way through the dense crowds that jammed the Tverskaya Street in Moscow on the 7th of November, I was caught, tossed up into the air, and passed along by dozens of stalwart youths.

"How warmly excited they get over a strange face!" said Eastman. A young Russian Communist remarked: "But where is the difference? Some of the Indians are as dark as you." To which another replied: "The lines of the face are different, the Indians have been with us long. The people instinctively see the difference." And so always the conversation revolved around me until my face flamed. The Moscow press printed long articles about the Negroes in America, a poet was inspired to rhyme about the Africans looking to Soviet Russia and soon I was in demand everywhere—at the lectures of poets and journalists, the meetings of soldiers and factory workers. Slowly I began losing self-consciousness with the realization that I was welcomed thus as a symbol, as a member of the great American Negro group—kin to the unhappy black slaves of European Imperialism in Africa—that the workers of Soviet Russia, rejoicing in their freedom, were greeting through me.

II.

Russia, in broad terms, is a country where all the races of Europe and of Asia meet and mix. The fact is that under the repressive power of the Czarist bureaucracy the different races preserved a degree of kindly tolerance towards each other. The fierce racial hatreds that flame in the Balkans never existed in Russia. Where in the South no Negro might approach a "cracker" as a man for friendly offices, a Jewish pilgrim in old Russia could find rest and sustenance in the home of an orthodox peasant. It is a problem to define the Russian type by features. The Hindu, the Mongolian, the Persian, the Arab, the West European—all these types may be traced woven into the distinctive polyglot population of Moscow. And so, to the Russian, I was merely another type, but stranger, with which they were not yet familiar. They were curious with me, all and sundry, young and old, in a friendly, refreshing manner. Their curiosity had none of the intolerable impertinence and often downright affront that any very dark colored man, be he Negro, Indian or Arab, would experience in Germany and England.

In 1920, while I was trying to get out a volume of my poems in London, I had a visit with Bernard Shaw who remarked that it must be tragic for a sensitive Negro to be an artist. Shaw was right. Some of the English reviews of my book touched the very bottom of journalistic muck. The English reviewer outdid his American cousin (except the South, of course, which could not surprise any white person much less a black) in sprinkling criticism with racial prejudice. The sedate, copperhead *Spectator* as much as said: no "cultured" white man could read a Negro's poetry without prejudice, that instinctively he must search for that "something" that must make him antagonistic to it. But fortunately Mr. McKay did not offend our susceptibilities! The English people from the lowest to the highest, cannot think of a black man as being anything but an entertainer, boxer, a Baptist preacher or a menial. The Germans are just a little worse. Any healthy-looking black coon of an adventurous streak can have a wonderful time palming himself off as another Siki or a buck dancer. When an American writer introduced me as a poet to a very cultured German, a lover of all the arts, he could not believe it, and I don't think he does yet. An American student tells his middle-class landlady that he is having a black friend to lunch: "But are you sure that he is not a cannibal?" she asks, without a flicker of a humorous smile!

But in Petrograd and Moscow, I could not detect a trace of this ignorant snobbishness among the educated classes, and the attitude of the common workers, the soldiers and sailors was still more remarkable. It was so beautifully naive; for them I was only a black member of the world of humanity. It may be urged that the fine feelings of the Russians towards a Negro was the effect of Bolshevist pressure and propaganda. The fact is that I spent most of my leisure time in non-partisan and anti-Bolshevist circles. In Moscow I found the Lux Hotel where I put up extremely depressing, the dining room was anathema to me and I grew tired to death of meeting the proletarian ambassadors from foreign lands, some of whom bore themselves as if they were the holy messengers of Jesus, Prince of Heaven, instead of working-class representatives. And so I spent many of my free evenings at the Domino Café, a notorious den of the dilettante poets and writers. There came the young anarchists and Menshevists and all the young aspiring fry to read and discuss their poetry and prose. Sometimes a group of the older men came too. One evening I noticed Pilnyak the novelist, Okonoff the critic, Feodor the translator of Poe, an editor, a theater manager and their young disciples, beer-drinking through a very interesting literary discussion.[12] There was always music, good folk-singing and bad fiddling, the place was more like a second-rate cabaret than a poets' club, but nevertheless much to be enjoyed, with amiable chats and light banter through which the evening wore pleasantly away. This was the meeting place of the frivolous set with whom I eased my mind after writing all day.

The evenings of the proletarian poets held in the Arbot were much more serious affairs. The leadership was communist, the audience working class and attentive like diligent, elementary-school children. To these meetings also came some of the keener intellects from the Domino Café. One of these young women told me that she wanted to keep in touch with all the phases of the new culture. In Petrograd the meetings of the intelligentsia seemed more formal and inclusive. There were such notable men there as Chukovsky the critic, Eugene Zamiatan the celebrated novelist and Maishack the poet and translator of Kipling.[13] The artist and theater world were also represented. There was no communist spirit in evidence at these intelligentsia gatherings. Frankly there was an undercurrent of hostility to the Bolshevists. But I was invited to speak and read my poems whenever I appeared at any of them and treated with every courtesy and consideration as a writer. Among those sophisticated and cultured Russians, many of them speaking from two to four languages, there was no overdoing of the correct thing, no vulgar wonderment and bounderish superiority over a Negro's being a poet. I was a poet, that was all, and their keen questions showed that they were much more interested in the technique of my poetry, my views on and my position regarding the modern literary movements than in the difference of my color. Although I will not presume that there was no attraction at all in that little difference!

On my last visit to Petrograd I stayed in the Palace of the Grand Duke Vladimir Alexander, the brother of Czar Nicholas the Second. His old, kindly steward who looked after my comfort wanders round like a ghost through the great rooms. The house is now the headquarters of the Petrograd intellectuals. A fine painting of the Duke stands curtained in the dining room. I was told that he was liberal-minded, a patron of the arts, and much liked by the Russian intelligentsia. The atmosphere of the house was theoretically non-political, but I quickly scented a strong hostility to Bolshevist authority. But even here I had only pleasant encounters and illuminating conversations with the inmates and visitors, who freely expressed their views against the Soviet Government, although they knew me to be very sympathetic to it.

During the first days of my visit I felt that the great demonstration of friendliness was somehow expressive of the enthusiastic spirit of the glad anniversary days, that after the month was ended I could calmly settle down to finish the book about the American Negro that the State Publishing Department of Moscow had commissioned me to write, and in the meantime quietly go about making interesting contacts. But my days in Russia were a progression of affectionate enthusiasm of the people towards me. Among the factory workers, the red-starred and chevroned soldiers and sailors, the proletarian students and children, I could not get off as lightly as I did with the intelligentsia. At every meeting I was received with boisterous acclaim, mobbed with friendly demonstration. The women workers of the great bank in Moscow insisted on hearing about the working conditions of the colored women of America and after a brief outline I was asked the most exacting questions concerning the positions that were most available to colored women, their wages and general relationship with the white women workers. The details I could not give; but when I got through, the Russian women passed a resolution sending greetings to the colored women workers of America, exhorting them to organize their forces and send a woman representative to Russia. I received a similar message from the Propaganda Department of the Petrograd Soviet which is managed by Nicoleva, a very energetic woman. There I was shown the new status of the Russian women gained through the revolution of 1917. Capable women can fit themselves for any position; equal pay with men for equal work; full pay during the period of pregnancy and no work for the mother two months before and two months after the confinement. Getting a divorce is comparatively easy and not influenced by money power, detective chicanery and wire pulling. A special department looks into the problems of joint personal property and the guardianship and support of the children. There is no penalty for legal abortion and no legal stigma of illegitimacy attaching to children born out of wedlock.

There were no problems of the submerged lower classes and the suppressed national minorities of the old Russia that could not bear comparison with the grievous position of the millions of Negroes in the United States today. Just as Negroes are barred from the American Navy and the higher ranks of the Army, so were the Jews and the sons of the peasantry and proletariat discriminated against in the Russian Empire. It is needless repetition of the obvious to say that Soviet Russia does not tolerate such discriminations, for the actual government of the country is now in the hands of the combined national minorities, the peasantry and the proletariat. By the permission of Leon Trotsky, Commissar-in-chief of the military and naval forces of Soviet Russia, I visited the highest military schools in the Kremlin and environs of Moscow. And there I saw the new material, the sons of the working people in training as cadets by the old officers of the upper classes. For two weeks I was a guest of the Red Navy in Petrograd with the same eager proletarian youth of new Russia, who conducted me through the intricate machinery of submarines, took me over aeroplanes captured from the British during the counter-revolutionary war around Petrograd and showed me the making of a warship ready for action. And even of greater interest was the life of the men and the officers, the simplified discipline that was strictly enforced, the food that was served for each and all alike, the extra political educational classes and the extreme tactfulness and elasticity of the political commissars, all communists, who act as advisers and arbitrators between the men and students and the officers. Twice or thrice I was given some of the *kasha* which is sometimes served with the meals. In Moscow I grew to like this food very much, but it was always difficult to get. I had always imagined that it was quite unwholesome and unpalatable and eaten by the Russian peasant only on account of extreme poverty. But on the contrary I found it very rare and sustaining when cooked right with a bit of meat and served with butter—a grain food very much like the common but very delicious West Indian rice-and-peas.

The Red cadets are seen in the best light at their gymnasium exercises and at the political assemblies when discipline is set aside.

Especially at the latter where a visitor feels that he is in the midst of the early revolutionary days, so hortatory are the speeches, so intense the enthusiasm of the men. At all these meetings I had to speak and the students asked me general questions about the Negro in the American Army and Navy, and when I gave them the common information, known to all American Negroes, students, officers and commissars were unanimous in wishing that a group of young American Negroes would take up training to become officers in the Army and Navy of Soviet Russia.

The proletarian students of Moscow were eager to learn of the life and work of Negro students. They sent messages of encouragement and good will to the Negro students of America and, with a fine gesture of fellowship, elected the Negro delegate of the American Communist party and myself to honorary membership in the Moscow Soviet.

Those Russian days remain the most memorable of my life. The intellectual Communists and the intelligentsia were interested to know that America had produced a formidable body of Negro intelligentsia and professionals, possessing a distinctive literature and cultural and business interests alien to the white man's. And they think naturally, that the militant leaders of the intelligentsia must feel and express the spirit of revolt that is slumbering in the inarticulate Negro masses, precisely as the emancipation movement of the Russian masses had passed through similar phases.

Russia is prepared and waiting to receive couriers and heralds of good will and interracial understanding from the Negro race. Her demonstration of friendliness and equality for Negroes may not conduce to promote healthy relations between Soviet Russia and democratic America. The anthropologists of 100 per cent pure white Americanism may soon invoke Science to prove that the Russians are not at all God's white people. I even caught a little of American anti-Negro propaganda in Russia. A friend of mine, a member of the Moscow intelligentsia repeated to me the remarks of the lady correspondent of a Danish newspaper: that I should not be taken as a representative Negro for she had lived in America and found all Negroes lazy, bad and vicious, a terror to white women. In Petrograd I got a like story from Chukovsky, the critic, who was on intimate terms with a high worker of the American Relief Administration and his Southern wife. Chukovsky is himself an intellectual "Westerner," the term applied to those Russians who put Western European civilization before Russian culture and believe that Russia's salvation lies in becoming completely westernized. He had spent an impressionable part of his youth in London and adores all things English, and during the World War was very pro-English. For the American democracy, also, he expresses unfeigned admiration. He has more Anglo-American books than Russian in his fine library and considers the literary section of the *New York Times* a journal of a very high standard. He is really a maniac of Anglo-Saxon American culture. Chukovsky was quite incredulous when I gave him the facts of the Negro's status in American civilization.

"The Americans are a people of such great energy and ability," he said, "how could they act so petty towards a racial minority?" And then he related an experience of his in London that bore a strong smell of cracker breath. However, I record it here in the belief that it is authentic for Chukovsky is a man of integrity: About the beginning of the century, he was sent to England as correspondent of a newspaper in Odessa, but in London he was more given to poetic dreaming and studying English literature in the British Museum and rarely sent any news home. So he lost his job and had to find cheap, furnished rooms. A few weeks later, after he had taken up his residence in new quarters, a black guest arrived, an American gentleman of the cloth. The preacher procured a room on the top floor and used the dining and sitting room with the other guests, among whom was a white American family. The latter protested the presence of the Negro in the house and especially in the guest room. The landlady was in a dilemma, she could not lose her American boarders and the clergyman's money was not to be despised. At last she compromised by getting the white Americans to agree to the Negro's staying without being allowed the privilege of the guest room, and Chukovsky was asked to tell the Negro the truth. Chukovsky strode upstairs to give the unpleasant facts to the preacher and to offer a little consolation, but the black man was not unduly offended:

"The white guests have the right to object to me," he explained, anticipating Garvey, "they belong to a superior race."

"But," said Chukovsky, "*I* do not object to you, *I* don't feel any difference; we don't understand color prejudice in Russia."

"Well," philosophized the preacher, "you are very kind, but taking the scriptures as authority, I don't consider the Russians to be white people."

From *Crisis*, vol. 27 (December, 1923–January, 1924), pp. 61–65, 114–18.

3. Selected Poems, 1912-1925

In the years following World War I, Claude McKay's basic commitment was to poetry and to the truth of his experience as a black man. His political radicalism had its roots in these twin concerns.

Before leaving for the United States in 1912, McKay had already produced *Songs of Jamaica* and *Constab Ballads,* his two volumes of Jamaican dialect verse. In these early works, he identified with the black peasantry of rural Jamaica and recorded as his own their tribulations and joys. At the same time, a deeply sentimental attachment to all things British prevented McKay from facing all the liabilities blacks suffered as a result of British imperialism. By trying to remain faithful to the black peasantry while simultaneously proclaiming his attachment to British traditions, McKay betrayed in the dialect verse not only his own youthful naiveté, but also the deeply ambivalent nature of Jamaican colonial society.

Under the influence of his English mentor, Walter Jekyll, he sought escape by imitating such Romantic pessimists as Leopardi and Schopenhauer and gloomily proclaiming the inevitability of life's injustices.[1] His adherence to Social Darwinism only deepened the pessimism of these early poems. The black man's lowly status appeared predetermined by nature's inexorable laws. McKay's natural urge to rebellion, evidenced in numerous dialect poems, was thereby deflected but not subdued.

Jamaica had not provided McKay with the experience necessary to recognize the pervasive malevolence of European racism. Once in the United States, however, he encountered a racial caste system that dispensed entirely with the social niceties that often masked racial prejudices in British Jamaica. In 1912 the American system of race relations was frankly designed to prevent blacks from achieving a human existence equal to that of the dominant whites. It would be no exaggeration to say that for blacks there prevailed a policy of spiritual genocide. As a laborer the Negro had his place, but despite all constitutional guarantees he had in fact no status as a citizen. The black man's normal human aspirations were consequently frustrated at every turn. As McKay so forcefully demonstrated in his polemical review of *He Who Gets Slapped,* the Negro was trapped within a viciously restrictive circle of racial discriminations.

In his poetry written after 1912, McKay expressed with unabashed directness the inner turmoil and anguish such entrapment entailed for him, and indeed for all blacks. Against white racists, he boldly proclaimed a counter-hatred and contempt which few black poets before him had dared acknowledge in themselves, much less articulate in verse. In contrast to his dialect poetry, McKay's American verse reveals a far more realistic appreciation of the Negro's actual status in Western Civilization.

McKay realized he could not come to terms with the American environment simply by echoing those clichés of Romantic disillusionment which had sustained Walter Jekyll in his peculiar Victorian isolation. In his American poetry, McKay instead harkened back to earlier Romantic traditions of rebellion and revolution. And against the fatalism of the Social Darwinists he opposed the more hopeful and equally "scientific" theories of Marx and Engels, who held men and their institutions—not "nature"—responsible for human society, its ills and ultimate fate. By 1917, McKay had freed himself to concentrate on the black man's actual isolation and despair in the midst of western society. As a consequence, he achieved in his American poetry a more consistent unity of theme and style than had been true in earlier, dialect efforts.

After 1912 McKay wrote no more dialect verse but instead adopted the more traditional sonnet forms and shorter lyric modes common to English poetry. He would henceforth project in all his verse the image of the romantic revolutionary, defiant of all injustices. Despite the conventionality of his poetic forms and the echoes of a standardized English Romanticism throughout his verse, McKay's despair, anger, alienation, and rebellion marked a new and important departure in American literature. For his angry rebelliousness laid bare for all to see a genuinely intolerable estrangement, which was shared in varying degrees by all black Americans. As McKay clearly revealed in such poems as "Outcast" and "In Bondage," blacks were not only alienated from the society which oppressed them, but also from their own human potentialities and from the fullness of life itself. The only alternative to such a living death was uncompromising resistance, a continuous exertion of human will against the forces of death. It is his development of this great theme of the black man's struggle for self-realization that links McKay as a pioneering forerunner to writers as diverse as Richard Wright, Ralph Ellison, James Baldwin, and LeRoi Jones. From 1917 through 1925, McKay's poems appeared in a wide spectrum of journals—*Seven Arts, Pearson's,* the *Liberator, Cambridge Magazine,* the *Workers' Dreadnought,* the *Messenger,* and *Bookman*—to name a few. Many were reprinted in America's black press. "If We Must Die" in particular reached a wide audience throughout the United States.

During his visit to England in 1920, he published *Spring in New Hampshire,* a small selection of new verse. His major collection, *Harlem Shadows,* came out in 1922. It brought together the best poems he had written since leaving Jamaica.

With the exception of four dialect poems, the poems included here all appeared between 1917 and 1925. Four poems, "In Memoriam: Booker T. Washington," "Invocation," "A Roman Holiday," and "Mulatto," were never included in McKay's collected poetry. "In Memoriam: Booker T. Washington" was found in manuscript among the William Stanley Braithwaite Papers at the Harvard University Library. It demonstrates the influence of the famous Tuskegee educator on the young McKay. "Invocation" appeared in *Seven Arts.* "A Roman Holiday" first appeared along with "If We Must Die" in the *Liberator.* Together with that more famous poem, it seems to have been intended as the first half of a two-part sonnet sequence. "Mulatto" originally appeared in *Bookman,* September 1925, and was reprinted by Wagner in *Les poètes nègres des Etats-Unis.* All the other poems in this volume were included in *Harlem Shadows* and again in the posthumous *Selected Poems.*

Because the original manuscripts have in most instances been lost, it is practically impossible to determine the exact chronological order in which McKay wrote his poetry. The poems which follow appear with the dates of their original publication. All were written during McKay's most creative years as a poet. After the appearance of *Harlem Shadows* McKay was increasingly preoccupied with prose, and with a few exceptions his later poetry is clearly inferior to that written before 1922. From 1923 until 1933, he devoted himself to fiction. After 1933, his journalistic essays and expository prose were clearly superior in quality to his efforts as a poet. The poems included here therefore represent a distillation of McKay's most important themes from his most fruitful years as a poet.

A MIDNIGHT WOMAN TO THE BOBBY * [2]

No palm me up,[a] you dutty brute,
You' jam mout' mash [b] like ripe bread-fruit;
You fas'n now, but wait lee ya,[c]
I'll see you grunt under de law.

You t'ink you wise,[d] but we wi' see;
You not de fus' one fas' wid me;
I'll lib fe see dem tu'n you out,
As sure as you got dat mash' mout'.

I born right do'n beneat' de clack [e]
(You ugly brute, you tu'n you' back?)
Don' t'ink dat I'm a come-aroun',[f]
I born right 'way in 'panish Town.

Care how you try, you caan' do mo'
Dan many dat was hyah befo'; [g]
Yet whe' dey all o' dem te-day? [h]
De buccra dem no kick dem 'way? [i]

Ko [j] 'pon you' jam samplatta [k] nose:
'Cos you wear Mis'r Koshaw clo'es [l]
You t'ink say you's de only man,[m]
Yet fus time [n] ko how you be'n 'tan'.[n']

* The notes accompanying the first three poems in this section appeared in the original editions of *Songs of Jamaica* and *Constab Ballads*. [Ed.]
[a] Don't put your hands on me.   [b] Your damned mouth is all awry.
[c] You are fast (meddling, officious) now, but wait a little, d'you hear?
[d] You think you're wise.
[e] The clock on the public buildings at Spanish Town.
[f] Day-laborers, men and women, in Kingston streets and wharves, famous for the heavy weights they carry, are called come-arounds.
[g] No matter how you try, you can't do more than your predecessors (all that were here before).
[h] Yet where are they all today?
[i] Did not the buccra (white man) kick them away (dismiss them)?
[j] Look.
[k] A piece of leather cut somewhat larger than the size of the foot, and tied sandal-wise to it: said of anything that is flat and broad.
[l] Mr. Kershaw's clothes, i.e., police uniform. Col. Kershaw, Inspector-General of Police in 1911 (when this poem was written) and for many years before.
[m] A mighty fine fellow   [n] When I knew you first.
[n'] Look what sort of figure you cut.

You big an' ugly ole tu'n-foot [o]
Be'n neber know fe wear a boot;
An' chigger nyam you' tumpa toe,[p]
Till nit full i' like herrin' roe.

You come from mountain naked-'kin,[q]
An' Lard a mussy! you be'n thin,
For all de bread-fruit dem be'n done,
Bein' 'poil' up by de tearin' sun: [r]

De coco [s] couldn' bear at all,
For, Lard! de groun' was pure white-marl;
An' t'rough de rain part [t] o' de year
De mango tree dem couldn' bear.

An' when de pinch o' time you feel
A 'pur you a you' chigger heel,[u]
You lef' you' district, big an' coarse,
An' come join [v] buccra Police Force.

An' now you don't wait fe you' glass [w]
But trouble me wid you' jam fas'; [x]
But wait, me frien', you' day wi' come,
I'll see you go same lak a some.[y]

Say wha'?—'res' me? [z]—you go to hell!
You t'ink Judge don't know unno well? [a]
You t'ink him gwin' go sentance [b] me
Widout a soul fe witness i'?

From *Songs of Jamaica,* pp. 74–76.

[o] Turned-in foot.

[p] And chigoes (burrowing fleas) had eaten into your maimed toe, and nits (young chigoes) had filled it.

[q] Naked skin, i.e., with your shirt and trousers full of holes.

[r] Having been spoilt by the hot sun. Pronounce "bein' " as a monosyllable.

[s] An edible root (*Colocasia antiquorum*).

[t] During some months.

[u] And when you felt hard times spurring you in your chigger-eaten heel.

[v] Came and joined.

[w] You don't wait for the right and proper moment.

[x] With all your infernal forwardness and officiousness.

[y] Same like some = just as others before you did.

[z] What's that?—arrest me?

[a] D'you think the magistrate doesn't know your tricks? Unno or Onnoo is an African word, meaning "you" collectively.

[b] Pronounce the *a* "ah," but without accent.

THE APPLE-WOMAN'S COMPLAINT

While me deh walk 'long in de street,
Policeman's yawnin' on his beat;
An' dis de wud him chiefta'n say—
Me mus'n' car' me apple-tray.

Ef me no wuk, me boun' fe tief;
S'pose dat will please de pólice chief!
De prison dem mus' be wan' full,[c]
Mek dem's 'pon we like ravin' bull.

Black nigger wukin' laka cow
An' wipin' sweat-drops from him brow,
Dough him is dyin' sake o' need,
P'lice an' dem headman boun' fe feed.

P'lice an' dem headman gamble too,
Dey shuffle card an' bet fe true;
Yet ef me Charlie gamble,—well,
Dem try fe 'queeze him laka hell.

De headman fe de town police
Mind [d] neber know a little peace,
'Cep' when him an' him heartless ban'
Hab sufferin' nigger in dem han'.

Ah son-son! dough you 're bastard, yah,
An' dere's no one you can call pa,
Jes' try to ha' you mudder's min'
An' Police Force you'll neber jine.

But how judge bélieve pólicemen,
Dem dutty mout' wid lyin' stain'?
While we go batterin' along
Dem doin' we all sort o' wrong.

From *Constab Ballads*, pp. 57–58.

[c] The prisons must want occupants, and that is why they are down upon us like angry bulls.
[d] The mind of the chief of the town police is never happy, except, etc.

We hab fe barter-out we soul
To lib t'rough dis ungodly wul';—
O massa Jesus! don't you see
How pólice is oppressin' we?

Dem wan' fe see we in de street
Dah foller dem all 'pon dem beat;
An' after, 'dout a drop o' shame,
Say we be'n dah solicit dem.

Ah massa Jesus! in you' love
Jes' look do'n from you' t'rone above,
An' show me how a poo' weak gal
Can lib good life in dis ya wul'.

CUDJOE FRESH FROM DE LECTURE

'Top *one* minute, Cous' Jarge, an' sit do'n 'pon de grass,
An' mek a ᵉ tell you 'bout de news I hear at las',
How de buccra te-day tek time an' bégin teach
All of us dat was deh ᶠ in a clear open speech.

You miss somet'ing fe true, but a wi' mek you know,
As much as how a can, how de business a go:
Him tell us 'bout we self, an' mek we fresh ᵍ again,
An' talk about de wul' from commencement to en'.

Me look 'pon me black 'kin, an' so me head grow big,
Aldough me heaby han' dem hab fe plug ʰ an' dig;
For ebery single man, no car' ⁱ about dem rank,
Him bring us ebery one an' put 'pon de same plank.

Say, parson do de same! ʲ Yes, in a diff'ren' way,
For parson tell us how de whole o' we are clay;
An' lookin' close at t'ings, we hab to pray quite hard
Fe swaller wha' him say an' don't t'ink bad o' Gahd.

ᵉ Make I = let me.   ᶠ There.
ᵍ Over: meaning, "He gave us a new view of our origin, and explained that we did not come from Adam and Eve, but by evolution."
ʰ Plough, i.e., pick up the ground with a pickaxe.
ⁱ Care: no matter what their rank.
ʲ Do you say that parson does the same?

But dis man tell us 'traight 'bout how de whole t'ing came,
An' show us widout doubt how Gahd was not fe blame;
How change cause eberyt'ing fe mix up 'pon de eart',
An' dat most hardship come t'rough accident o' birt'.

Him show us all a sort [k] o' funny 'keleton,
Wid names I won't remember under dis ya sun;
Animals queer to deat',[l] dem bone, teet', an' headskull,
All dem so dat did live in a de ole-time wul'.

No 'cos say we get cuss mek fe we 'kin come so,
But fe all t'ings come 'quare, same so it was to go:
Seems our lan [n] must ha' been a bery low-do'n place,
Mek it tek such long time in tu'ning out a race.

Yes, from monkey we spring: I believe ebery wud;
It long time better dan f'go say we come from mud:
No need me keep back part, me hab not'in' fe gain;
It's ebery man dat born—de buccra mek it plain.

It really strange how some o' de lan' dem advance;
Man power in some ways is nummo soso chance; [o]
But suppose eberyt'ing could tu'n right upside down,
Den p'raps we'd be on top an' givin' some one houn.' [p]

Yes, Cous' Jarge, slabery hot fe dem dat gone befo':
We gettin' better times, for those days we no know; [q]
But I t'ink it do good, tek we from Africa
An' lan' us in a blessed place as dis a ya.[r]

Talk 'bouten Africa, we would be deh till now,
Maybe same half-naked—all day dribe buccra cow,
An' tearin' t'rough de bush wid all de monkey dem,
Wile an' uncibilise,' [s] an' neber comin' tame.

---

[k] All sorts.　　　　　[l] The queerest animals.
[m] It is not because we were cursed (Gen. ix. 25) that our skin is dark; but so that things might come square, there had to be black and white.
[n] Africa.　　　　　[o] No more than pure chance.
[p] Hound: equivalent to the English slang phrase "giving someone beans [hell]."
[q] Do not know: have no experience of.
[r] This here.　　　　　[s] Wild and uncivilized.

I lef' quite 'way from wha' we be'n deh talk about,[t]
Yet still a couldn' help—de wuds come to me mout';
Just like how yeas' get strong an' sometimes fly de cark,[u]
Same way me feelings grow, so I was boun' fe talk.

Yet both horse partly [v] runnin' in de selfsame gallop,
For it is nearly so de way de buccra pull up:
Him say, how de wul' stan', dat right will neber be,
But wrong will eber gwon [w] till dis wul' en' fe we.

From *Songs of Jamaica*, pp. 55–58.

[t] I have run right away from what we were talking about.
[u] Makes the cork fly.
[v] Almost.
[w] Go on.

PASSIVE RESISTANCE

There'll be no more riotin',
Stonin' p'lice an' burnin' car;
But we mean to gain our rights
By a strong though bloodless war.

We will show an alien trust
Dat Jamaicans too can fight
. An' dat while our blood is hot,
They won't crush us wi' deir might.

Hawks may watch us as dey like,
But we do not care a pin;
We will hold "the boys" in check,
There'll be no more riotin'.

We are sorry, sorry much
For the worry given some;
But it will not last for aye,—
Our vict'ry day shall come.

There are aliens in our midst
Who would slay us for our right;
Yet though vipers block the way
We will rally to the fight.

We'll keep up a bloodless war,
We will pay the farthings-fare
An' we send the challenge forth,
"Only touch us if you dare!"

From the Kingston *Daily Gleaner* (April 6, 1912).

IN MEMORIAM: BOOKER T. WASHINGTON

I vividly recall the noon-day hour
      You walked into the wide and well-filled hall:
      We rose and sang, at the conductor's call,
Dunbar's Tuskegee hymn. A splendid tower
of strength, as would a gardener on the flower
      Nursed tenderly, you gazed upon us all
      Assembled there, a serried, sable wall
Fast mortared by your subtle tact and power.
O how I loved, adored your furrowed face!
      And fondly hoped, before your days were done,
You would look in mine too with paternal grace.
      But vain are hopes and dreams!—gone: you are gone,
Death's hand has torn you from your trusting race,
      And O! We feel so utterly alone.

From an unpublished manuscript in the William S. Braithwaite Papers,
Harvard University Library. The poem was written shortly after Washing-
ton's death in 1915.

INVOCATION

Ancestral Spirit, hidden from my sight
By modern Time's unnumbered works and ways
On which in awe and wonderment I gaze,
Where hid'st thou in the deepness of the night?
What evil powers thy healing presence blight?
Thou who from out the dark and dust didst raise
The Ethiop standard in the curtained days,
Before the white God said: Let there be light!
Bring ancient music to my modern heart,
Let fall the light upon my sable face
That once gleamed upon the Ethiopian's art;
Lift me to thee out of this alien place
So I may be, thine exiled counterpart,
The worthy singer of my world and race.

From *Seven Arts,* vol. 2 (October, 1917), p. 741.

THE TROPICS IN NEW YORK

Bananas ripe and green, and ginger-root,
   Cocoa in pods and alligator pears,
And tangerines and mangoes and grape fruit,
   Fit for the highest prize at parish fairs,

Set in the window, bringing memories
   Of fruit-trees laden by low-singing rills,
And dewy dawns, and mystical blue skies
   In benediction over nun-like hills.

My eyes grew dim, and I could no more gaze;
   A wave of longing through my body swept,
And, hungry for the old, familiar ways,
   I turned aside and bowed my head and wept.

First appeared in *Liberator,* vol. 3 (May, 1920), p. 48. Reprinted from
Selected Poems, p. 31.

FLAME-HEART

So much I have forgotten in ten years,
So much in ten brief years! I have forgot
What time the purple apples come to juice,
And what month brings the shy forget-me-not.
I have forgot the special, startling season
Of the pimento's flowering and fruiting;
What time of year the ground doves brown the fields
And fill the noonday with their curious fluting.
I have forgotten much, but still remember
The poinsettia's red, blood-red, in warm December.

I still recall the honey-fever grass,
But cannot recollect the high days when
We rooted them out of the ping-wing path
To stop the mad bees in the rabbit pen.
I often try to think in what sweet month
The languid painted ladies used to dapple
The yellow by-road mazing from the main,
Sweet with the golden threads of the rose-apple.
I have forgotten—strange—but quite remember
The poinsettia's red, blood-red, in warm December.

What weeks, what months, what time of the mild year
We cheated school to have our fling at tops?
What days our wine-thrilled bodies pulsed with joy
Feasting upon blackberries in the copse?
Oh some I know! I have embalmed the days,
Even the sacred moments when we played,
All innocent of passion, uncorrupt,
At noon and evening in the flame-heart's shade.
We were so happy, happy, I remember,
Beneath the poinsettia's red in warm December.

First appeared in *Spring in New Hampshire* (1920), p. 30. Reprinted from *Selected Poems*, p. 13.

MY MOTHER

The dawn departs, the morning is begun,
The Trades come whispering from off the seas,
The fields of corn are golden in the sun,
The dark-brown tassels fluttering in the breeze;
The bell is sounding and children pass,
Frog-leaping, skipping, shouting, laughing shrill,
Down the red road, over the pasture-grass,
Up to the schoolhouse crumbling on the hill.
The older folk are at their peaceful toil,
Some pulling up the weeds, some plucking corn,
And others breaking up the sun-baked soil.
Float, faintly scented breeze, at early morn
Over the earth where mortals sow and reap—
Beneath its breast my mother lies asleep.

First appeared in the *Liberator*, vol. 3 (March, 1921), p. 24. Reprinted from
Selected Poems, p. 22.

THE PLATEAU

It was the silver, heart-enveloping view
    Of the mysterious sea-line far away,
    Seen only on a gleaming gold-white day,
That made it dear and beautiful to you.

And Laura loved it for the little hill,
    Where the quartz sparkled fire, barren and dun,
    Whence in the shadow of the dying sun,
She contemplated Hallow's wooden mill.

While Danny liked the sheltering high grass,
    In which he lay upon a clear dry night,
    To hear and see, screened skillfully from sight,
The happy lovers of the valley pass.

But oh! I loved it for the big round moon
    That swung out of the clouds and swooned aloft,
    Burning with passion, gloriously soft,
Lighting the purple flowers of fragrant June.

First appeared in *Harlem Shadows* (1922), p. 19. Reprinted from *Selected
Poems*, p. 25.

ADOLESCENCE

There was a time when in late afternoon
    The four-o'clocks would fold up at day's close,
Pink-white in prayer. Under the floating moon
    I lay with them in calm and sweet repose.

And in the open spaces I could sleep,
    Half-naked to the shining worlds above;
Peace came with sleep and sleep was long and deep,
    Gained without effort, sweet like early love.

But now no balm—no drug nor weed nor wine—
    Can bring true rest to cool my body's fever,
Nor sweeten in my mouth the acrid brine,
    That salts my choicest drink and will forever.

First appeared in *Harlem Shadows*, p. 14. Reprinted from *Selected Poems*, p. 27.

AFRICA

The sun sought thy dim bed and brought forth light,
The sciences were sucklings at thy breast;
When all the world was young in pregnant night
Thy slaves toiled at thy monumental best.
Thou ancient treasure-land, thou modern prize,
New peoples marvel at thy pyramids!
The years roll on, thy sphinx of riddle eyes
Watches the mad world with immobile lids.
The Hebrews humbled them at Pharaoh's name.
Cradle of Power! Yet all things were in vain!
Honor and Glory, Arrogance and Fame!
They went. The darkness swallowed thee again.
Thou art the harlot, now thy time is done,
Of all the mighty nations of the sun.

First appeared in the *Liberator*, vol. 4 (August, 1921), p. 10. Reprinted from *Selected Poems*, p. 40.

OUTCAST

For the dim regions whence my fathers came
My spirit, bondaged by the body, longs.
Words felt, but never heard, my lips would frame;
My soul would sing forgotten jungle songs.
I would go back to darkness and to peace,
But the great western world holds me in fee,
And I may never hope for full release
While to its alien gods I bend my knee.
Something in me is, lost, forever lost,
Some vital thing has gone out of my heart,
And I must walk the way of life a ghost
Among the sons of earth, a thing apart.

For I was born, far from my native clime,
Under the white man's menace, out of time.

First appeared in *Harlem Shadows*, p. 45. Reprinted from *Selected Poems*, p. 41.

ENSLAVED

Oh when I think of my long-suffering race,
For weary centuries, despised, oppressed
Enslaved and lynched, denied a human place
In the great life line of the Christian West;
And in the Black Land disinherited,
Robbed in the ancient country of its birth,
My heart grows sick with hate, becomes as lead,
For this my race that has no home on earth.
Then from the dark depth of my soul I cry
To the avenging angel to consume
The white man's world of wonders utterly:
Let it be swallowed up in the earth's vast womb,
Or upward roll as sacrificial smoke
To liberate my people from its yoke!

First appeared in the *Liberator*, vol. 4 (July, 1921), p. 6. Reprinted from *Selected Poems*, p. 42.

IN BONDAGE

I would be wandering in distant fields
Where man, and bird, and beast, lives leisurely,
And the old earth is kind, and ever yields
Her goodly gifts to all her children free;
Where life is fairer, lighter, less demanding,
And the boys and girls have time and space for play
Before they come to years of understanding—
Somewhere I would be singing, far away.
For life is greater than the thousand wars
Men wage for it in their insatiate lust,
And will remain like the eternal stars,
When all that shines to-day is drift and dust.

But I am bound with you in your mean graves,
O black men, simple slaves of ruthless slaves.

First appeared in *Spring in New Hampshire,* p. 31. Reprinted from *Selected Poems,* p. 39.

THE LYNCHING

His Spirit in smoke ascended to high heaven.
His father, by the cruelest way of pain,
Had bidden him to his bosom once again;
The awful sin remained still unforgiven.
All night a bright and solitary star
(Perchance the one that ever guided him,
Yet gave him up at last to Fate's wild whim)
Hung pitifully o'er the swinging char.
Day dawned, and soon the mixed crowds came to view
The ghastly body swaying in the sun.
The women thronged to look, but never a one
Showed sorrow in her eyes of steely blue.

And little lads, lynchers that were to be,
Danced round the dreadful thing in fiendish glee.

First appeared in the *Cambridge Magazine,* vol. 10 (Summer, 1920), p. 56.
Reprinted from *Selected Poems,* p. 37.

TO THE WHITE FIENDS

Think you I am not fiend and savage too?
Think you I could not arm me with a gun
And shoot down ten of you for every one
Of my black brothers murdered, burnt by you?
Be not deceived, for every deed you do
I could match—out-match: am I not Afric's son,
Black of that black land where black deeds are done?
But the Almighty from the darkness drew
My soul and said: Even thou shalt be a light
Awhile to burn on the benighted earth,
Thy dusky face I set among the white
For thee to prove thyself of higher worth;
Before the world is swallowed up in night,
To show thy little lamp: go forth, go forth!

First appeared in the *Liberator,* vol. 2 (September, 1919), p. 25. Reprinted from *Selected Poems,* p. 38.

THE WHITE HOUSE *

Your door is shut against my tightened face,
And I am sharp as steel with discontent;
But I possess the courage and the grace
To bear my anger proudly and unbent.
The pavement slabs burn loose beneath my feet,
A chafing savage, down the decent street;
And passion rends my vitals as I pass,
Where boldly shines your shuttered door of glass.
Oh, I must search for wisdom every hour,
Deep in my wrathful bosom sore and raw,
And find in it the superhuman power
To hold me to the letter of your law!
Oh, I must keep my heart inviolate
Against the potent poison of your hate.

First appeared in the *Liberator,* vol. 5 (May, 1922), p. 16. Reprinted from *Selected Poems,* p. 78.

* "My title was symbolic . . . it had no reference to the official residence of the President of the United States. . . . The title 'White Houses' changed the whole symbolic intent and meaning of the poem, making it appear as if the burning ambition of the black malcontent was to enter white houses in general." Claude McKay: *A Long Way from Home* (1937), pp. 313–14. See also letter to Alain Locke, below, pp. 143–44. [Ed.]

A ROMAN HOLIDAY

'Tis but a Roman Holiday;
Each state invokes its soul of basest passion,
Each vies with each to find the ugliest way
To torture Negroes in fiercest fashion.
Black Southern men, like hogs await your doom!
White wretches hunt and haul you from your huts,
They squeeze the babies out of your women's womb,
They cut your members off, rip out your guts!
It is a Roman Holiday: and worse:
It is the mad beast risen from his lair,
The dead accusing years eternal curse,
Reeking of vengeance, in fulfillment here—
Bravo Democracy! Hail greatest power
That saved sick Europe in her darkest hour!

From the *Liberator,* vol. 2 (July, 1919), p. 21.

IF WE MUST DIE [3]

If we must die, let it not be like hogs
Hunted and penned in an inglorious spot,
While round us bark the mad and hungry dogs,
Making their mock at our accursed lot.
If we must die, O let us nobly die,
So that our precious blood may not be shed
In vain; then even the monsters we defy
Shall be constrained to honor us though dead!
O kinsmen! we must meet the common foe!
Though far outnumbered let us show us brave,
And for their thousand blows deal one deathblow!
What though before us lies the open grave?
Like men we'll face the murderous, cowardly pack,
Pressed to the wall, dying, but fighting back!

First appeared in the *Liberator,* vol. 2 (July, 1919), p. 21. Reprinted from
Selected Poems, p. 36.

THE WHITE CITY

I will not toy with it nor bend an inch.
Deep in the secret chambers of my heart
I muse my life-long hate, and without flinch
I bear it nobly as I live my part.
My being would be a skeleton, a shell,
If this dark Passion that fills my every mood,
And makes my heaven in the white world's hell,
Did not forever feed me vital blood.
I see the mighty city through a mist—
The strident trains that speed the goaded mass,
The poles and spires and towers vapor-kissed,
The fortressed port through which the great ships pass,
The tides, the wharves, the dens I contemplate,
Are sweet like wanton loves because I hate.

First appeared in the *Liberator,* vol. 4 (October, 1921), p. 7. Reprinted from *Selected Poems,* p. 74.

BAPTISM

Into the furnace let me go alone;
Stay you without in terror of the heat.
I will go naked in—for thus 'tis sweet—
Into the weird depths of the hottest zone.
I will not quiver in the frailest bone,
You will not note a flicker of defeat;
My heart shall tremble not its fate to meet,
My mouth give utterance to any moan.
The yawning oven spits forth fiery spears;
Red aspish tongues shout wordlessly my name.
Desire destroys, consumes my mortal fears,
Transforming me into a shape of flame.
I will come out, back to your world of tears,
A stronger soul within a finer frame.

First appeared in the *Liberator,* vol. 4 (October, 1921), p. 7. Reprinted from *Selected Poems,* p. 35.

AMERICA

Although she feeds me bread of bitterness,
And sinks into my throat her tiger's tooth,
Stealing my breath of life, I will confess
I love this cultured hell that tests my youth!
Her vigor flows like tides into my blood,
Giving me strength erect against her hate.
Her bigness sweeps my being like a flood.
Yet as a rebel fronts a king in state,
I stand within her walls with not a shrcd
Of terror, malice, not a word of jeer.
Darkly I gaze into the days ahead,
And see her might and granite wonders there,
Beneath the touch of Time's unerring hand,
Like priceless treasures sinking in the sand.

First appeared in the *Liberator*, vol. 4 (December, 1921), p. 9. Reprinted
from *Selected Poems*, p. 59.

MULATTO

Because I am the white man's son—his own,
Bearing his bastard birth-mark on my face,
I will dispute his title to his throne,
Forever fight him for my rightful place.
There is a searing hate within my soul,
A hate that only kin can feel for kin,
A hate that makes me vigorous and whole,
And spurs me on increasingly to win.
Because I am my cruel father's child,
My love of justice stirs me up to hate,
A warring Ishmaelite, unreconciled,
When falls the hour I shall not hesitate
Into my father's heart to plunge the knife
To gain the utmost freedom that is life.

First appeared in *Bookman*, vol. 72 (September, 1925), p. 67. Reprinted
from Wagner, *Les poètes nègres des Etats-Unis*, p. 580.

LIKE A STRONG TREE

Like a strong tree that in the virgin earth
Sends far its roots through rock and loam and clay,
And proudly thrives in rain or time of dearth,
When dry waves scare the rain-come sprites away;
Like a strong tree that reaches down deep, deep,
For sunken water, fluid underground,
Where the great-ringed unsightly blind worms creep,
And queer things of the nether world abound:
So would I live in rich imperial growth,
Touching the surface and the depth of things,
Instinctively responsive unto both,
Tasting the sweets of being, fearing no stings,
Sensing the subtle spell of changing forms,
Like a strong tree against a thousand storms.

First appeared in the *Survey Graphic*, vol. 53 (March 1, 1925), p. 662.
Reprinted from *Selected Poems*, p. 45.

ST. ISAAC'S CHURCH, PETROGRAD

Bow down my soul in worship very low
And in the holy silences be lost.
Bow down before the marble Man of Woe,
Bow down before the singing angel host.
What jewelled glory fills my spirit's eye,
What golden grandeur moves the depths of me!
The soaring arches lift me up on high,
Taking my breath with their rare symmetry.

Bow down my soul and let the wondrous light
Of beauty bathe thee from her lofty throne,
Bow down before the wonder of man's might.
Bow down in worship, humble and alone,
Bow lowly down before the sacred sight
Of man's Divinity alive in stone.

First appeared in the *Survey Graphic*, vol. 53 (March 1, 1925), p. 662.
Reprinted from *Selected Poems*, p. 84.

II.

THE EXPATRIATE
YEARS
1923–1934

4. An Article and Letters, 1925-1932

The literary history of the United States in the 1920s is above all the story of her expatriate writers in Europe. Although Claude McKay is seldom mentioned in accounts of the period, he shared in the confusion, excitement, and hard work of those years when the best in American literature was created by her "writers in exile." [1] From 1923 until February 1934, he lived and worked successively in Germany, France, Spain, and Morocco.

During his years abroad, McKay dedicated himself to mastering the art of prose fiction and produced three novels—*Home to Harlem* (1928), *Banjo* (1929), and *Banana Bottom* (1933)—plus a collection of short stories, *Gingertown* (1932). In the process he led a successful revolt against the genteel treatment of black life in Negro American fiction.

Thus, in fiction, no less than in poetry, McKay proved an innovator. As a poet, he expresed the black man's alienation in the midst of a dehumanizing environment and demonstrated the necessity of rebellion against the forces of death. In his fiction, he looked beyond these themes toward an affirmation of black life, "as one great part of the whole of life" (p. 145).

In opposition to W. E. B. Du Bois' emphasis on a "talented tenth" guiding the Negro masses to freedom, McKay pushed forward in his novels and stories the ignorant black folk of farm and city as the potential directors of their own fate. He tried to show that they were the living basis upon which any valid black identity had to be constructed. For McKay, the true exemplars of the race were uprooted but self-sufficient urban drifters, such as Jake and Banjo in his first novels, and the durable peasant farmer, Jubban, in *Banana Bottom*. Only by wedding themselves to such men in their natural, unself-conscious striving for fellowship could the educated "leaders" of the race achieve genuine liberation for themselves and their people.

All of McKay's fiction pointed toward the need for a black community identifying itself as such and accepting confidently its own unassailable humanity and cultural values. To participate fully in a larger national or international community, blacks in the United States and the West Indies had first to fulfill their own potentialities as members of identifiable ethnic groups. To be Americans or Jamaicans in any effective sense, they must first be themselves, not rootless imitators of middle-class Anglo-Saxons.

McKay's unapologetic celebration of lower-class blacks shocked and outraged the Negro middle class, which felt he was merely trying to capitalize on the white "Negro vogue," a parallel movement to the Harlem Renaissance in the late 1920s. For his part, McKay maintained that black writers, like all others, should attempt "to comprehend life" (p. 155). He insisted that black writers could not be bound by the necessities of propaganda, however laudable its purposes. He felt they must instead embrace in art all the emotional and intellectual potentials of life itself. Only then could they do justice to the full complexity of their own humanity.

This section opens with McKay's answer to those critics who felt he had betrayed his race in his novels and short stories. In the main, the letters which follow this opening statement further document his revolt against those who would limit in any way the black writer's choice of subject matter. McKay had perhaps even more sympathy for the black "Babbittry" of his race than Sinclair Lewis had for the white equivalent. Like Lewis, however, he felt bound to point out their limitations. Even such venerable intellects as W. E. B. Du Bois and Alain Locke failed to escape McKay's censure, as his letters to them reveal.

A NEGRO WRITER TO HIS CRITICS

The following article is a retrospective piece whose original appearance coincided with the publication of McKay's collection of short stories, Gingertown. *In it, McKay reviews his earlier creative efforts, the critical furor they aroused, and his reasons for choosing to write of black lower-class existence.*

When the work of a Negro writer wins recognition it creates two widely separate bodies of opinion, one easily recognizable by the average reader as general and the other limited to Negroes and therefore racial.

Although this racial opinion may seem negligible to the general reader, it is a formidable thing to the Negro writer. He may pretend to ignore it without really succeeding or being able to escape its influence, for very likely he has his social contacts with the class of Negroes who create and express this opinion in their conversation and through the hundreds of weekly Negro newspapers and the monthly magazines.

This peculiar racial opinion constitutes a kind of censorship of what is printed about the Negro. No doubt it had its origin in the laudable efforts of intelligent Negro groups to protect their race from the slander of its detractors after Emancipation, and grew until it crystallized into racial consciousness. The pity is that these leaders of racial opinion should also be in the position of sole arbiters of intellectual and artistic things within the Negro world. For although they may be excellent persons worthy of all respect and eminently right in their purpose, they often do not distinguish between the task of propaganda and the work of art.

I myself have lived a great deal in the atmosphere of this opinion in America, in sympathy with and in contact with leaders and groups expressing it and am aware of their limitations.

A Negro writer feeling the urge to write faithfully about the people he knows from real experience and impartial observation is caught in a dilemma (unless he possesses a very strong sense of esthetic values) between the opinion of this group and his own artistic conscientiousness. I have read pages upon pages of denunciation of young Negro poets and story-tellers who were trying to grasp and render the significance of the background, the fundamental rhythm of Aframerican life. But not a line of critical encouragement for the artistic exploitation of the homely things—of Maudy's wash tub, Aunt Jemima's white folks, Miss Ann's old clothes for work-and-wages, George's Yessah-boss, dining car and Pullman services, barber and shoe shine shop, chittling and corn-pone joints —all the lowly things that go to the formation of the Aframerican soil in which the best, the most pretentious of Aframerican society still has its roots.

My own experience has been amazing. Before I published *Home to Harlem* I was known to the Negro public as the writer of the hortatory poem "If We Must Die." This poem was written during the time of the Chicago race riots. I was then a train waiter in the service of the Pennsylvania Railroad. Our dining car was running between New York, Philadelphia and Pittsburgh, Harrisburg and

Washington and I remember we waiters and cooks carried revolvers in secret and always kept together going from our quarters to the railroad yards, as a precaution against sudden attack.

The poem was an outgrowth of the intense emotional experience I was living through (no doubt with thousands of other Negroes) in those days. It appeared in the radical magazine the *Liberator,* and was widely reprinted in the Negro press. Later it was included in my book of poetry *Harlem Shadows.* At the time I was writing a great deal of lyric poetry and none of my colleagues on the *Liberator* considered me a propaganda poet who could reel off revolutionary poetry like an automatic machine cutting fixed patterns. If we were a rebel group because we had faith that human life might be richer, by the same token we believed in the highest standards of creative work.

"If We Must Die" immediately won popularity among Aframericans, but the tone of the Negro critics was apologetic. To them a poem that voiced the deep-rooted instinct of self-preservation seemed merely a daring piece of impertinence. The dean of Negro critics [William S. Braithwaite] denounced me as a "violent and angry propagandist, using his natural poetic gifts to clothe [arrogant] and defiant thoughts." [2] A young disciple characterized me as "rebellious and vituperative."

Thus it seems that respectable Negro opinion and criticism are not ready for artistic or other iconoclasm in Negroes. Between them they would emasculate the colored literary aspirant. Because Aframerican group life is possible only on a neutral and negative level our critics are apparently under the delusion that an Aframerican literature and art may be created out of evasion and insincerity.

They seem afraid of the revelation of bitterness in Negro life. But it may as well be owned, and frankly by those who know the inside and heart of Negro life, that the Negro, and especially the Aframerican, has bitterness in him in spite of his joyous exterior. And the more educated he is in these times the more he is likely to have.

The spirituals and the blues were not created out of sweet deceit. There is as much sublimated bitterness in them as there is humility, pathos and bewilderment. And if the Negro is a little bitter, the white man should be the last person in the world to accuse him of bitterness. For the feeling of bitterness is a natural part of the black man's birthright as the feeling of superiority is of the white man's. It matters not so much that one has had an experience of bitterness, but rather how one has developed out of it. To ask the Negro to render up his bitterness is asking him to part with his soul. For out of his bitterness he has bloomed and created his spirituals and blues and conserved his racial attributes—his humor and ripe laughter and particular rhythm of life.

However, with the publication of *Home to Harlem* the Aframerican elite realized that there was another side to me and changed their tune accordingly. If my poetry had been too daring, my prose was too dirty. The first had alarmed, the second had gassed them. And as soon as they recovered from the last shock, they did not bite their tongues in damning me as a hog rooting in Harlem, a buzzard hovering over the Black Belt scouting for carcasses and altogether a filthy beast.

If my brethren had taken the trouble to look a little into my obscure life they would have discovered that years before I had recaptured the spirit of the Jamaican peasants in verse, rendering their primitive joys, their loves and hates, their work and play, their dialect. And what I did in prose for Harlem was very similar to what I had done for Jamaica in verse.

The colored elite thought that if animal joy and sin and sorrow and dirt existed in the Belt as they did in ghettos, slums, tenderloins and such like places all over the world, they had no place in literature, and therefore my book was a deliberate slander against Aframerica. From being too much of a rebel I was now a traitor who should be suppressed. . . .

Here I may well protest publicly that my affection for Aframerica is profound. During my first couple of years in the States as a student I had a real admiration for the many colored students I came to know and the refined colored society I was introduced into at Tuskegee, Manhattan (Kansas), Kansas City, Wichita, Denver and later for the smart set of musicians and theatrical persons I met in New York.

But it was not until I was forced down among the rough body of the great serving class of Negroes that I got to know my Aframerica. I was perhaps then at the most impressionable adult age and the warm contact with my workmates, boys and girls, their spontaneous ways of acting on and living for the moment, the physical and sensuous delights, the loose freedom in contrast to the definite peasant patterns by which I had been raised—all served to feed the riotous sentiments smoldering in me and cut me finally adrift from the fixed moorings my mind had been led to respect, but to which my heart had never held. During the first years among these Negroes my only object in working was to possess the means to live as they did. I forgot poetry.

I did not grow up in the fear of skeletons in the closet, whether they were family, national or racial, sacred cows and the washing of dirty clothes in public. And I have often wondered why many subjects that seemed to me most beautiful and suitable for literature and by which art might have done better than society—subjects that intellectual persons of both sexes discuss over the dinner table and in the salon and that people in the street gossip about, should be publicly shocking in print and taboo in art.

What does it matter that the superior class of Negroes are all aware of the existence of the Jakes and Strawberry Lips and Billy Biasses, the Congo Roses, Susies and Madam Lauras of the race; * that they sometimes get up round robins for the white landlord to put them out of the nice Black Belt streets when they flaunt themselves too boldly in the face of Colored Respectability. The best Negroes will gossip and joke about such people in their drawing rooms, but as soon as they are captured as characters between the covers of a book and made to live in black and white, these same people set up a howl of protest, and all their organs from the littlest newspaper in Alabama to the heaviest magazine in New York burst forth in denunciation of the writer as a traitor to his race.

Their idea is that Negroes in literature and art should be decorous and decorative. These nice Negroes think that the white public, reading about the doings of the common Negroes, will judge them by the same standards. I should be the last person to defend the intelligence of any public simply because it read. However, the whites may know more about the blacks on the inside than the blacks think. Who knows that there may not be a potential writer among the young men of the vice squad doing the Belts who is making careful use of his eyes and ears while chasing a job? Or that there may not be an intellectual among the white bohemians who are privileged guests at exclusive Negro speakeasies and in the homes of the colored smart sets? . . . Negro apprentices to the craft of writing may be quite raw in dealing with the material to their hand, but their work will have that authentic ring of one who has. lived familiarly and freely in the atmosphere of his creation. And if they sin a little on the side of crude realism—why, no people more than a suppressed minority needs self-criticism to save itself from

* All characters in *Home to Harlem.* [Ed.]

the miserable soul-stifling pit of self-pity. If aspiring Negro writers are made afraid and artistically inarticulate from fear and pressure within their own circles, the truth may come from without, perhaps in unpleasant and inartistic form.

On the "broader" side (literally at least) my work has been approached by some discriminating critics as if I were a primitive savage and altogether a stranger to civilization. Perhaps I myself unconsciously gave that impression. However, I should not think it was unnatural for a man to have a predilection for a civilization or culture other than that he was born unto. Whatever may be the criticism implied in my writing of Western Civilization I do not regard myself as a stranger but as a child of it, even though I may have become so by the comparatively recent process of grafting. I am as conscious of my new-world birthright as of my African origin, being aware of the one and its significance in my development as much as I feel the other emotionally.

One of my most considerate critics suggested that I might make a trip to Africa and there write about Negro life in its pure state. But I don't believe that any such place exists anywhere upon the earth today, since modern civilization has touched and stirred the remotest corners. I cherish no Utopian illusions about any state of human society. Poets may dream, but dreams are ferment of the stuff of experience. The poet of a subject people may sing for the day of deliverance without being afflicted by fanciful visions of any society of people in which the eternal problems of existence would not still exist. A Negro poet living in a purely Negro community would automatically become free of the special problems of race and color, of foreign arrogance insisting upon an aristocracy of color or stock and that a man of parts was inferior because the group of people he belonged to was suppressed by brute power.

But I can see no reason why an Aframerican intellectual should go to any part of Africa to undertake an experiment in living unless he felt irresistibly forced to do so. Negroid Africa will produce in time its own modern poets and artists peculiar to its soil. The Aframerican may gain spiritual benefits by returning in *spirit* to this African origin, but as an artist he will remain a unique product of Western Civilization, with something of himself to give that will be very different from anything that may come out of a purely African community.

I don't know if I ever suggested the superiority of pure-black over pure-white virtues, although I will confess that I do prefer virtues that are colorful to the sepulchral kinds. Some sympathetic critics have rebuked me for making my black drifters finer than the white, when I thought I was being specially impartial. I may have sinned in my book *Banjo* by being too photographic, too much under the fetid atmosphere of the bottoms of Marseilles.

But there was factually a remarkable difference between the attitude of the white and the black drifters. Most of the blacks, and especially the Aframericans, were virtually taking a holiday away from the United States—a country where they had less freedom of movement and contact with white people than in Europe. They could return when they wanted to, but preferred to exist as they could on the beach because Europe was new-found land to them.

But the whites were Europeans who had been rounded up in America to be dumped upon the shores from which they had been trying to escape. Some of them came from unimaginably poor and austere regions, others from countries ruled by dictatorships under which they dreaded to return and had been mercifully set down upon the more hospitable shores of Provence. One sees at once why these men were despondent and lacking in the irresponsible holiday spirit of the blacks.

From all this I should say that we are all floundering in a mass of race, color, national consciousness and all the correlative consciousnesses. Besides, many of us who are trying to see and live tolerantly and temperately are worried by a guilty conscience. White and colored. In spite of our professions we become very self-conscious and rather uneasy as soon as we open a book in which there are white and colored characters in action or in conflict. We are prone to put too much stress on the identity of the characters, having an automatic reaction to them not just as people but rather as types representative of our separate divisions. And we are quick to pounce upon exaggerated types that we think were presented with bias, forgetting that bias may be in our own minds. But as one finds this trait even among the great major groups of people who own and inherit the earth—to a despairing extent to anyone who puts the artistic record of life above patriotism and prejudice—it may be forgiven among the poor minorities, especially the colored, who often find it rubbed into them that their state is due to their lack of "white" virtues.

In a tale some characters will almost always be finer than others. One may have the highest ideals of human brotherhood, but the fact under our ideals is that humanity is actually divided into races and nations and classes. And individuals do bear the marks of their special group. A sincere artist can represent characters only as they seem to him. And he *will* see characters through his predilections and prejudices, unless he sets himself deliberately to present those cinema-type figures that are produced to offend no unit of persons whose protest may involve financial loss. The time when a writer will stick only to the safe old ground of his own class of people is undoubtedly passing. Especially in America, where all the peoples of the world are scrambling side by side and modern machines and the ramifications of international commerce are steadily breaking down the ethnological barriers that separate the peoples of the world.

From *New York Herald-Tribune Books*, March 6, 1932.

LETTERS TO ARTHUR A. SCHOMBURG

The three letters which follow were written by McKay in the spring and summer of 1925, three years before the publication of Home to Harlem. *They clearly reveal that as a novelist he quite early anticipated conflict with middle-class reformers within the race. He felt their ceaseless battle to win a measure of justice in America prevented them from understanding the viewpoint of the creative writer. All three letters are to his friend Arthur A. Schomburg (1874–1938), the black bibliophile whose personal library formed the basis for the New York Public Library's renowned Schomburg Collection of Negro Literature and History.**

> Poste Restante
> Toulon (Var)
>
> April 28, 1925

My dear Schomburg:

At last I have finished my book in the way I want it to be and I am having it typed. The next thing for me to have now is a publisher who will pay me something in advance, "a few hundred dollars" for I'll soon be at the end of my rope. Being so long away

---

* See McKay's sketch of Schomburg in *Harlem: Negro Metropolis,* pp. 139–42. [Ed.]

from America, I am out of touch with the publishing market. I therefore want to trust the placing of my book and the driving of a good pecuniary bargain with *you*. I will tell you the most likely publishers.

If you are willing to undertake this hard job please let me know and I will send you the ms. as soon as it is typed off. I think the best firm to try at first is Alfred A. Knopf's, failing that, Harcourt and Brace, my poetry publisher, and failing them, Boni and Liveright. I am certain to suit one of these. But Knopf first of all as you might get an advance more easily out of him. I want that advance to live on while I am waiting for the proofs and planning my novel of a West Indian near-white in America.[3]

Now when I send you the ms., Schomburg, great though the temptation is, I hope you won't keep it by you to *read it*. Unless you can do it in one night! I want you to rush the placing of it—because my future as a writer or anything—all depends on my getting that novel published as quick as possible.

I have reached the point where I can no longer expect to get charity from anyone. I *must* make good by my own worth. Another thing—I want you to guard the secret of the title of the book *— also that I have sent it to you.

It is necessary that no one should know that I have finished, especially *certain* groups of liberals so-called in New York, until the book is announced by the publishers themselves. If it is known that I have finished, my precarious supply of bread-and-butter may be cut off entirely. . . .[4]

I am waiting now to hear from you. I may be leaving Toulon before you reply but your letter will be forwarded without delay. I shall not be going near Paris, however, as I cannot afford it.

I think you will like my novel. It's a comedy, a satire on white and black, and I don't make virgins of my colored girls. No sir! It will shock some of our ultrarespectable hypocritical Negroes, but I think I'm nearer the truth and tragedy and gaiety of Negro life than Miss Jessie Fauset.[5]

Ever your friend,
CLAUDE

---

* "Color Scheme." [Ed.]

Poste Restante
Finistère, France

July 17, 1925

Dear Schomburg,

Just got your letter. As I said when I sent the ms. I leave the business of the book entirely in your hands (I could do nothing else when I am far away this side of the waters) and whatever suggestions I offer concerning the marketing are merely *suggestions.* You are on the spot and must be allowed your own discretion in the matter.

I never expected you to war with that NAACP crowd. I have nothing against the officers white and black, although [Joel] Spingarn and Mary Ovington [6] are *mes bêtes noires*—can't stick them as individuals—but as I said in a previous letter the influence of the organization may be bad for aspiring Negro artists and other individual Negroes who believe in exercising freedom of thought and action that seem contrary to the aims of the NAACP. That's why I welcome criticism of them whether it comes from the Garvey group, the Owen and Randolph paper [the *Messenger*] or the [New York] *Amsterdam News*—fair, keen criticism and protest is good for the souls of organizations and people.

In the matter of the medal, however, I think you're flogging a dead horse. The very thought of a Spingarn medal to reward the intelligence of American Negroes annoys me.[7] (You may quote this whenever you want to.) I should have liked to be an American Negro just for the chance of refusing it in ringing words. Put any other race or national group of America in that position and see how ridiculous it looks. For a Negro to win real achievement of any sort in America is reward sufficient, the recognition of a Negro's merit by any authentic intellectual group in America is medal enough. The Spingarn medal therefore seems to me the cheapest of decorations (and I hold all such baubles as trash) an insult to the intelligence of the American Negro—like a tick attached to a thoroughbred horse. But if it pleases the vanity of the Spingarns and the NAACP to recognize Negro talent by such a showy smug gesture, let them have their peacockish pleasure. Let the whole colored officialdom of the NAACP have the medal. Doubtless they are working for it (and many others outside the organization), working to show the pompous Professor Spingarn how much they merit his notice.

The fact, my dear Schomburg, merely demonstrates how far below the general average is the American Negro's feeling for genuine self-respect, for real achievement in contemporary thought as expressed in science, literature and art. Just picture the Spingarn medal being offered to any other race or national group in America —even the Jews of the ghetto would resent the words accompanying [the award].[8] You and the *Amsterdam News* have missed the real point. It is not a joke, it is an insult to the intelligence of 15 million colored Americans—a people bigger than Belgium.

[Walter] White however is a good personal friend thinking of friendship from the personal point of view.[9] When I was sick, broke and alone over here he organized a little charity for me to which Joel Spingarn kindly contributed 50 dollars.[10] Walter likes me personally and so could be of help with the book if it didn't offend him personally, but it might for he's a propaganda angel when I am not. However much I resent organized cruelty against weak people or individuals, I always want to write the truth about things as I feel and see it. American Negroes have been living their lives behind closed shutters (I mean the better-off ones) not allowing the light in for fear of cracker insults and mud. For the sake of artistic self-expression the light should be let in. I am never afraid of light. I love sun and truth as I see it.

I am terribly anxious to hear what you have made for me. I'm about broke and don't want to stay in Bretagne over long. But I must stay till I hear *definitely* from you. In the meantime if I get some cash I will pull out again so continue to write to Thomas Cook et fils, Place de la Madeleine, Paris.

Ever,
CLAUDE

Brittany, France
[Undated, 1925]

My dear Schomburg,

This enclosed excerpt from [Alain] Locke's letter worries me extremely. I have *never* said I don't want *Walter* to know about my book for Walter is really one of my best friends. Certainly you could not have said that to Locke. Did you?

Do, my dear Schomburg, try to keep yourself out of all back-biting gossip. When we must fight our enemies or friends, let us come out openly and do it, but you must know how the Negro belts are just rotten-crazy with spiteful, nonsensical malice and if we get mixed up in that sea of shit we shall never be able to do any real revolutionary work along artistic or social lines.

Best regards,
Ever CLAUDE

LETTER TO ALAIN LOCKE

In 1925 Alain Locke edited the New Negro, *an important collection of black poetry and prose, which in effect introduced the Harlem Renaissance or New Negro Movement to the American reading public. Upon receiving a complimentary copy of the book, McKay wrote Locke the following letter of grievance. Locke stubbornly refused to admit to any fault in his handling of McKay's work. Although both men shared an essentially similar commitment to cultural pluralism, they remained temperamentally poles apart. As a philosopher and critic, Locke expected McKay to see the wisdom of his judgment. As an artist who consistently celebrated the free spirit, McKay rejected Locke's attitude as obtusely presumptuous.*

Chez Thomas Cook et fils
Marseilles, France

August 1, 1926

My dear Locke,

I received a copy of the *New Negro* a few days ago. Many thanks to you and the Bonis.[11]

However, I am displeased about my representation in it. I remember writing to you that "White Houses" was *not* the title of the poem published under that title in the *Survey Graphic*.[12] In the *Liberator* it had appeared under the title "The White House." That is a symbolic title. When you change it to "White Houses," the poem immediately becomes cheap, flat Afro-American propaganda. What does a man of creativity, a poet, care about entering a lot of uninteresting white houses? The whole symbolical import of my poem is lost under the title you have chosen to give it and allowed to remain after I had called your attention to it. If you understand how an artist feels about *the word* that he chooses above *other words* to use—if you know that artistic creation is the most delicate of all creative things—if you want to pit against how a craftsman, a gold-smith, an engraver, might feel about someone changing his design —then you will understand how I feel about "The White House." I do hope you will set this matter right in the future editions of your work.

I also wish you had asked me about the "Negro Dancers" in the *Liberator*. As the magazine was defunct there was no one but me to ask and, of course, I would have vetoed their publication.[13]

Dear Locke, in your letter you mention petty differences and misunderstandings. I wish you would see how these are the things that make for discord between people who should stand together on a common platform. I eliminated "Negro Dancers" from my *Harlem Shadows* because I did not consider the poems up to the level of my other work. The process of elimination reflects the growth of an artist, that process is his inalienable privilege. By printing in 1925 poems that I eliminated from *Spring in New Hampshire* in 1921 and *Harlem Shadows* in 1922 (and without any commentary note), you've broken up the artistic pattern that I have been trying to work out. I cannot understand why you have done it. You knew my address. You might easily have consulted me. That is the very ordinary and usual procedure among literary people. Besides, we—you and I—are something of friends and friendship calls for greater courtesy, I hold, than among strangers!

I hope you enjoy Paris. I am working hard on my novel. [I] hope to have my book of short stories out this year and my novel will be finished this month.[14] If you're having a new edition of *New Negro,* I should like "Negro Dancers" eliminated and other poems that I have substituted.

CLAUDE

LETTERS TO JAMES IVY *

Chez Thomas Cook & fils
67 La Canabiére
Marseille (Bouches-du-Rhône)
France . . .

May 20, 1928

My dear Ivy,

Oh yes I remember you all right and thanks for your letter. Naturally, I expected the colored brethren to cuss me out and themselves crazy in their rhetorical darky way after they got through licking their fat lips over *Home to Harlem*. But their craziness does not move me in any way. I am an artist interested in imaginative portrayals of life and artistic truth. The average Aframerican is so thin-skinned, he cannot stand up like a man before the artistic presentation of any phase of Negro life. He is afraid of [the] white man's ridicule and mockery. He sees Negro life falsely as a propagandist, and a very unintelligent propagandist at that, and he wants only to see in art a what-will-look-good-to-the-white-public side of it. The sincere Negro artist cannot take any stock of the criticism of black Babbittry because it is ignorant. I don't think a sincere artistic presentation of Negro life in America, no matter whether it is high, low or middle, will ever please the black Babbitts because what they want is not a picture but [a] whitewash or veneer.

Poor hopeless lost souls in the hot desert of [the] white man's prejudice, I understand perfectly their attitude, but I cannot side with nor pity them, as I do not believe in human pity. I believe in human intellect and understanding and Babbitts, black or white, do not have intellect and understanding. They are lost souls and I am finding myself through instinct, intellect and understanding by digging down in the roots of my race and getting in warm contact with it and seeing it, in spite of all the black-and-white raging and clamor, as one great part of the whole of life. . . . So let the howling go on. The noisier the merrier. I've given the old colored beans something

* James Ivy (1901–   ), black educator and journalist, edited the NAACP's *Crisis* magazine from 1950 until his retirement in 1966. [Ed.]

to chew on. I have seen only the criticisms in the *Pittsburgh Courier* anyway. I suppose it hurt the editors' patriotism the way I treated the Smoky City.[15]

Of course, I had monies from many friends. [Eric] Walrond [16] and [Harold] Jackman [17] have helped and somebody, I don't remember who, did send me a contribution of money from a number of Harlemites among whom were Mrs. [A. Philip] Randolph and Hubert Harrison and Grace Campbell.[18] I was grateful and happy, especially in realization of the fact that Negroes are poor and cannot give away money with the careless gesture of white people unless someone is insensitive enough to take it out of them with Garvey graft, and buncombe. But since I have been over here I have gotten plenty of money from white admirers of myself and my poetry—sums ranging from hundred, five hundred, thousand francs through to two hundred dollars that I had at different times.[19] I have worked very little—surely not more than a year in all at different intervals. Of course I have lived roughly and very cheaply, but with my sensual love of life I have had a tolerably good time. Preacher Ferris writes out of the acrimony of his disappointed and frustrated spirit. He is a bad writer with two books to his credit and he lives under the delusion of thinking himself a writer and thinker.[20] The man is just as badly botched in his whole make-up as the nigger newspaper for which he writes.

I am glad you are on the *Messenger*. It is a good magazine. Do [Chandler] Owen and [A. Philip] Randolph still have it? Under them it was a splendid magazine during and right after the War. It had the *Crisis* licked miles and miles, it was so well-edited and strong in its opinion. It was on the same level with the New York *Nation* which I think is the best American magazine from a journalistic point of view. But afterwards the tone of the *Messenger* went down a great deal in my opinion. I don't know why and how, one cannot always tell how decay begins, the same thing happened to the *Liberator*. I haven't seen the *Messenger* however since I left America in '22. You might let me see a copy with your stuff.

The reviews in the big-boss press are great, all of them, and the book is selling in spite of its stark realism. I am working hard on the second one [*Banjo*], which is about the life of Negro boys on the beach here, as I have seen and lived it myself. I want to finish this month. Then I am going to travel and may look in on America again. I hope we meet again some day. Are you teaching in a college? How is your French? Couldn't you get a job up North? Let me hear from you again and good luck to you.

Yours sincerely,
CLAUDE MCKAY

Chez Thomas Cook et fils
2 Place de la Madeleine
Paris, France

September 20, 1929

My dear Ivy,

I beg you to forgive my long silence, but getting back to Paris in the spring I found myself with plenty of business to go through with my representative [William Aspenwall Bradley], besides a painful intimate affair which lasted for weeks and made me unfit for any kind of work. To get away from myself I dashed about a great deal with old friends, the show people of *Blackbirds* [21] and Aframericans holidaying in Paris. But I was very unhappy all the time and managed to cut loose last month (towards the end) and am here near the frontier working on my next novel,[22] but not yet decided where in Spain I shall settle down to finish it. Barcelona is the most attractive place, but I am sure it must be pretty awful with the exhibition on and the town overcrowded with visitors. However, I'll stay in Spain as I feel more in harmony with its culture than that of France.

It was good to get your last letter and the review of *Banjo*. I really don't think it as good a story as *Home to Harlem* from the esthetic point of view. It doesn't run smoothly enough and is clogged up with "the problem of the Negro." However, I had to get that out of my system. Now I can go on with real creative work. It must be a choice between story telling and essays on the race problem. I don't mind doing an essay now and then, but I don't want that to destroy my creative energies.

Ray is not altogether myself.* Most people think so, because he is an intellectual, but I merely use him as a vehicle. There is a little of me in all my chief characters!

Frank Harris was ill at Nice this spring.[23] I was there for Easter but did not try to see him. No, I don't think he is a great writer

* Ray, McKay's fictional Negro writer, appeared in both *Home to Harlem* and *Banjo*. [Ed.]

in spite of your protest. He has one little story about Jesus' resurrection which I think is a masterpiece—it is so well done—a masterpiece as [Ernest] Dowson's "Cynara," but that does not make Dowson a great poet.[24] Harris is efficient, a great journalist, but he lacks the magic, the soul, the stuff of gold or whatever you want to call it that makes a great writer of a man. He is in a class a little higher than [H. L.] Mencken.

I had a wonderful time of it in Africa living among the Arabs and making friends.[25] I did not want to leave if it were not that the French are masters there, and I prefer to live under the French in France where the government is more liberal bossing its own people. They do treat the Arabs badly. I was treated decently because I was a tourist and wore Egyptian clothes. The French are the cleverest propagandists in the world. They hate colored people, yet pretend they are liberal because they have a liberal tradition to live up to. I dislike them because they are the most nationalistic people in the world, and they are never tired of saying they are the nation destined to keep the torch of civilization burning.

My work has been reviewed in one of the leading weeklies of Paris and they have attacked me.[26] I expect more when it is translated, but I shall be prepared for them when I write my travel book.

Don't you make enough to take a trip abroad? So many of the Negro teachers and professors do Europe every summer. Locke never misses one and Harold Jackman was here this summer and many Fisk and Atlanta teachers.

[Claude McKay]

LETTER TO W. E. B. DU BOIS

Alain Locke was not the only black critic who incurred McKay's displeasure. He was also offended by W. E. B. Du Bois, the editor of the NAACP magazine, Crisis, *who in June 1928 published one of McKay's poem's in the same issue of* Crisis *in which he denounced McKay's new novel,* Home to Harlem.

c/o Thomas Cook & Son
Calle de Fontanella 19
Barcelona, Spain

June 18, 1928

Mr. W. E. B. Du Bois
69 Fifth Avenue
New York City

Dear Mr. Du Bois,

I think I beseeched you over a year ago *not* to publish those poems I sent to the *Crisis* towards the end of 1925.

I must remind you again that those poems were sent to *Crisis* for a special purpose. I was ill. I had no money. I wrote to a number of New York publications, including the *Crisis,* frankly stating my situation and asking them to help me by buying a poem or more. I received prompt replies and help from some of the publications. Others that did not accept had the courtesy, with one exception, to return my poems. The exception was the *Crisis* (the only Negro publication I wrote to) which neither replied nor returned my poems. About a year and a half later, when I saw two of the poems in the *Crisis* I was surprised, because, as I said then in a letter to you (the duplicate unfortunately is in Paris) I thought the poems had gone astray in the mails. You replied with a check for the published ones and stated that Miss [Jessie] Fauset was in charge when I wrote and she, I suppose, had no time to waste on a non-influential and down-and-out fellow writer.[27]

I had expected you, after receiving my letter, to return and not make use of the remaining poems. I wrote to my agent in New York to call in all the prose and verse that I had sent out to various magazines. These were all returned and if I did not list the *Crisis* it was because I had already written to the Editor and I took it as a matter of course that a Negro publication of a recognized high standard would not fail to conform to the common rules of journalistic ethics.

My reasons for not wanting any of the things I sent out long ago published now are private and tactical, and I particularly resent the publication of my poem in the same number of the *Crisis* in which, in criticizing my novel, the Editor steps outside the limits of criticism to become personal. I should think that a publication so holy-clean and righteous-pure as the *Crisis* should hesitate about printing anything from the pen of a writer who wallows so much in "dirt," "filth," "drunkenness," "fighting," and "lascivious sexual promiscuity."

But I have no objection to the quoted phrases as criticism, if you did not also choose (to employ the Coolidgism) to question my motive in writing my book and bring it down to the level of the fish market. Now this is personal and you have been an editor long enough to know that it has nothing to do with criticism. And so I will reply personally to you, Mr. Du Bois, by retorting that nowhere in your writings do you reveal any comprehension of esthetics and therefore you are not competent or qualified to pass judgment upon any work of art.

My motive for writing was simply that I began in my boyhood to be an artist in words and I have stuck to that in spite of the contrary forces and colors of life that I have had to contend against through various adventures, mistakes, successes, strength and weakness of body that the artist-soul, more or less, has to pass through. Certainly I sympathize with and even pity you for not understanding my motive, because you have been forced from a normal career to enter a special field of racial propaganda and, honorable though that field may be, it has precluded you from contact with real life, for propaganda is fundamentally but a one-sided idea of life. Therefore I should not be surprised when you mistake the art of life for nonsense and try to pass off propaganda as life in art!

Finally, deep-sunk in depravity though he may be, the author of *Home to Harlem* prefers to remain unrepentant and unregenerate and he "distinctly" is not grateful for any free baptism of grace in the cleansing pages of the *Crisis*.

Yours for more utter absence of restraint,

CLAUDE MCKAY

LETTER TO MAX EASTMAN

McKay felt that the task of black writers remained essentially that of all artists, namely to "comprehend life in its universal aspects." In the following letter he criticizes Max Eastman's book The Literary Mind: Its Place in an Age of Science *and uses the opportunity to set forth his own ideas on the general function of literature.*

Apartado 26
Correo Español
Tangier, Morocco

April 25, 1932

My dear Max,

I made some notes on your book to write you about three months now at least, but I couldn't, because all my time was taken trying to get part of my new work off to [Eugene] Saxton * (you know why) and I wanted to write you a long, full letter.

I read the book twice and thought it your most brilliant prose work since the *Enjoyment of Poetry*.[28] I hope it sold well, which it deserves, and netted you a neat sum. It makes me think more again of something that has always puzzled me and that is why a first-rate critic of poetry like you has never been offered a permanent place as poetry critic on one of the first-rate American reviews instead of having to drudge your life out lecturing awful stuff. It can't be your radicalism, you couldn't be too radical in poetry criticism for the *New Republic,* the *Nation* or the *Forum.* So it may be because you are too conservative! And that your competence as a critic of poetry was overshadowed by the modernist movement that has so skillfully and with the aid of the advanced intellectuals taken, held and dominated the field of poetry in America for the last twenty years.

Well, I was tickled to death by your forthright attack and demolition of the ultra modernists in poetry and prose and their praiseful critics. Personally, I believe that a good many of the unintelligible poets and prosateurs really lack that high mental equipment that makes for clarity of expression of a high order. I say this because often when I take the time to go through the odd punctuation and trick phrasing and get down to the bone of their stuff I find it as banal as Eddie Guest's [29] or (in the case of T. S. Eliot, for example) as pedantic and commonplace as Martin Tupper.[30] I except a few whom I regard as crusading revolutionists against the dead weight of formal respectability under which modern literature is buried. Like James Joyce whom I consider a Don Quixote of contemporary literature, but that is the James Joyce of *Ulysses.*[31]

As for the younger generation of new humanists, I think they are battling for their existence. Some of them sound too intelligent,

---

* Eugene Saxton was McKay's editor at Harper and Brothers in New York. [Ed.]

from the stuff I've read, to be altogether with the older humanists, so I have a hunch they are also in revolt against the movement, proletarian as well as bourgeois (see Mencken),[32] that would make literature a thing of mass expression or a popular ballyhoo instead of a skilled and arduous profession.

However, although I found the book exhilarating and enjoyed your tilts at and decapitation of the literary pontiffs, I can't for the life of me work up any enthusiasm over the thesis, which, fundamentally, is the conflict between science and literature. Because I can't see why there should be any conflict except for morons, even though such morons happen to be seated in the authoritative places of academic literature. I could understand better a conflict between religion and science since religion is supernatural and had to surrender the major part of its premises when Science turned its light upon them.

I mention religion because it seems to me the best analogy of illustrating what I feel about the matter of Science and Literature. The great literature and music and painting and architecture that grew out of the periods when the elite of humanity believed in gods and God are still wonderful works of art to us who do not believe —and in spite of their scientific errors! Dante's hell has a magical power over me even though I don't believe in hell and I can adore the presence of the gods and the angels and the saints in Homer and Milton and the great Renaissance painters even as I do the Koran in Mohammedan architecture.

So I believe that when a real artist has something to say or sing or sculpt or paint about human life he'll do it forthright without in the least imagining that he was handicapped or limited by the progress of science. And if his intelligence and comprehension are of a high order he cannot but feel that his work is facilitated by the discoveries of science, even though Science should lay its operating hand upon his body and soul and lay bare the why and wherefore of his creative energy and of the material by which he works. For instance, if science could prove what *is* the literary mind then it would be so much the better for the future generations of *littérateurs*.

Also it would be easier to determine real from fake literary excellence, just as the science of photography has chased a lot of cheap painters to cover and out of business, which I believe is responsible for (if one dare not say the Cult of Unintelligibility) the Cult of Bunk in modern art and the confusion of real masters like

Cézanne and Monet with the gang of geometrical tricksters.[33] And while I am on it I must say that I was a little surprised you did not mention modernist painting too for there can be no doubt that it is correlative to the modernist literary movement. And more, my idea is that both are a kind of bourgeois attitudinizing of the social revolutionary ferment. I thought of that when I was in Moscow and used to frequent Meyerhold's theater.[34] I noticed that the audience was mostly members of the old intelligentsia and whenever I met a proletarian he was an intellectual. And when I talked to Meyerhold he seemed like a lost person who did not know what the new social order was all about, but thought that a revolutionary art form in the theater was necessary to interpret the revolution. Meanwhile all the proletarians who could get or buy tickets were crowding the Bolshoi Theater to see the ballet.

I agree with your statement that poetry is a communication of experience, but so are painting and music in varying degrees. So I think poetry could stand a more definite definition, but that is difficult since it overflows into other art forms just as music does into poetry.

I can't see any fundamental conflict between science and literature as long as literature has the vast province of social manners [in which] to disport itself [and], even the field of science also which has great need of the literary hand to interpret it. I remember your saying once that many scientific treatises were impossible because their authors did not know how to write. I think the poet or storyteller can make effective use of scientific discoveries by allusions without usurping the role of the specialists. The danger is that he may bore the general reader.

Aldous Huxley knows a huge lot about science but when he puts the technical knowledge of the making of a phonograph and the recording of a disc in his novel, he becomes tiresome unless you are technically interested. For that one would prefer to go to a straight popularizer. You know the popular science book that tells us all about the nature of electricity and photography and so on. Tennyson too becomes thin and dated with his Darwinian references in *In Memoriam*.

But this doesn't seem to me to imply science encroaching upon and limiting the sphere of literature, but rather literature remaining upon its own unassailable ground. Rather it shows that these pious souls who want to make "literary truth" take the place of "scientific fact" are foolish and wrong just as were their spiritual forebears before them who accepted "literary truth" as revealed religion. Today you and I smile at the supernatural pretensions of "literary truth," but that "truth" remains great literature for us all the same and we don't care a damn that it was created in an unscientific atmosphere.

I can't imagine any intellectual of these times who keeps abreast of the thought currents of this age accepting a "literary truth" as against a "scientific fact." I could understand one accepting a "religious truth" but then that lies outside the pale of reason. The intellectual fogeys who want "literary truth" to be scientific or to function today as it did in the time of the Hebrew prophets or the Greeks or even up until the eighteenth century ought to get themselves transferred from this earth to some other planet. But I think that if the intellectual idea of "literary truth" were analyzed it would prove at bottom to be nothing more than a "wise saying" or a "beautiful phrase" delivered in an unique and startling manner—an addition to the sum of the universal wisdom of mankind.

Such a wisdom exists telling of the passion, the folly and sagacity, success and failure, pain and joy of living life. It existed long before modern science and I believe it will continue to exist as vigorous and independent as ever as long as humanity retains the faculties of feeling [and] thinking—the inexhaustible source from which great and authentic literature springs, whether it be cerebral or sentimental, realistic or romantic.

A Jamaican slave sang: Rock stone a ribber-bottom no
                                        feel sun-hot
when he wanted to say that his master sitting all day in the shade did not know what hard toil in the sun meant. And that saying has became a classic in the folk language of the peasants.

And when Lady Macbeth cries, "Not all the perfumes of Arabia can sweeten this little hand" [sic], all those who have set their hand to any deed that they regretted will recognize that as universal poetry.

I cite and accept these with enthusiasm as *literary* truths and I don't think your citation from Pascal was a particularly pregnant and happy one.[35] And I couldn't agree with you at all when you state on page 241 that "Science has withdrawn intellect from literature." That may hold true for those who lack a comprehensive intellect and the futurists ought to take comfort from such a statement and go on being unintelligible. If science has rid literature from its false pretensions, then so much the better it seems to me for the future of literature which will have to stand on its own intrinsic merit, and although our age may not be very favorable to the creation of great literature I am convinced that intellect and a real one is absolutely necessary for the making of a literary masterpiece.

Therefore I believe M. Benda [36] rests upon sound ground when he demands that artists make "an attempt to comprehend life." They should and only so far as they do comprehend life in its universal aspects will their work have more than a contemporary interest and take rank to stand the test of time. . . .

I hope you will be coming over this summer. I haven't heard from you since your card from Bermuda and don't know where you are and what doing since. You would love it here for a change, I think. The garden has sprung full of wild flowers with lovely poppies of various kinds and daisies.

I suppose you are doing a new book. . . . I struggled through revising the first part of my new stuff and have sent it to Saxton, asking him at the same time for money, for I have enough just for a couple of weeks more. I am afraid to look at the summer in the distance with my work half done before me. [37]

I hear that in spite of the slump the authors are doing pretty well and that many of the newer men have a permanent contract and draw a monthly allowance. And of course I wish I was in on that too.

I have just met an American here who knew you by sight, has seen you at parties in New York. And he spoke most flatteringly of you and Eliena * together. I hope I see you both this summer.

> With my best as ever,
> CLAUDE

---

* Eastman's wife. [Ed.]

5. Experiments in Fiction, 1928-1941

As a writer of fiction McKay is best known for his celebration of black folk culture in *Banana Bottom* and for his vigorously drawn picaresque heroes in *Home to Harlem* and *Banjo*. McKay rejoiced that such characters as Jake and Banjo refused to "go down and disappear under the serried crush of trampling white feet." [1] He pointed out that their survival was "baffling to civilized understanding . . . a challenge to civilization itself." [2]

McKay's appreciation of the black folk's vitality and health was heightened by his awareness that they also suffered from constant assaults upon their basic human integrity. In his short stories, particularly, he wrote with insight and sympathy about the isolation and loneliness of men and women circumscribed by poverty and color prejudices and cut off from any effective communication with each other, even within their own community.

McKay's short stories have received little critical attention. It is significant, however, that he was naturally drawn to the form in his earliest attempts at fiction and that *Home to Harlem* was originally a short story. After the success of *Banjo,* he published his collection of short stories, largely because he did not want to become known solely as an author of picaresque tales but wished to establish himself as a writer "of many moods." Late in life, he remarked that "some of my best material is in the book of short stories, *Gingertown.*" [3]

The stories selected for inclusion in this volume illustrate the importance of the short story in the development of McKay's fiction. The first selection, "He Also Loved," is excerpted from *Home to Harlem*. It is narrated by Jake's intellectual friend, Ray, who uses it to warn a college friend of the hypocrisy involved in a blanket condemnation of all low-life characters. The story stands alone as an individual chapter, and it originated as an independent short story before *Home to Harlem* was expanded into a novel.

"Mattie and Her Sweetman" and "The Strange Burial of Sue" are from *Gingertown*. Together, they demonstrate the difference between McKay's treatment of urban Harlem and rural Jamaican life. In the Harlem stories, McKay's characters are far from their rural origins and isolated from one another in an essentially cold, abrasive, urban environment. Repressed internally by self-doubts and externally by poverty and white prejudices, they have little opportunity for fellowship, except that which can be found in cabarets, "parlor socials," and pool halls. As McKay notes, "Living for Mattie was harder than working."

The characters in his Jamaican stories, on the other hand, are usually more at ease with one another and with their environment. But even in Jamaica, Anglo-Saxon values intrude to challenge the serenity of the peasant's customary relationships. As "The Strange Burial of Sue" makes clear, Jamaicans are nevertheless capable of rallying to preserve the basic stability of their ways, and no member of the community is left to die alone.

The final story, "Yeoman Abdul's Funeral," is taken from "Harlem Glory," an unpublished novel which McKay began in 1940 but never completed. Although written at a later date than the other stories in this selection, it is nevertheless included here in order to illustrate the continuity and direction of his fictional themes. The novel relates the fortunes of Buster South, a black bon vivant, who returns to Harlem and the Great Depression after a madcap European expatriation. Upon his return, he becomes involved in two quite different movements, which are agitating the common people of Harlem. One is led by a self-proclaimed god, who calls himself Glory Savior and is McKay's fictional prototype of Father Divine. The other is directed by a gaudily attired Moslem of Afro-American origin known as Omar. Omar represents another actual character, Sufi Abdul Hamid, who in the early 1930s began a boycott movement against Harlem merchants, which eventually forced them to hire black clerks. The fictional Omar forms an organization called the Yeomen of Labor and begins a similar campaign. Abdul, a dark-skinned Moslem from the Middle East residing in Harlem, joins Omar and becomes a valuable aide. During a demonstration, Abdul becomes involved in an altercation and is stabbed to death. His funeral is described in the excerpt which concludes this section.

No claim is made that the stories which follow are a wholly representative sampling of McKay's fiction. On the whole, however, they do enable one to see more clearly those aspects of McKay's fiction which tend to be obscured by the picaresque and primitive in *Home to Harlem* and *Banjo*.

HE ALSO LOVED

It was in the winter of 1916 when I first came to New York to hunt for a job. I was broke. I was afraid I would have to pawn my clothes, and it was dreadfully cold. I didn't even know the right way to go about looking for a job. I was always timid about that. For five weeks I had not paid my rent. I was worried, and Ma Lawton, my landlady, was also worried. She had her bills to meet. She was a good-hearted old woman from South Carolina. Her face was all wrinkled and sensitive like finely-carved mahogany.

Every bed-space in the flat was rented. I was living in the small hall bedroom. Ma Lawton asked me to give it up. There were four men sleeping in the front room; two in an old, chipped-enameled brass bed, one on a davenport, and the other in a folding chair. The old lady put a little canvas cot in that same room, gave me a pillow and a heavy quilt, and said I should try and make myself comfortable there until I got work.

The cot was all right for me. Although I hate to share a room with another person and the fellows snoring disturbed my rest. Ma Lawton moved into the little room that I had had, and rented out hers—it was next to the front room—to a man and a woman.

The woman was above ordinary height, chocolate-colored. Her skin was smooth, too smooth, as if it had been pressed and fashioned out for ready sale like chocolate candy. Her hair was straightened out into an Indian Straight after the present style among Negro ladies. She had a mongoose sort of a mouth, with two top front teeth showing. She wore a long mink coat.

The man was darker than the woman. His face was longish, with the right cheek somewhat caved in. It was an interesting face, an attractive, salacious mouth, with the lower lip protruding. He wore a bottle-green peg-top suit, baggy at the hips. His coat hung loose from his shoulders and it was much longer than the prevailing style. He wore also a Mexican hat, and in his breast pocket he carried an Ingersoll watch attached to a heavy gold chain. His name was Jericho Jones, and they called him Jerco for short. And she was Miss Whicher—Rosalind Whicher.

Ma Lawton introduced me to them and said I was broke, and they were both awfully nice to me. They took me to a big feed of corned beef and cabbage at Burrell's on Fifth Avenue. They gave me a good appetizing drink of gin to commence with. And we had beer with the eats; not ordinary beer, either, but real Budweiser, right off the ice.

And as good luck sometimes comes pouring down like a shower, the next day Ma Lawton got me a job in the little free-lunch saloon right under her flat. It wasn't a paying job as far as money goes in New York, but I was glad to have it. I had charge of the free-lunch counter. You know the little dry crackers that go so well with beer, and the cheese and fish and the potato salad. And I served, besides, spare-ribs and whole boiled potatoes and corned beef and cabbage for those customers who could afford to pay for a lunch. I got no wages at all, but I got my eats twice a day. And I made a few tips, also. For there were about six big black men with plenty of money who used to eat lunch with us, specially for our spare-ribs and sweet potatoes. Each one of them gave me a quarter. I made enough to pay Ma Lawton for my canvas cot.

Strange enough, too, Jerco and Rosalind took a liking to me. And sometimes they came and ate lunch perched up there at the counter, with Rosalind the only woman there, all made up and rubbing her mink coat against the men. And when they got through eating, Jerco would toss a dollar bill at me.

We got very friendly, we three. Rosalind would bring up squabs and canned stuff from the German delicatessen in One Hundred and Twenty-fifth Street, and sometimes they asked me to dinner in their room and gave me good liquor.

I thought I was pretty well fixed for such a hard winter. All I had to do as extra work was keeping the saloon clean. . . .

One afternoon Jerco came into the saloon with a man who looked pretty near white. Of course, you never can tell for sure about a person's race in Harlem, nowadays, when there are so many high-yallers floating round—colored folks that would make Italian and Spanish people look like Negroes beside them. But I figured out from his way of talking and acting that the man with Jerco belonged to the white race. They went in through the family entrance into the back room, which was unusual, for the family room of a saloon, as you know, is only for women in the business and the men they bring in there with them. Real men don't sit in a saloon here as they do at home. I suppose it would be sissified. There's a bar for them to lean on and drink and joke as long as they feel like.

The boss of the saloon was a little fidgety about Jerco and his friend sitting there in the back. The boss was a short pumpkin-bellied brown man, a little bald off the forehead. Twice he found something to attend to in the back room, although there was nothing at all there that wanted attending to. . . . I felt better, and the boss, too, I guess, when Rosalind came along and gave the family room its respectable American character. I served Rosalind a Martini cocktail extra dry, and afterward all three of them, Rosalind, Jerco, and their friend, went up to Ma Lawton's.

The two fellows that slept together were elevator operators in a department store, so they had their Sundays free. On the afternoon of the Sunday of the same week that the white-looking man had been in the saloon with Jerco, I went upstairs to change my old shoes —they'd got soaking wet behind the counter—and I found Ma Lawton talking to the two elevator fellows.

The boys had given Ma Lawton notice to quit. They said they couldn't sleep there comfortably together on account of the goings-on in Rosalind's room. The fellows were members of the Colored Y.M.C.A. and were queerly quiet and pious. One of them was studying to be a preacher. They were the sort of fellows that thought going to cabarets a sin, and that parlor socials were leading Harlem straight down to hell. They only went to church affairs themselves. They had been rooming with Ma Lawton for over a year. She called them her gentlemen lodgers.

Ma Lawton said to me: "Have you heard anything phony outa the next room, dear?"

"Why, no, Ma," I said, "nothing more unusual than you can hear all over Harlem. Besides, I work so late, I am dead tired when I turn in to bed, so I sleep heavy."

"Well, it's the truth I do like that there Jérco an' Rosaline," said Ma Lawton. "They did seem quiet as lambs, although they was always havin' company. But Ise got to speak to them, 'cause I doana wanta lose ma young mens. . . . But theyse a real nice-acting couple. Jerco him treats me like him was mah son. It's true that they doan work like all poah niggers, but they pays that rent down good and prompt ehvery week."

Jerco was always bringing in ice cream and cake or something for Ma Lawton. He had a way about him, and everybody liked him. He was a sympathetic type. He helped Ma Lawton move beds and commodes and he fixed her clotheslines. I had heard somebody talking about Jerco in the saloon, however, saying that he could swing a mean fist when he got his dander up, and that he had been mixed up in more than one razor cut-up. He did have a nasty long razor scar on the back of his right hand.

The elevator fellows had never liked Rosalind and Jerco. The one who was studying to preach Jesus said he felt pretty sure that they were an ungodly-living couple. He said that late one night he had pointed out their room to a woman that looked white. He said the woman looked suspicious. She was perfumed and all powdered up and it appeared as if she didn't belong among colored people.

"There's no sure telling white from high-yaller these days," I said. "There are so many swell-looking quadroons and octoroons of the race."

But the other elevator fellow said that one day in the tenderloin section he had run up against Rosalind and Jerco together with a petty officer of marines. And that just put the lid on anything favorable that could be said about them.

But Ma Lawton said: "Well, Ise got to run mah flat right an' try mah utmost to please youall, but I ain't wanta dip mah nose too deep in a lodger's affairs."

Late that night, toward one o'clock, Jerco dropped in at the saloon and told me that Rosalind was feeling badly. She hadn't eaten a bite all day and he had come to get a pail of beer, because she had asked specially for draught beer. Jerco was worried, too.

"I hopes she don't get bad," he said. "For we ain't got a cent o' money. Wese just in on a streak o' bad luck."

"I guess she'll soon be all right," I said.

The next day after lunch I stole a little time and went up to see Rosalind. Ma Lawton was just going to attend to her when I let myself in, and she said to me: "Now the poor woman is sick, poor chile, ahm so glad mah conscience is free and that I hadn't a said nothing evil t' her."

Rosalind was pretty sick. Ma Lawton said it was the grippe. She gave Rosalind hot whisky drinks and hot milk, and she kept her feet warm with a hot-water bottle. Rosalind's legs were lead-heavy. She had a pain that pinched her side like a pair of pincers. And she cried out for thirst and begged for draught beer.

Ma Lawton said Rosalind ought to have a doctor. "You'd better go an' scares up a white one," she said to Jerco. "Ise nevah had no faith in these heah nigger doctors."

"I don't know how we'll make out without money," Jerco whined. He was sitting in the old Morris chair with his head heavy on his left hand.

"You kain pawn my coat," said Rosalind. "Old man Greenbaum will give you two hundred down without looking at it."

"I won't put a handk'chief o' yourn in the hock shop," said Jerco. "You'll need you' stuff soon as you get better. Specially you' coat. You kain't go anywheres without it."

"S'posin' I don't get up again," Rosalind smiled. But her countenance changed suddenly as she held her side and moaned. Ma Lawton bent over and adjusted the pillows.

Jerco pawned his watch chain and his own overcoat, and called in a Jewish doctor from the upper Eighth Avenue fringe of the Belt. But Rosalind did not improve under medical treatment. She lay there with a sad, tired look, as if she didn't really care what happened to her. Her lower limbs were apparently paralyzed. Jerco told the doctor that she had been sick unto death like that before. The doctor shot a lot of stuff into her system. But Rosalind lay there heavy and fading like a felled tree.

The elevator operators looked in on her. The student one gave her a Bible with a little red ribbon marking the chapter in St. John's Gospel about the woman taken in adultery. He also wanted to pray for her recovery. Jerco wanted the prayer, but Rosalind said no. Her refusal shocked Ma Lawton, who believed in God's word.

The doctor stopped Rosalind from drinking beer. But Jerco slipped it in to her when Ma Lawton was not around. He said he couldn't refuse it to her when beer was the only thing she cared for. He had an expensive sweater. He pawned it. He also pawned their large suitcase. It was real leather and worth a bit of money.

One afternoon Jerco sat alone in the back room of the saloon and began to cry.

"I'll do anything. There ain't anything too low I wouldn't do to raise a little money," he said.

"Why don't you hock Rosalind's fur coat?" I suggested. "That'll give you enough money for a while."

"Gawd, no! I wouldn't touch none o' Rosalind's clothes. I jes kain't," he said. "She'll need them as soon as she's better."

"Well, you might try and find some sort of a job, then," I said.

"Me find a job? What kain I do? I ain't no good foh no job. I kain't work. I don't know how to ask for no job. I wouldn't know how. I wish I was a woman."

"Good God! Jerco," I said, "I don't see any way out for you but some sort of a job."

"What kain I do? What kain I do?" he whined. "I kain't do nothing. That's why I don't wanna hock Rosalind's fur coat. She'll need it soon as she's better. Rosalind's so wise about picking up good money. Just like that!" He snapped his fingers.

I left Jerco sitting there and went into the saloon to serve a customer a plate of corned beef and cabbage.

After lunch I thought I'd go up to see how Rosalind was making out. The door was slightly open, so I slipped in without knocking. I saw Jerco kneeling down by the open wardrobe and kissing the toe of one of her brown shoes. He started as he saw me, and looked queer kneeling there. It was a high, old-fashioned wardrobe that Ma Lawton must have picked up at some sale. Rosalind's coat was hanging there, and it gave me a spooky feeling, for it looked so much more like the real Rosalind than the woman that was dozing there on the bed.

Her other clothes were hanging there, too. There were three gowns—a black silk, a glossy green satin, and a flimsy chiffon-like yellow thing. In a corner of the lowest shelf was a bundle of soiled champagne-colored silk stockings and in the other four pairs of shoes—one black velvet, one white kid, and another gold-finished. Jerco regarded the lot with dog-like affection.

"I wouldn't touch not one of her things until she's better," he said. "I'd sooner hock the shirt off mah back."

Which he was preparing to do. He had three expensive striped silk shirts, presents from Rosalind. He had just taken two out of the wardrobe and the other off his back, and made a parcel of them for old Greenbaum. . . . Rosalind woke up and murmured that she wanted some beer. . . .

A little later Jerco came to the saloon with the pail. He was shivering. His coat collar was turned up and fastened with a safety pin, for he only had an undershirt on.

"I don't know what I'd do if anything happens to Rosalind," he said. "I kain't live without her."

"Oh yes, you can," I said in a not very sympathetic tone. Jerco gave me such a reproachful pathetic look that I was sorry I said it.

The tall big fellow had turned into a scared, trembling baby. "You ought to buck up and hold yourself together," I told him. "Why, you ought to be game if you like Rosalind, and don't let her know you're down in the dumps."

"I'll try," he said. "She don't know how miserable I am. When I hooks up with a woman I treat her right, but I never let her know everything about me. Rosalind is an awful good woman. The straightest woman I ever had, honest."

I gave him a big glass of strong whisky.

Ma Lawton came in the saloon about nine o'clock that evening and said that Rosalind was dead. "I told Jerco we'd have to sell that theah coat to give the poah woman a decent fun'ral, an' he jes brokes down crying like a baby."

That night Ma Lawton slept in the kitchen and put Jerco in her little hall bedroom. He was all broken up. I took him up a pint of whisky.

"I'll nevah find another one like Rosalind," he said, "nevah!" He sat on an old black-framed chair in which a new yellow-varnished bottom had just been put. I put my hand on his shoulder and tried to cheer him up: "Buck up, old man. Never mind, you'll find somebody else." He shook his head. "Perhaps you didn't like the way me and Rosalind was living. But she was one naturally good woman, all good inside her."

I felt foolish and uncomfortable. "I always liked Rosalind, Jerco," I said, "and you, too. You were both awfully good scouts to me. I have nothing against her. I am nothing myself."

Jerco held my hand and whimpered: "Thank you, old top. Youse all right. Youse always been a regular fellar."

It was late, after two a.m. I went to bed. And, as usual, I slept soundly.

Ma Lawton was an early riser. She made excellent coffee and she gave the two elevator runners and another lodger, a porter who worked on Ellis Island, coffee and hot home-made biscuits every morning. The next morning she shook me abruptly out of my sleep.

"Ahm scared to death. Thar's moah tur'ble trouble. I kain't git in the barfroom and the hallway's all messy."

I jumped up, hauled on my pants, and went to the bathroom. A sickening purplish liquid coming from under the door had trickled down the hall toward the kitchen. I took Ma Lawton's rolling-pin and broke through the door.

Jerco had cut his throat and was lying against the bowl of the water-closet. Some empty coke papers were on the floor. And he sprawled there like a great black boar in a mess of blood.

MATTIE AND HER SWEETMAN

In the neighborhood of 135th Street and Lenox Avenue a parlor social was taking place in the flat of a grass widow called Rosie.

Rosie had sent out invitations to a number of chambermaids, bellhops, waiters, longshoremen, and railroad men whom she knew personally. She asked them to bring their friends and to tell their friends to bring their friends.

The price of admission was twenty-five cents. Soda pop and hard drinks were sold at prices a little more than what was paid in the saloon. At ten o'clock Rosie's place began filling up with guests. It was that type of apartment called railroad flat. The guests put their wraps in Rosie's bedroom and danced in the dining-room and parlor.

Rosie kept the soda pop and beer cold in the ice-box in the kitchen. Whisky, wine, and gin were locked up in a cabinet whose key was secured by a red ribbon suspended from her waist.

The parlor social was good company. There was a fascinating mélange of color: chocolate, cocoa, chestnut, ginger, yellow, and cream. The people for whom these parlor maids and chambermaids worked would have gazed wonder-eyed at them now. Aprons and caps set aside, the maids were radiant in soft shimmering chiffon, crêpe de Chine and satin stuff. How do they do it? those people would have commented, wearing the things they do on their wages?

In that merry crowd was one strange person—a black woman in her fifties. She wore a white dress, long white gloves, black stockings and black shoes, and a deep-fringed purple shawl. She was of average height and very thin. Her neck was extraordinary; it was such a long, excessively skinny neck, a pathetic neck. Her face was much finer than her neck, thin also, but marked by a quiet, dark determination.

She danced with a codfish-complexioned strutter wearing a dress suit. He was tall with a trim ready-to-wear appearance and his hair was plastered down, glistening with brilliantine. His mouth wore a perpetual sneer. The woman danced badly. Her partner was a good dancer and tried to make her look as awkward as he could. The music stopped and they found seats near the piano.

"What youse gwina drink, Jay?" she asked.

"Gin," he said, casually.

"Rosie!" the woman called.

Rosie bustled over, a marvel of duck-chested amiability. Rosie's complexion was a flat café-au-lait, giving the impression of a bad mixture, coffee over-parched, or burned with skimmed milk, and the generous amount of powder she used did not make the effect any pleasanter.

"Whaz you two agwine to hev, Mattie?" She knew, of course, that Jay was Mattie's sweetman and Mattie did the paying.

"One gin and one beer," said Mattie.

"Gwine to treat the pianist to something?" Rosie knew how to tease her guests into making her parlor socials things worth giving.

"You throw me a good ball a whisky, sistah," said the pianist, a slight-built, sharp-featured black, whose eyes were intense, the whites appearing inflamed. . . .

Hands waved at Rosie from a group seated at a small table wedged against the mantelpiece, and an impatient young man called:

"Seven whiskies, Rosie, and four bottles a ginger ale jest that cold as you c'n makem."

"Right away, right away, mah chilluns." Rosie started a quick-time duck step to the cabinet.

Two girls pushed their way through a jam of men blocking the way between the dining-room and the parlor. The smaller was a satin-skinned chocolate; the other, attractive in a red frock, was cocoa. The cocoa girl saw Jay with Mattie and cried: "Hello, Jay! Howse you?"

"Hello, you Marita!" said Jay.

"Having a good time?"

"Kinder," he sneered.

Marita was the waitress at Aunt Hattie's pigs'-feet-and-chittlings joint. Jay went there to eat sometimes. Marita rather liked him, put more food than ordinary in his dish, and chatted with him. She would have liked to keep company with Jay, but he made her realize that he had no desire to go with a girl in the regular way. He never felt that sort of feeling that would urge a fellow on to rent a room for two and live, a good elevator boy, in the Black Belt. For it was easier going with the Matties and grass-widows of Harlem. Marita couldn't imagine herself down to the level of Jay's women. Not yet —when she was young and strong and pretty. But she rather admired his casual way of getting along and felt a romantic fascination for the sneer that sharp living had marked him by.

The pianist turned his inflamed eyes to the ceiling and banged the piano. Jay left Mattie alone to jazz wih Marita.

"What a scary way she's dressed up!" said Marita as they wiggled past Mattie.

Jay grinned. Marita went liltingly with his movement. He disliked toting a middle-aged black hen round the room. Not that he minded being Mattie's sweetman. He was very proud of his new job. For three months before he met her he had been dogged by hard luck. The bottom had been eaten out of his nigger-brown pants. A flashy silk shirt, the gift of his last lady, had given way around the neck and at the cuffs. For thirteen weeks it had not seen the washtub, and when it did it went all to pieces. The toes of his ultra-pointed shoes were turned pathetically heavenward and the pavement had gnawed through his rubber heels down to the base of the leather.

Meeting Mattie at a parlor social in the Belt's Fifth Avenue had materially changed Jay's condition. He had been taken to 125th Street and fitted to a good pair of shoes. Mattie chose also a decent shirt for him. But it was not silk. He hadn't achieved a new suit yet. The choice was between that and an overcoat. Mattie's resources could not cover both at once. One would have to wait until she could put by enough out of their daily living to get it. And so she decided that a heavy, warm overcoat was more necessary, for it was mid-January and in his ruined summer suit Jay had been freezing along the streets of Harlem.

It was not quite a month since Mattie and Jay had come together, and docile as she seemed, she was well worn in experience and carried a smoldering fire in her ugly black body. Years ago she had had a baby for a white man in South Carolina. But being one black woman who did not feel proud having a yellow pickaninny at any price, she had got rid of the thing, strangling it at birth and, quitting relatives and prayer-meeting sisters, made her way up North.

Marita's girl pal discovered friends and went to drink with them. Marita followed, and Jay danced after her and got in with the gang. They were making rapid time with Old Crow whisky. They sent Rosie over to the pianist with a double drink of whisky to spur him on.

"Play that theah 'Baby Blues,' " she said. "Them good spenders ovah theah done buys you this drink and ask foh it."

The pianist tossed off his whisky, turned his eyes to the ceiling, and banged, "Baby blues, Baby blues."

Mattie stood up and went over to Jay. "Le's dance," she said. She loved dancing as a pastime, but it wasn't in her blood, and so she was a bad dancer.

"Not now," Jay said, angrily. "Ahm chinning with the gang."

He was putting away a lot of the boys' good liquor and it was working on him in a bad way for Mattie. Disappointed, she looked round for Rosie. Rosie was bustling about in the kitchen getting new glasses. Mattie gulped down two stiff drinks of gin and returned to her seat by the piano. . . .

Baby Blues! Baby Blues!

"Le's do this heah sweet strut, gal." And before Jay, Marita was on her feet and poised for movement. Her pal was jigging with one of the chocolate boys. The space was filled thick and warm with dancers just shuffling round and round. Hot cheeks, yellow, chestnut, chocolate, each perspiring against each.

"Is that theah thing you' lady now?" Marita asked.

"She ain't a bad ole mammy as she looks," said Jay. "She's good giving. Fixed *me* up all right."

"Did she buy you this heah dress suit? Youse the only one here all dressed up so swell."

Jay grinned for the compliment.

"No. I hired this off a ole Greenbaum. The other was so bad. But she got me these heah shoes and a swell overcoat. And she's gwina get me a nifty suit."

"But youse kinder rough on her, though. You ain't treating her right, is you?"

Young and pretty, Marita disapproved of Mattie, old and ugly, having Jay; but she also resented with feminine feeling Jay's nastiness to the older woman.

"I ain't soft and sissified with no womens," said Jay. "Them's all cats, always mewing or clawing. The harder a man is with them the better."

"Think so?" Marita said. Her resentment rose to anger and she wanted to stop wriggling, but Jay's casual manner (which said, I don't care whether you dance or quit) held her tethered to him.

Mattie, sitting alone, had swallowed her sixth glass of gin. Rosie, feeling sympathetic, went and gossiped with her for a while.

"Ain't dancing, honey?"

"No, but I guess I'll take the next one."

"Don't you sit heah and get too lonely drinking all by you'se'f and that yaller strutter a yourn having such a wicked time."

"I don't mind him fooling with his own crowd when we goes to a pahty, 'causen Ise pass their age."

Finished "Baby Blues."

Jay went back to the waiters' table. One of his poolroom pals came in and joined the group, greeting Jay with enthusiasm and praising his rig-out.

In the poolroom where Jay loafed and played, he had become the hero of the place since his new affair. Colored boys who washed water-closets and cleaned spittoons for a living, with no hope of ever doing better, envied the way Jay could always get on to some woman to do everything for him. They wished they had Jay's magic. Jay might have his bad days getting by sometimes, but his luck never deserted him. He toted a charm.

The pianist turned his face to the ceiling and began a plaintive "Blues." He cast down his eyes for a moment and said to Mattie, "Ain't you gwina dance, sistah?"

Mattie essayed a smile. "Guess I will."

She crossed over to Jay and asked, "Wanta dance this with me?"

Jay glared at her, "Wha's scratching you? I don't wanta dance. Ahm having a good time heah."

The sneer deepened under the influence of the mixed drinks working on his temper. Mattie lingered near the table, but nobody asked her to sit down. Turning to go, she said to Jay hesitatingly, "Well—any time you feels like dancing with me Ise ready."

"Oh, foh Gawd's sake," he exclaimed, "gimme a chance! Shake a leg, black woman."

Everybody within hearing turned to look at Mattie, some with suppressed giggling, others with pity, Marita and her pal were ashamed and could not look at Mattie. For there is no greater insult among Aframericans than calling a black person black. That is never done. In Aframerican literature, perhaps, but never in social life. A black person may be called "nigger" as a joke in Aframerica, but never "black," which is considered a term of reproach in the mouths of colored people quite as contemptuous as "nigger" in the mouths of whites. And so Aframericans have invented pretty names such as low-brown, seal-skin brown, chocolate, and even prune as substitutes for black.

Oh, Blues, Blues, Brown-skin Blues: the piano wailed.

"That was a mean one," said Marita.

"Oh, mean hell. I guess the ole mug likes when you handle her rough. Don't she, Jay?" said his pal.

"Ain't nobody wanting their bad points thrown up to them as nasty as that," declared Marita.

Her pal agreed. The girls imagined themselves growing old some day and ridden by a special passion like Mattie.

And Mattie by the piano, thinking that everybody was laughing at her, called for another gin. She wanted not to care. She knew she did not belong to a fast parlor-social set where everybody was young or acting young. Rosie with her hostess's tricks looked like a vampire beside her. But although she was ugly and unadjustable, she loved amusement and was always ready to pay for it.

Mattie worked hard doing half-time and piecework, washing and ironing and mending for white people. Her work was finely done and her patrons recommended her to their friends. She earned twenty to thirty and forty dollars a week.

Living for Mattie was harder than working. Having an irresistible penchant for the yellow daddy-boys of the Black Belt, she had realized, when she was much younger, that because she was ugly she would have to pay for them.

She occupied a large rear room on the second floor of a private house, situated in the cheapest section of the Belt. The price was moderate and she was allowed the use of the kitchen and the spacious back yard for laundry work.

Mattie's coming and going quietly through the block was remarked by the good and churchy neighbors of the African Methodist, the Colored Methodist, and the Abyssinian and Cyrenian churches. And they marveled at her, a steady, reliable worker, refusing to be persuaded into membership in a church. . . .

Mattie brooded. Nevah befoh I been slapped like that by an insult so public. Slam in the face: Black woman! Black woman! Didn't I know I was that and old and no beauty?

Oh, mamma, sweet papa. Blues, Blues, seal-skin, brown-skin Blues. The pianist was gone on a wailing Blues.

Mattie got up to go home. She looked round for Jay. He had hurt her, but her pride had fallen, humbled and broken, under desire. Jay was not in the room. Mattie found him in the kitchen with his poolroom pal and a boozy gang over a bottle of gin.

"I'm gwine along home, Jay," she said. "Youse coming?"

Jay was going drunk. "Why you nosing and smelling after a fellah like that foh?" he demanded.

"Don't get mad, Jay. I ain't bothering you. If you wanta stay—"

"Oh, beat it outa here, you no-'count black bitch."

Mattie slunk off to Rosie's bedroom and put on her coat. She saw Jay's overcoat and felt it and after a slight hesitation slipped it on over hers. Outside it was snowing. She dove her hands into the deep pockets and said: "A man's clothes is that much more solid and protecting than a woman's is." She went home, southward, along Lenox Avenue.

The gang finished the gin. Jay suggested to the waiters they should all go and hunt up a speakeasy. Marita and her pal said they were going home.

"No, you come on along with us," said Jay.

"Not me. I gotta work tomorrow," said Marita.

"Me too. That don't make no difference," said the darkest waiter. The others joined him asking the two girls to change their minds; but the girls went home.

The fellows stood up, arguing just what they should do next, when Rosie elbowed through them and waved a bottle of gin in their faces.

"Le's have another round," said the mulatto waiter.

"You'd bettah," said Rosie. "Wha's this heah talk about you all going when is jest the time to start in on some real fun."

The boys sat down again, each waiter paying a round of drinks. The waiters had been paying all along. Jay and his friend had not paid for anything. The darkest waiter was soft. He began sifting a pack of cards, crying: "Coon-can! Coon-can! Le's play coon-can!"

"Ahm feeling high, ahm feeling cocky," said Jay.

The bottle of gin was finished and they were now ready to leave, but Jay could not find his overcoat.

"Ain't nobody could take it 'cep'n' the one that done buys it." Rosie grinned maliciously.

Jay was mad and blew Mattie to hell with curses. Just a hussy trick to get me home to bed. Ain't got no shame nor pride, that woman. But I'll punish her some more.

Outside the snow had turned to sleet and a high wind was driving through the shivering naked trees.

"It'll be some sweet skating on the sidewalk tomorrow," said one of the waiters.

"And bitter cold, too," said Jay. And the thought of his overcoat gave him a comfortable, warm, and luxurious feeling.

The boys had decided to visit a certain speakeasy. They walked along Fifth Avenue, and Jay stopped before an apartment house.

"It's here, fellahs," he said.

"All right," said the chocolate boy. "Le's go on in and look the fair browns ovah."

Jay, with his hands in his pockets and his dress suit slightly damp, gleaming in the far-flung flare of the arc-light, was the picture of perfect aplomb.

"But, buddies, I ain't got no money on me," he announced.

"And I ain't got none, neither," said Jay's pal.

The waiters exchanged eye-flecks with one another.

"Well," said the mulatto waiter, "after Rosie she done ate up so much I ain't none so flush to treat anybody else again 'cep'n' mahself. What about you fellahs?"

His workmates took his cue and said they had just enough each for himself.

"Tell you what, then; we'll call this show off until some other night," said the mulatto.

The waiters said good night to Jay and his pal. They were unanimous about not treating them in the speakeasy. If Jay hadn't any money to pay in the speakeasy, let him go home to Mattie. They had seen and felt so much as servitors, that they had not wasted any pity on Mattie. There were women whose special problems made them stand for that kind of hoggishness. But, neither had they any servile praise for Jay's attitude.

The waiters saw Jay and his pal out of sight, then entered the apartment house and rang the bell of the speakeasy. They worked. Creatures of service, waiters—that moment serving up a rarebit, this moment a cocktail, next a high-ball; bellhops in livery with ridiculous buttons before and behind, leaping up like rabbits at the touch of a knob. And they were fool spenders having that curious psychology of some servants who never feel life such good living as when they are making a big splurge imitation of their employers. . . .

"Come on buddies," said the mulatto. "We may be suckers all right in Rosie's joint, but we won't be suckers in a cat dog bite mah laig hear the player piano crying fair chile baby oh boy house."

Jay said good-bye to his pal and hurried homewards, head bent against the sleety wind, his hands in his trousers pockets, and thinking aloud: Well I was setting for an all-night laying-off, but I guess I'll have to warm up the ole black hen tonight, after all.

But Mattie, too, had been thinking hard in the meanwhile.

I don't know what love is, but I know what's a man!

The cabaret song was singing in her head. She remembered when she first left Dixie and "went N'oth" to Philadelphia, how she had liked a yellow man and he had laughed in her ugly face and called her "black giraffe." She had forgotten the incident, it was so long ago, but Jay made her remember it now. She had hated that man deeply and wanted to do him real hurt. And now she felt the same kind of hatred for Jay.

She lay in bed without sleeping, waiting for Jay, but not in the mood he anticipated. Dawn was creeping along the walls when the bell rang. Mattie raked up a window and craned out her giraffe neck. She had on a white nightcap and looked like a scarifying ghost.

"Who's it?"

"It's me—Jay."

"Wait a minute."

Mattie opened the closet where she kept her soiled linen and took out a little bandanna bundle that she had made of Jay's rags of a suit, his old greasy cap, his old shoes, and the remains of his silk shirt.

"Theah's you' stuff. Take a walk."

The bundle fell against Jay, nearly knocking him over. Mattie raked down the window. The sleet blew in Jay's face and the wind sang round his rump. He turned up his collar and walked shivering toward Lenox Avenue.

From *Gingertown* (Harper and Brothers, 1932), pp. 55–71. Copyright reserved by Hope McKay Virtue. Reprinted by permission.

THE STRANGE BURIAL OF SUE

"She's the biggest bitch in the banana walk, begawd she is," said young Burskin as he tossed down his three ha'pennys' worth of rum and set the glass down on the counter for another. "Sue Turner is worser than a bitch, I say, and says it to the wul'."

There were seven black and brown men in the grogshop, barefooted, with pantaloons rolled up over their knees and their broad gleaming machetes in their hands. All morning they had been chopping down bananas and wrapping them in the dried leaves, fine long bunches to be shipped abroad. And finished now, with money in their pockets, they were come to the grogshop for a drink before going to eat.

The young man who was vilifying Sue was a very freckled, foolish-faced mulatto, thick and able-bodied. He let flow his stream of vilification as if he were telling it to the hills and ravines, for the men in the place were clearly unsympathetic to him by their sullen silence.

Everybody in the village knew that Sue was free-loving. And there had never been any local resentment against her. She was remarkably friendly with all the confirmed concubines and the few married women, and she was a picturesque church member.

Customers drifted in and out of the grogshop, men dropping in for the midday swig, and even school children for a pint bottle for their parents and biscuits. And Burskin, like a mad red mule, kept on gnashing his teeth and telling all the intimate things that had passed between him and Sue.

Peasant matrons stopped to listen, and passed on, ashamed and afraid for themselves. Only the children found it funny. Burskin was really alone in carrying on that way.

Sue's house was not very far away down the hill on a slope of fat banana land running down to the gully. And at last the news reached her of what was going on up at the grogshop. Sue was a notoriously strong brown woman. She had wrestled with many of the men and pretty often came off victor. Only the dwarfish baker Patton had really put her down beaten with the jiu-jitsu tricks he brought back from Colon.

She tore up the hill to the grogshop; raging and jumping upon Burskin like a mad beast, she bore him to the ground and mauled him. Burskin was a strong-set fellow, but he was no match for Sue. And all the time she was mauling him he never said a thing. It was as if something in him was appeased by Sue's beating. When the grogshop-keeper and a couple of drinkers got her up, his face was bloody, but his expression was contented and he went quietly on home.

The grog shop-keeper demonstrated his appreciation of Sue by setting up a round of drinks for all the people in the shop. Among them was Mrs. Sam Bryan, who congratulated Sue for giving Burskin sweet hell. The first and only child that Sue had, now a big girl, was for Mrs. Sam's husband. But that had not troubled Mrs. Sam nor the other children that Sam had outside besides the four with his wife. Mrs. Sam was famous in the village for having said she didn't mind what virtue her husband found in other women; he always had to come back under his own roof. And she and

Sue were the friendliest of neighbors. Sue's girl lived sometimes with her mother, sometimes with her father, and was equally at home in both families.

According to the peasant-folk idea of goodness Sue was a good woman. Which means she was kind. Sue's mother used to be a "market woman." That is, she used to tramp to Gingertown twice a week on Wednesday and Saturday, the big market days, to buy provisions for the better-off peasant women who were pregnant or had young children or otherwise incapacitated or did not care to go marketing. Sometimes she toted the goods in a large basket on her head, and when there were plenty she rode a hampered donkey. And from her various patrons she received enough for her own provisioning.

When Sue was born people called her the "market baby," because, they said, she was begotten on the market route and nobody, not even her mother, knew who was her father. As a little girl Sue trotted along to market in the footsteps of her mother. And when she grew up she did the same work. She even went farther than her mother—to the city market on drays which involved two or three days' going.

Sue was buxom and stout, and there was keen rivalry between the draymen as to which would have her go in his dray. Besides her market work she was good at nursing in time of illness, and became the most favored nurse of the mountain region. Nearly everybody who was sick wanted Sue as nurse, and she didn't make any difference between those who could give her something and those who hadn't anything to give. It was while she was nursing Mrs. Sam Bryan through a childbirth illness that she conceived for Sam. But that and her notorious free-loving ways, especially with adolescents, had never diminished her popularity among the peasant women nor made her any less wanted.

But it was a wonder, though, when Nat Turner married Sue. He was a good-tempered quadroon and had never been reckless about love or liquor or anything except perhaps hard and steady work. It was his mother who courted his first wife for him and married them.

When the smallpox epidemic broke out in the village it laid low Turner's mother and wife and little son. It was Sue who nursed them while her own mother was also down. In those days the peasants trooped to the town to get the medicine from the distributing center, but they also wrapped the smallpox victims in long broad cool banana leaves, waiting nine days for the change in the crisis for better or worse.

There were many deaths in those close-linked mountain villages. Every day for three harrowing weeks there was a death, and one day there were as many as five. Sue's mother went under, also Turner's wife and his mother, but his little son came through. And towards the end of her long nursing, after the death and burial of Turner's mother, Sue also became ill in his house, but it was a slight attack that did not spoil her happy face, and when she became well the marks it left were just like friendly freckles.

She stayed on in Turner's house after the epidemic had passed over, and after some months he married her, although she would have lived with him all the same without privilege of ceremony. But Turner was indeed a steady man, steadiest of the older young men of the mountain land, apparently undemonstrative and un-emotional, and, knowing who Sue was, he must have badly wanted to hold her steadily by him so that she might not lightly quit one day for somebody else.

About as different as a teal from a lamb was Sue to the first Mrs. Turner. For his first wife Turner had seemed incapable of great emotion, but he became blindly attached to Sue. And there was no doubt that Sue was attached to her husband, too, for his fine hus-bandly qualities and the security she derived therefrom, his simple fidelity and the freedom with which she could carry on as before. And she didn't change, either, in her ways towards the village women. Her good-heartedness was now strengthened by material power. Turner had a dray and a hired drayman that went to the far markets with the peasants' provisions. And now when Sue went along she could afford to bring back her neighbors' provisions without charging anything. She still helped to nurse when she was needed, and many were the very poor village girls who got from her the rags to wrap their little bastards in.

The village bucks swapped rakish tales about Sue, withal they had a real regard for her. There was no malice in their gossip, as there was when the subject was the runted "free-for-all" black cat whom they also dubbed "Stinky-sweety."

One day an indiscreet relative was trying to broad-hint Turner about Sue's doings, and Turner remarked that he felt proud having a wife that was admired of other men. That remark provoked a great deal of peasant thinking and comment, and the folk were divided as to whether Turner was wise or foolish.

Burskin was not like the village bucks who ganged and played together and exchanged their adolescent experiences. He was a freckled, chestnut-skinned boy and was raised by his wrinkled-black grandmother. His brown mother had died before he could remember her.

He was never a playful boy, and was always sort of tongue-tied and comically grave. When he arrived at the age to leave elementary school he had made just half the classes that the average boy usually made. His father was ambitious for him and paid for a year of further study. But Burskin's head couldn't stand it. So his father took him to Gingertown, where he was apprenticed to a cooper's trade.

But after two years at it the master cooper said that Burskin would never learn the trade and he sent him home. Burskin returned to work with his father in the field. He was born for that. Heavy, patient, plodding, perfect for digging and planting in the soil. He was expert at clearing the land and limbing the trees.

Two years in the town had not drawn Burskin even a little out of himself. He was still the same. The lads used to tease him about his lack of interest in girls.

"Why no get you one stucky?" * he was asked. "Even Stinky-sweety. If you no know how, she wi' show you."

Burskin's father's sugar-cane field adjoined Turner's sugar-mill, and it was natural that Sue should notice her young neighbor when he returned from Gingertown. He was just at that curious age.

The Burskins had no sugar-mill, and always did their sugar-making in Turner's sugar-house. And it was while Burskin was engaged in this work that Sue grew interested in him, so withdrawn and heavy with his adolescent load.

Sue came down one day to supervise the sugar-mill and the house while her husband was occupied at home getting banana suckers to plant a field. Burskin's father was attending to the boiling down of the liquor into sugar, a hired woman was feeding the canes to the mule-drawn mill and young Burskin was bringing them in on a donkey.

Sue chatted a little with Burskin while he unloaded the canes in the mill-bed. Burskin had carried a bundle of the canes on his head, and Sue twitted him that it was a poor bundle and that she could tote one three times as heavy. And she offered to carry a few bundles for Burskin.

So when Burskin returned for another load, driving the donkey

* Sweetheart.

before him, Sue went along, following him down the foot-track leading to the Burskin field, half hidden by the long leaves of the cane growing on either side.

They reached the clearing where there was a heap of cane. Fat juicy lengths cut short for the mill. Canes of all colors: ribbon cane, black cane, governor cane, white cane, sukee cane. It was fine cane land, dark, loamy earth.

The cane-cutters, two of them, had piled up a splendid heap and were now cutting on the other side of the little brook that sounded through the field. Sue and Burskin could not see them over the tall canes, but the agitation of the long leaves as the machetes were laid to their roots indicated where they were. They were singing in the island dialect:

> Chop the sugar-cane, boy, O chop the sugar-cane,
> Chop it down, chop it down, chop it down.
> Sugar cake an' rum foh them people in a town,
> Gingertown, Gingertown, Gingertown.

> Cockish liquor * sweet, boy, O chop the sugar-cane.
> Drink it down, drink it down, drink it down.
> Sugar cake an' rum foh them people in a town
> Gingertown, Gingertown, Gingertown.

The cutters made up new verses as they sang and from the neighboring fields other voices came joining theirs.

Sue sprawled on the warm leaves swinged by the sun and chatted with Burskin, while the donkey cropped the young cane shoots. She was the kind of woman that could make a lad tell her everything about himself without being self-conscious of doing it. Burskin told Sue he hadn't seen a girl yet he wanted for a stucky and that he had never been with one.

"Not even when you was at Gingertown?"

Burskin said no.

Their conversation lapsed awkwardly. Then Burskin remarked that they had stayed overlong, and began loading the donkey. As he loaded he exclaimed over a fine piece of black cane, saying it was

---

* A strong drink the peasants make from fermenting the juice of the cane.

just what he wanted for his granny. For she had no teeth and that piece of cane was soft and full of rich juice and could easily be masticated by her gums.

"Gimme it!" Sue said.

"No, it's granny's. You got good teeth foh bite any kind a cane."

Sue sprang up, threatening to wrest the cane from the husky Burskin. She grabbed at it and they closed and struggled together, Burskin warming joyously to it and making a low, cackling sound. Then Sue tossed him, and they rolled and rolled over and over in the rustling cane leaves. And during a queerly quiet moment their mouths came together and he felt a strange sweet quivering awakening him to a new experience.

That week of sugar-making was the most delicious in Burskin's life. The smell of the white cane liquor bubbling into hot brown sugar in the huge boilers was sweeter to his nostrils than at any other time. And he worked with a new zest, scooping up the warm sugar out of the wide wooden cooler and ladling it into the tins for the market. His grandmother felt a different sounding to his walk in the house, remarked the changed expression of his features, and knew that something had happened to him.

Soon Burskin became a constant visitor to the Turner home. And besides his intimacy with Sue, Turner showed him every friendly consideration. Turner habitually accepted any person whom Sue liked. And as Burskin was quiet and hard-working after the manner of Turner, the men had much in common.

They went fishing and bird-shooting together. And every Sunday Burskin partook of the Turner family dinner. Sunday was the great guest day of the village. An invitation to a good dinner was much looked forward to from those who went to the week-end far market and brought special edibles such as ham, cheeses, and tinned things from the town.

From the beginning of his friendship with the family, whenever Burskin had to go to the far market with sugar or yams, he went by the Turner dray. Sue went often with the dray instead of her husband. And Burskin went as often as she did and he could find stuff to sell. Sometimes it was very little that could have been disposed of in the local market. But naturally Burskin preferred to go to the far market always while Sue was going. Thus they often had the week-end off away by themselves, for the drays left the mountain country for the town markets on Friday afternoon and returned before dawn on Sunday. It needed an extra day when they went to the city market.

More than any of Sue's other admirers Burskin was liked by Turner, who treated him like a brother. Each helped in the other's field work. Friendly peasants had a custom of lending days to one another. And Burskin would lend Turner a day, cutting bananas or planting yams, which Turner would return with his hired man when Burskin was clearing corn land or engaged in sugar-making. It was even Turner who suggested to Sue that she should sometime take a meal of home-cooked food to Burskin as a change from the rough field-cooked food, as his grandmother was too old to do it.

Turner never tired of Burskin and his constant visits, but they began to irk on Sue after a time. The close friendship lasted from the end of the October rainy season until Easter, when Burskin met a rival in the tall and shiny black Johnny Cross, who had arrived from Panama with eye-catching American-style suits and a gold watch and chain and rings of Spanish gold.

Johnny Cross was welcomed by many of the village families with fiddling and feasting. It was the night of one of the Easter-time tea-meetings in the village that Sue got off with him. It was a big admittance-free tea-meeting (so the village yard dances are called) and the revenue came from the sale of fancy cakes put up at auction and bought chiefly by the bucks for their sweethearts. At these meetings there were two special cakes, one formed like a crown and the other like a gate, symbolizing the crown and the gate of the village. The leading youths of a village always banded together to prevent an outsider getting away with the gate and the crown.

But Johnny Cross was fixed with more money than the village bucks could muster for a year. He bought the crown cake and gave it to the queen of the palm-booth as a gesture of courtesy, and he bought the gate and gave it to Sue. And that night he danced with Sue nearly all the time, and most of all the mountain jig. She was a strong wild dancer, and she flashed some bold movements as they jig-a-jigged around the stout bamboo pole in the center of the barbecue supporting the palm booth. . . .

Sue was obviously worried by Burskin's first-love importunacy. Burskin would show up at the most embarrassing moments when she was with Cross: down at the bridge at nightfall when she was coming from shopping, or in the shadow of the great cotton tree in the late evening when she was going home from the field. Clearly

Burskin was watching them. Besides, he was insolent when he visited her house and saw Johnny Cross there.

To the neutral Turner, Johnny Cross was quite as welcome as Burskin had been and all the previous friends of the family.

Sue decided to shake Burskin off and began with tricks. She would announce that she was going to the far market, and Burskin would gather together the best stuff of his field to go, too. But when the dray was all loaded to start she pretended to be unwell and her husband had to go instead. Three times she turned that trick. And the fourth time Burskin amazed all the market folk at the loading-place by pulling out of going to market at the last moment and asking Turner to dispose of his stuff.

Late that night, raving with jealousy, Burskin went to Sue's house and almost beat through her front door with his fist, hoping to find Johnny Cross there. But only the two frightened children appeared, for Sue had gone to a dance at another village with Johnny Cross. Burskin could not sleep that night, but prowled like a mad beast up and down the village.

By morning he had calmed down and decided to go and beg Sue to be good to him again, as in the old days. But the children had told Sue what had happened, when she came home a little before daybreak on Saturday morning and that just turned her completely mad against Burskin. And when he went to her house that forenoon Sue drove him away like a dog. Burskin attempted to plead with her, but Sue picked up the wash-clothes bat and threatened to beat his brains out if he didn't quit her place.

Burskin quit Sue's place for the grogshop, where he drank himself drunk and exploded.

When Turner came home that Sunday morning and heard what had happened, his wrath was a terrible thing. More terrible because he could not express it like Sue. He had accepted Burskin on the level, as a friend of Sue and the family and had never shown that he knew of any irregular relations between him and his wife, and it seemed incredible that the boy should take such a low advantage of his hospitality by proclaiming the intimacies between him and Sue in public. The silver pieces he had brought back from the market for Burskin were like burning metal in his hand. He took them down to the grogshop and left them in the care of the keeper. The men of the village noted the silent change in Turner, his profound anger, and could not say a decent word to him about the matter.

They were ashamed, thinking of it. Turner was determined to "bring Burskin before the judge." He said as much as that.

Burskin retaliated by bringing a counter-suit against Sue for assaulting and wounding him. Thereby he hoped that Turner would retire his plaint, for in his heart he did not nourish any real anger against Sue, although he was bruised badly. But her angry hand laid upon his body seemed to have cooled and cured him of his trouble and he went around now in a hang-dog manner.

Sue was a member of the village church. After her marriage to Turner she was baptized in the Cane River and received into the church. But the little brown parson had never approved of her. He was hard on the sin of fornication. He couldn't preach a sermon in which fornicators were not dragged in. Once he had preached a sermon naming poor old Ma Jubba, who lived in a one-roomed dirt hut with her two sons and their concubines. The parson said he had heard that Ma Jubba slept in the same bed with her elder son and his woman and apparently took an unholy pleasure in her son's sin.

Ma Jubba was so old and gray and toothless and bent over on her shiny bamboo staff that it had never entered the common mind of the village that there could be anything wrong about her sleeping on the same banana-rush bed with her son and his concubine.

It took the young brown graduate of the Baptist college to think and say so publicly. His grandfather had slept like that on the old slave plantation. And it may be that he was so hard on fornication because everybody knew he was a child of it, as the son of the black servant and the quadroon busha * of the Cane Valley estate. He was quite a boy when his mother became respectable by marrying a peasant shopkeeper of Gingertown.

The young parson was not so much liked as the white man before him. The country people said he was too much of a self-righteous busybody and that he was shrewd and practical and full of holy tricks. There was a story of how, his horse having eaten of the nightshade, he gave him stimulants and hastily rode to the horse-market, nine miles away, to swap him. He swapped the horse for another, and that same night it died on the hands of the new owner.

The parson thought it was his business to read Sue out of church membership. And did, publicly. He never made it quite clear whether it was because Sue had beaten Burskin or Burskin had

---

* Manager or overseer. [Ed.]

slandered Sue. Burskin was not a member of the flock and could not be dealt with. Turner was very wroth and said he would never put foot in the church again.

Because of her husband Sue felt a little troubled. He was such a sure prop to her. Surely she would never dream of comparing much less measuring him with any of the bucks with whom she dallied. Who else on that mountain top would have given her the solid security and freedom that Turner did? She knew the history of her mother and of her own girlhood. Turner had taken her child by Sam Bryan as his own. He was going to educate her a little, and how proud she would be to see her daughter become a postmistress or a schoolmistress. And as Turner never reproached her, she felt sometimes, as a wave of feeling swept her, how good it would have been if her will had been as strong as her body to save him all that pain and shame. And in those moments she would experience a deep and deadly hate for Burskin.

As for him, whenever he spied Sue or her husband any place, he hastily disappeared to avoid them. Not that he was so afraid of physical violence, but he was now thoroughly ashamed of his crazy acting. He tried through go-betweens to get Turner to compromise, but Turner replied that Burskin had gone beyond the point where any man could compromise with him. As Burskin had apparently felt that proclaiming Sue in public only could assuage his hurt vanity, so Turner must have had a vague feeling that the decision of the law courts and the spending of money would wipe out the disgrace. He had already paid five guineas for lawyer's fee, and he had mentioned having a barrister down from the city, but Sue had opposed that.

During the interval before the time fixed for the hearing of the case Sue was strangely restless. She developed a mania for toting heavy loads on her head, although there were Turner's mules and horses to do that, and a girl who stayed and worked with them for her keep. She would bring in heavy logs of firewood from the forest and insist on chopping and splitting them herself. She heaved upon her head baskets of yams and bunches of bananas as if they were the weight of a feather pillow. She rode the vicious kicking mule down and over the hills from the local market until he sweated white. She worked in the fields as never before, digging and planting like a farm-loving man. Sue used to place bets sometimes to demonstrate that she could equal or even surpass a man's work, but the way she carried on now seemed a little mad. As if she wanted to burn up all her splendid strength.

One midday she was coming up the hill from the river with a back-breaking tub of wet clothes, and a terrible pain seized her coming up the hill. She could barely reach the barbecue, and then she could not lift the tub down. She flung it from her head, breaking it. When Turner and his hired black came home from the banana-field, and the two children from school to lunch, they found no food, but dead ashes in the fireplace, and Sue moaning in bed with a killing pain in the pit of her belly.

They got some medicine from the local pharmacist and sent for a doctor in Gingertown. Gingertown was thirteen miles away. The messenger came back to say the doctor was called away from home and probably could not come to see Sue until the next morning.

All that afternoon the village matrons and concubines and maidens streamed down to Sue's house to offer advice and help. And as the news spread more came from neighboring villages. The leaders of the church came also to watch and to pray. The pain never eased, nor Sue's moaning, and sometimes it thrust sharply deeper into her and she cried out fearfully.

Night came, and in the midst of her suffering the folk began to gossip that Burskin might have set the obeah magic upon Sue. But Sue heard and whispered that it was a natural illness. The woman who held her in her arms said she had said something about a miscarriage. And the women began speculating in undertones if Sue had not been making a baby for Burskin and gotten rid of it because of her hatred for him.

Around midnight Sue beckoned Turner to the bed and tried to embrace him. The women laughed and cried "Shame!" at Sue and Sue made a wry grin and died in the midst of the laughter.

The doctor drove up in his buggy in the morning only to give permission to bury. The rural constable had suggested a post-mortem, but Turner said he did not want his dead wife to be butchered and quartered, and the doctor considerately gave his permission for interment. But most of the village murmured against that, being in favor of a post-mortem, so that they might know exactly what had been wrong with Sue. She was always so vital and vigorous yet had died that way. There was something of a mystery in her death and it was haunting.

The sickness and death of Sue gave the opportunity for a great tribute to her popularity. The whole mountain range turned out to assist at the burial. On foot, muleback, and horseback. There were carpenters and grave-diggers enough to make and dig half a dozen coffins and graves. Prosperous peasants brought hampers of food-stuffs on donkeys. Pigs and goats were killed. Mrs. Sam Bryan, as boss of the culinary department, helped by many women, prepared great boilers of food and roasting pigs and salted fish. And the crowd was fed in a booth over the barbecue.

It was taken as a token by the peasants that Sue's burial took place on the same day the court trial should have been held. Some persons had suggested a church service. The crowd was so huge it would have overflowed the church and made a splendid parade.

But the little brown parson was awfully solemn and quietly re-fused a church service, and Turner, remembering that Sue had re-cently been read out of church membership, did not urge it. All he wanted was a decent burial.

The service was to be held over the grave, and the grave was dug right next to Sue's flower garden. But instead of the soothing funeral hymns, such as "Crossing Jordan," "At the Pearly Gates," and "The Angels Are Waiting to Receive You," the parson chose such hell-fire ones as "Too Late, Too Late," "Backsliders, Repent," and "That Lost Soul."

The crowd felt strange singing the hymns, and a feeling of im-pending woe ran communicating through it. For his text the parson took, The Barren Fig Tree. But before he began the sermon he began swaying and clapping his hands and led off singing again, "Get right with God before you're dead and gone to hell."

> Get right with God before you're dead
> . . . . before you go to hell
> . . . . get right with God.

And as the hymn ended, the parson threw up his hands and began a prancing fit, crying: "O God! she's gone to hell. Dead in sin and gone to hell. Sue Turner is gone to hell."

Fear and confusion shook the crowd. Never before in the history of the hills had the black folk gathered around a grave and heard the preacher damn a soul to hell. Not even when it was a suicide.

In the midst of his sacred antics Turner went up to the parson, shook his fist in his face, and said, "Sue no gone a no hell!"

The preacher shouted louder, "She's gone to HELL!"
But Turner grabbed him and pushed him and said: "Get offen
mah wife graveside. Gwan 'bout you' damn business."
A great sympathetic murmur ran through the crowd.
The preacher cried, "Sinners, repent!"
But Turner cried:. "You no gwina hold no revival meeting ovah
mah wife grave. Gwan away. I wi' bury mah wife mahself."

The parson retired, and in the commotion some one cried out:
"If Sue gone a hell I gwine there too," and he had to be held back
from flinging himself into the open grave. It was Burskin.

Turner took the parson's place over his wife's grave. The only
precedent to that was in the early days of religion among the freed
slaves of the hills, when a black deacon insisted on burying his own
mother because he said he wanted to do the last best thing for her.

The taciturn Turner became strangely loose-tongued. He took as
his text: "I am the resurrection and the life." But he did not preach
a regular sermon. Instead he called upon those who had any griev-
ance against Sue to say so now. And as nobody said anything, he
called upon those who had anything to say in favor of Sue to say it.

Mother Buckram stood forth to tell in her cracked age-thinned
voice how Sue had nursed her through her last painful attack of
rheumatism. And Stinky-sweety, who had had a baby and didn't
know who was its daddy, had a crying fit telling that it was Sue who
had regularly been helping them along. And now all the women,
weeping and wailing, wanted to pay tribute to the generosity of
Sue. Tell how she had chosen and bought things for them better
than they could have done themselves.

And the hell-fire panic loosed its grip on the crowd. And there
was singing of soothing hymns, hopeful hymns, and mingling of
farewell tears.

The coffin was put in the hole and Turner threw in the first
handful of earth saying, "Ashes to ashes and dust to dust." And
he was conscious of Burskin beside him, blubbering like a baby.
And he felt compassionate towards him.

The earth was shoveled in and Turner felt the first shovelful
falling on the box like a heavy sounding in his heart. But he stood
through it dry-eyed until the grave was filled and piled into shape
and banked with flowers and two flaming dragon-bloods planted at

the head and the foot. Then he spread out his hands and said, "Lord,
letteth now thy servant depart in peace."

From *Gingertown* (Harper and Brothers, 1932), pp. 221–42. Copyright
reserved by Hope McKay Virtue. Reprinted by permission.

YEOMAN ABDUL'S FUNERAL

Yeoman Abdul had died in the Harlem Hospital from his stab
wound and Omar had arranged to give him a Moslem funeral. The
Yeomen's Hall on Lenox Avenue was converted into an improvised
funeral chapel. The spacious and rather dilapidated old hall was
formerly one of the largest and gaudiest Negro saloons and cabarets
in pre-Prohibition Harlem.

The funeral was held on a Saturday evening. The body had been
on view all day and a stream of humble Harlemites had passed
through the building to see it. The casket was set upon a bier right
before the platform. The body was tightly swathed in white and
Abdul's red fez was set on his head. There were floral contributions
sent by individuals and societies. From the ceiling in the forefront
of the platform right over the casket, there was suspended a red
banner in the middle of which was fixed a huge golden crescent.

Apparently Omar had underestimated the strength of his move-
ment among the people of Harlem, or he would have obtained one
of the big casinos for the funeral service. Long before the hour for
the service, the hall was packed. Secret and mystical societies,
which Omar never imagined might have been touched by his move-
ment, were unexpectedly represented. There were delegations from
the Builders of the Pyramids, the Sheiks of Arabia, the Mullahs of
Morocco, the Daughters of Medina, all wearing marvellously colorful
regalias and turbans or fezzes. Besides the Afro-American proselytes,
there was a representative group of Moslems from Egypt, East
Africa, West Africa and North Africa; the majority of them, how-
ever, wore conservative American clothes. Few Afro-Americans in
Harlem were aware of the large colony of Africans in their midst.
Like colored Americans, the Africans were of varying complexion,
from ebony to ivory and the so-called typical African of legend and

history could be more easily identified among the Afro-Americans than the Africans of Harlem.

By the time the service began the sidewalks were animated by a crowd vastly greater than that inside the hall. Omar had requested an imam from Egypt to conduct the funeral service. The imam was a brown man who without his robes might have been just an ordinary American mulatto. In his burnoose and turban he seemed very foreign.

"Allah, il la ha, il la la hi, Mohammed Rasul lu, la hi" (God is great and Mohammed is his prophet). For half an hour the imam chanted and prayed in Arabic, continually repeating the refrain "Allah, il la ha," etc. And the women of Harlem wept and moaned and men murmured, "Amen," although they did not understand the words.

The imam ended in English, clipped, precise, effective. "Many of you not seen before Moslem funeral, nor been in any Moslem meeting. In Moslem land a funeral is simple thing. No casket, no flowers. We think more of spirit of dead than body. We Moslems worship the spirit of our great and good souls. They are our saints. We keep them inside hearts. So I can only say you people of Harlem to do for Abdul, what his people in Africa would do. Carry Abdul in your hearts, think well of Abdul, remember Abdul.

"He came a stranger to live among you. He found death here. But also he found life here among you, his life work. He saw great work for people of Harlem to accomplish. He joined in that work. He followed your great leader, Omar. He was a faithful follower. He died as a soldier among you, for you. Remember Abdul."

The imam called Omar to speak. Omar, long-booted and spurred, in white cape and turban stepped to the front of the platform. Omar began with telling how first Abdul joined his Yeomen of Labor, in the beginning of its formation. They had accused him in the colored newspapers of being a labor fakir, and racketeering in a strange religion. And Abdul had come to him, simply affirming his faith, and saying that any man who worked for his people in the spirit and with the name of God must be a good man. Abdul was a martyr for the cause of colored people and the cause must go on as a monument to Abdul.

"Friends and followers, people of Harlem, they accuse me of being a racketeer. But if I wanted to be a big shot racketeer, I would have continued in partnership with Glory Savior. I would have trained you to shout: 'I'm a Glory Soul—with no body, no sex, no problem of race or color.' Glory Savior has many mansions, glory homes, glory lands, glory cars, glory boats, glory cattle. I have nothing but this old building, which belongs to the Yeomen. I have nothing but my faith in my people. I have faith that you will turn your back on the old glory stuff and rise up to save yourself as a people."

A loudspeaker had carried Omar's voice to the street. And as he finished the audience exploded with applause. The imam stood and stretched out his hands over the casket in an appeal for silence. But the frenzy was prolonged. The contagion carried to the crowd outside and swept the block, the people shouting, "Omar! Omar!" So great was the tumult that one frightened soul turned in a police alarm under the impression that the grand emotional demonstration was a riot starting. Police cars clanging dashed to the scene. The cops were ready to swing into action. But Omar, warned of the danger, had hurried outside through a side door. Pushing his way into the thick of the crowd, dominating with his size and conspicuous uniform, he thrust aloft his hand and thundered: "It's a funeral! Silence! A funeral!" The police, also subdued, contributed their best effort to relieve the situation and help the traffic, restricting the crowd to the sidewalk, and keeping it circulating.

It was a people's funeral. The professional strata, the smart fringe of the neighborhood's life were not represented. But the intelligentsia, by proxy was perforce represented by the newspapermen. Foremost among them was the editor of *The Nugget,* liveliest of Harlem's weeklies. He was a highly educated person out of a leading New England college, who had increased his culture by post graduate studies abroad. He considered himself the peer (and was educationally qualified to be) of his white fellows, even though not accepted in their group and was consequently a little embittered generally and specially skeptical about any movement of the colored masses. He despised Negro journalism and even himself for being identified with it, when his talents entitled him to a superior field. But even his cynicism was momentarily disarmed by the overwhelming emotional demonstration of the people.

So he said to the *Nugget* photographer, who was pleased to have flashed some excellent aspects: "That was really an impressive crowd. But I can't understand how those people were so patient and serious all the time listening to that imam, though they couldn't understand the language he was speaking. Do you think our common people, dumb as they are, could really work up any enthusiasm for a new religion?"

"They listen to the Catholic priests doing their stuff in Latin, which they don't understand either," said the photographer. "Yet there are many colored Catholics, thousands of them. If you have colored Catholics, why can't you have colored Buddhists or Moslems or what else?"

"Perhaps you're right," said the editor.

From the unpublished manuscript "Harlem Glory," by permission of Hope McKay Virtue.

III.

LOOKING FORWARD—
THE FINAL SEARCH
FOR COMMUNITY
1934–1948

6. Letters and Essays, 1934-1948

With his return to the United States in February 1934, Claude Mc-Kay entered upon the final phase of his long and turbulent career. The Great Depression was at its height, and the United States, along with the rest of the world, was beset by massive unemployment and unparalleled misery. Whether they willed it or not, writers everywhere were being swept into the resultant social and political turmoil. The letters and essays included in this section document McKay's involvement with the great public issues that dominated the American literary scene through World War II.

In many respects, McKay's position in the 1930s was unique. To begin with, he was technically still a British subject. He would not become an American citizen until 1940. During his twelve years abroad, he had maintained a friendly correspondence with many individuals in the United States, and had directed his fiction toward an American public. But as a novelist, he had also antagonized important groups whose influence upon the literary scene, particularly among black writers, loomed large after his return.

For one thing, he had quite early abandoned Communist party politics. Although he had been extravagantly feted by the Russians in 1922 and 1923, he had foreseen that their dominance over the Third Communist International would be narrowly partisan and self-serving. He clearly recognized that he could not submit to Bolshevik discipline without violating his own revolutionary and artistic ideals. After leaving Russia, therefore, he had maintained his independence and had devoted himself to fiction. As he witnessed the emergence of full-blown Soviet totalitarianism under Stalin and saw European Communists transformed into servants of the Moscow party line, McKay abandoned his faith in Marxist Communism. It is ironic that upon his return to the United States in 1934, the Russian-directed American Communist party was attracting to its cause many of the leading writers and intellectuals in the United States. Most would eventually experience the same process of disillusionment that McKay had undergone in the previous decade.

In the early 1930s McKay's close friend, Max Eastman, was defending Leon Trotsky against Stalinist vilification, and many people assumed McKay had become a follower of Trotsky. McKay soon made plain his disenchantment with all shades of Communist political thought. For the remainder of his life, he was a persistent critic of American Communist activities. Unlike many former Communists, however, he never became a political conservative, but always affirmed his belief in the necessity for some form of democratic socialism.

McKay returned to New York City eager to contribute in any way he could to the further development of black American literature and group life. Unfortunately, as a novelist he had scarcely endeared himself to the few well-established Negro middle-class organizations which might have been able to find him a position commensurate with his abilities. Furthermore, his reputation for outspoken independence often made even those who shared his ideas shy away from him for fear of incurring his displeasure. Others in Harlem merely resented his having remained so long abroad and considered him a foreigner who had long since lost touch with the American scene.

Finally, McKay's attitude regarding the racial problem, particularly his stand on the issue of integration, offended most left-wing groups and almost all established middle-class opinion, both inside and outside the black community. In brief, McKay advocated the intensive development of all aspects of Negro group existence. Irrespective of white help or hindrance, he wished to see blacks organized as a powerful, cohesive ethnic group, capable of demanding equality with all others in every phase of America life. Throughout his writing career, McKay had communicated this desire as a fundamental impulse at the heart of black experience. He regarded the great energies expended on civil-rights agitation, revolving always around the issue of integration, as above all a reflection of black middle-class goals. Their single-minded emphasis on integration, he felt, was ultimately detrimental to the larger goal of freedom for the black masses.

McKay was not opposed to integration, nor did he propose that blacks abandon their struggle for full civil liberties within the American system. He only pointed out that the continued drive for civil rights and the integration of Negroes *as individuals* into American society would mean little if the black masses remained disorganized and hopelessly sunk in poverty, ignorance, and social confusion. For the good of the nation as a whole, he maintained, American Negro leaders should recognize the difference between a destructive segregation based on racism and the natural tendency for blacks, as well as other ethnic groups, to aggregate in their own communities for the cultivation of their own particular identities and ways of life.

Despite all his efforts at clarification, McKay was dismissed by most opinion makers as just another black nationalist and was even accused by one journalist of "wallowing in the black fascist trough."

Essentially, McKay was advocating, in the 1930s and 1940s, the development of "black power," a general term that only gained wide currency in the late 1960s, after it became evident that the achievement of abstract legal victories in the area of civil rights would not by itself materially improve the position of Negroes in the United States. By then both McKay and his ideas lay buried and well nigh forgotten by the black communities he had wished to serve upon his return to the United States in the 1930s.

As an opponent of Communism, a critic of Negro middle-class leadership, and an uncompromising advocate of cultural pluralism, McKay found himself in the 1930s and 1940s almost completely isolated from the main currents of American opinion. The extent of McKay's isolation following his return can be seen in his letters to Max Eastman which open this section. These letters also provide a vivid picture of the general poverty and social disarray which greeted McKay upon his return from abroad.

McKay's plans for establishing a black literary magazine, which he also discusses in these letters, reveal that he wished to carry on the democratic, dogma-free journalism that had characterized the old *Masses* and the *Liberator*. He would soon learn that those days were gone forever.

The articles which follow his letters to Eastman are divided topically into five groups. The first group consists of three articles and a circular letter, in which McKay registers his opposition to Communism and explains his reasons for maintaining as a creative writer an independent, critical view of all political parties.

The second topical group consists of five articles, beginning with the essay, "For Group Survival," and concluding with his "Reply to George Schuyler." In these articles, McKay discusses the need for a strongly cohesive Negro community life, outlines the grassroots labor movements of Harlem, and defends his ideas concerning black unity.

The third group consists of two articles in which McKay looks at two related topics: in "Anti-Semitism and the Negro," he denies that anti-Semitism exists in depression Harlem, and in a "Reply to Ted Poston," he answers charges that he himself is antiwhite.

In the fourth set of articles—"Nazism vs. Democracy," "The Negro in the Future of American Democracy," and "Out of the War Years"—McKay addresses himself to the special importance of World War II for the future of American race relations and American democracy in general.

Finally, in the two articles on North Africa and in his review of John Gunther's *Inside Asia,* McKay tries to point out the pernicious effects of Western imperialism, not only for North Africa and Asia, but also for Europe herself in the two decades before World War II.

Following these articles, the remainder of the book traces, through his last letters to Max Eastman, McKay's final, tragic isolation and his movement toward Catholicism.

During the last fourteen years of his life, McKay had to struggle incessantly against the personal bitterness that inevitably flows from poverty, illness, and social isolation. The letters and articles gathered here show that he succeeded better than he might have believed. The man's basic humanism and his great personal integrity stand out. Equally important, the questions that he raised in his articles have with the passage of time become increasingly important to all Americans, black and white, who seek a just and lasting resolution to the nation's racial problems. No writer can ask for more in the way of success than the continued relevance of his work.

LETTERS TO MAX EASTMAN

168 West 135th Street
New York City

May 9, 1934

Dear Max,

I have an offer to teach English, literature or language, I don't know which, in a Southern college. I understand it is as good as certain and that one of the foundations which give money for Negro education will eke out the salary.

In the meantime do you know of any noble-hearted body whom

the *Crisis* has spared a little who might be taking a vacation for the summer and could lend me a studio or country place where I could write and study in preparation? I don't know if I shouldn't even take a teacher's course at Columbia for the summer to get me in shape as I have no practical experience! *

I don't know exactly what you said to Lieber ¹ when you went to see him about me, but he wrote me a note about my writings that made me kind of mad and at this time I can't afford to get mad at anybody! It was all about plot and not as tactful and suggestive as Bradley might have done it. I know that I am nothing to get enthusiastic about as a plot spinner, but [*Home to*] *Harlem* and *Banjo* were not plotted, but they sold very well and made me money. *Banana Bottom* which I tried to do on a plot did not come through at all. I know perfectly well the kind of criticism and stimulation I need to work well. At this moment the magical thing would be an advance of a couple of hundred dollars to start either a novel about Morocco or an autobiographical piece. Money would certainly move my brain in the right direction! And if Lieber could start something he would be surprised at the result! I haven't heard from him since you were there, and I went to see him right afterwards.

Do you come into town every Thursday? I want to come up some evening and get my stuff, especially some books of which I have great need. I have been doing some reading down at the Big Library,** but the difficulty of carfare is quite formidable.

I have noticed the appearance and the [*New York*] *Times* review of your book.² Congratulations and I hope you have not forgotten my copy. Last Sunday I had dinner with a group of colored Communists. I couldn't convince them that because you and I remain good friends I am not a Trotskyite. I argued against proletarian literature and the idea of my writing a proletarian Negro novel, and when I told them that I had been at a party at [Carl] Van Vechten's to meet Emma Goldman and that I liked her *personally* more than many Communists, some of them were sorry they had eaten with me.³

I hope your book will stir up another big controversy and sell. Did you see Louis Fischer's article on Trotsky? ⁴ I thought some of it was very good, although the Third Communist International seems to me by far a greater tragedy than Trotsky. For Trotsky is still a

---

* For reasons that are not entirely clear, the teaching position never materialized. [Ed.]
** The New York Public Library at 42nd Street and Fifth Avenue. [Ed.]

heroic figure even though there is something of the quixotic about him, but the Communist International looks like a stuffed carcass and it seems to me it will be so as long as its [seat] remains in Russia. I don't think the Russian Bolshevists are entirely to blame. I don't see how the Communist International could exist and grow as a fermenting revolutionary body there, while they are building up Russia to take a place as a powerful world state among the nations.

Sincerely,
CLAUDE

147 West 142nd St.
New York City

July 11, 1934

Dear Max,

We have a plan on to found a magazine and I do wish you would send me some pointers on the best way to organize it so that if it goes through and is established I'll have the controlling power and could not be maneuvered out in case of a difference or a schism. I know you can tell me how from your experience.

The thing is to be built up around me, and if it is . . . I want it to be done on a solid basis. Also could you tell me how much it will cost to bring out a first issue of 1000 copies (approximately about 15 pages, more or less *Nation*-size)? I want to submit same to a business committee. And for anything in general you may have to say about this I shall be grateful.

I have seen Miss Shepherd * twice since you left. One night we did Harlem together—a friend of mine footing the bill. She sent me to see the head of the New York State Employment Bureau—a man named Kaufman. He was nice but nothing has come of it so far.

I should have seen Miss Shepherd again, but she is too neurotic for my purpose. She spends all the time talking about you, which may be all right for the good of her own soul, but it is hell for me. And then I don't know *what* I should say. Perhaps [it was] all wrong what I did [say].

The second time I saw her she seemed very desperate. I don't know what she really wants—whether she expected to go to Chilmark ** or not. One moment she talks as if she would go and the

---

* Max Eastman's elderly secretary. [Ed.]
** The location of Eastman's summer home on Martha's Vineyard. [Ed.]

next as if she couldn't. Anyway her company and state of mind are not helpful to me in my present state.

I am getting a manager. Not a word from Lieber since he said he had sold that poem. I thought he would have been able to see my publishers about reprints, etc., but evidently he is not my man. [I] am still sponging along and trying to make the best of it.

Sincerely,
CLAUDE MCKAY

313 West 137 St.
New York City

August 24, 1934

Dear Max,

Here is a card for the first affair we are giving for the magazine. I know it is all right to use your name and hope you will be back by that time and able to attend.

I had a letter from Peggy Tucker today.[5] She said you had written to her about me. She seems to have had some unpleasantness recently. She is going to Mexico for about a month and hopes to see us when she gets back.

I have so much work to do, trying to get my verse together and worrying about the magazine and hardly anybody helping me. I am desperately hungry most of the time, lacking even pennies to mail letters and go to the library where I am looking through old magazines for some poems.

The exasperating thing is that I am doing part-time work writing history to prove that African blacks were the founders of civilization, for an eccentric old Negro who titles himself Professor.[6]

I have to do that for my room and wouldn't mind it so much if the old fool was not always butting in on me with senile talk about ancient African glory.

I think that woman in Morocco is a little cracked. She has written asking me to get her a room in Harlem, but with all the scandals going on between her and the Moors in Tangier (she has written about them herself), I don't think it is advisable.[7]

Hope you have an agent in mind you can recommend me to. Love to you and Eliena.

Sincerely,
CLAUDE

313 West 137th St.

New York City

August 25, 1934

Dear Max,

I am in an awful jam, trying so hard to have a place to sleep by doing hack work and existing on strong black coffee to hold down hunger. It's a long time since I have had a dollar of my own. Can't even find enough carfare to scout around and do that article on Harlem.

I am enclosing a copy of the letter from my publisher. I thought I could get all the poems together and in their hands by September, but I can't even find time to type them, much less to overhaul them.

I have been trying to find an agent, without success, and *I ask you again, will you please* let me know of any reliable ones you may hear of.

Sincerely,

CLAUDE

313 West 137th St.

New York City

September 11, 1934

Dear Max,

The soirée was a great success. The large studio was crowded with enthusiastic people, with a few whites. Only there is little money to show for it. I put Harold Jackman (a popular sheik and school teacher you met at our other party) at the door and he got tight and deserted his post at that late hour, when bohemian-minded people prefer to drop in at a party—and many just walked in. Some even brought their admittance fee to me and [Arthur] Schomburg. So far we made about twenty-five bucks, expenses paid leaving about seventeen, but we still have to collect tickets.

[I] wish you had been there. Glenway Wescott [8] came and wants to meet or see you again. I have found an interesting woman who is going to take charge of the social side. We were born and grew up in the same village, and she is pretty well fixed as a policy manipulator. Her father and mine were near and dear neighbors and church officers together, and she is very sentimental about the old association. . . .

Schomburg was an efficient master of ceremonies. The circular

I sent out about starting the magazine was turned into news by an enterprising agency and has been published in all the Negro newspapers. So I am still "news," and I think if I once get the first issue out, it is going to go. The enthusiasm for the kind of magazine I want to do is surprising. All the young artists in Harlem are interested and there are some fine ones. . . . I have decided finally on the name *Bambara*. It is one of the finest tribes of the African Sudan, noted for its well-planned community life and its art work, mainly decorative head-dresses and masks made of antelope's horns. What think you? . . . Thanks for my little check. I used it to clean myself up and be prepared for the party. . . . I made a short introductory speech and read the Morocco poem which was applauded.* Although there is no money yet and existing [is] still a big problem, I feel much better. If only my head was not such a chronic nuisance . . . like a permanent hang-over. . . . Love to you and Eliena.

Sincerely,
CLAUDE

P.S. Since there is no money to pay for contributions at the outset, I want to make the magazine cooperative—the contributions paid from whatever is left over [after] expenses, as we used to do on the *Liberator*. I think such a plan will keep the group together and interested: What do you think?

FOR A NEGRO MAGAZINE **

Ten years ago all the literary circles of America were enlivened by talk of a Negro Renaissance. Appreciative and interpretative articles in newspaper and magazines were duly followed by a fat little crop of Negro books by white and colored authors. The vogue for Negro music attained its peak. African Negro sculpture found a place in modern art circles beside the art of other peoples.

Looking back to that period today the Negro Renaissance seems to have been no more than a mushroom growth that could send no roots down in the soil of Negro life.

About this apparent setback there are many opinions. Some think that the field was over unscrupulously exploited. Others that

---

* "A Farewell to Morocco." See Claude McKay, *Selected Poems*, p. 88. [Ed.]

** This circular letter appeared in the summer of 1934. [Ed.]

the national interest in the artistic expression of the Negro was only a passing fad.

But we believe that any genuine artistic expression can transcend a fad; that the Negro's contribution to literature and art should have a permanent place in American life; that American life will be richer by such contribution; and that it should find an outlet and a receptive audience.

Therefore, our aim is to found a magazine to give expression to the literary and artistic aspirations of the Negro; to make such a magazine of national significance as an esthetic interpretation of Negro life, exploiting the Negro's racial background and his racial gifts and accomplishments.

We want to encourage Negroes to create artistically as an ethnological group irrespective of class and creed. We want to help the Negro as writer and artist to free his mind of the shackles imposed upon it from outside as well as within his own racial group.

We mean to go forward in the vanguard of ideas, trends, thoughts and movements. But we are not demanding that the creative Negro should falsely accept nostrums and faiths that he does not understand. We realize that there are creative persons whose reaction to life is instinctive and emotional like actors who say their lines grandly without knowing what they really are about. We are not demanding that writers and artists should be more intellectual and social-minded in their work than they are constitutionally capable of being.

Nevertheless we have standards to which we will hold our contributors, such as:

SINCERITY OF PURPOSE
FRESHNESS AND KEENNESS OF PERCEPTION
ADEQUATE FORM OF EXPRESSION

The magazine is to be established under the editorship of CLAUDE McKAY, who has often been referred to as a pioneer of the so-called Negro Renaissance.

Mr. McKay has returned to this country after over 11 years' residence abroad, during which time he has traveled extensively and written a number of novels. He has not only kept in close touch with the social and artistic trends of American Negro life in their purely racial as well as radical phases, but he has also an international outlook on the Negro besides a store of experience from his long residence in different countries of Europe and [Africa].

From his mature experiences and broad outlook we believe that he will forge an adequate and keen instrument for the expression of genuine Negro talent.

LETTERS TO MAX EASTMAN

Oct. 25 [1934]

Dear Max:

Here I am in this camp sixty miles away from Harlem. Mr. Hudson sent your letter to Commander Howe who turned it over to a young assistant, Mr. Hale. He sent for me and of course my problem was a problem, as I am not a citizen and had not lived the required four years in New York. He suggested relief under an alias, but there was the possibility of publicity (especially in the Harlem sheets), and any publicity might prove harmful not only for me, but the State Department official who made it possible for me to get back and the consul who gave me the visa: for it is stipulated that he should make sure the immigrant would not become a public charge. What I wanted anyway was not so much relief, which is kind of demoralizing, as a little job, and I told Mr. Hale that; so he suggested my coming to this camp, which was started last May for the down-and-out of the Welfare Department.[9] He took me to the Municipal Lodging House, where I was signed up as a laborer and given a ticket to get here. But he promised to write to the director, Captain Clarke, about me and ask him to let me work on a four-sheet mimeograph[ed] weekly the camp put out. Hale thought I could put in the rest of the hours writing for myself.

So here I am. The place reminds me something like my police and railroad days: barracks life: two in one cell, ship-plan: lights out at 11: barracks food, good enough, but slovenly served. The pay is $1 a day but 50 cents is taken for maintenance [and] you are paid for six and charged maintenance for 7. You get no wages until after you have worked $15 which is held until you are leaving. But withal it is infinitely better to be here than as I was in New York. The *big* drawback is that I see no chance of creative work. And a life like this should be endurable only if it can be compensated by creative work. But there are two of us in each cell with a little board fixed to the wall for toilet things and no chair, no space for any. And I cannot ask for a room, for the camp is overcrowded, with all new men sleeping in open dormitories. I am going to see if I can train myself to write in the office, while the other fellows are around. [I] don't know if I will be able to do it.

I tried several persons for jobs in the city without success. Any of those colored places could have found me a place, even to address envelopes. But I have no pull, and I guess they are really afraid of me!

I wish you could scrape a little money together somewhere and send me, not [a] check (cash), so I can buy typing material (I have no ribbon) and laxative (the food!); and make a trip to New York to get my big suitcase or place it somewhere.

It is a terrible existence, but I am keeping faith for one objective—just to do that bohemian-life book—I mean the 1923–27 period—Berlin and Paris—I carry around bits of papers in my pocket and jot down scenes and characters as they come. I have only one determination, to make it a success. And I will do it.

The camaraderie here is as good as could be expected. The ignorant men are all right; the intelligent are naturally sad. One of the supervisors was a globe-trotter and knows most of the bohemian crowd I knew in Paris, besides all the aristocrats! He used to be wealthy. The director, Captain Clarke, has been nice; [he] has a vast contempt of Communists, however, [and] confuses them with socialists, anarchists, and what not. Says the Communists sent paid agitators here, not so of course. But in writing, not a word of that! In writing please use my passport name, Festus C. or F. C. McKay; and if any mail, please place in envelope. Camp Greycourt, Greycourt, N.Y.

[Claude McKay]

General Delivery
Chester, New York *

[November, 1934]

Dear Max,

Maybe you're away, and I hear too that letters are delayed in being delivered sometimes. The camp is so large, over 700 men, and there is no regular postal service, so this time I am writing to Croton.

First, I am enclosing the letter young Mr. Hale sent to me and I want to suggest, merely suggest and leave the matter to your judgment, that you try to see him. You will have to telephone for an

* I give this address—it's three miles or so from the camp and I walk out there sometimes.

appointment as he is always besieged by people. You see he *did* promise that he would keep me in mind for some kind of a job and asked me to write to him when I got here. But he must be reminded and kept after I suppose; he is so busy.

It is really awful up here—barracks life and the men are the worst bums of the Bowery and Municipal Lodging House, chronic criminal dead souls. The railroad, freight boats, and Marseille were heavens in comparison. The food is good, but the way they eat it, slopping over the place, turns one's stomach and kills your appetite. . . . I am working in the canteen now counting checks and serving over the counter [and] that is something of an experience. I haven't done that since I worked in my brother's grocery as a kid . . . but a doorman's or watchman's job in N.Y. would be better. I thought I would have had something from that agency where you went to see me, but all the jobs were for women's [day] work and nothing ever turned up. . . . I cannot complain here. There is more food than I can eat and a bed . . . but it isn't just bread alone, I am finding out. Now I can understand why people commit suicide rather than become paupers. The situation is hopeless, even for the born bums. They are sent up here to be *rehabilitated*: this dreary Camp, "Grey" court is a good name, fine stone building, large grounds—they get one dollar a day and the city takes 50 cents for maintenance. They get a canteen book and spend the other 50 cents in cigarette tobacco and soda pop. They have a recreation room etc., but no women. They are prisoners. They hate each other. No hope to save anything, excepting the few who will not smoke. And when they draw a little money, they buy a thing called rubber alcohol which sells for 40c a pint. They put water in it, but it drives them crazy. And when they get drunk, they are sent away. The first week I came up 25 were sent away—last week 14. And the chief topic of conversation is, "when you may be sent money," for they are all nearly of the drunkard class and can't keep away from it, even the best ones—the clerks, college men—bum drinkers, and the downfall of most of them is drinking. And when they are sent away, *back* to the Municipal Lodging House—so the place is a kind of sanatorium.

Yet, if I could get a chance to write it would not be unbearable, but the rooms are cells—two men to a room and no chance to think, much less write. It would be presumptuous to ask for a place—there are not rooms enough. This is an *Emergency* Relief place. I guess it was like this in Russia when the Revolution came.

Strangely this place does bring back to me something of the feeling I had in Russia of people working to clear away a wreck.

I was hoping Harper would publish the poems. But see Saxton's letter! It knocked me down and out. I wrote a series of sonnets on cities which I read at the Librarian's Conference, [and] they were so applauded.[10] All the librarians wanted to know when the poems would be published. I said I hoped soon, but it was a vain hope. . . . I wish you would get the ms. back from Saxton. . . . I don't know if any agent would handle it. There are just about 50 poems and would be worthwhile out if *Harlem Shadows* was republished. And fancy when I saw Saxton in Paris he wanted to publish *Harlem Shadows* alone! Now even with the new poems he won't do it. . . . I don't see why I couldn't take a CWA [Civil Works Administration] job without using the name Claude. It could be fixed up, I think. Well, it's a handicap to get fame.

I wonder if my last letter made you sick? I know how it is when you can't do anything, and the outlook is all so dreary. I have an expatriate story in mind—a good one that ought to go—*if* I could write it out. I have it sketched on slips of paper. I know what's wrong with me is [birth] pains—too many abortions. The lusty child is crying to be born but needs the right doctor. Love again to Eliena and please write.

CLAUDE

General Delivery
Chester, N.Y.

November 10, 1934

Dear Max,

I received your letter at last, also the underwear, which I was greatly in need of and am very grateful. In spite of the ennui, the bleakness and desolation of this atmosphere, it was better, perhaps, for me to come here and get into the mood of having a job (such as it is) again. I never doubted my own capabilities that I could do anything at all if an opportunity was offered. Only I am overwhelmed by the feeling that this is such a waste of energy—nothing to gain by experience. I suppose I could be reconciled to it, like the majority here, if I felt I was old and worn out, but I feel more and more like a caged wild animal.

Saxton's rejection of the poems gave me an awful jolt. I wonder if there is no agent I can get to undertake placing them? I *do* need a good understanding person. For instance it was suggested that I might have *Home to Harlem* republished in a Modern Library edition, but that would mean a great deal of negotiation that an agent only could do well.

I have the makings of a short story that came to me out of the book I told you I wanted to write. And I have sketched it out and even started to write it. It is an expatriate story of America and abroad. When the short-story idea came I dropped doing the outline of the book to take it up, thinking that if I wrote the short story and it hit the mark, it would buoy me up to carry on the bigger thing and with assurance. And it will be easier to do the short story under these conditions.

About my valises you might enquire at the Elks Club, 272 West 136th St. near 8th Ave., asking for Darrell Campbell, the "exalted ruler," who is a friend. He promised to get them from 313 W. 137 [Street]. And I am not sure whether he left them at the club or at his home. If at the club they are not so safe, I think, and I would much rather you keep them for me—if you have room. They are heavy. One has books including those I took from you, excepting *The Unpossessed* which I loaned to Harold Jackman, 442 Manhattan Avenue. The Club is open generally in the afternoon.

The camp is upon a hill above the village of Greycourt between Monroe and Chester. It was a prison for women formerly and it was turned over to the Welfare Department for a relief camp. It was started last May.

I haven't written to Schomburg since I came here. He said I should have sent him a letter which he would forward to one Mr. Peabody who was interested in Negro creative work, but Schomburg has started me off on so many plans which never came to anything that I was just fed up. . . . Lieber told me that Saxton remarked to him that he thought the American public was not interested in Negro authors enough to justify publication. And he thought the successes of the nineteen twenties were the result of a fad only! Lieber didn't want to tell me but finally did. And that is one reason I am determined to get my chance over all obstacles to put over another book. I know that if I only get my break to write it I will find a publisher—and a public too. But the odds are working hard against me. Heywood Broun [11] promised to get me an assignment to write some Harlem articles but didn't come through; also I wrote a Father Divine thing for Freda Kirchwey,[12] but perhaps it didn't click. It was nice of [Carl] Van Vechten, but he didn't come nor even respond to that invitation to my party.

CLAUDE

General Delivery
Chester, New York

Nov. 25, 1934

Dear Max,

Did you have any time to see that Mr. Hale of 902 Broadway? I think that if you did see him, it might help the situation a little. He did tell me to write, you know, and promised that he might do something by way of a job in N.Y. later. Therefore, if you could also put in a word, let him know that it was you who wrote to Mr. Hudson, he might do something more quickly about my letter, or even to better my situation up here. For instance, if he did say a word to the Captain here, it is just possible, he could find me a private corner with a table where I could put my typewriter and write. I have a story, I think a good one, an expatriate theme with [an] American throwback. It's a hell of a job to work it off in this suffocating atmosphere, but I am trying to do it.

I thank you for the letter and your note. I am writing Posselt [13] to take the ms. of the poems from Saxton. I'll tell him about the other things I have and that I am doing too. But the Marseille novel is out of it.* Must be revised. [The publisher John] Day wrote Lieber that he would publish if I revised it.

This canteen job is not bad. I get up at 6, have breakfast and begin work at 6:45. We close at 10 p.m. But I have every other day off. It is the atmosphere that is awful. Ninety percent of the men are from the flop houses. And to live, eat and sleep among them is so awful, it destroys all zest for living. The hopelessness of it is contagious. They get, we get 50 cents a day and maintenance. $2.50 a week. The food is good enough but cooked for a multitude of 800 it becomes quite unpalatable. The administration gives a canteen book worth 2 dollars once a week to each man. That is you take it if you want it. The majority take, so they can buy ice cream, sweets, cigarettes, etc. from the canteen. That leaves 50 cents a week. Most of them drink. But as they don't make enough to buy good liquor they buy a thing called rubber alcohol, which makes them besotted. But the rules are strict against drunkenness. Still

---

* "Romance in Marseille," McKay's unpublished novel (see p. 33). [Ed.]

they drink and every week a batch is fired, without money, back to the sidewalks and breadlines of New York. They all live in fear of being fired or given some disagreeable job when they are delinquent. And that is the general daily topic of conversation. . . .

I guess I could write a great story about this place. But it would have to be anon. For by right I should not be holding a relief job. I am paying the penalty of being too naively international-minded. And maybe all that, in a subtle way, works against my doing the best I could creatively. I do not feel so intellectually free and strong as I should. I am in the position of one to whom a patron might say, "Well if you don't like it, you didn't have to take it."

As soon as I am able I must get my first [citizenship] papers. It is just too bad that it will be nearly a year since my return and nothing has been done. But I have never had the money.

I hope this won't strike you as whining. . . . But, I am trying to find myself, myself. I know that if I am not vigorous, strong and frank and forthright in my writing, I'll never come back in a big way, and so I have to analyze myself.

I see the ad of your new book in the *Times*. Is it published? [14]

Sincerely,
CLAUDE

Hello to Eliena.

General Delivery
Chester, N.Y.

December 3, 1934

Dear Max,

I have an idea and a proposal to make. I think Joel Spingarn may be able to help about a job if he were approached from the right angle. I would write to him myself, but a letter from a friend ought to do more. You know early last summer, he did send me another $25.00, when he learned that I didn't get the Guggenheim award.

My idea is that you explain my present position to him, where I am and what I am doing, and that I need a congenial job of any kind, where I may have a chance to write, and preferably in the city, where I can have access to the library.

Spingarn has a wide contact with publishers and firms and I think he could get me a place somewhere with a little exertion—

proof-reading, or typing, author's reading, addressing envelopes, filing, even a doorman's place.

Up here I am in an impasse and the only thing to do is get out as soon as I can. I have not made any headway with my short story, in which lies the background of my novel. . . . I have not asked the Captain for any special privileges although Hale wrote to me and said he would "co-operate." But one should be shrewd about asking favors under certain conditions and be able to gauge their feasibility. The Captain himself, although he is director, has to share one room with another official, two beds to a room. Of course he has a *room* and not just a cell like myself. He told me one day that his greatest desire was also to write, but he couldn't find the time nor the opportunity. He dabbles in poetry and prose too, bad stuff. One has to be wary with people who have the writing bug and can't get it off. They are the most capricious and cutting in the world. And the Captain and ninety percent of the crew here are Irish, as moody and chameleon-like as the Moors.

This place after all is a labor camp for down-and-out men, mostly bums, and the individual must lose his identity and become just a brass check among the rest. And the men are like children, jealous of the slightest favor shown to one of their numbers—say he has a racket—no working-class pride exists here—no hope of a better nobler life for workers.

A few weeks ago we had a youngish enough man, who used to sit beside me at meals. He couldn't eat, couldn't get used to the food. We talked a little, he had traveled extensively to the West Indies, South Seas, Europe. He couldn't make it up here and became very ill and was sent down to Bellevue Hospital, where he died last week. Then it came out that he had been a wealthy man-about-town, the son of the wife of a former South American ambassador. His mother was a millionaire, and living in Europe, but he had run through his inheritance and she wouldn't help him any more. . . . Up here it is better for men who have known any decent living to hide it, for the crowd makes you feel uncomfortable about it.

If you want to get some idea of what the place is like, you might drive up here some afternoon, when you have a little leisure. The Captain will be glad to show you around. He is always here excepting Thursday and Friday.

Don't think I could get more than a chapter or two of a book out of a place like this. It is too much of a sordid let-down in life to dwell on. *Et moi, je n'aime pas la souffrance*—neither in literature nor in life. There is nothing here of that Rembrandt-like color and the keen wits-testing competition and desire just to live which relieve slum life of its sordidness.

Just now the book that is taking shape in my mind is coming out of my experiences abroad. Whether poetry or prose, my writing is always most striking and true when it is a little reminiscent and nostalgic. The vividness of *Home to Harlem* was due to my being removed just the right distance from the scene. Doing *Banjo* I was too close to it. *Banana Bottom* was a lazy dream, the images becoming blurred from overdoing long-distance photography. The European perspective appears exactly right for a sharp poignant, expatriate book, after which an African one should follow.

I hope you will win the film suit and make some money. You never did explain to me how it was taken out of your hands, and so I know nothing about it. Was any Soviet person involved in it? [15] And as I am on it, have you heard from Trotsky recently? I saw advertisements of your new book in the *New York Times,* but no announcement of its publication. And what about the *Modern Monthly?* I heard there was a poem of mine in one issue, but I did not even receive a copy.[16]

Freda Kirchwey has accepted an article of mine about that Father Divine of Harlem, but she says she isn't sure when it will be printed as it is not topical. . . .[17] Please don't forget Spingarn, tell him I exhausted all ways hunting a job and that I am not standing on any dignity, since I haven't any left, and I am willing to fit into anything that can be found for me. . . . Relying on you to do this:

Sincerely,
CLAUDE

General Delivery
Chester, N.Y.

December 16, 1934

Dear Max,

I want to risk leaving this place to go back to the city at the end of this week. But I'd like to be assured of some food, while I am hunting round for something. Before I came up here Mr. Hale was arranging for me to get my food at some place downtown, but I chose the other alternative of coming here as a chance to break into practical earning-a-living work, thinking I could also muscle in some creative [work] and never imagining by a long sight the place could be so appalling.

I don't want to worry you now you're preparing your lectures, but could you deputy anybody to see this Mr. Hale, so I could be assured of some food when I get there—writing won't do, I think not. That will make me feel better about coming. I have completed the rough draft of that story and I have a good title for it: "Enigmatic Expatriate." It's about a strange little old man moving in the circle of intellectual bohemians abroad, although he is not one of them and cannot be. Of his going from place to place following the bohemian caravan and his being sensitive or having a complex about the word "insanity" or "lunacy." And he does not want to return home. I bring him along up to the time of the great bank failures, when he loses his money in one. And decides to go home—*happy.* Then he confesses that he had been put in an asylum in America by his relatives—because of his money. He had managed to get out and go abroad where he could live eccentrically. But all the time he preferred America and now that he had no money and nothing to fear he was happy to return at last. Of course it is much more elaborately worked out than I can convey to you. I want some seclusion to work over the leads and cues and fair-type it. And I want also to see Russell about my poems.[18] I asked him to get them from Saxton and don't know if he did. I want to come back and see what can be done. I have about 9 dollars coming when I leave and with it I can rent a room for about 2 weeks and have carfare to scout around, while I am getting my meals some place.

Yours sincerely,
CLAUDE

General Delivery
Chester, N.Y.

December 19, 1934

Dear Max,

I have written Spingarn enclosing your [correspondence] and commenting: (where he says I am a "very bad person to help" and you add, "which is true,") "I don't know if this is altogether so. I worked under Max on the *Liberator* loyally and efficiently until he gave it up and went abroad. . . ." And of the whole *Liberator* group, like moths attracted to a flame around you I am one of the few you're still very friendly with. We had *one* important difference

—that was in Moscow and it was over an abstract intellectual point—regarding the Negro problem and the *Liberator*. I had different views from yourself and stated them. . . . Since then the C. P. [Communist party] of America has carried on its propaganda among Negroes from the very acute angle of my position. . . . But it remains a debatable matter. . . . It was purely intellectual—never degenerating into [a] personal wrangle as say between you and Frank Harris and the *Liberator* remnant now.[19] As far as I can remember we have never had any real personal differences. And you must admit that while on the *Liberator* my conduct was all right. I never had any differences with any of the staff (I worked with Floyd, Crystal, Bob Minor and all the others).[20] I had to meet all kinds of people in my capacity as assistant editor, even prejudiced Southerners. Mike Gold was the only person I couldn't get on with—rather he didn't want to with me either. I don't think it was necessary to my life to swallow his petty manners.

I know I have made enemies but who hasn't? And when I think of the many literary and artistic persons and their enemies, the don't-speak-to-me-anymore-once-friends, I feel as if I have not done so badly. I am no angel and I am not patting myself on the back. Human beings as I see them seem to fall into three major categories: those who want to pat and pet another like a dog, those who want to kick another around like a dog, those who want to lie down with others like swine. I have never been able to run much with any group, but I don't think it is because I am unfriendly. It is because of my unattachedness. Nearly all individuals who have known me would have to confess that they sheered away because there was no means of establishing contact. That is a terrible limitation among social-minded persons I admit, but it is congenital. I have always lived introvertedly even in the midst of friends and rackets.

I don't think I am "suspicious." On the contrary, I approach people with a very simple frankness. Naturally, I have instinctive hints, suggestions and leads about people, but they are not born of suspicion. This is not a defense of myself. In Paris, in Barcelona, anywhere when I have a little money I have so-called friends. Any down-and-out person soon loses friendly contact. You know yourself that no people are more insulting and difficult than people with money, but they never lack so-called friends. I suppose I could continue getting a meal and a flop here and there in Harlem and invitations to drinking parties, but the personal price to pay is too high. People are not satisfied unless they can get you by the very guts and make you puke up your soul. I heard they used to say in Harlem they couldn't see how I could hold myself together so well although broke. They wanted me to be like a hog in the gutter.

Thank you for your Croton offer.* I was speculating to leave Monday, but probably I shall start before, and grasp the opportunity to see you on Sunday. I like my story more than anything I've done since the short-story form of *Home to Harlem*. I read it to an intelligent old derelict here and he remarked it was very poignant, pathetic and *American*. But he said I should find out how people are spirited away to asylums, so that no one can pick flaws in the plan. He says that what I write is true, his people tried to put him away also when he had money. The opening of the story is a kind of running fresco of bohemians abroad and [after] all is unfolded the old man walks quickly into the picture.** Thanks very much for Croton, but I don't think I ought to go up until I'm clear about food.

Your letter was returned because you left off the very necessary "general delivery," which is equivalent to "Poste Restante" in Europe. If I should miss seeing you, you may write to 200 West 146th St., N. Y. C. c/o D. Campbell, where I'll ask them to send my mail temporarily.

Gee, I'd like so much a *job,* a little job! This work here would be all right if it were not for the abysmal misery and indecency. Even one's natural functions must be performed openly, as if to rob us of the last vestige of reticence, but the supervisors have doors to their toilets.

C McK

ANOTHER WHITE FRIEND

McKay left Camp Greycourt in December 1934, and returned to New York City. For a while he lived with Selma Burke, the black sculptress who was then an art student and model. Together they

---

* Eastman had invited McKay to stay at his home at Croton-on-Hudson, just north of New York City. [Ed.]
** This story seems never to have been published, and the manuscript is not among the McKay Papers in the James Weldon Johnson Collection at Yale. [Ed.]

shared a small apartment on West 63rd Street in the infamous Hell's Kitchen area, where the Lincoln Center for the Performing Arts now stands. It was there he began his autobiography. Toward the end of 1935, he finally found a job with the Federal Writers' Project in New York, and in 1937 he finished his autobiography, A Long Way from Home.

In the excerpt from A Long Way from Home *which follows McKay relates the story of an unusual friendship and in the process tells of his life in Harlem during World War I.*

I had already bought my ticket [for England in 1919], when a few days before the date of sailing I received a letter containing a soiled scrap bearing one of my poems, which had been reprinted in the New York *Tribune*. The letter was from another white friend, quite different from those before mentioned.

Ours was a curious friendship and this was the way it came about. Coming off the dining car one night, I went with another waiter to his home in one of the West Forties. His wife had company and we played cards until a late hour.

When I left I went to eat in a Greek place on Sixth Avenue. While I was waiting for the steak and looking at a newspaper, a young fellow came in, sat down at my table, and taking my cap from the chair, put it on. Before I could say a word about such a surprising thing, he said in a low, nervous voice: "It's all right, let me wear your cap. The bulls are right after me and I am trying to fool them. They won't recognize me sitting here with you, for I was bareheaded."

The Greek came with my steak and asked what the fellow wanted. He said, "A cup of coffee." He was twenty-three, of average height and size, and his kitelike face was decent enough. I saw no bulls, but didn't mind his hiding against me at all if he could get away that way. Naturally, I was curious. So I asked where the bulls had got after him, and why. He said it was down in the subway lavatory, when he was attempting to pick a man's pocket. He was refreshingly frank about it. There were three of them and he had escaped by a ruse that cannot be told.

He was hungry and I told him to order food. He became confidential. His name was Michael. He was a little pick-pocket and did his tricks most of the time in the subways and parks. He got at his victims while they were asleep in the park or by getting friendly with them. He told me some illuminating things about the bulls, and so realistically that I saw them like wild bulls driving their horns into any object.

When I was leaving the restaurant, Michael asked if he could come up to Harlem, just to get away from downtown. I said that it was all right with me. Thus Michael came to Harlem.

The next morning when Manda, my girl friend, pushed the door open and saw Michael on the couch she exclaimed: "Foh the land's sake! I wonder what will happen next!" That was the most excitable state I had ever seen her in since our friendship began. I told her Michael was a friend in trouble and I was helping him out for awhile. She accepted the explanation and was not curious to know what the trouble was about. Like most colored southerners, she was hostile to "poor white trash," and the situation must not have been to her liking, but she took it as she did me. There was always a certain strangeness between Manda and me. Perhaps that helped our getting along comfortably together.

Manda was a pleasant placid girl from the Virginia country. She also was the result of a strange meeting. One late evening, when I got off the train, I ran into two of the fellows (an elevator runner and a waiter) who had worked with me at the women's club. We decided to give an impromptu party. It was too late to get any nice girls. So we said, "Let's go down to Leroy's and pick up some." Leroy's was the famous cellar cabaret at the corner of One Hundred Thirty-fifth Street and Fifth Avenue, and Harlem called it "The Jungle." Leroy's was one of the cabarets where you could make friends. Fellows could flirt with girls and change tables to sit with them. In those days the more decorous cabarets would not allow visiting between tables.

We knew the kind of girls to approach. In the Harlem cabaret of that time (before Van Vechten's *Nigger Heaven* and prohibition made the colored intelligentsia cabaret-minded) there were generally three types of girls. There were the lady entertainers who flirted with the fellows impersonally to obtain nice tips and get them to buy extra drinks to promote the business of the house. Some of them were respectably married and had husbands who worked in the cabarets as waiters or musicians.

Another class of girls was more personally business-like in flirting. They didn't make the fellows spend too much in the cabaret, and had a preference for beer as a treat, for they expected them to spend on the outside. They were easily distinguishable by the confederate looks that passed between them and their protectors, who usually sat at separate tables.

And there were the lonely girls, the kitchen maids, laundresses and general day workers for New York's lower middle classes, who came for entertainment and hoping to make a friend from some casual acquaintance they might pick up.

Five of us went down to Leroy's. We noticed three girls of the last-mentioned type sitting together, chummy over large glasses of beer. We got their eyes. They were friendly, and we went over to their table. A waiter brought more chairs. We ordered a round of drinks, and, without palavering, we told the girls that we were seeking partners for a party. They were willing to join us. As we got up to go, we noticed at a neighboring table another girl all alone and smiling at us. She had heard our overtures. She was different from the girls who were going with us, not chic, brown with a plump figure, and there was a domestic something about her which created the impression of a good hen.

The elevator operator, who was a prankish fellow, challenged the girl's smile with a big grin and said: "Let's ask her too." The three girls giggled. The other girl was so odd—her clothes were dated and the colors didn't match. But she wanted to come, and that astonished them. We thought she was a West Indian, and were surprised to find out that she was from the South.

We all went to my room in One Hundred Thirty-first Street, where we had a breakdown. In the party Manda was as different as she looked. She lacked vivacity, and since the other fellows preferred the nimbler girls, I had to dance with her most of the time. As host, I did not want her to feel out of the fun. She made herself useful, though, washing the glasses when they got soiled and mixed up, and squeezing lemons for the gin.

By dawn we were tired and everybody was leaving. But Manda said she would stay awhile and clean up. She wasn't going to work that day and I wasn't either. From then on we became intimate friends. She was a real peasant type and worked as a laundress in a boarding house. She always came to look me up when I got in from a trip. She had a room in One Hundred Thirty-third Street near Fifth Avenue, but I went there only once. I didn't like its lacey and frilly baby-ribboned things and the pink counterpane on the bed.

We didn't have a lot to say to each other. When she tidied the room she was careful about the sheets of paper on which I was writing. And if she came when I was writing or reading she would leave me alone and go into the basement to cook. There is always an unfamiliar something between people of different countries and nationalities, however intimate they may become. And that something between me and Manda helped rather than hindered our relationship. It made her accept little eccentricities on my part— such as the friendship with Michael, for instance. And so we sailed smoothly along for a couple of years. Manda was a good balance to my nervous self.

The cabarets of Harlem in those days enthralled me more than any theater downtown. There were so intimate. If they were lacking in variety they were rich in warmth and native excitement. At that time the hub of Harlem was One Hundred Thirty-Fifth Street between Fifth Avenue and Seventh. Between Seventh Avenue and Eighth the population was still white. The saloons were run by the Irish, the restaurants by the Greeks, the ice and fruit stands by the Italians, the grocery and haberdashery stores by the Jews. The only Negro businesses, excepting barber shops, were the churches and the cabarets. And Negro Harlem extended from One Hundred Thirtieth to One Hundred Forty-fifth Streets, bounded on the East by Madison Avenue and on the West by Seventh Avenue. There, coming off the road like homing birds, we trainmen came to rest awhile and fraternize with our friends in the city—elevator runners and porters—and snatch from saloon and cabaret and home a few brief moments of pleasure, of friendship and of love.

On the morning after my meeting with Michael, Manda said she had been to see me twice the night before. She had telephoned the commissary and was told that my dining car was in. She went to the kitchen in the basement and prepared a big breakfast of ham and eggs and fried potatoes with coffee. I asked Mr. Morris, my landlord, to join us, for I wanted to introduce Michael to him.

He, too, had no liking for "poor white trash." He was a strapping light-brown man and doing well with the lease of two private houses and an interest in one of the few Negro-owned saloons. He came from the South, but had been living many years in the North. When he was a young man in the South, he had "sassed" a white man. And for that he was struck. He struck back, and barely escaped with his life. He was a kind landlord and a pleasant mixer, especially in saloons. But he could be bitter when he got to talking about the South. He was decent to Michael, who was a northerner, for my sake. I had been his tenant for a long time and I exercised the freedom of a friend in that house. We drank together and I got my friends sometimes to patronize his saloon (thus contributing my little to help Negro business).

So Michael came to make Harlem his hideout, while he performed his petty tricks downtown. I told Mr. Morris and Manda that he was the ne'er-do-well son of a former boss, and had taken a liking to me. Whatever they really thought of him I never knew, for they never said. But they were aware that our relationship was not a literary one; they knew that he was not one of those white folks who were interested in the pattern of words I was always making. For Michael made no pretense of being intellectual. However, they liked him, for there was a disarming cleanliness and wholesomeness about his appearance, so that they never imagined that he was what he was. And it would never have occurred to them that I could be friendly with a crook. One never can tell about appearances, and so we all make mistakes by it. For example, when some of my strutting railroad friends came to know Manda, they couldn't believe their eyes: seeing is less penetrating than feeling.

When I was away on the railroad, Michael used my place if he needed it. He did not have a key, but I instructed Morris to let him in. I never felt any concern about anything, although I had some dandy suits in my closet and three Liberty Bonds in my trunk. Michael was profoundly sentimental about friendship, the friends of his friend, and anyone who had befriended him. He could even feel a little sorry for some of his victims after he had robbed them. That was evident from the manner in which he talked about their embarrassment. His deep hatred was directed against the bulls, and his mind was always occupied with outwitting and playing tricks on them. There were two classes of them, he said: the burly-brute, heavy-jawed type, which was easy to pick out, and the dapper college-student type, which was the more dangerous. He said that the best victims to single out were men in spectacles, but that sometimes the bulls disguised themselves and looked Harold Lloydish.

When Michael had no money he ate at the house. The landlord and Manda were sympathetic. At least they could understand that a wild and perhaps disinherited scion might be reduced to a state of hunger. The tabloids often carried sentimental stuff about such personages. When Michael had something he was extravagant. I remember one day when he brought in a fine ham. Manda cooked it in delicious Virginia style, thinking, as she said, that Michael's father had relented and that we were eating a slice of his inheritance.

Michael and I exchanged looks. I felt like saying something impish to stir up Manda's suspicion. But Michael was now well established as a disinherited son instead of a "poor white trash" and I decided not to risk upsetting his position.

Also I was fond of Manda and had no desire to disturb her black Baptist conscience. She was a good woman. When she did my shirt and things in the laundry of the house where she worked, she brought her own soap and utilized her own spare time. And she would never take home any discarded rags or scraps of food that were not actually given to her.

Michael didn't hit it off so well with the fellows from the railroad, though, except for the lackadaisical one, who liked everybody. Michael was not a boozer, nor hard-boiled. In appearance he was like a nice college student. He was brought up in a Catholic home for boys which was located somewhere in Pennsylvania. He was put in there when he was about nine and kept there for twelve years. . . . Oh yes, and besides bulls, he hated priests and the Catholic Church.

I liked him most when he was telling about his escapades. There was that big-time representative of an ancient business who had his bags checked in the Grand Central Terminal. Michael managed to get the ticket away from him and refused to give it back unless the man paid twenty-five dollars. The man did not have the money on him and was afraid of a scandal. He had to telephone a friend for it and was even ashamed to do that. He walked along Broadway with Michael until they found a drugstore from which he could telephone. And he begged the lad to remain out of sight, so that his friend should not think the money was for him. "Gee!" Michael said. "And I was scared crazy all the time, thinking he would call a cop and have me arrested. But I faced it out and got the dough. The big stiff."

And there was the circus performer who had all his money at home. So Michael went along with him to get his. But when the actor got in, he sent his wife out, and she chased Michael with a rolling pin.

One afternoon, as I was dressing to go to work, I was suddenly made self-conscious by Michael remarking: "If I had your physique, I wouldn't work."

"What would you be, then," I asked, "a boxer?"

"Hell, no, that's too much bruising work, and only the big fists are in the money."

"Well, you should worry," I said, "if you haven't a swell physique. You don't work anyway."

"Oh, I'm different; but you—well, it's queer, you liking a woman like Manda."

"Why, I thought you liked her," I said. "She's nice to you."

"I know she is, and she's a fine one all right; but that's not what I mean. I mean she's so homely, she couldn't do any hustling to help you out. See what I mean?"

"Ugly is but lovely does," I said.

"That's nothing," he said.

"A whole lot more than you think," I said.

"Money is everything," he said. "When I have money I get me a pretty woman."

"Every man has his style and his limit," I said. "I prefer my way to yours."

"I know that without your saying so. Say, you don't like the way I live, eh? Be frank."

"I never said anything about that," I said.

"But you wouldn't live the way I do, would you?"

"Perhaps because I can't. One must find a way somehow between the possible and the impossible."

"But ain't it hell to be a slave on a lousy job?"

When I made no answer he went on: "Do you think you'll ever get a raise out of your writing?"

"I don't know. I might. Anyway, my writing makes it possible for me to stand being a slave on a lousy job."

Weeks passed sometimes and I never saw Michael, although he was often in Harlem, for usually when I was in he was out. He was as busy at his job as I was on mine, with shiploads of soldiers returning from Europe and the railroad service engaged to its utmost capacity. Doubling-out became like a part of the regular schedule, there was so much of it.

One day when I was in the city Michael dropped in. Seeing a revolver on the table, he asked what was the meaning of it. I said that the revolver had been in my possession for some years, ever since I used to manage an eating place in a tough district of Brooklyn. But why was I carrying it, he asked, when it might get me into trouble with the police? He never carried one himself, although his was a dangerous trade, for he was safer without it if he were picked up by the bulls.

I explained that I, like the rest of my crew, was carrying the revolver for self-defense, because of the tightened tension between the colored and the white population all over the country. Stopping-over in strange cities, we trainmen were obliged to pass through some of the toughest quarters and we had to be on guard against the suddenly aroused hostility of the mob. There had been bloody outbreak after outbreak in Omaha, Chicago, and Washington, and any crazy bomb might blow up New York even. I walked over to a window and looked out on the back yard.

Michael said: "And if a riot broke in Harlem and I got caught up here, I guess I'd get killed maybe."

"And if it were downtown and I was caught in it?" said I, turning round.

Michael said: "And if there were trouble here like that in Chicago between colored and white, I on my side and you on yours, we might both be shooting at one another, eh?"

"It was like that during the war that's just ended," I said, "brother against brother and friend against friend. They were all trapped in it and they were all helpless."

I turned my back again and leaned out of the window, thinking how in times of acute crisis the finest individual thoughts and feelings may be reduced to nothing before the blind brute forces of tigerish tribalism which remain at the core of civilized society.

When I looked up Michael was gone.

There was nearly three months' silence between us after that. It was broken at last by the pencilled scrawl and newspaper clipping which I mentioned earlier. Immediately I wrote to Michael, telling him that I had quit the railroad and was going abroad and that I would like to see him before leaving.

He came one evening. Manda made a mess of fried chicken, and we had a reunion with my landlord and Hubert Harrison, who was accompanied by a European person, a radical or bohemian, or perhaps both.

Hubert Harrison entertained us with a little monologue on going abroad. He was sure the trip would do me good, although it would have been wiser for me to accept the original proposal, he said. He asked me to send him articles from abroad for the *Negro World* (the organ of the Back-to-Africa Movement), which he was editing.

At first Michael was uneasy, listening to our literary conversation. He had never heard me being intellectual. And he was quite awed by the fact that it was pure poetry and not a fine physique that had given me a raise so quickly. He thought that that poem in the New York *Tribune* had had something to do with it. And with a little more liquor he relaxed and amused us by telling of his sensations when he saw that poem over my name in the newspaper. And then he surprised me by saying that he was thinking about getting a job.

The European woman was charmed by the novel environment and she idealized Michael as an American proletarian. She thought that Michael was significant as a symbol of the unity of the white and black proletariat. But when she asked Michael what division of the working class he belonged to, he appeared embarrassed. After dinner we went for awhile to Connor's Cabaret, which was the most entertaining colored cabaret in Harlem at that time.

Michael came down to the boat the day I sailed. Mr. Gray * also was at the pier. I introduced them. Mr. Gray was aware that Michael was poor, and whispered to me, asking if he might give him something. I said, "Sure." He gave Michael ten dollars.

As the boat moved away from the pier, they were standing together. And suddenly I felt alarmed about Mr. Gray and wondered if I should not have warned him about Michael. I thought that if I were not on the scene, Michael might not consider himself bound by our friendship not to prey upon Mr. Gray. But my fear was merely a wild scare. Michael was perfect all the way through and nothing untoward happened.

[*After spending a year and a half in England, McKay returned to America and rejoined the* Liberator. *One day Michael showed up at the* Liberator *office, and he and McKay had a final meeting.*]

. . . I went downstairs and found Michael. I brought him up to my office. Michael had read in a newspaper that I was working on the *Liberator* and he had looked up the address and called to see me. In two years Michael had changed almost beyond recognition. The college-lad veneer had vanished. A nasty scar had spoiled his right eyebrow and his face was prematurely old, with lines like welts. After I went abroad he had landed a job as a street-car conductor. He had worked a few months and becoming disgusted, he drifted

---

* A fictitious name McKay gave to the English admirer of his poetry who paid his fare to England in 1919. [Ed.]

back to petty banditry. He was copped and jailed in a local prison, where he made criminal friends more expert than himself. Now he was in with a gang.

We chatted reminiscently. I related my radical adventures in London. I exhibited what I had accomplished by way of literature on the side. And I presented him with a signed copy of the book [*Spring in New Hampshire*]. Michael looked with admiration at the frontispiece (a photograph of myself) and at me.

"Jeez," he said, "you did do it, all right. You're a bird."

"What species?" I asked.

Michael laughed. "What are you wanting me to say? You are an eagle?"

"Oh no," I said, "that's a white folk's bird. Blackbird will do."

"There you're starting again," Michael said. "You know I haven't been in Harlem since you left."

I said that I was living in the same place and invited him to come up. I told him that my landlord, Mr. Morris, had asked after him.

Michael shook his head. "It ain't like before. I'm in with a rotten gang. We'se all suspicious of one another. If I came around to see you, they'd soon get wise to it and want to mess around there, thinking there was something to make."

I said I wouldn't care, since there was nothing. And knowing them might be another exciting diversion, I thought.

Michael's face became ugly. "No, you're better off without knowing that gang. They couldn't understand you like me. They're just no good. They're worse than me. And lookit that guy what send you out to me. He was looking at me as if I wasn't human. I know that my mug ain't no angel's since that wop bastard gashed me, but all the same I ain't no gorilla."

"Couldn't you find another job and start working again?" I asked.

He shook his head. "It's too late now. I can't get away or escape. I'm not like you. Perhaps if I had had some talent, like you."

I knew that he was doomed. I had a pocket edition of Francis Thompson's "Hound of Heaven" on my desk. It was one of my favorite things. Michael looked at it. I said that Thompson was an Irish poet.

"I read a lot, whenever I get a chance," he said, "newspapers and magazines."

I read a little from "The Hound":

I fled Him, down the nights and down the days;
I fled Him, down the arches of the years;
I fled Him, down the labyrinthine ways
Of my own mind; and in the mist of tears
I hid from Him, and under running laughter.
   Up vistaed hopes I sped;
      And shot, precipitated,
Adown Titanic glooms of chasmèd fears,
From those strong Feet that followed, followed after. . . .
In the rash lustihead of my young powers,
   I shook the pillaring hours
And pulled my life upon me; grimed with smears,
I stand amid the dust o' the moulded years—
My mangled youth lies dead beneath the heap. . . .

I told Michael something of the writer's way of living. And I gave him the book.

"Can you spare it?" he asked. I said I was always "sparing" books, dropping them everywhere, because they were too heavy to tote.

"I guess when the gang sees me with these here," said Michael, "they'll be thinking that I'm turning queer. . . ."

I never saw Michael again. Just before I left for Europe the following year I received a pathetic scrawl informing me that he had been caught in a hold-up and sentenced to prison for nine years. . . .

From *A Long Way from Home* (New York: Lee Furman, 1937), pp. 45–56, 106–8. Reprinted with the permission of the publisher and Hope McKay Virtue.

After 1935 McKay's employment with the New York City division of the Federal Writers' Project inevitably led to his involvement in the political controversy which whirled like a restless wind throughout the New York literary scene.

In the three selections which follow, McKay details the reasons for his opposition to Communism, states his own political position, and urges creative writers to adopt a position of critical independence when writing about politics and politicians. The first selection, "An Open Letter to James Rorty," first appeared in the Socialist Call; *the other two articles were first printed in the* New Leader, *which, like the* Call, *was in the 1930s an anticommunist left-wing publication.*

AN OPEN LETTER TO JAMES RORTY *

Dear James Rorty:

I was invited to join the League of American Writers [21] and was under the impression that it was an organization composed of all writers of left liberal and radical persuasion. On the membership list I saw such names as Bruce Bliven, John Chamberlain, Waldo Frank, Horace Gregory, Josephine Johnson, Archibald MacLeish and Vincent Sheehan.[22]

But the night of the opening meeting of the Congress at Carnegie Hall, when I listened to Earl Browder [23] attacking Waldo Frank [24] and Trotskyists and Anarchists, I felt that the Congress was being used for official Communist propaganda and walked off the platform. And I did not attend any other meetings.

That same evening I read your article in the *Socialist Call*. You state that "the primary test by which writers were chosen to take part in the Congress was . . . their attitude toward the Moscow trials." [25]

But I don't think I was chosen for that, because all my Communist acquaintances are aware that I do not accept the official Soviet version of the Moscow trials. I am even a little further than that to the right. I don't like any dictatorship.

Now Mr. Rorty, the points you make in your article are interesting, the facts illuminating. But I'd like to know precisely what you propose to do about them? As I see the situation, it appears to me not merely a difference of tactics between radical factions, but fundamentally a part of the great struggle between genuine democracy and dictatorship. More and more today the world is being divided into two great camps of people who still believe in democracy and people who prefer dictatorship.

But because there exists on the left flank of bourgeois democracy a regime of proletarian dictatorship in Russia some liberal intellectuals argue that as Russia is a proletarian state they should suspend criticism of its mistakes and criticize only the fascist dictatorship maneuvers which menace the social progress of the world.

But these intellectuals are either led or maneuvered by those

---

* James Rorty (1891–1973) was a poet, radical editor, and co-founder of the *New Masses* who abandoned communism in 1932.

who give their allegiance to the Comintern, who believe only in the principle of dictatorship and have nothing but contempt (which is sometimes concealed) for genuine workers' democracy. Such a situation naturally produces intellectual confusion.

Personally, I don't believe in Utopia nor that there is any state which can put itself above criticism. And it seems to me that more than any the Soviet state stands in need of radical criticism and analysis always and precisely because it is generally admitted by radical workers that it is perhaps the greatest social experiment in the history of the human race.

Also I think intellectuals unworthy of their name when they abdicate the right to independent thinking, discussion, and criticism.

I regard the independent intellectuals as the spiritual descendants of the prophets and skeptic philosophers, who always fearlessly opposed and criticized the priests, while the Communist and Fascist intellectuals, intolerant of criticism, stem straight from the scribes who always blindly and faithfully served the hierarchy of the priests. There has never been and never can be any compromise between the two types of intellectuals.

I lived under the Communist dictatorship, a Fascist dictatorship and a colonial dictatorship and found each system different in its social development with some good features and some bad. But in the intellectual sphere I felt something which was common to each of them. And that was a feeling of fear among those who desired to think and express themselves independently.

I came to the conclusion that any regime was bad under which people were afraid to think and talk independently. For throughout the ages it is the persistence of independent thought and criticism against reaction, which made social progress possible.

I am against all dictatorships, whether they are social or intellectual. *I believe in the social revolution and the triumph of workers' democracy, not workers' dictatorship.* Finally, I would like to ask what you and other intellectuals like yourself propose to do?

Complaining and denouncing are not enough. The scribes are highly organized and can accomplish much. Is it not possible to have an organization of independent writers?

"I Believe in the Social Revolution and the Triumph of Workers' Democracy," *Socialist Call* (July 17, 1937), p. 8.

COMMUNISM AND THE NEGRO

My attention has just been called to an article in the Federal Writers' Project in the issue of the *New Leader* of July 23, in which it was stated that I have fought against "Communist domination of the Negroes on work relief." It would be more correct to say that I have resented Communist persecution of non-Communist workers.

To fight Communist domination I would have to fight the union of the unemployed and WPA workers and I stand by the principle of unionism. It must be admitted that more than any other group the Communists should be credited with the effective organizing of the unemployed and relief workers.

From the administration they have won the right of Federal relief workers to organize and it is inevitable that the Communists will be politically powerful in the unions they control just as, for example, the Socialists formerly dominated the needle trades' unions.

I am opposed to the Communists, not, like the Trotskyites and other opposition Communists, on account of their opportunist interpretation of Marxian ideas, but because I do not accept the basic political ideology of Communism.

(1) I reject absolutely the idea of government by dictatorship, which is the pillar of political Communism.

(2) I am intellectually against the Jesuitical tactics of the Communists: (a) their professed conversion to the principles of Democracy which is obviously false since they defend the undemocratic regime in Russia and loudly laud its bloodiest acts; (b) their skunking behind the smoke screen of People's Front and Collective Security, supporting the indefensible imperialistic interests of European nations and deliberately trying to deceive the American people; (c) their criminal slandering and persecution of their opponents, who have remained faithful to the true traditions of radicalism and liberalism.

More important than the fear of the Communists dominating the Negroes on work relief (especially through the talents of their colored members among the Federal writers!) is my concern about the Communists capturing the entire colored group by cleverly controlling such organizations as the so-called National Negro Congress.[26]

Experience since the Emancipation should have taught the various colored leaders that it is a mistake to deliver the colored people over to any one political party. The colored minority has special problems to face and should itself organize its powers for social and political preferments, similar to other American minorities.

It would be bad enough for the colored minority to be owned by any purely American party, as it formerly was by the Republican party. But it would be disastrous if it were captured by a Communist party, which, despite its professions to the contrary, is the highly controlled Propaganda Bureau of the Communist International, which is dominated by the Russian Government.

For in the eventuality of a crisis developing between the United States and Soviet Russia, the colored minority might find itself in a very vulnerable and unenviable position. As a member of this group and also as a radical thinker, I am especially concerned about its future and the danger of its being maneuvered through high-powered propaganda into the morass of Communist opportunism.

"Negro Author Sees Disaster If the Communist Party Gains Control of Negro Workers," *New Leader* (September 10, 1938), p. 5.

ON THE LEAGUE OF AMERICAN WRITERS: A STATEMENT OF PRINCIPLE

The Communist-controlled League of American Writers draped the banner of Democracy over the facade of its Third Congress. And writers who ostentatiously proclaim belief in the democratic principles of freedom of expression gave support to an organization whose policy and tactics, if carried out on a national scale, would foster undemocratic ideals and inevitably lead to the strict regimentation of American literature.

I had thought that the amazing attack on Waldo Frank, the former President of the League, which was delivered by Commissar Browder at the opening of the Second Congress in 1937, would have started a revolt among League members—at least all those who entertain serious ideas about the business and purpose of writing.

Because of an honest statement of intellectual doubt regarding events in Soviet Russia, a distinguished writer and profound social thinker was reprimanded by a little politician, who takes his orders from Moscow. But the general membership of the League was not perturbed.

Unwittingly I was tricked into signing the call for that Second Congress and I attended the opening meeting at Carnegie Hall. But when I heard Commissar Browder purging Waldo Frank, I knew that I was in the wrong place and walked off the platform.

Following that incident, I received several communications inviting me to affairs sponsored by the League. But I have never responded. I felt that if for sentimental reasons which are not relevant to the craft of writing, famous writers were willing to lend their prestige and enormous influence to setting up the beginning of a dictatorship in American letters, I still possessed the democratic right to make my little protest.

That Second Congress of American Writers was challenged by John Chamberlain, James Rorty and others and on the eve of the Third Congress, Frances Winwar and Babette Deutsch resigned.[27]

The names of other nationally known writers who had stellar places in the Second Congress are absent from the roster of the Third.

There must be a lot of doubt in the minds of many as to the executive leadership of the League of American Writers, whether it is actually working to promote the spirit of democracy, tolerance and freedom of literary expression, which distinguishes modern writing and which has been extinguished under all the totalitarian regimes.

Evidently the League is not run in that spirit of free enquiry which sets the iconoclastic writer apart from the scribe. The League is primarily political and extremely partisan.

It fights Fascist totalitarianism, but proscribes as Fascists, Trotskyists and Reactionaries the writers who are opposed to Communist totalitarianism.

It invites German writers who have fled the Hitler terror to speak from its platform; it does not extend any invitation to Russian writers who have fled the Stalin terror, of which there are many abroad and who also staunchly believe in that Democracy which is touted by the League.

"Millions of Books in Soviet Russia" was one of the slogans of the Second Congress of the League. There was no reference to the fact that no writer can exist or publish material in Russia who does not support the Stalin regime. No mention of the great poets Mayakovsky and Yesenin [28] who had wholeheartedly embraced Communism, but who ominously preferred the way out by self-purge, just before the great purge liquidated scores of their fellow writers and artists. At its Second Congress the League's watchword was the battle for Democracy in Spain. It would have been an unbelievably noble gesture if this year the League had invited such writers as are informed of the facts to expose Russia's role, along with the Nazis and Fascists, in helping to destroy Democracy in Spain.

But the League is run on the Stalinist principle of rule or ruin. In the domestic field its interest in Democracy is qualified by its lust for power. It sabotaged the New York Writers' Project in an attempt to gain control of it through its stooges. And its underhand methods resulted in the liquidation of a group of writers selected to do special work, because of outstanding ability.[29]

It was prominent League members such as Heywood Broun and Max Lerner and the scribes of the *Daily Worker* and the *New Masses,* who attacked liberal Governor LaFollette [30] as a Fascist, when he issued his extraordinary progressive manifesto. It little mattered to them that much of Governor LaFollette's program could be embodied in the New Deal and that soon afterwards President Roosevelt honored him with a special invitation to the White House.

I specially refer to the slandering of Governor LaFollette, because it was precisely similar tactics by Communist scribes in Germany, which helped prepare the way of the Nazi accession to power. German liberals and social democrats were unscrupulously libeled by Communist scribes in the pay of Stalin.

They were denounced as social fascists and enemies of the people, so that all issues were confused and the people were not made aware of who were their real enemies. In 1931 I was visiting a contributor to the *Tagebuch* [31] in Berlin and he informed me that he was so disgusted with the streamlined attacks of the Communist scribes directed against the liberals that he was making plans to retire to a remote part of the Austrian Tyrol!

Perhaps some of the distinguished German exiles who were honored guests at the Writers' Congress could furnish specific illuminating items regarding the methods of the Communists, which may enlighten the innocents of the Writers' League. It is ironical that exiled German liberals should be exploited by an organization whose unprincipled leadership is fundamentally opposed to their tolerant ideas of culture.

When creative writers become political-minded, they owe it to the public to dig down to the facts and interpret them. The public expects more from them than from ordinary politicians. But instead of promoting scientific social enquiry and research, the League of American Writers prefers to vilify and silence those writers who adhere to such principles of free enquiry, because they are contrary to the real purposes of the League's leadership. For the League's purpose is to defend the domestic and foreign policies of Soviet Russia against all criticism.

The development of such a League in this country will inevitably result in the formation of another opposed to its aims. And soon American writers may find themselves ranged into two actively hostile camps. And instead of the dream of that republic of letters to which men of different nations and races expressing divergent opinions may belong, American writers may wake up when it is too late to find themselves in the grip of a rigid dictatorship of letters.

Perhaps because I am subject to very special limitations, I may value the possession of free intellectual inquiry and expression even more than the large majority of writers who were born to it. To me it is a precious thing. We need more of it in America.

But also I have lived under dictatorships where there was none at all. I have seen men risking imprisonment and banishment to smuggle newspapers and books across frontiers. I have seen them whispering on street corners and in cafes, afraid of being overheard by spies. I have seen them trample underfoot the official rags published by dictatorships.

And because of my experience and my convictions I am opposed to any organization of intellectuals of the Left or the Right, which is basically undemocratic, such as the League of American Writers.

"Where the News Ends," *New Leader* (June 10, 1939), p. 8.

In his "Circular Letter for the Creation of a Negro Writers' Guild" and the five articles that follow it, McKay tells why he believes that the first goal of American Negroes should be the overall improvement of their community life. The articles, "Harlem Runs Wild" and "Labor Steps Out in Harlem" are particularly good examples of McKay's interest in and reportage of the several grassroots community movements that agitated Harlem during the Depression years.

CIRCULAR LETTER FOR THE CREATION
OF A NEGRO WRITERS' GUILD

217 West 126th Street
New York City, N.Y.

October 23rd, 1937

Dear Friend and Confrère:

For some weeks a number of creative writers and journalists have been meeting informally in round-table conversations pertaining to closer contact between Negro writers.

From these conversations there developed one clear and definite idea: we agreed that the time was ripe for Negro writers to draw closer together in mutual fellowship. We felt that as members of a distinct group we specfically could make a special contribution in the interest of the work and lives of our intellectuals. We thought that the achievement of our writers of the past should receive more appreciation from a social and historical as well as literary perspective, precisely as other groups of people measure their cultural development by the achievements of their talented members.

We agreed that a democratic association of Negro writers was needed. We thought that such an association, properly founded and directed, would be beneficial to all our writers and especially to those younger and potential ones who may look to the older for inspiration.

To the timid and the obstreperous among us who are frightened by the bugbear of segregation and isolation, whenever a matter of special group organization is under consideration, we desire to say that we are not thinking in terms of narrow sectarianism, but rather in universal aspects of group culture. We think that it is possible to establish through intellectual fellowship something like a living counterpart of the unparalleled Schomburg collection of Negro books in the domain of scholarship.

In our conversations we agreed that the Negro's authentic talent in literature and art should be encouraged more, and nurtured and developed within the group. Friends and sympathizers of other groups may do much to help by way of material encouragement and constructive criticism, but they cannot generate in Negroes that energy which produces real creative expression. Negroes themselves must produce that.

As a result of our conversations it was suggested that I should communicate with the talented creative writers and journalists of our group for the purpose of forming an association.

Thereupon, I approached a few of our writers, including James Weldon Johnson. Mr. Johnson, who has been aptly called the "dean of Negro letters," was very sympathetic to the idea of an association of the Negro literati and also willing to lend his prestige as a writer and his experience in organizational work to the plan.

I am, therefore, inviting you to a preliminary meeting which will be held at the above address on Monday, November 1st, 1937, at 8 p.m.[32]

Yours sincerely,
CLAUDE McKAY

FOR GROUP SURVIVAL

In this twentieth year of the Russian Revolution, fifteenth year of Italian Fascism, and the fourth year of Nazism, it should hardly be necessary for any Negro to advocate the aggregate organization and development of his group against the passive Uncle Tom and Do-Nothing policy of integration.

If a scheme is put forward to establish something beneficial and exclusively for Negroes, such as a hospital, a school or a bank, the black cry of segregation is heard. No sane Negro believes in or desires legal segregation, in which his racial group will be confined by law to ghettoes. For such a system of segregation will inevitably result in congestion and increased crime, disease and filth.

But it is one of the most natural phenomena of human life every-where that people possessing special and similar traits will agglom-erate in groups. And it is a physical impossibility to compel two dif-ferent groups of people to live promiscuously together against their will. Different groups agglomerate for different social reasons; such as a common nationality, a common religion, a common language, class interests, or special characteristics of race or color.

It would seem a most elementary law of self-preservation and survival that wherever a distinct group of people is living together, such a people should utilize their collective brains and energy for the intensive cultivation and development of themselves, culturally, politically and economically. The intellectual leaders and profes-sional members of such a group should be zealous in promoting the special interests of the mass of their community. For it is the living reality of the common mass which makes possible the more cultured existence of the intellectual leaders and the professional members of the community.

The United States of America are uniquely a national composite of various groups. In the so-called "melting pot" we have distinguishable groups with special interests, who are none the less American and proud to be identified with the general interest of the nation. There are Italians, Finns, Irish, Scandinavians, Jews, Chinese and others, all more or less living together in groups. These people in building up themselves fraternally, culturally, politically and economically as groups are contributing their special part to the greatness of the American nation as a whole.

To these diverse groups must be added the Negro group. The Negroes, who were emancipated from slavery before the great waves of European immigration swept into America, still remain the lowest group of Americans, socially and economically. Ever since its emancipation from chattel slavery the Negro group as a whole has been hopelessly divided and half paralyzed by the ideology of segregation. The difference between an aggregated group of people and a group segregated by law has never been defined, clarified and explained by Negro leaders. Unique efforts to establish institutions for the special benefit of the Negro people have encountered opposition because of the ideology of segregation. Handicapped by the fear of segregation, the Negro group has never launched out in confidence to develop the positive potentialities of its position as a special group.

When Booker T. Washington founded the great institution of Tuskegee as a practical demonstration of what Negroes might accomplish for themselves, culturally and economically, as a people, he was opposed by leading Negro intellectuals of the North. Yet although Mr. Washington may have followed a mistaken lead in national politics, his social basis was sound. He did not fold his arms and whine and wait for integration. He accomplished something different. He attracted national attention because he had something different to offer. Tuskegee Institute stands a fine monument to him and is perhaps the greatest all-Negro institution in the world.

The Negro group still has a long way to go and a great deal to learn. Of all the groups in America the Negro might learn most from the Jewish group. The American Jewish group is a conglomeration of Jews from different countries, such as Russia, Poland, Germany,

Hungary, the Balkan states. Similarly the American Negro group has been augmented by Negroes from the various West Indian islands and from South America.

Not all Jews live in Jewish communities, but the majority of them are socially conscious and aware of the necessity of aggressive group organization and the development of Jewish community life. There are Jewish Youth organizations, a Jewish Historical Society, Jewish Publications Society, Jewish Physical Culture, Jewish Legion, Jewish War Veterans, Jewish Occupational Committee, etc. There are a Jewish Agricultural Society, Jewish Labor Committee and, perhaps the most important of all, the United Hebrew Trades with its militant membership—an integral part of American organized labor. In the national field there exists the B'nai Brith, a society organized in 1843 for Jewish unity. In the international field there is the Alliance Israelite Universelle, which was organized in 1860 for the emancipation, education and defense of the Jewish masses in all lands.

Jews organize Jewish hotels, theaters, clubs, stores, printing establishments, colleges and hospitals, without segregating themselves from national institutions. In fact they have broken down 100 per cent barriers of American prejudice and discrimination by building up institutions inferior to none which are a credit to the entire American nation. . . . I am not trying to present the Jewish people as one harmonious whole. There are differences among them as there are among all other groups. The interests of Jewish capitalists are at variance with the interests of Jewish workers. Yet Jewish labor has won such concessions as it has from the Jewish employer class and put itself in the front ranks of the American labor movement, because the moral sentiment of the majority of the Jewish community was on the side of the workers.

The Irish, the Germans, the Scandinavians, the Italians, the Jews—all the European immigrants who poured into America, were not from the wealthy classes. They were, in the majority, poor workers and peasants fleeing from class prejudice, poverty, aristocratic and royal exploitation in Europe. They came here as individuals and in families. They had to start from the bottom to build themselves up. They also had to face prejudice and discrimination, although not in the same degree as the Negro. Those who had a common nationality or religion or language found it necessary to develop group unity to fight for and find a place in the national life.

After their emancipation the black people found themselves up against white prejudice and discriminatory laws and practices. The possessing white majority would not yield any solid ground in their social system to the dispossessed black minority. For over half a century Negroes remained good Lincoln Republicans. The Negro group was practically the ward of the Republican party. Perhaps its leaders could not understand that guardians do not like to have wards on their hands forever, that they expect their wards to grow up sometime and think and act independently. But a few choice plums were distributed to outstanding Negroes and the Negro group applauded. Uncle Tom slave, Uncle Tom free!

The Negro people remained a special group. They were excluded from trains and trams, hotels and restaurants, schools and theaters and other public places. They were kicked out of the Christian churches. They were effectively segregated. But the only thing more than any other that Negroes started out to build exclusively for themselves was the Negro church. Because the Negro people are so profoundly religious-minded, they have always neglected their material interests for the spiritual.

Despite constant discrimination and virtual segregation leading Negroes declare: We want integration. Now I believe that all sane Negroes want integration. But how are they going to get it? Can the integrationists demonstrate to the black minority how they may be integrated into the white majority? Can they point to a group of blacks blissfully integrated in the white Utopia? Why do the integrationists preach integration and yet practice segregation by residing in the Black Belt, while most of them represent Negro concerns and institutions? The Negro group is *not* integrated because a few Negroes are employed here and there in white institutions according to their intellectual attainments; or because some have special places in the Republican, Democratic, Socialist and Communist parties.

The integration of a minority in a majority group depends entirely upon the goodwill of the majority and not upon the desire of the minority. I can see no indication anywhere that the white majority is ready to let down the barriers to include the black minority. The few philanthropic white individuals and organizations interested in Negro welfare do not represent the will of the white majority. The Communists have a program of local autonomy and complete social equality for Negroes, but they are only a small minority. There is the great organized labor movement. Yet the integrationists are not visualizing the Negro group as integrated in a new order of proletarian society, but in the present set-up of capitalist society.

Organized labor, just as white in complexion as white capitalists, is not indulging in a pipe-dream of integration in the capitalist control of society. The advance guard of organized labor makes a militant fight. Much more an integral part of this nation than the black minority, militant labor has its own banks, schools, printing establishments, clubs and cooperatives.

The educated Negro has long labored under the illusion that he could ignore and neglect his own group and find the place in white society for which he thought his education entitled him. But thinking Negroes should realize that we are living in a changing world under a new era and that the age of individualism is dead. Thinking Negroes must realize that in this age of the radio, the control and direction of the masses is the big problem alike of democracies and dictatorships.

And what of the Negro masses? Must they remain abandoned to the fine theory of integration and the care of white philanthropists? Is it possible that the educated Negro can feel no kinship with his own people? Certainly if the Negro leaders abdicate their right to leadership of their own people others must step in.

With the world's attention fixed upon events in Hitler's Germany today, it seems to me that the attitude of the Negro apologists of integration is not merely defeatist, but also criminal. The German Jews had come closer to integration and assimilation than Jews in any other country. As a group they were not strongly organized for emergencies. They were fairly unorthodox, intermarried freely with the best German families. They were tolerated and accepted by the majority of Germans.

Yet now under a political change of regime, the Jews of Germany are being systematically reduced to the status of Negroes in America. Perhaps if the German Jews had been more strongly organized as a group, they might have been better prepared to fight against the evil of Nazism. Perhaps some Negroes fondly imagine that in the event of a reactionary change in this nation's government, they will be treated better than the Jews of Germany. But Jews at any rate have this advantage over Negroes. Thousands of them cannot be differentiated from white Christians.

It seems to me that the argument for the intensive group organization of Negroes is a very simple and elementary one. Negroes must organize as a group to obtain the utmost out of their special situation. Negro leaders should get together and plan to lead their people out of their present state of apathy and confusion. As a group we are the most supine to ruthless exploitation by others. There are numerous Negro associations. It seems to me that what the group lacks is coordination of organization and leadership and a definite purpose.

A Negro community may be likened to any uncongenial small town where a businessman may be compelled to reside for business reasons, even though he prefer to live in a large up-to-date city. Such a person would naturally be interested in the town as a whole; the fire department, streets, housing, lighting and police. Because if there is a fire, an epidemic or a riot, he or a member of his family may be a victim. Similarly, any group-conscious Negro should be interested in the intensive development and advancement of his community.

This excerpt from an article by a Jewish intellectual might be pondered with profit by Negro leaders: "Today no minority group has a right to consider itself adjusted to the life of the majority unless it is economically assimilated. To be economically differentiated means to be denied protection of one's right to live by leaving one's livelihood at the mercy of the majority group."

That is the real issue the Negro has to face—the economic issue upon which integration depends. Negro leaders who evade the practical issue of group organization and development to shibboleth the empty slogan of "integration" without being able to demonstrate a practical plan of integration are not only betrayers but lynchers of the soul of the race.

From *Jewish Frontier,* vol. 4 (October, 1937), pp. 19–26.

HARLEM RUNS WILD

Docile Harlem went on a rampage last week, smashing stores and looting them and piling up destruction of thousands of dollars worth of goods. But the mass riot in Harlem was not a race riot. A few whites were jostled by colored people in the melee, but there was no manifest hostility between colored and white as such. All night until dawn on the Tuesday of the outbreak white persons, singly and in groups, walked the streets of Harlem without being molested. The action of the police was commendable in the highest degree. The looting was brazen and daring, but the police were restrained. In extreme cases, when they fired, it was into the air. Their restraint saved Harlem from becoming a shambles.

The outbreak was spontaneous. It was directed against the stores exclusively. One Hundred and Twenty-fifth Street is Harlem's main street and the theatrical and shopping center of the colored thousands. Anything that starts there will flash through Harlem as quick as lightning. The alleged beating of a kid caught stealing a trifle in one of the stores merely served to explode the smoldering discontent of the colored people against the Harlem merchants.

It would be too sweeping to assert that radicals incited the Harlem mass to riot and pillage. The Young Liberators [33] seized an opportune moment, but the explosion on Tuesday was not the result of Communist propaganda. There were, indeed, months of propaganda in it. But the propagandists are eager to dissociate themselves from Communists. Proudly they declare that they have agitated only in the American constitutional way for fair play for colored Harlem.

Colored people all over the world are notoriously the most exploitable material, and colored Harlem is no exception. The population is gullible to an extreme. And apparently the people are exploited so flagrantly because they invite and take it. It is their gullibility that gives to Harlem so much of its charm, its air of insouciance and gaiety. But the façade of the Harlem masses' happy-go-lucky and hand-to-mouth existence has been badly broken by the Depression. A considerable part of the population can no longer cling even to the hand-to-mouth margin.

Wherever an ethnologically related group of people is exploited by others, the exploiters often operate on the principle of granting certain concessions as sops. In Harlem the exploiting group is overwhelmingly white. And it gives no sops. And so for the past two years colored agitators have exhorted the colored consumers to organize and demand of the white merchants a new deal: that they should employ Negroes as clerks in the colored community. These agitators are crude men, theoretically. They have little understanding of and little interest in the American labor movement, even from the most conservative trade-union angle. They address their audience mainly on the streets. Their following is not so big as that of the cultists and occultists. But it is far larger than that of the Communists.

One of the agitators is outstanding and picturesque. He dresses in turban and gorgeous robe. He has a bigger following than his rivals. He calls himself Sufi Abdul Hamid. His organization is the Negro Industrial and Clerical Alliance. It was the first to start picketing the stores of Harlem demanding clerical employment for colored persons. Sufi Hamid achieved a little success. A few of the smaller Harlem stores engaged colored clerks. But on 125th Street the merchants steadfastly refused to employ colored clerical help. The time came when the Negro Industrial and Clerical Alliance felt strong enough to picket the big stores on 125th Street. At first the movement got scant sympathy from influential Negroes and the Harlem intelligentsia as a whole. Physically and mentally, Sufi Hamid is a different type. He does not belong. And moreover he used to excoriate the colored newspapers, pointing out that they would not support his demands on the bigger Harlem stores because they were carrying the stores' little ads.

Harlem was excited by the continued picketing and the resultant "incidents." Sufi Hamid won his first big support last spring when one of the most popular young men in Harlem, the Reverend Adam Clayton Powell, Jr., assistant pastor of the Abyssinian Church —the largest in Harlem—went on the picket line on 125th Street. This gesture set all Harlem talking and thinking and made the headlines of the local newspapers. It prompted the formation of a Citizens' League for Fair Play. The league was endorsed and supported by sixty-two organizations, among which were eighteen of the leading churches of Harlem. And at last the local press conceded some support.

One of the big stores capitulated and took on a number of colored clerks. The picketing of other stores was continued. And soon business was not so good as it used to be on 125th Street.

In the midst of the campaign Sufi Hamid was arrested. Sometime before his arrest a committee of Jewish Minute Men had visited the Mayor and complained about an anti-Semitic movement among the colored people and the activities of a black Hitler in Harlem. The *Day* and the *Bulletin,* Jewish newspapers, devoted columns to the Harlem Hitler and anti-Semitism among Negroes. The articles were translated and printed in the Harlem newspapers under big headlines denouncing the black Hitler and his work.

On October 13 of last year Sufi Hamid was brought before the courts charged with disorderly conduct and using invective against the Jews. The witnesses against him were the chairman of the Minute Men and other persons more or less connected with the merchants. After hearing the evidence and defense, the judge decided that the evidence was biased and discharged Sufi Hamid. Meanwhile Sufi Hamid had withdrawn from the Citizens' League for Fair Play. He had to move from his headquarters and his immediate following was greatly diminished. An all-white Harlem Merchants' Association came into existence. Dissension divided the Citizens' League; the prominent members denounced Sufi Hamid and his organization.

In an interview last October Sufi Hamid told me that he had never styled himself the black Hitler. He said that once when he visited a store to ask for the employment of colored clerks, the proprietor remarked, "We are fighting Hitler in Germany." Sufi said that he replied, "We are fighting Hitler in Harlem." He went on to say that although he was a Moslem he had never entertained any prejudices against Jews as Jews. He was an Egyptian * and in Egypt the relations between Moslem and Jew were happier than in any other country. He was opposed to Hitlerism, for he had read Hitler's book, *Mein Kampf,* and knew Hitler's attitude and ideas about all colored peoples. Sufi Hamid said that the merchants of Harlem spread the rumor of anti-Semitism among the colored people because they· did not want to face the issue of giving them a square deal.

The Citizens' League continued picketing, and some stores capitulated. But the Leaguers began quarreling among themselves as to whether the clerks employed should be light-skinned or dark-skinned. Meanwhile the united white Harlem Merchants' Association was fighting back. In November the picketing committee was enjoined from picketing by Supreme Court Justice Samuel Rosenman. The court ruled that the Citizen's League was not a labor organization. It was the first time that such a case had come before the courts of New York. The chairman of the picketing committee remarked that "the decision would make trouble in Harlem."

One by one the colored clerks who had been employed in 125th Street stores lost their places. When inquiries were made as to the cause, the managements gave the excuse of slack business. The clerks had no organization behind them. Of the grapevine intrigue and

---

* Sufi Hamid posed as an Egyptian but was actually native American. See McKay's *Harlem: Negro Metropolis,* p. 190. [Ed.]

treachery that contributed to the debacle of the movement, who can give the facts? They are as obscure and inscrutable as the composite mind of the Negro race itself. So the masses of Harlem remain disunited and helpless, while their would-be leaders wrangle and scheme and denounce one another to the whites. Each one is ambitious to wear the piebald mantle of Marcus Garvey.

On Tuesday the crowds went crazy like the remnants of a defeated, abandoned, and hungry army. Their rioting was the gesture of despair of a bewildered, baffled, and disillusioned people.

From *Nation,* vol. 140 (April 3, 1935), pp. 382–83.

LABOR STEPS OUT IN HARLEM

There are new steps attracting attention in Harlem. Not the gay capriccios of Father Divine and his angels on parade nor those of the Black Elks or pro-African societies strutting along in amazing uniforms, led by prancing drum majors and bands playing stirring music. The new steps are those of labor on the march in Harlem.

Three years ago picketing was as rare as an elephant in Harlem —for Harlem was a Hades of unskilled, unorganized labor and of bootleg skilled labor. Skilled Negro workers considered themselves fortunate when hired by either white or colored employers at half the wages paid to organized white workmen. And the unskilled Negro masses, cut off by the Depression from their usual occupations downtown, worked desperately for anything they could get. Yet Harlem in its worst hard times, as in its days of brightest prosperity, was never labor conscious. The social aspirations of the masses were channeled into racial and religious movements like the Back-to-Africa mirage and Father Divine's Kingdom of Heaven.

But in 1934 a powerful black Negro appeared on the streets, with a sonorous voice and a crude workingman's accent. He was an arresting figure in high boots—colorful cape, Sam Browne belt, and bright turban. Harlem didn't wonder much at the strange costume. It is accustomed to the marvelous apparel of the black dervishes and Amerindian and East Indian fakirs who walk its streets hotly purveying snake medicine and herbs as cures for deadly diseases. It was the things the big Negro in uniform said which moved the people. He preached labor organization. He said: "Wake up and demand jobs in Harlem from white employers." To the dark army of unemployed, skilled and unskilled, shuffling without aim and without hope along the streets, he said: "Do what white workers are doing elsewhere. Organize and fight for jobs. The New Deal calls for redistribution of income. We Negroes were never in the 'income' class. Let *our* New Deal slogan be, 'Share the jobs!' "

Formerly labor agitation in Harlem was carried on exclusively by colored and white Socialists and Communists. It was mainly theoretical. From the stepladder the comrades preached the unity of black-and-white labor under the symbol of a black-and-white handclasp. But, unheeding, the Negro masses went by. Even in Harlem, the largest Negro city in the world, the best-paid labor is white, hired by white employers who exploit the colored community. The symbol of the black-and-white handclasp is ideal; the real thing in Negro experience is the strong white hand against the black. Elevator operators, waiters, porters, maids had seen their jobs downtown shrink away during the Depression and their places taken by white workers. Yet except on special issues, such as lynching and the sensational trial of the Scottsboro boys, the Negro masses remained indifferent to radical propaganda, even though the Communists, ambitious to build a proletarian mass movement in Harlem, approached and made a united front with Father Divine.[34]

While that neo-African "God" and open-shop advocate staged his spectacular parades of prancing, hollering Negroes through the streets of Harlem, more balanced minds among the masses listened to the black labor preacher. He did not stop at the theory and symbol of black-and-white organization. He shouted: "A symbol is fine but Negroes can't eat symbols. When we organize and get better jobs, white workers will respect us and shake our hands." He was more a preacher than a labor leader. He knew amazingly little of the history of labor in America, less of the modern labor movement and its social and international implications. And so he confused the necessity of organization among Negro workers with ideas of Negro labor and Negro capital cooperating to build up a new economy based on race.

On this foundation he established the Afro-American Federation of Labor, which nevertheless attracted some of the hardest-thinking youths in Harlem. They were high school and college graduates, trapped jobless in the Depression. Young men and women, they mounted stepladders on Fifth, Lenox, and Seventh Avenues and harangued the crowds that collected. The Afro-American Federation of Labor picketed little grocery stores and clothing shops on the avenues of Harlem. It obtained little jobs for Negro clerks. That was a new thing in Harlem. Until then the average Harlem boy and girl with a grade-school education had never had a chance at such jobs, which would be filled by a similar type of youth in any normal community. The Afro-American Federation of Labor had initiated a movement that was destined to alter the economic aspect and perspective of Harlem.

But the respectable colored citizens began to wonder, to doubt whether it was a wise movement. The ministers said that picketing was a dangerous weapon which might develop into a boomerang; employers should be approached in a Christian way. A hoary political leader posed the question, Were Negroes competent enough to become clerks? A brown business man said that good-will between whites and blacks was worth more than jobs; therefore picketing was wrong. Prominent social workers feared that if the blacks boycotted white business in Harlem, the downtown business men might retaliate by discharging their colored workers. From a white source the founder of the Afro-American Federation of Labor was denounced as a Black Hitler. The Negro newspapers pounced upon and widely circulated the slander.

The Federation challenged the bigger business men of Harlem by invading 125th Street, its principal thoroughfare, and picketing their stores. A few merchants whose business wasn't good anyway took advantage of the agitation, hired a small number of Negro clerks, and made a special bid for Negro customers. But the majority of the storekeepers, scenting danger, formed a Harlem Merchants' Association to resist the demands of the agitators. The merchants gave an interracial banquet in the heart of Harlem and invited representative Negroes, who made good-will speeches, lauded the merchants, and denounced irresponsible Negro trouble-makers.

The leader of the Harlem movement was tempestuous and careless in his speech. He planted his stepladder on the corner and exhorted the people to support him, while detectives for the merchants wrote down his phrases. He soon got into trouble with the police and was arrested for disorderly conduct. The first case against him was dismissed. But he was continually heckled and harassed by the merchants' henchmen, white and colored. Finally, on the application of a storekeeper, an injunction was granted against him, the court ruling that a labor organization and picketing must not be based on the issue of race.

The would-be leader of the Harlem masses rejected the advice of sympathizers who urged him to make a study of American labor and seek fraternal affiliation, since it was impossible for him to create an independent labor unit. He was soon to find out for himself that it was impossible, and the Afro-American Federation shortly afterward disappeared. When it collapsed, its leader shed his picturesque uniform, shaved off his thick beard, married, and immersed himself in the study of Oriental philosophies. For all his absurdities, he was a significant type—one of the first Negroes to become a labor leader not from studying socialism or communism but simply because he was able to see the practical economic necessity of organizing the depressed masses of Negro workers.

Some of the young agitators of the Afro-American Federation of Labor joined the Communist party. Others gave themselves to abortive and futile Afro-American and pan-African movements. As there was no organization to support them, the majority of the Negro clerks who had obtained jobs through the Federation were dismissed. With the liquidation of the movement, the picketing of stores was terminated and labor agitation discontinued in Harlem. For a few weeks the Negro masses were apparently indifferent and quiescent. Then suddenly they went wild in the historic riot of March 19, 1935. The outburst awoke city officials, politicians of all shades, labor leaders, and the Negro intelligentsia to the intolerable labor situation and miserable living conditions of Harlem. The Mayor appointed a committee to determine the cause of the riot. While its investigation was still in progress, a new labor movement was launched.

This was the Negro Labor Committee, organized in July 1935, as a result of a conference of 110 Negro and white delegates from various trade unions. The Negro Labor Committee, endorsed by the American Federation of Labor, consists of 25 colored and white members of a number of outstanding trade unions. Its purpose is to give aid and counsel to unions engaged in organization and strike activities among Negro workers, to adjust the grievances of organized Negro workers in the various unions, and to weed out of the ranks of labor racial and other prejudices. It seeks to remedy the acute problem of the Negro worker's relationship to organized labor through the existing unions.

At the same time another union was formed from the debacle of the Afro-American Federation of Labor—the Harlem Labor Union, Inc. This organization retained the main features of the defunct Federation, with one important difference. It was not officially a racial organization although in practice it was. Its leaders were less spectacular. They wore no uniforms. And strangely they had no following among Harlem's young elite. Their support came from the most depressed masses.

The president of the Harlem Labor Union, Ira Kemp,[35] is a member of the African Patriotic League, an organization closely related to the Harlem Labor Union, and apparently, its political whip. He is the Republican nominee for assemblyman on La-Guardia's ticket. Like his gaudier predecessor, he knows almost nothing of the history and purpose of the organized movement. He talks well, expressing standard opposition to organized white labor, which he says does not give colored labor a fair deal. During the strike at the Negro *Amsterdam News* in 1935, he agitated against the employees, declaring that the walkout was fostered by white men who desired to destroy Negro business.

Ira Kemp is black and long and lean. He plants his stepladder on the crowded corner and harps on white discrimination against colored people. He illustrates his pungent talk with items of discrimination against Negro painters, carpenters, and other skilled workers in the national trade unions. He paints a convincing picture of Harlem as a hotbed of bootleg labor, where skilled Negroes can work at their trade only by undercutting the white scale of wages. Individuals in the crowd shout: "Yeah, man, that's true. The white union gave me a hell of a run-around until I had to get out." Kemp waxes more eloquent with sympathetic responses. He declares that the AFL is notoriously indifferent to Negro workers, but that the CIO is more dangerous to the Negro because it is out to consolidate the existing labor standards by organizing the whites in the superior and the Negroes in the inferior positions. He declares that the Negro organizers of the national unions are traitors to their race because they are not agitating for more and better jobs for Negroes. They are being used by the white leaders to maintain the status quo. "Share the jobs!" Kemp shouts. "The Harlem Labor Union is fighting for more and better jobs for Negroes. Let the Negro organizers of the national unions demand bigger and better jobs for Negroes. The Negro Labor Committee hands out a white and a black hand clasped on paper. Can black folks eat a white handshake?" "No, never!" roars the crowd. "Then tell 'em to share the jobs," Kemp shouts back.

Naturally the racial Harlem Labor Union finds itself in sharp conflict with the Negro Labor Committee. Further complicating the picture is the CIO, the launching of which marked the start of a fairly successful drive to organize clerks of all kinds and other workers as well in Harlem. The Negro Labor Committee has endorsed the CIO, but some unions which support the Committee remain loyal to the AFL, which has a conservative Negro following. Thus Harlem has become the theater of a three-sided labor battle. It is a battle that is waged with an incessant distribution of handbills—each side accusing the other of racketeering, fooling the workers, selling out to the employers—dual and triple picketing and stepladder propaganda. Meanwhile the white business man takes advantage of the situation and plays one side against the other, and the little colored business man, up to now immune, stands outside the arena quizzically watching developments. One day the Harlem Labor Union pickets a store; the proprietor recognizes the union and employs colored clerks signed up with it. A few days later the CIO, supported by the Negro Labor Committee, signs up some of the clerks and pickets the same store. A huge placard in the window advises the Harlem housewife to buy there because the store has signed a contract with the Harlem Labor Union.

At the headquarters of the Negro Labor Committee I saw Frank Crosswaith,[36] the chairman, busy conferring with Negro organizers from the Painters' Union, the Retail Grocery and Dairy Stores Union and the Laundry Workers' Union. They were all earnest, alert men, fully aware of the vast new field the CIO has opened up to labor and of its benefit to Negro workers if they take advantage of it. Crosswaith is a nervous, intellectual type. I have heard him disposed of in conversation as a lover of roses. I observed a lovely rose in his buttonhole, which he keeps fresh by sticking it in a tiny vial neatly attached under the lapel of his coat. He showed me the little outfit and explained that he had always been a natural lover of roses and wore one every day. And he did not mind if some people considered it an affectation in a labor leader. He has been a member of the Socialist party for more than twenty-four years, has studied at the Rand School of Social Science, has been a lecturer member of the Trade Union Committee for Organizing Negroes, organizer for the Elevator Operators' Union and the Pullman Porters' Union, and is now organizer for the International Ladies Garment Workers.

Crosswaith admitted that labor conditions were still bad among Negroes in Harlem and that the Harlem Labor Union stood on tenable enough ground when it demanded more and better jobs for Negroes in the Negro community. He also agreed that Negroes stood a better chance of obtaining and holding clerical positions in their own communities than in districts where they were strangers. But as a trade unionist and Socialist, believing in the need for the solidarity of labor, he was opposed to the Harlem Labor Union because it is an independent organization whose terms are easier than those of the national unions. Others imagine that since the independent union thrives on the patriotic sentiment of the community, they may win the good-will of the Negroes by dealing with it. On the whole, however, the leadership of the independent union has not gained the confidence of the serious members of the community, even though they may be dissatisfied with the national unions.

It rests with the Negro organizers to agitate for more and better positions for Negroes within the unions and to look out for their special interests. In other industrial areas besides Chicago and New York the colored communities are taking direct action to secure more and better jobs. White workers, themselves fighting grimly for more wages and fewer hours, cannot be expected to stop or turn aside for the colored workers. The latter will have to make the special fight which their special position demands. That fight does not stop with making Negroes members of national unions. It must be carried on to protect them, once they are in the unions, against the intrigues of reactionary white workers and Machiavellian employers. Only in this way will Negroes in time gain confidence in the labor movement.

Like the IWW in its great days, the CIO is reaching down to the mass of Negro workers which the AFL always ignored. But there are many potential Harlem Labor Unions in the colored communities with the slogan, "Share the jobs!" They will have to be reckoned with. For the Negro group will not remain contented with the white workers in the superior and the colored worker in the inferior position throughout the ranks of labor. When Negro radicals and labor leaders realize this fact and act upon it, they will have contributed more to the advancement of the cause of labor and interracial relations than they ever do by the unctuous mouthing of slogans.

From *Nation,* vol. 145 (October 16, 1937), pp. 399–402.

ON ADAM CLAYTON POWELL, JR.: A RESPONSE

The exuberant young minister of the Abyssinian Baptist Church asserts that my article "Labor Steps Out in Harlem," which was published in the *Nation*, is a masterpiece of inaccuracy.[37] Yet he marshals no facts to refute the statements contained in that article, which dealt with three important labor organizations in Harlem, namely the Afro-American Federation of Labor, the Negro Labor Committee and the Harlem Labor Union, Inc. If there are glaring inaccuracies, as the reverend columnist maintains, I eagerly wait to be corrected by the responsible officials of the aforementioned organizations. Until then I stand by my article.

I know all about the Citizens' Committee and the dubious role of Adam Clayton Powell, Jr., who marched in Sufi's picket line after Sufi had denounced him from a stepladder in Seventh Avenue. I did mention the Citizens' League and Mr. Powell when I wrote for the *Nation* an article on the Harlem riot of March 19, 1935. But in my recent article I did not mention the Citizens' League because it is dead. Also I did not mention Sufi, who underwent a metamorphosis from Aframericanism to Orientalism. But I gave the credit due to his organization, whose spirit lives again in the Harlem Labor Union.

Powell refers to "his friend Kemp" who is "Republican nominee for Assemblyman." Now this friendly salute is not merely a journalistic euphemism. It is common local knowledge that Ira Kemp is a good friend of Adam Powell, Jr., and that Powell endorsed Kemp's independent labor movement and gave it his blessing from the pulpit of the Abyssinian Baptist Church, when he exhorted his congregation to support Ira Kemp.

Yet while supporting Kemp who is a rabid anti-Communist, the ineffable young preacher granted permission to a Communist group to use the Abyssinian church for a propaganda meeting. When the conservative trustees prevented the meeting, the vacillating young man tried to squirm out from under his agreement but the Communists impaled him on the cross he made for himself by staging a demonstration before the church, which remains one of the memorable events of Harlem. This incident illuminates the opportunistic, careerist character of the preacher–columnist—a man who flirts with reds on one hand and on the other supports red-baiters such as Ira Kemp.

I can proclaim the fact that I, Claude McKay, do not happen to be a "friend" of Ira Kemp. I have listened to him on the street corners. And of course, I have talked to him about his labor organization. But I told him very frankly that he could not fight the organized labor movement with an independent and exclusively Negro organization. I told him that if he were ambitious to become a labor leader he would have to change some of his ideas and tactics and seek affiliation with the national labor forces.

However I do have a profound sympathy for and faith in the inarticulate Negro worker that Ira Kemp represents. And I reiterate loudly and clearly that as long as thousands of depressed Negro workers remain discontented and outside of the organized labor movement, they are a challenge to and indictment of that movement.

Very ingeniously the cleric scribe seeks to tie me up with "Trotskyism" and Negro Nationalism. This do I think of Negro Nationalism in the United States. It is the brain child of the American Communists and the real Negro nationalists are the Communists. They have advocated the creation of a separate Negro state within the American nation, without taking into account the simple fact that if this country were ever to establish a Communist form of government, Negroes, according to Communist theory, would automatically become the most important political factor in any region where they are a majority. Therefore local autonomy for Negroes is necessary only under the present social set-up.[38]

But the Communists and Negro "thinkers" like the Rev. Adam Powell, Jr., would reject such autonomy as segregation. They refuse to face the fact of the actual status of Negroes in the American social system and promote instead the mirage of African nationalism for American Negroes.

It is shamefully inconsistent that the man who shepherds the largest flock of Negroes in the world in a church should decry the efforts of Negro communities to build themselves up socially and politically to the American standard of living by declaring that such aspiration is Nationalism.

No one has ever been asinine enough to image that all the Negroes in New York could find jobs in Harlem. No dealer, however chauvinistic, could advocate the driving out of white businessmen from the Negro community and in the same breath demand that the white employers should give Negroes better jobs. But any Negro leader who declares that Negroes should not demand better jobs in their community and organize their consumers' power and establish cooperatives for cheaper buying is a moron and a danger to the group. The intensive building up of Negro communities to standard levels would be beneficial to the entire nation and especially to the bigger white businessman.

But like so many of the loose-thinking would-be intellectuals of our group, Adam Powell, Jr., confuses nationalism with racialism. Bigoted leaders of the common folk such as Ira Kemp are not really nationalists but racialists. All suppressed minorities develop naturally some ego of racialism. However, because the Fascists and the Nazis have perverted the noble use of the word "race" to serve their ignoble imperialist ends, it has become fashionable for liberals and radicals to disparage "race." But race is a blanket word for the entire human species and cannot be easily discarded. One may challenge the so-called scientific divisions of the human race, but we cannot abolish the instinct and the reality of race.

In trying to label me a Trotskyite, the Rev. Powell, Jr., opportunistic "friend of Kemp," and booster of Crosswaith in the same breath, is merely playing some kind of game, which is not cricket, with his erstwhile Stalinist friends. It should be hardly necessary for me to state that I am neither Trotskyite nor Stalinist for I am not a Communist. But I will also say that I do have a high respect for Trotsky as a thinking man and none for Stalin.

Political acrobats like young Powell are quite exercised because I am intellectually independent and not specifically labeled with any "isms." Dr. Alain Locke in reviewing my career in *New Challenge* takes a similar attitude.[39] I do not expect such intellectual weaklings and turncoats to understand my mind. My faith in the cause of social justice and a new social order broadly based upon the dignity and democracy of labor has never wavered. But my intellect is not limited to the social interpretation of Marx and Lenin. It reaches beyond Voltaire and Mohammed and Jesus and finds its roots in the logic of the Greeks who actually used their brains to think, who approached social theories and problems with open minds; and from them extracted the genuine and rejected the spurious.

It would be expecting the impossible from the young student of theology who caters to the most fundamental form of Negro religion on Sunday that he should understand my type of mind.

"Claude McKay Versus Powell," New York *Amsterdam News* (November 6, 1937), p. 4.

NEGRO EXTINCTION OR SURVIVAL:
A REPLY TO GEORGE S. SCHUYLER

By describing me as "wallowing in the black Fascist trough" and ornamenting his column with similar phrases, George S. Schuyler brings into the field of Negro journalism the low, unbridled language of the barrack room and the soldier's mess.[40]

I am quite capable of replying to him in like language, for I also had semimilitary training as a policeman. But sometimes one of the unpleasant duties of a policeman is to arrest rude and boisterous soldiers who have run amuck. Therefore, I will not reply to Mr. Schuyler in his idiom, but mainly because I do sincerely believe that Negro life and manners must be reoriented and that one of the first steps in that direction should be the raising of the standard of Negro journalism.

There has been quite a lot of illogical Negro nonsense about an article on "Labor [Steps Out] in Harlem," which I wrote for the *Nation*. In that article I reviewed the labor situation as it exists in Harlem and gave an account of the three labor organizations which have dominated the situation.

There has been no challenge of the facts marshalled in my article. I got them straight before I wrote. But evidently certain individuals and would-be leaders did not like the slant of my article. They thought, perhaps, that they did not get enough space or praise and that some persons whom they disliked got too much.

I said that Harlem was the Hades of bootleg labor and I repeat that statement. Harlem is not only hell for black, but also for white labor. For example, there are apparently more plumbers' stores concentrated in the Harlem area than in any other section of New York City.

Yet it is in recent weeks only that these stores are being picketed to get their workers unionized. But there is another side to that picture. There are many colored plumbers in Harlem who are working clandestinely for less than the standard wages, because the plumbers' union accepts white men only.

A similar condition prevails among electrical workers. There are hundreds of electricians in Harlem doing bootleg work. The electricians' union bars Negroes. My article in the *Nation* dealt exclusively with labor in Harlem. Not with Negroes working elsewhere in New York City and who are organized in unions. Not with the Pullman porters and railroad waiters who work outside of Harlem.

Not with the cafeteria union, whose 1000 Negro members are working downtown. Anyone with eyes in his head who ferrets round Harlem will find hundreds of Negro painters, carpenters and plumbers and electricians working at bootleg jobs.

Harlem has been a neglected area for black as well as white labor. It was the neglect of Harlem which made possible the advent of leaders of the ignorant common folk, such as Sufi and Ira Kemp. Frank Crosswaith, chairman of the Negro Labor Committee, stated frankly to me that it was in 1935 only that he started active labor organizational work in Harlem.

Until then he was busy with labor organization elsewhere and as a Socialist lecturer throughout the United States.

Now this attacking me through my *Nation* article from covert white and overt black sources is significant. George S. Schuyler is not reviewing my article, but rather reopening the debate in which we participated over Station WEVD last spring. That debate was summarized in Schuyler's favor in the *Pittsburgh Courier,* obviously by Schuyler himself; printed with important items omitted in the *Amsterdam News;* and finally fully published in the *Jewish Frontier* for October, under the title, "American Negro Dilemma, Group Survival vs. Integration."

I think the suitable title should have been, "Negro Survival or Negro Extinction." It is illogical to pose the issue of the integration of American Negroes in American life. It would be logical to raise the question of integrating Hawaiians, Puerto Ricans, and Virgin Islanders in the American social system.

But American Negroes are an integral part of the American nation, even as the Irish, the Finns, the Italians, the Germans, the Jews and other groups are. The Negroes have a special status, which is below the general American level. That's all!

The issue between the Schuyler school of thought and myself is this: Does the Negro group desire to survive or to be exterminated? Schuyler in his debate really argued for the extermination of the Negro group. He maintained that "all schemes for racial organization of Negroes imply segregation and isolation."

Now I remember Schuyler as a journalist who collaborated on the *Messenger* under the able editorship of Randolph and Owen. I had thought of him as a black man who had great faith in the Negro people. I was not sure if I were not mistaken, because I had lived abroad for many years. To make sure I decided to consult the Schuyler dossier.

I was amazed to discover that almost every important point in my radio debate had been advocated much more forcibly by George Schuyler himself a few years ago. In the *Pittsburgh Courier* of February 14, 1931, George S. Schuyler broadcast a call for 5000 young Negroes to organize the Young Negroes' Cooperative League. Wrote Schuyler:

> One of the worst tragedies in the world is the individual trained to do a specific thing and not in a position to do it. Turn a machine gun on a crowd of red caps . . . and you would slaughter a score of Bachelors of Arts, Doctors of Law, Doctors of Medicine, Doctors of Dental Surgery. . . . I have devoted a great deal of time to the study of this problem. . . . We cannot depend upon philanthropy. . . .
>
> The white folks have enough to worry about. . . . We will get economic opportunity quicker by creating it than by waiting for Nordic philanthropists to hand it to us on a platter. . . .
>
> The Negro writer, artist, professional person—the intelligentsia owe it to the masses upon whom they live as does the flea upon the hound, to take the leadership and not permit the masses of Negroes to wander aimlessly and hopelessly in the mire of poverty and degradation. . . . The talented tenth must do this out of intelligent self-interest. . . .
>
> The Negro of education, especially the intellectual, has no business standing by with folded arms sneering cynically at his struggling brethren. . . . It is the duty of the intelligent Negro of today to make things better and more hopeful for the young Negroes of tomorrow. . . .
>
> We need a great campaign of mass education for the purpose of organizing the masses of Negroes. . . . Unless the Negro masses are able to organize their economic power effectively and intelligently, there will be no berths for the Negroes of education and culture. . . .

Schuyler had a generous response from young Negroes. He announced that he was going to England to study the cooperative movement there. He went to Europe and West Africa. He returned to America and did nothing for the thousands of Negroes whom he had incited to follow him.

Today he denounces his own brain child as black fascism. The man who once adjured Negro writers and artists to become social-minded now declares that Negro art is "race racketeering." He who exists upon Negro business (in his own words) "as does the flea upon the hound" now sneers at "those who talk a great deal about Negro business."

He who lampooned the NAACP in that nauseating satire, *Black No More*,[41] is now business manager of the *Crisis*.

Like a mad dog, he dashes here and there and bites everybody. He is the supreme advocate of Uncle Tom Do-Nothingness. Unconvincingly he declares for a mild "cooperation between white and colored people," a kind of diluted form of Urban Leaguism, without recognizing the fact that if co-operation between white and colored is to be effective and not merely charitable patronage, the Negro group must make special efforts to lift itself up to the white standard of living.

Schuyler's inept attempt to slander me merely discredits himself. As a traveler and writer I have submitted my record to examination in my autobiographical travel book, *A Long Way from Home*. In my book I have not been too proud to criticize myself. And I am not afraid to face criticism.

But ever since I began thinking independently I have been interested in the progressive labor movement and in socialism and communism. But I have never aligned myself with any political party. Why? Because I believe that the approach of the writer and artist to social problems is radically different from the approach of the politician.

George S. Schuyler went to Africa and learned nothing, but that there "slaves [exist] today, even as they do in America. . . . Slavery is the oldest African institution. . . . And African slavery was introduced into Europe not by Europeans, but by Africans."

I lived for over three years in Africa. And there I learned that it is possible for different groups of people to exist side by side in social competition without any group surrendering its soul and advocating its own extinction. Besides the lesser groups were three major groups, native Moors, Jews and Europeans, each group preserving its own unique identity.

Appropriately, Scribe Schuyler commended the young Pharisee Powell for his miserable meandering upon my article in the *Nation*. From ancient times the Scribes and Pharisees have worked closely together in deceiving the people. Today they have made a league

with death and a covenant with hell for the extermination of the
Negro group.

But where are the young Negroes who once responded so bravely
to Schuyler's call? Why don't they shout their denunciation of the
man who led them astray, this false prophet of the Yellow Peril
within the group, this falsifier of the truth, who vomits his filth upon
all those who disagree with him?

"McKay Says Schuyler Is Writing Nonsense," New York *Amsterdam News*
(November 20, 1937), p. 12.

*In both "Anti-Semitism and the Negro" and his "Reply to Ted
Poston," McKay denies that anti-Semitism existed in Harlem during
the Depression and warns that it should not be allowed to become
an issue. Whether McKay was right or whether he was merely deny-
ing the existence of a budding black anti-Semitism in hopes that it
would die an early natural death remains difficult to determine.*

ANTI-SEMITISM AND THE NEGRO

A series of meetings and articles airing the idea of anti-Semitism
among Negroes have agitated a wave of discussion in Harlem. I par-
ticipated in one of the meetings and from the handling of it, con-
cluded it was Communist-inspired. The audience was large and
colored, consisting of ordinary workers, relief workers, householders,
a few professional persons and students and a small sprinkling of
whites. The principal speakers were Negro intelligentsia and were
vague, unconvincing and apologetic about anti-Semitic sentiment
among Negroes. The intelligent audience put the pep in the meeting,
which the speakers lacked.

The discussion was initiated by speakers who had apparently
agreed upon a formula and obviously followed the Communist
"party line" and insisted that the greatest problem confronting the
Negro group was Fascism and anti-Semitism.

But the members of the audience thought differently: each re-
iterated that the problem of their group was the Negro problem.

They stressed the fact that the Negro group lived under Fascist rule in the South and a special regime in the North, that it was excluded from free participation in the industrial life of the nation and relegated to menial status, that it was intolerably circumscribed in the educational, political and social fields.

A young Jewish visitor contributed a thought to the discussion: she agreed that the Negro problem was bad but not as grave as anti-Semitism, because the Negro status was fixed and accepted by the group. This statement stirred up shouts of protest among the audience: some said the Negro was disabled by the white majority here precisely as the Jewish minority by the Hitler regime.

As to anti-Semitism among Negroes, I have consistently maintained that the evil does not exist and that it is a real danger for certain parties to seek to capitalize upon such an issue.

The first omen appeared in 1933, when Harlem Negroes started campaigning for clerical jobs under the leadership of an unusual man who called himself Sufi Abdul Hamid.

Previously in Chicago, the Sufi had labored with others in a similar campaign and succeeded in placing colored clerks in department, chain, and private stores there. In New York, he donned a white turban, red-and-blue cape and military belt, exhorted crowds from a stepladder and picketed Harlem stores.

Two main features of his platform were the stressing of racial solidarity and an anti-Communist stand. Several times he was arrested for disorderly conduct and also for fomenting race hatred between white and colored, but always he obtained an acquittal. He won national publicity (for which he was avid) when a clever reporter featured his movement as pro-Fascist and sensationally labeled him the Black Hitler.

The Sufi's propaganda made a special appeal to the large body of white-collar Harlemites who were unemployed at that time. Some were graduate students, who in normal times might have been absorbed as social workers by welfare organizations such as the Urban League or by the Negro colleges.[42]

Negro communities are unlike other American communities in many respects. And one of the most glaring is the discrimination practiced by white middlemen catering to the consumers of the communities. They have never employed colored youths in clerical positions in their establishments and, in this respect, Harlem, the largest Negro community in the world, is no exception. Under the Depression, the residents were notoriously apathetic. The Sufi's propaganda moved them, opened their eyes, pushed them forward to fight for jobs and better living conditions.

The movement gained momentum and some employers conceded the Negro's right to better jobs in the community. The Sufi encountered not only the opposition of whites, who denounced him as racist, fascist, and Black Hitler, but also blacks, who declared he was a trouble-maker, who wanted to drive the white people out of Harlem. He denied that he was pro-Nazi, emphasizing that he could not be an admirer of Hitler, who, if he hates Jews, despises Negroes, regarding the latter as less than human.

The Sufi's activities were arrested when he was enjoined from agitating on the ground that a labor organization could not be operated on the basis of race. Then, the Sufi turned from the unemployment struggle to the cult of mysticism, one of the most profitable enterprises in Harlem and which is far removed from the interests of the merchants and the attentions of the courts. Yet, when recently he died tragically, he was still branded with the stigma of Black Hitler.[43]

The majority of Harlem's merchants and landlords are Jewish, and perhaps a similar situation exists in all large black belts of America. If Harlem's middlemen were not Jews, they would be Anglo-Saxons or Germans or Irish or some other white group. But the Jews on the whole are among the more recent of the immigrant groups coming to America, who had to adjust themselves to existing conditions and fit into special avenues.

Negroes were among the oldest, most exploited and disadvantaged and neglected groups. The Jewish middlemen studied their needs as determined by their economic status and made special concessions, whereby Negroes could obtain goods upon easy terms, such as the installment plan, for example.

Social conditions must inevitably be bad for any segregated group, unable to climb above the last rung of the economic ladder. Except that the inhabitants are colored, Harlem is like any other abandoned slum district.

It is congested. Housing conditions are notoriously bad; the rents are too high compared to the earning capacity of the average Negro. Most families take in lodgers to eke out the rent. Many tenements are firetraps. Unemployment is general; petty crimes are prevalent; prostitution is open in all the blocks.

But the Jewish middlemen are not directly responsible for the deplorable conditions existing in Harlem or any other black belt. Such conditions are the heritage of the system of Negro slavery; they are the by-product of the policy of special economic discrimination and prejudice which the ruling white majority has perpetrated against the colored minority.

The nation as a whole is responsible, including many sycophantic Negro leaders who batten upon the misery of their group. No anti-Jewish demonstrations have ever occurred in Harlem. The only anti-white demonstrations on record were those which were directed against the Italian middlemen, during the war in Ethiopia.

To me the relationship between Negroes and Jewish middlemen is similar to that of the slum dwellers of the East Side, which has been so eloquently described in [Michael Gold's novel] *Jews without Money*. The sweatshop workers of the East Side had to organize and fight for better living and working conditions against the exploiters of their own group.

So likewise the Negro group must organize as workers, consumers and tenants to win concessions, which will improve their economic status. For the health of the Negro and the whole nation, the Augean stables of the black ghettoes must be cleaned.

Nothing constructive can be gained by any attempt to identify the Negro group with anti-Semitism and thus link it to the Nazi-Fascist movement. There are signs pointing in that direction. At the height of the Sufi activities, there was an organization known as Jewish Minute Men, which started investigating anti-Semitism in Harlem.

At present there is another organization known as the Anti-Defamation League which, I understand, is ferreting out anti-Semitic sentiments among Negroes.

Any such snooping seems to me a waste of time and money. Wherever they are in close contact with Negroes, as in Harlem, the Jews could contribute more to better human relationship by facing the real issue of the acute social and economic misery among the Negro group and helping to ameliorate conditions. Thus, they may set an example to the rest of white America, as they have in other social achievements.

Merely contributing to Negro charity cannot solve the problem, nor will the flattery of political stooges, who will betray their own group as well as those who place their confidence in them. The Negro group must be encouraged and permitted to organize as such and shoulder its social and political responsibilities like the Jewish, the Irish, the Italian and every other American group.

There are certain gangsters of opportunism who for political purposes are seeking to stir up and fan the latent primitive antagonisms and illogical prejudices of one group of people against the other.

Such vandals of the spirit of progress and tolerance are set to destroy all that still remains noble in the human race in its eternal struggle against the savage and the beast in man's nature. One is aware of the Fascist enemy by the stripes of the tiger; he does not dissimulate.

But the Communist hyena disguised as shepherd dog is the sinister enemy that works havoc in the sheepfold under cover of darkness. He is assiduous in unhappy Harlem, often prowling behind the scenes, ready to pounce upon every social issue and convert it into an empty slogan and seeking by any means to discredit the wary individuals and groups that keep him out.

"Everybody's Doing It: Anti-Semitic Propaganda Fails to Attract Negroes; Harlemites Face Problems of All Other Slum Dwellers," *New Leader* (May 20, 1939), pp. 5–6.

A REPLY TO TED POSTON'S REVIEW OF "HARLEM: NEGRO METROPOLIS"

Many intellectuals are iconoclasts and rebels against tradition. But when the noblest traditions of a great civilization come crumbling upon us in what we believe to be the wrong way, we are constrained to revise our ideas. And so even the most ordinary of traditions assumes an extraordinary importance, such as, for example, that of authors in general not replying to unfavorable reviews of their books. But as the *New Leader* has published the review of my book, *Harlem: Negro Metropolis,* as a feature about me, perhaps I may be permitted to air my reaction to the innovation.[44]

In the first place: in no part of my book have I ever hinted for economic segregation as helpful to the life of the Negro minority in the American commonwealth. What I do advocate is the greater social and cultural development of the sprawling, backward Negro community-breeding place of crime and disease, mumbo-jumbo jungle of cultists and occultists, paradise of policy players.

I advocate the uplifting of the Negro community to American standards—that encouragement and aid be given to the development of more community enterprises, that Negro workers be permitted to organize with or without white workers. And I believe that the cultivation and expansion of Negro communities will be beneficial not only to the Negro people but to the entire nation. Otherwise they will remain cesspools of poverty and iniquity and a menace to the American standard and conception of life.

The reviewer of my book in the *New Leader* is apparently pleased with my presentation of the Communist movement in Harlem since he apparently hates the Communists from personal motives.

Now I do not hate the Communists as such. It is the Communists' program and propaganda tactics that I combat. Because I consider them to be harmful not only to the racial group of which I am a member, but to humanity as a whole to which I also belong. But I do realize that the Communists manipulate real issues to promote their propaganda. In my racial group they thrive upon the economic barriers with resultant poverty and misery, social discrimination and degradation, and the insults that people of dark complexion descended from the African race must endure.

I don't believe that one can effectively fight Communist propaganda just by hunting down Communists and crying, "Here they are fixed in high or low or just ordinary working-class places." I believe that Communist or Fascist persons have a human right to live and work if they can find any. If Communists are barred from lucrative employment in the labor world as Negroes are barred, it is natural that both will find common ground upon which they may meet. I advocate the greater development of Negro communities by Negroes themselves, precisely because that is one way of combating the Communists.

I am not, as your reviewer asserts, antiwhite, any more than perhaps Jews are anti-German. Intelligent Jews cooperate with liberal German exiles from Nazi Germany, but not with German Nazis and Russian Communists who agreed to sell them out to Nazi Germany. And certainly the Jews will not give up their rights to think and plan for themselves as a group of people and criticize even their best friends among the Gentiles.

Similarly, I hold that Negroes should think for themselves as a minority group in the adjustment of their group life to the white world. And I have quoted Mr. Philip Randolph, the outstanding Negro intellectual and labor leader, who has declared that the Negro group must cooperate, but only with other American groups.

Nobody who has carefully read my book with an open mind would say that I was antiwhite, whatever that ironical charge may mean to a Negro when (as was the case of your reviewer) it is made by another Negro! Dorothy Canfield, reviewing *Harlem: Negro Metropolis* in the Book-of-the-Month Club News, says of the author: "He neither accuses white people nor pities Negroes." [45] But I am not resentful of your reviewer's statement, for ideas seduce me so that I am more interested in the fact that the enormous disparity between the colored and the white world is such that only a member of the Negro group can inform, if he cannot convince, the white that another member is "antiwhite."

The Negro Labor Committee of Harlem cannot be compared with the United Hebrew Trades, which was created to protect the interests of Jewish workers in the world of labor. The Negro Labor Committee is more like an arbitration board. I have stated its aims in my book, which are mainly to adjust differences between white trade unionists and Negro workers. The average Harlemite is hardly aware of its existence, because the Harlem Labor Union dominates the scene. Once Mr. Crosswaith, the Chairman of the Socialist Negro Labor Committee, and I were discussing the merits of the independent Harlem Labor Union in the presence of Mr. Edward K. Welsh,[46] a member of the Negro Labor Committee. I pointed out that although the independent union did not operate in the tradition of the best trade-union standards, it was getting jobs for many Negroes in Harlem's stores. Mr. Crosswaith said: "But what's a job —a mere job! I'm interested in Negroes getting a trade-union job at trade-union wages." This was a praiseworthy statement, only it was made at a time when thousands of Negroes wish that they had WPA jobs at less than trade-union wages and others are on relief!

The *New Leader* should ask its reviewer to retract the statement: "McKay declares that he (Sufi) was not anti-Semitic, but only 'anti-Jewish.' " It is a lie. No such statement appears in any passage of my book, and the other vicious, almost unprintable words attributed to the Sufi should not have been published in a reputable newspaper like the *New Leader* unless they were verified. The Sufi always denied that he was anti-Semitic or anti-Jewish. The New York courts acquitted him of the charges of anti-Jewish propaganda; the police declared that they never heard him make statements against the Jews as such.

Any casual observer can verify that there is no anti-Semitism among the Negro masses of Harlem. It perhaps exists in the imagination only of irresponsible intellectuals who may be interested in some form of personal racketeering.

Anti-Semitism is a disease of Europe and white Christianity. And Afro-American victims of the fiery cross must not be dragged into the vortex of anti-Semitism. There is confusion enough in Harlem. And my book and its reviewer bear witness to that fact. In this crisis of civilization, Negroes stand sorely in need of inner strength and resolution to face the test of American Democracy.

"Claude McKay Replies to Poston on Solution of Negro Problems," *New Leader* (December 7, 1940), p. 5.

THE BUSINESS OF NUMBERS

The following selection is excerpted from McKay's last book, Harlem: Negro Metropolis. *McKay's chapters in this book on Father Divine, Sufi Abdul Hamid, and other Harlem folk leaders and institutions, such as the numbers game, will make it a valuable sourcebook for a long time to come.*

Playing numbers is the most flourishing clandestine industry in Harlem. It is the first and foremost of the rackets and the oldest. Exciting the masses' imagination to easy "hits" by the placement of tiny stakes with glittering quick returns, it squeezes Harlem in its powerful grip. To the Negro operators it is not so enormously profitable today as in its halcyon period, when its foundations were laid and it spread with impunity, not fearing white competitors and the action of the law. At that time the operators ("kings" and "queens" as they were called) each had a turnover of a quarter of a million dollars yearly. But after a span of unbelievably fabulous, gold-years, the law of the land at last became aware of them and

Federal and Municipal investigations compelled well-known operators to retire to private, comfortable and even luxurious lives. Through fear or careless management the business of some slipped from their hands and they were reduced to penury. And others were driven from the field by white overlords.

Through all the changes Harlemites have played the game increasingly and apparently will as long as Harlem exists. Numbers is a people's game, a community pastime in which old and young, literate and illiterate, the neediest folk and the well-to-do all participate. Harlemites seem altogether lacking in comprehension of the moral attitude of the white world towards its beloved racket.

In its early years these whites in and around Harlem who were aware of the game were tolerantly amused, and contemptuously called it "the nigger pool," or "nigger pennies"! "Numbers" was the only game on which a penny could be put up as a wager. But a lucky penny makes six dollars for the player, minus the small percentage for the collector who places the bet. The white world never imagined that the pennies of Harlem's humble folks were creating fortunes of thousands of dollars and "kings" and "queens" in Harlem.

But suddenly in 1928 the nation became aware of the state of affairs when a wealthy Harlem Negro, Caspar Holstein, was kidnaped and held for $50,000 ransom. Holstein was considered to be worth half a million dollars. He was outstanding and upstanding in the community. He operated the Turf Club, which was the rendezvous of Harlem's fastest set. He owned the premises. Prominent in Negro Elkdom, he was exalted ruler of one of the best lodges. He was known as Harlem's philanthropist—the only one! He donated money to Negro colleges and charitable institutions. He provided scholarships for brilliant Negro students who were too poor to enter high school and college. Through his club he tided needy individuals and families over difficult times. And although he used his personal income, he did not attach his name to such gifts.

There was also an artistic side to Holstein's extraordinary activity. He was *persona grata* among Harlem's elite. And he gave pecuniary assistance to struggling and aspiring writers and artists. In collaboration with the Negro magazine *Opportunity,* he set up a fund for literary prizes. He did not exclude white organizations from his generosity and thus he contributed donations to the League for Mutual Aid. Holstein was born in the Virgin Islands and when the island of St. Thomas was devastated by an earthquake, he gave a large sum of money, organized relief, shipped food and clothing to the victims, and lumber and skilled workmen to rebuild the houses.

Locally Holstein dealt in real estate, but everybody was aware of his real business as a race-track broker and a numbers banker. He was one of the big six among the numbers bankers. He was liked, he was respected, he was trusted. Sometimes faced with the payment of unusually large sums to winners, some numbers bankers defaulted and fled Harlem. But Holstein was renowned for his reliability. He paid fully the heaviest winnings. His fame spread and his business increased.

The kidnaping occurred on the night of September 21, when Holstein was leaving a friend's house in 146th Street. A white man approached, flashed a detective badge and said that Holstein was wanted at police headquarters in Harlem. Holstein replied that he would go willingly, although he knew of no reason why the police should want him. Another white man came up and between them they walked Holstein to a waiting car. In the car a third accomplice was sitting beside the chauffeur. All were white. Holstein was roughly shoved in. The car started, but instead of turning south toward the police station, it headed north to the Bronx. Aware then that he was tricked, Holstein struggled with his captors. They covered him with their guns, overpowered and blindfolded him and drove to a hideout in the Bronx.

The gangsters had reasoned that Holstein, carrying on an illegal business, was just another gangster who would gladly toss them a large sum and hush up the affair. But Holstein enjoyed being munificent voluntarily; otherwise he was a very stubborn man. He insisted that his property was in collateral and that he did not possess any considerable amount of negotiable funds. Ascertaining that Holstein dealt regularly with the Chelsea bank in Harlem, the kidnapers telephoned there to ask if Holstein's check would be honored for a large sum. But already the bank was notified that Holstein had disappeared in a suspicious manner, and it gave a noncommittal reply. Holstein's close associates had telephoned the bank. They were worried by his absence even for a short while, without any of them being informed of where he was. For his affairs demanded his constant personal attention.

Soon Harlem was agitated by the rumor of Holstein's kidnaping. Some thought that rival numbers bankers had had him "taken for a ride." But a message was received at the Turf Club demanding a payment of $50,000 for his release. The police started hot on the trail. The Negro sergeant (now Lieutenant Battles) was then the glamor boy of the police in the eyes of Harlemites, at a time when Negroes on the police force were a rarity and none was an officer. Battles was a friend of the kidnaped man and knew the places in which the right information could be picked up. A bootleg basement spot in 125th Street yielded the clue.

It put the police on the trail of one Michael Bernstein, a beer runner of the Bronx. Scenting the police on their heels, the kidnapers released Holstein on the fourth day of his detention. But upon his return to Harlem, Holstein pretended that he did not know who were his kidnapers or where he had been held. He said that he was blindfolded when he was taken and could not identify his captors or his environment. The police intensified their activity and within a few hours Michael Bernstein and his accomplices, Peter Donohoe, Anthony Dagustino and Moe Schubert were apprehended. But in court Holstein still refused to identify the men. His attitude was evasive. He admitted that he had been beaten and tortured to reveal the extent of his bank account, but said he had not been permitted to see his captors. Holstein's reticence fed the gossip that his kidnaping was perhaps a hoax engineered by himself.

But he was not the type of man who would foolishly give his clandestine business a sensational publicity which finally helped to ruin it. Always he was extremely reserved about his affairs. Had he desired, he might have allowed his vanity to feed and inflate itself upon his charitable acts, but many of his large gifts were covered under anonymity. Often when he gave donations under his name to respectable institutions he suggested that it should not be published, because he was averse to placing such institutions in a compromising position. Many "innocents" among the respectable of Harlem were quite unaware of his real business affiliations. Although he was one of the fabulous six of Harlem's numbers operators, he never paraded his prosperity in the flashy big-shot-of-Harlem way of the "kings" and "queens." He was very conservative in his appearance and his habits. He dressed quietly, like a dignified broker, and abstained from drinking liquor and smoking. To obtain his release, he made a deal (which was eventually confirmed) not to squeal on his kidnapers.

The Holstein case hit the front page and won national notoriety. It was the first time a wealthy Negro was kidnaped and held for ransom. It made the world aware of another phase of Harlem. For ten years Harlem was nationally advertised as the headquarters of the Garvey Black-Star-Back-To-Africa movement. And carried forward by the impetus of the ascendant literary and artistic bohemianism of New York, the Negro renaissance spurt of the latter nineteen twenties had stimulated national interest in the creative possibilities of Harlem. But Holstein's kidnaping flashed the searchlight on a Harlem underworld, different from the drab ugly tenements nauseating with odors of fried pork chops and rot-gut gin. This was an underworld comparable within its dimensions to the dazzling dynamic underworld of the whites, a world in which the shrewd enterprising members of the Negro minority chiseled out a way to social superiority by the exploitation of the potentialities of their own people. That "nigger-pool" was not such a contemptible thing after all. And it was destined amazingly to stimulate the speculative propensities of the Negroes and establish itself as the new game of the white and black masses of all the United States.

And now others besides the big racket monopolists of the white underworld discovered an interest in the Harlem game. Federal agents ferreted out information about the "kings" and "queens" of the black masses, who paid no income taxes. And as they probed, they uncovered startling facts. The secret "nigger-pool" was no child's play. But, disarming as black laughter in Harlem, albeit loosely organized, it was a formidable parasitic growth within the social body of the blacks.

And the great black bottomless pool had spawned independent auxiliaries. The avid playing of numbers enormously multiplied the appetites of the credulous in the science of numerology. Harlem was set upon a perpetual hunt for lucky numbers. House numbers, car numbers, letters, telegrams, laundry, suits, shoes, hats, every conceivable object could carry a lucky number. Any casual thing might become unusual with the possibility of being endowed with a lucky number: a horse in the street, the first person you meet, an automobile accident, a fire, a fight, a butterfly fluttering on the air, a funeral, even a dog posing against a wall! And dreams! Harlem is haunted by numbers.

Dreaming of numbers is an inevitable condition of the blissful state of sleeping. And so the obsession of signs and portents in dreams as interpreted by numbers created a business for local numerologists. They compiled books of dreams interpreted by playing numbers. Dream books of numbers were published by Prince Ali, Madame Fu Futtam, Professor Konje, Red Witch, Moses Magical and many others. Such are the best sellers of Harlem.

"Hot" lucky numbers are peddled on the streets. Some are offered with a phial of oil or a box of incense to elude the curiosity of the police. But many are brazenly sold in a little piece of folded paper. And the occult chapels have multiplied and increased their following by interpreting dreams by numbers and evoking messages from the dead with numbers attached to the messages and by figuring out signs and portents by numbers.

The religious playing of numbers naturally increases the development of mysticism in Harlem. The numbers must be guessed and played at hazard. When such numbers do not win, the addicts of the game will readily resort to those psychic types of persons who profess to be mediums of numbers. It may be crudely manifested in Harlem, but this mystical abnegation is not a Negroid monopoly. It exists among the international gamblers of Monte Carlo as well as the *aficionados* of the Spanish lottery. In fact I have been amused in foreign parts by some gamblers taking me as a kind of fetish and touching my skin before placing a bet.

The early history of the founding and growth of the numbers industry in Harlem is unknown to the millions who ardently participate in the game today. It has a Mediterranean background and might parallel the story of a small smuggler in Spain or Sicily building himself up to great power by the active cooperation and admiration of the common people.

In the first decade of the Negroes' big trek to Harlem, 1910–1920, a few Puerto Ricans and Cubans joined them and established barber shops in the black belt. They had a large patronage, chiefly among the British West Indians, many of whom had worked in Cuba and Central and South America, before coming to the United States, and thus were familiar with Latin-American customs. Then the Spanish-American colony did not border on the Negro district as it does today, but was concentrated in the east nineties.

The numbers game had its first start in these Spanish barber shops. Originally it was known as *bolita* or *paquerita*. The British West Indians called it "numbers" and popularized it. It was introduced to Harlem by a Spaniard from Cataluña, who was nicknamed Catalan by the Spanish-speaking Harlemites. Catalan devised his system of playing the numbers from the financial figures of the Stock Exchange. Familiar as he must have been with the method of the Spanish lottery, this could not have been a difficult job. The playing number was deduced from the totals of domestic and foreign sales. Its computation was not mathematical. Figures were arbitrarily chosen and put together to make a unit of three. To the uninitiated it was an extremely puzzling thing; to the players who were given the key, it was simple. As the financial figures printed in the newspapers are exact, there could be no trickery.

The numbers game has gripped all of Harlem precisely because there is no obvious trickery in it. It is an open, simple and inexpensive game of chance. Any winner gets an enormously sweet profit. Who would not thrill to a Cinderella penny placed on a number, say 391, and bringing the player 6 dollars? Make it 10 cents and it is 60 dollars, if you win. And the average Harlemite reasons that he may as well invest a dime on a lucky number as he might in a glass of beer or a piece of candy.

Of course the operator of the numbers game is more fully insured against loss than the moguls who run the gambling Bank of Monte Carlo. For a thousand different numbers are played every day and only one can win. And there is only one chance in a thousand of a person winning. Yet not a day passes but somebody does win. The stakes may be small or big, more often small, but still that is a great incentive for everybody to play.

Catalan was the sole numbers operator in Harlem for many years. The barbers gathered up the numbers slips and the money for him and he hired a few collectors to pick up numbers here and there. Nobody knew the extent of his wealth. He was unassuming and lived modestly. Once he went to Spain and it was rumored that he purchased there a fine piece of property. But shortly after the ending of the World War he returned to Spain again to settle down.

Before leaving he made over his business in Harlem to a Cuban Negro named Messalino, who was his chief aide and confidant. Messalino was quite a different type of man. He was flashy, amiable, man-about-town. As lieutenant to Catalan, his flair for extravagance was checked by the latter's thriftiness and simplicity of living. But when Catalan made his exit, deeding to Messalino the Harlem field, the latter splashed forth gorgeously. He bought a big car and hired a chauffeur in uniform. He entertained lavishly. Catalan had checked accounts and paid winners from his small apartment. Messalino rented an office and installed clerks with adding machines and typewriters. He expanded the game, exciting community interest and making all Harlem numbers-minded. He was the first of the dazzling line of numbers kings.

With the speculative propensities of the simple people aroused, other Negroes became aware of the huge operating profits and

Messalino was challenged by rival numbers bankers. The post-war expansion of Harlem brought the considerable Puerto Rican colony to the border of the black belt. And new rival bankers sprang from their group. The common people became enchanted by lucky numbers and Harlem a huge factory humming with the alluring activity of the game.

The operation of the game became more complex with its hectic spread. An army of collectors was organized to solicit players. Over the collectors were controllers, who received the money with the slips, which they turned over to the bankers. Each collector was remunerated with 10% of monies collected. And from any client who played the lucky number he was entitled to 10% of his win. The controller's reward was 5% of the total sum turned over to the banker. A competent controller is a powerful asset in the setup and may have as many as 50 collectors in charge.

The chances of winning were increased by the combination plan of six ways of playing a number. No. 915 could be played thus:

915
519
159
195
591
951

A player might put six cents on this number, allotting one cent to each component.

The magnetism of the game was heightened by its illegitimate link to the Stock Exchange. Harlem folk thought that they too had a little part in the ramifications of the stock market. The widespread playing and the increase and rivalry of bankers had brought into existence a type known as the tipster. The tipster made it his business to discover the lucky number prior to the publication of the financial reports in the newspapers. This was done by establishing contact with minor employees of the Stock Exchange, who perhaps were not aware of the purpose for which the figures were used.

The tipster played the number himself and also informed a few confidential persons, who agreed to share their winnings with him. The tipster did not always receive full advance information, sometimes he could give only the first and second figures of the lucky number. At other times his lead was wrong, as the earlier Stock

Exchange reports were subject to correction before final publication. However, the tipster idea was a profitable one, and in the dizzying era of Prohibition the tipster was a mighty man in the numbers business. One ingenious Harlemite actually rigged up an office in the Wall Street district and was highly regarded as "the Negro with a office in Wall Street." He organized a syndicate to play his tips. The bankers were afraid of him, as his tips were generally good winners. Sometimes he played both ends against the middle by tipping off bankers and players. The informed bankers held in their collectors on such occasions and remunerated the tipster. Sometimes the method was employed to break the smaller competing bankers and run them out of the racket. In the hectic Harlem of the late nineteen twenties, "the Negro in Wall Street" became an affluent Harlemite. He purchased a yacht, upon which he played host to members of Harlem's smart set. His prosperous reign continued until the Seabury investigations of 1931, when the Stock Exchange discontinued the publication of the Clearing House reports from which the lucky numbers were computed.

The advent of Prohibition gave impetus to the growth of the numbers racket. As the widest-open bootleg area in New York, Harlem was a rich field for other rackets. From barber shops the numbers business spread to scores of cigar and candy stores, which were actually bootleg joints. Like the bootleg liquor business, the firmly established numbers game received the proper police protection as soon as the law caught up with it. Many of the Harlem police played the numbers regularly. And bankers and controllers paid handsomely for protection. They paid district captains and leaders who had powerful influence with the police and the courts.

In those days the collectors of slips had no fear of being arrested. If they were arrested, there were special lawyers to handle their cases and there were special numbers bondsmen who were well paid by the bankers to obtain bail for offenders. If the cases were too flagrant to be dismissed, the sentences invariably would be light. Arrested collectors used substitute names. When they were important officials of the game, the bankers provided real substitutes to be sentenced in their place. It was the bounden duty of the bankers to provide legal aid for their employees. If a banker shirked this responsibility, he would be boycotted by all collectors and his business ruined.

The Seabury investigation of 1931 turned the light and the heat on the operators of the game and their protectors. The "kings" and "queens" of Harlem were paraded before public opinion. But a few of the biggest ones eschewed the spotlight. Some of them, Cubans, Puerto Ricans and British West Indians, preferred a sea change instead and skipped to their respective islands. But many inside facts were extracted from those who faced inquiry.

One of the leading "queens" who testified was a Madam Stephanie Saint Clair, who later became the spouse of the Harlem labor and cult leader, Sufi Abdul Hamid. She revealed that the operators of the numbers game were often double-crossed by their "protectors." In spite of sums of money paid for their protection, collectors were regularly arrested to provide business for bondsmen and lawyers.

From then on Harlem's banker "kings" and "queens" were doomed to an agitated reign. For the white lords of racketeering decided to put in a controlling fist. They organized a syndicate to dominate the Negro operators. The big boss of the syndicate was Dutch Schultz. He summoned the Negro bankers to get into his syndicate on his terms or get out of the racket.

The small fry of the Negro bankers paid the tribute but the bigger ones resisted. Their motives for resisting were as much moral as financial. Curiously the Negro racketeers put the white gangsters in the class of unregenerate criminals. They felt that they who had a respectable enough status in the colored community could not join an association of white criminals! Some of these Negroes had amassed a fortune, enough to retire from the business. One man went into the garage and taxicab business. A Cuban returned home to buy an estate and enter politics. And a British West Indian went back to buy up an entire township of his island. One big "king" attempted to carry on an independent game. His collectors were beaten up by gangs. His best controller was scared out of Harlem. And one night the top of his car was shot away by machine guns when he was motoring in the Bronx. He gave up the fight.

The numbers game in Harlem now came under the undisputed control of the big white booze raiders. The game was efficiently organized. And it was more smoothly operated. The lucky number was taken from the Mutuel reports instead of the organs of the Stock Exchange. Thus the tipster was eliminated. There was no syndicate to break bankers, who disappeared when they could not pay off. But the winners were exceeding few compared to the golden harvest years of the reign of the Negro kings. And the éclat in the atmosphere, which formerly made Harlem hum like a beehive, went out of the game forever.

When Prohibition was delivered the *coup de grâce* in 1933, Harlem, the vast depot of bootleg, was eclipsed. The bottom fell out of the gigantic underworld business which Dutch Schultz and his cohorts had built up. And now instead of secondary importance the numbers game assumed the proportions of a major racket. The large corps of gangster employees had to be paid wages and politicians and officials their graft.

To meet expenses Dutch Schultz attempted to reduce the cost of operating the numbers game. He had established the extensive chain of Dutch Masters cigar stores in Harlem as fronts for the running of the numbers business. And under him the game had its widest expansion in other cities with thousands of whites participating. But in Harlem he depended exclusively upon colored controllers and collectors.

In an economy drive Dutch Schultz tried to get them to take a reduction on their percentages. The Negroes refused. Schultz tried to coerce them. They went on strike and paralyzed the playing of numbers in Harlem. They maintained that if colored bankers had paid the high rate for many years, they would not work for less under white bankers.

Dutch Schultz was powerless to take action against them. For in Harlem the numbers game is an intricately intimate transaction. Most people play with friends or relatives only. Sometimes a collector is a person out of work, who picks up numbers from his friends. The friends get others to play and so the person is helped collectively. When the controllers and collectors went on strike, Dutch Schultz attempted to replace them with white ones. But the whites couldn't make the machinery work. The numbers business was not so easy to handle as the booze business. Most collections are made in the privacy of the players' homes. And excepting bohemian and courtesan circles, colored folk are not comfortable with whites penetrating into their homes. The strikers were supported by the players.

Dutch Schultz found himself up against a formidable passive resistance. And his murderous gorillas were powerless to help him there. Finally he withdrew his demands and consented to the controllers and collectors operating on the old basis. But some of them did not return to work for the white syndicate. They had learned that Dutch Schultz was in reality not so mighty and were no longer afraid. It was the beginning of the end of Dutch Schultz's supremacy in Harlem. New Negro bankers started secret operations in their homes. Others withdrew from the syndicate. It disintegrated and when Dutch Schultz was assassinated in 1934, the numbers business in Harlem had already passed out of his control.

But the come-back of Negro bankers could not revive the glory of the "kings" and "queens" of Harlem. The phrase fell into disuse and "numbers bankers" or "racketeers" became current. The new crop of native operators did not do enough business to dazzle the world. The game had spread amazingly underground and developed into a clandestine national pastime. The invisible white syndicate now held the power and the secret of the gaudy "kings" and "queens."

But one unusual aspect of the illicit game is its siring of a legitimate respectable bantling. When Dutch Schultz horned into the numbers arena and the Negro operators went on strike, the business of the little storefronts run by the latter faced ruin. But many held on and increased their stocks of candy and cigars with hot dogs and soda drinks. The men left their wives or children to carry on while they hunted work elsewhere. The transformed places won the patronage of new clients. The owners were surprised to discover that they could successfully compete with whites who formerly monopolized such small businsses in Harlem. Today there are hundreds of such places, which do not need the numbers game to exist.

Caspar Holstein was one of those who quietly dropped out of the numbers racket when the national searchlight was trained on it. Aside from the kidnaping case, he had managed to keep out of the spotlight during the notorious period of the investigations. He stayed on in Harlem, using his assets to do other things. His real estate holdings had increased and he had acquired the Liberty Hall property of the Back-To-Africa movement, when it went bankrupt.

He gave much of his time to the social welfare of the Virgin Islands. From 1917 until 1931 the government of the islands was administered by the United States Navy. The people agitated for the return of civil government, which they had had under the Danish administration of the islands. Holstein had actively assisted the islanders in their efforts. An American Negro Commission was appointed to investigate and report on the islands in 1927. A civil governor, Paul M. Pearson, was appointed in 1931.

But the change from military to civil administration did not come up to native expectations. The new governor proved unpopular and a mass movement developed against his administration. An active participant in the movement, Holstein organized the Virgin Islanders here. He carried his crusade to the islands personally in 1935 and was wildly acclaimed by the population at the time of his visit. That year Governor Pearson was removed from his post.

For his aggressive part in Virgin Isles politics, Holstein drew the enmity of powerful politicians. Nemesis pursued him upon his return to New York. In his legitimate enterprises he had employed dummies, who now double-crossed him, involving litigation and heavy loss of property. His fine club became the scene of strange brawls and shootings and it was forced to close. He was under constant police surveillance and was arrested a few times, but could not be convicted. Finally in 1937 he was indicted as a numbers operator, although he had long since quit the racket. He received an indeterminate sentence and remained in prison for nearly a year.

Always a reserved person, even when his affairs projected him in the limelight, he is more withdrawn than ever since his release. Sometimes he may be seen entering his Turf Club, which is now deserted and unlit. Or he may be discovered sitting aloof in a café on Seventh Avenue, severely dignified and appearing as if he were in the wrong place, as he does not drink or smoke.

Perhaps he, more than anyone, is familiar with the small beginnings and the gigantic octopus growth of the numbers game in Harlem. But tight-lipped in retirement even as when he was big boss, he would be the last person to tell all he knows. Even if he likes one enough to loosen up a little, he is ever wary and delivers himself in generalities.

Said he: "When I was kidnaped and the police were hot on the trail of the gang, I overheard them debating one night whether they should turn me loose or bump me off without leaving a trace. They said it was no use making me promise to hold my tongue, for 'a nigger will always talk.' But one of them argued that if I didn't talk when I was tortured, then maybe I wouldn't to the police. He said maybe I was different and it would be plain stupid to bump me off and get nothing for it but a mess of trouble. So I was turned loose and I didn't talk."

From *Harlem: Negro Metropolis* (New York: E. P. Dutton and Co.), pp. 101–16. Reprinted with the permission of the publisher and Hope McKay Virtue.

In the three articles which follow, McKay gives expression to the ambivalence and irony with which Negroes viewed World War II. He also looks forward to the special role Negroes might play in the strengthening of democratic forces during and after the war.

NAZISM VS. DEMOCRACY: SOME HARLEM SOAPBOX OPINIONS

Last week in Harlem an Aframerican soap-boxer was hauled into court for pro-Nazi propaganda and anti-Semitic utterances and was remanded on bail of $1000. He was one of the many step-ladder personalities who agitate the common crowd on Lenox and Seventh Avenues, between 116th and 145th Streets, in New York City. These men sometimes put over an extraordinary performance in dissipating the somberness of Harlem with the gaiety of their quips.

It is interesting to listen to them and to hear remarks of individuals in the crowd. While not altogether pro-Nazi, they do gloat over the Nazis upsetting the international applecart, and they are not pro-British. Many of them declare that a Nazi victory might be better for the black people. It is not because they imagine the Nazis having any tenderness for black people. But they believe that a Nazi victory would stir the blacks from their present lethargy either to live or to die.

Often words such as these are tossed into the crowd: "The white folks don't care a damn about you." And the people argue, wondering how close the soap-boxers are to the truth. Is the nation as a whole interested in the mind of its black minority? We know that there is some official cognizance of it. After intensive propaganda, President Philip Randolph of the Pullman Porters decided last July to lead thousands of black workers to Washington and protest their exclusion from defense jobs. Whereupon President Roosevelt issued an executive order declaring that Negroes should not be barred from defense jobs.[47]

But Aframericans are aware that a presidential order or a governor's declaration does not prevent discrimination against them. They know that the blacks are not hired to any great degree. Every day brings tales of rejection of competent applicants. And they wonder among themselves whether official statements against racial discrimination in industry are designed for domestic or international effect.

Inevitably the Aframericans make comparisons between their status and that of the so-called non-Aryan peoples under the Nazi rule. They know, of course, that they have the freedom at least to let off steam on a Harlem sidewalk. But also they feel that they are permitted such liberty just as horses are allowed to neigh in a well-fenced paddock. If they are not subject to violence, it is because they are reduced to such abject docility.

Harlem's soap-boxers may be crude in their delivery, but their intelligence is sharp. When Marshal Pétain stated cryptically that the French democracy was fundamentally different from American democracy, a soap-boxer hooked it for the topic of his talk. And he informed the crowd that a black deputy from Martinique was included in the National Council set up at Vichy.[48] There are considerable groups of French, Spanish and Africans, besides the British West Indians in Harlem. And while the soap-boxer is frequently British West Indian and often American, he is sometimes Spanish or French.

It must be stated that the street-corner orators are generally supported in a decorous manner by the recognized black leaders and the national Negro newspapers. Negro leaders often refer to the "totalitarian South" and the "Fascist South." While the West Indian intellectual coterie is unstinted in its regular denunciation of British Imperialism. One of its leading spirits and president of the West Indian National Council, W. A. Domingo, was arrested and thrown into concentration camp in June, when he attempted to visit the island of Jamaica. The Jamaican Progressive League of New York and West Indian–American organizations immediately instituted agitation with petitions to the local government to procure his release. But they've had no success. Domingo is held on several counts, that his presence was likely to obstruct the British War effort. And this is one of them: "that he was likely to impede the speedy carrying out of the work of establishing United States naval and air bases in Jamaica." [49]

While the West Indians fight for a better life under British Imperialism, colored Americans carry on against American complacency. A. Philip Randolph and the Urban League emphasize the disparities in the industrial arena. The National Association for the

Advancement of Colored People is working on the issues of the status of black men in the Army and Navy and also in the British Forces. But all of this is only one struggle on the same front of social justice under democracy for the black race.

There are no indications that the black people are pro-Nazi. But there may be a dangerous feeling that life cannot be worse for them even if the Nazis should win. The blacks remember that the last World War against German Imperialism was fought "to make the world safe for Democracy." But during that war black soldiers were persecuted at home and abroad. They were goaded to riot in Texas and [13] of the ringleaders were hanged.[50] And immediately after the War was ended race riots flared (in 1919). Starting in the South, they spread to the big cities of Washington and Chicago.

Now this Second World War revolves around a moral issue which transcends that of the First: the Nazi ideal of the superiority of the German race and its destiny to rule the world. The black people are aware that their precarious status under democratic governments may be worsened if the Nazis should win. But, nonetheless, they must continue to fight for a better position under the democratic system. What craven souls they would be if they did not keep up the battle against the smug conscience of America! If they, so cruelly discriminated against, did not urge and push forward militantly to be among those who are fighting against the rule of hate.

When Aframericans denounce the "Fascist South," they stand on solid ground. For the medieval *sangre limpieza,* the blood test of the Nazis, is so rigidly applied in the South that not even the whitest colored individual can escape it. It is generally known that other features of Nazi racial decrees exist in the South. And although the nation may not be aware, Negro newspapers are full of stories of the harsh treatment, with resulting friction, under which drafted black men must serve in the South.

But the South is not the North. And although there are discriminatory practices in the North with rumblings of Fascist movements in recent years, the black people know that the differences between both sections are vast.

Here again comparison with Germany may be cited. In the later nineteen twenties, there were one or two German states in which the Nazis won the power, but so long as the national Government remained social-democratic, the Jews were not nationally persecuted. They could hope. But when the Nazis won national control in 1933, it was no longer a state or a party, but the entire nation organized against the Jews.

So likewise, even though the majority of black Americans live in the bitter South, as a people they can live in hope. But fight they must. In the North their soap-boxers can hold the street corners, their leaders can express their thoughts in print and demonstrate. Let us not forget that theirs is part of the nation's democratic struggle on the home front.

"Negroes Are Anti-Nazi, but Fight Anglo–U.S. Discrimination. Soap-Boxers in Harlem Typify Negro Resentments," *New Leader* (October 25, 1941). p. 4.

THE NEGRO IN THE FUTURE OF AMERICAN DEMOCRACY

Recently I attended a little meeting, which was sponsored by one of Harlem's earnest radicals. It was called for the purpose of discussing the problem of the Negro organizing along new lines. I had been under the impression that this would be a meeting of Negroes only, because the plan, as outlined to me, had emphasized the idea of the group organizing itself to achieve certain social and political ends.

However, I was surprised, not unpleasantly, to find a few white persons at the meeting and it was rather interesting that most of the important talking was done by an intelligent white radical. This person attached the highest importance to the idea of a new radical organization of Negroes along racial lines. Here was a white radical of broad outlook and keen intelligence advocating for Negroes a form of organization altogether different from that which the radical vanguard had hitherto followed in dealing with the Negro group.

The traditional idea of Socialists and Communists was that Negroes should think less as Negroes and more as workers, fighting in the common struggle of all workers: that Negroes should react to social conditions as a class, and with the working class in general, and not as a racial group.

After the white radical had finished explaining his point of view, a colored girl interrogated him. She possessed a keen mind, had been a sympathizer among the Communists and [had] visited the Soviet "Fatherland." She asked whether the new point of view was not contrary to the former radical approach to the Negro group, and if the old idea of the Negro participating in the workers' struggle upon an equal footing with his white brother should be scrapped or otherwise be regarded as a failure. The leader of the discussion explained that the question of social equality was not involved, but it was plain that the old radical attitude had proved a failure.

Now, it is a fact that the radical was expressing a point of view that is being discussed by other whites, liberals as well as conservatives. And certainly there must be some profound social reason for such an attitude on the part of alert social thinkers, contemplating the American scene and the Negro in the far background.

In my opinion, there are two main reasons for the new point of view. First, the failure of the experiment in International Socialism in Soviet Russia as the social salvation of exploited workers and oppressed peoples, with the resultant suppression of all free intellectual inquiry and artistic freedom. Second, the rise and spread of National Socialism in Europe, with its pseudo-scientific philosophy of Nordic superiority, ruthless persecution of so-called non-Nordic minorities and the Philistine regulation of intellectual and artistic pursuits.

Inevitably the two opposing forces on the continent of Europe are profoundly affecting the thought of social thinkers in America. Capitalist Democracy in Europe is beset by both systems. The orthodox Russian Communists had pledged their support of that Capitalist Democracy, whose destruction was once the first principle of their *raison d'être*. But it appears perfectly clear that the red word is not trusted by the directors of Democracy as such. A white lie is more to their liking than a red lie, and so they clearly demonstrated that if they must be nicked, they prefer to be nicked by Munich rather than by Moscow.

The problem of Europe is indeed frightening. And its most dreadful repercussion here is the vicious insidious propaganda, which is working to range social thinkers and the people into the opposing camps of Communism or Fascism. Thus the issue: Can Democracy be preserved and made to function with justice in these states?

As the stepchild to Democracy, the Negro is inevitably linked with this issue. And therefore it becomes obvious why he is receiving so much attention from all the political parties. For if the Democratic system must endure in this country, the Negro must perforce play a more positive and important part in it. As a group, Negroes will have to shoulder their share of the white man's burden, even though in so doing they shock the old South into a new attitude of life.

Alert, sensitive to the pulse of the national life as a whole, the white leaders and thinkers seem more aware of the potentialities of the Negro group than the Negroes themselves. They are also aware that the old-style Negro leadership cannot stand the test of these times. Shrewd political observers like Congressman Hamilton Fish, Arthur Krock of the *New York Times* and Dorothy Thompson of the *Herald Tribune* are concerned about the new Negro alignment. But there is no sign yet of a new national Negro leadership.

When the international crisis broke in 1914, the group possessed able spokesmen such as Dr. W. E. B. Du Bois, Booker T. Washington, and Monroe Trotter. And soon Marcus Garvey appeared on the scene to articulate the voice of the common blacks. Again, today Negroes are ripe for real leadership. But in the present crisis the group lacks a leading authoritative word. It has worthy outstanding men, of course. But we sorely need the broad outlook, the new spirit for these new times. Perhaps, it is just over the horizon.[51]

"Claude McKay Says," New York *Amsterdam News* (April 15, 1939), p. 11.

OUT OF THE WAR YEARS:
LINCOLN, APOSTLE OF A NEW AMERICA

Abe Lincoln's greatness as a man and as President has been glorified by the pregnant bigness of his time. In the eighteen fifties the United States needed a sterling leader as much as it did in the seventeen seventies. And the pivotal significance of Kansas and Nebraska in the struggle of free labor versus slave labor, with the abolitionist opposed to slavocrats and Horace Greeley, William Lloyd Garrison, John Brown, *Uncle Tom's Cabin* and Young Republicans, representing the militant new industrial society against the feudal system of Tory Democrats—all converged upon Abraham Lincoln to find national expression in his sane, balanced, soil-flavored voice.

Now Lincoln's eyes must have gazed far beyond the horizon into the expansion and future of the United States. And those eyes saw clearly that if this nation were dominated by the feudalism of the South, that the United States' arteries would harden and its expansion [would be] checked. And so Lincoln declared, in his speech of nomination for the Senate in 1858: "A house divided against itself cannot stand. This government cannot endure permanently half slave and half free."

Yet he disassociated himself from the impetuous John Brown and Horace Greeley and all those whose actions would have resulted in a split nation, leaving the South immersed and smug in its backward system. For Lincoln had glimpsed the glory of the United States moving forward as a single nation, subduing the Northwest and the Far West, with its ships ploughing the oceans. And as Lincoln's eyes saw more clearly he grew stronger in spirit and greater in stature. Perhaps it was the inner revelation, the hidden mysticism of the profound mind that urged him on to emerge as the great American apostle of the Industrial Revolution.

For in Lincoln's time the world after hundreds of years of relatively backward economic existence, was just on the threshold of the Age of Steam. Transport of men and materials was taking to steel rails and wheels. The spinning jenny, the power loom and the cotton gin had been invented. And factories were superseding handicraft systems, bringing a vast increase of cheap textiles to augment the wealth of the world and the progress of humanity.

At that epoch the slavocrats of the South with its impossible romantic attitude of life aspired to the leadership of the nation. Yet there were signs on every side that the burgeoning new age needed a new outlook, new blood, a new system of popular education, which the South did not possess and could not create. Then in 1860 Lincoln challenged the South and decreed the complete exclusion of slavery from the new territories. From compromise and tolerance Lincoln had moved out boldly at the opportune moment to take the leadership of the nation, and war between the North and the South was inevitable.

It was a bitter struggle and grim. But the North possessed the new ideas and weapons and the forces of progress were on its side. And released from its fetters the United States thundered ahead on steel rails from Maine to Florida, from New York to Chicago through Kansas to California. American steamships sailed the seven seas to China, Africa, India and Europe. The United States leaped forward and became the greatest industrial nation of the world.

We like to speak of Lincoln as the great Emancipator in thinking of the liberation of Negro slaves. But Lincoln was a much greater emancipator than that. It was the whole American nation he liberated to measure itself and take its stride as a leader in the general progress of the world. And Lincoln himself had no illusions about the situation, for he possessed the mind of a seer. Lincoln saw that the old South was hell-bent on secession and he knew that a separate Southern nation of slaves and slave-holders within the United States would be inimical to the interests of the entire nation, free whites as much as Negro slaves. And so in his first message to Congress he described the conflict as "a people's contest, a struggle for maintaining in the world that form and substance of government whose leading objective is to elevate the condition of man. . . ." And in his reply to Horace Greeley, who had attacked him on the issue of slavery, Lincoln said: "My paramount object in this struggle is to save the union and is not to save or destroy slavery."

It is not fashionable or perhaps wise in social thought to identify a nation and its people as one in their evolution. But it is obvious that nations, like plants and human beings, grow. And if development is thwarted they are dwarfed and overshadowed. And one nation's legitimate and natural expansion may be something quite different from another's ruthless aggression and exploitation. If the reactionary Southern states had won in the Civil War, this nation might have remained cramped and stagnant and backward as Czarist Russia. And so the grandeur of Abraham Lincoln is godlike as one sees him in his true perspective—a backwoodsman, self-educated, self-made, honest, but vacillating, a dreamer, a pioneer in overalls, epitomizing the spirit of the new America stepping out in the race among the nations of the industrial age.

Many of the loud-mouthed demagogues in high places in the eighteen fifties had no understanding of the real issues involved, just as many today do not, as the American nation faces another great crisis. But in my humble opinion America's stake in this war is greater than any nation's. The composition of the American population and its economy place this nation in a position of unalterable opposition to the Nazi idea of a "new order." It is interesting to imagine on Abraham Lincoln's birthday how he in sharp and clear phrases might have presented the basic fact of this plain truth to all of the American people, with the knowledge that idealism is like a castle in the air if it is not based on a solid foundation of social and political realism.

From the *New Leader* (February 13, 1943), p. 4.

Years before Frantz Fanon, McKay witnessed at firsthand the injustices of the French and Spanish colonial regimes in North Africa, and in the three articles which follow he points out not only the inevitability of colonial revolts, but the disastrous consequences to any democratic government which persists in a reactionary colonial policy.

NORTH AFRICA AND THE SPANISH CIVIL WAR

Returning from a recent trip abroad, where he had gone as a delegate to one of the literary pow-wows of the Popular Front, my colleague Langston Hughes brought me a letter of greeting, scrawled in bad French and English, which he had received from a young Moroccan.

This Moroccan I had befriended in his native land, using my wits to obtain a passport to enable him to travel in his own country.

At last he arrived in Paris and in a cafe there, he had probably mistaken Langston Hughes for a Moroccan. But he discovered that Mr. Hughes was an American Negro and also that he knew me, his American friend.

Mr. Hughes had also visited beleaguered Madrid and wrote excellent articles about the conditions prevailing there which were published in the Negro press. In none of those articles did I discover any significant reference to the native problem of North Africa and its relation to the Spanish Civil War. How many Americans are aware that the native North African problem is similar in some aspects to the Afro-American problem in the South?

The five-year revolt of the Moroccan warrior, Abdel-Krim, was actually one phase of the liberation movement of the Spanish people.[52] All during that campaign the voice of the Spanish people was loud in protest against the war in Morocco. The organized workers protested and also the middle-class organizations. Spanish women wailed that their men were being shipped for burial in the African cemetery.

Abdel-Krim would have won the independence of Spanish Morocco, if it were not for the intervention of the French.

The French Republic decided that it could not permit the existence of an independent native state contiguous to its Moroccan protectorate. Although there was no solidarity of purpose between the Spanish monarchists and the French republicans (especially in North Africa, where the lax and inefficient native policy of Spain, which had allowed Abdel-Krim to get away with his revolt, was much criticized by the French), the latter mobilized their war machinery to help the Spanish dictator, Primo de Rivera. Abdel-Krim was defeated by their allied forces and made a prisoner of the French.

Five years after the defeat of Abdel-Krim, the Spanish monarchy was overthrown: its blunders in Morocco were the main cause of the debacle. As soon as the republic was proclaimed, the Spanish labor organizations clamored for the abandonment of Spanish Morocco. They were supported by middle-class organizations, which passed resolutions advocating that the Spanish protectorate be granted its independence as soon as possible.

The Spanish workers, in regard to the status of Spanish Morocco, were even much more advanced than the native leaders themselves. After twenty years of protection, the native leaders did not consider the country ripe for independence.

So they sent a representative delegation to Madrid, petitioning the government of the young republic for reforms in the native system of administration. The petition was mild, asking for a free native press, freedom of movement for natives, native voice in fiscal matters, free native councils and higher education. That petition was remarkable for this phrase, roughly translated: "We natives consider ourselves as pupils and the Republic our teacher. . . ."

The native leaders had the support of the advanced Spanish workers in Morocco. In Madrid, the delegation was enthusiastically received by the population, photographed with the President of the Republic and other members of the government, feted with honors and promised their demands.

But when the delegation returned to Morocco, conditions became worse for the natives. Instead of more freedom of movement, passport regulations became more stringent. Things tightened up in Tetuán: it was no longer the clearing house for nationalist thought in Morocco. The natives murmured that the young Spanish Republic had come under the thumb of the reactionary elements of the old French Republic.

It is true that the Spanish peseta had been pegged by a large loan from the Bank of France.

If the first Spanish Republican government had reacted intelligently to the healthy, instinctive feeling of the Spanish people and abandoned Morocco, the face of Europe would be vastly different from what it is today.

Had the African cemetery been abandoned, imperialistic France and Fascist Italy would inevitably have clashed over it, but the hopeful new Spain might have been saved, even as old Spain saved itself from the World War. Better that the imperialistic French Republic and Fascist Italy had battled out their affair then, as they must in the future.

There would have been no Fascist Italy left to weld the Rome–Berlin axis and finally force through the Munich agreement.

By holding down its Moroccan colony, the Spanish Republic gambled dangerously with its own existence and lost.

The protectorate was easy of access to all the reactionary Spanish plotters and foreign agents. With the well-trained Foreign Legion ready for any reactionary adventure, Morocco was well cast for its new role in the Spanish tragedy.

The natives were disillusioned about the new Republic. Besides the harsh measures imposed, Jesuit propagandists had worked on their credulous minds, telling them that radical mobs would loot and burn their mosques as they had the churches in Spain. At last, when the executioner * of the Spanish Republic was ready, he struck from Morocco.

The nationalist movements of North Africa have progressed amazingly within the last five years. Controlling North Africa, France has felt the full pull of the movements. In North Africa, nationalism expresses itself differently from nationalism in Egypt or Ireland. Significantly, all the young nationalist leaders of North Africa were Socialists or Radical Socialists, many of them educated in France, and some being members of left parties there.

But when the French Popular Front was obliged to face the issue of defending the social rights and aspirations of the native people against French colonial aggression, precisely as the Spanish Republican government had done, it took the side of reaction.

In their wild efforts to cover up the shame, the Popular Front

* General Francisco Franco. [Ed.]

press and its apologists proclaim that the nationalists have been inspired by Fascist agents and that they are Fascist-minded.

Columnist Dorothy Thompson [53] writes authoritatively: "North Africa is in ferment, the populations stirred up by Fascist agitation." But Anne O'Hare McCormick,[54] who has visited North Africa and the Near East, is nearer the truth when she writes: "It is too easy to imagine that this fever inflaming Arabs . . . is merely the effort of Fascist propaganda. It is a self-starting movement of revolt against foreign rule."

When Soviet Russia was on friendlier terms with Fascist Italy than with the democracies, the nationalist movements were still agitating in North Africa! It was not a German Fuehrer nor an Italian Duce who stirred the feelings of the North Africans. It was the Egyptian leader Zaglul Pasha.[55]

North Africa, like the rest of the Moslem world, was looking to Egypt for leadership. For Kemal Ataturk [56] had abolished the caliphate and was striving to detach Turkey from Islamic internationalism—chiefly because the Arabs had turned against Turkey during the World War and fought on the side of the Allies.

The North Africans detest Fascist Italy. Fresh in their minds are the ruthless measures Italy employed in its conquest of Tripoli. In one instance, the entire Senussi tribe was bombed out of their fertile region, one of the finest in the country, and men, women and children were driven into the desert to die. Then Italian farmers were sent in to take possession.

I was in North Africa during the native boycott of Italian business which grew out of this incident, a boycott in which I participated. It started in Egypt and spread all through North Africa.

Italian farmers could not obtain native labor. Italian groceries and cafes depending on native patronage had to be liquidated. Perhaps it was the effect of that boycott more than anything which prompted Mussolini to pretend that he is a friend of Islam.

To the native North African mind, Fascism is synonymous with hooliganism and sheer bestial cruelty. Italy was not invited to participate in the international government of Tangier which was set up in 1924, and there started a systematic campaign of terrorism which everybody, natives and foreigners alike, agreed was Italian.

Rowdy Italian elements stirred up incidents with which the police were powerless to cope, as Italians did not come under the international regulations. Tangier was cowed by hooligans, and brawls and robberies were so frequent that wealthy natives and foreigners were afraid to walk the streets after dark.

Finally Italy was given a seat in the international government and immediately the hooliganism ceased.

One of the most significant items in the recent Italian agitation over Tunis was the report that the native population was demonstrating against Italy.

The North Africans are not fools. They have no desire to exchange the ruthless dictatorship of democracy for the more ruthless dictatorship of Fascism.

Yet in spite of the confused issues, which are deliberately and doubly confused by the Popular Front propagandists, the native struggle for social justice and national freedom must continue.

Spanish reaction first strengthened itself in Morocco by forcing the young Republic to betray the native workers in the colony before it began its offensive against the Spanish workers at home.

In exactly the same manner, French reaction fortified itself in North Africa under Blum when it compelled the Popular Front to liquidate its native sections.

And as soon as it felt strong enough and safe with Daladier, it challenged the workers in France.

The lesson is plain.

"Native Liberation Might Have Stopped the Franco Revolt," *New Leader* (February 18, 1939), pp. 2, 5.

NORTH AFRICAN TRIANGLE

As soon as you reach North Africa, if your eyes and perceptions are good, you are aware of the struggle for a living among three clearly defined groups—Christian, Jew, Moslem. But you also observe that the struggle has reached a certain balance, with each group held within its limits.

The Moslem natives form the largest group, but in the modern social and political set-up in North Africa they have been pushed down to the bottom. They are in the position of a subject people, with no voice in the affairs of state. The Europeans declare that the Moslems are naturally medieval-minded and backward, that they are in their present position because they refused to accept the French civil code, and that the real reason for their refusal was their polygamy. But to accept the French civil code a Moslem would have to abjure not only polygamy but the main tenets of his religion. Moreover, about three-fourths of the North African native population consists of peasants, shepherds, and hired workers so poverty-stricken that a man can barely afford one wife. Even the new middle class of native functionaries created by the French, who have been educated in the Franco-Arab schools, cannot maintain more than one wife decently. The Moslem wife is an expensive luxury. She can do no outside work to help her husband as the Christian and Jewish women can, and when the Moslem marries he must pay a good sum, the amount dependent on his means, to the parents of the bride. Only the very wealthy—pashas, caids, cadis, and other notables—can indulge in polygamy.

It is not polygamy that hinders the North African native from adopting the French civil code but his whole way of life, which is an integral, perhaps the most important, part of his religion. In a Moslem country you are born a Moslem and remain one all your life even if you never enter a mosque. Your birth and marriage, divorce and death are recorded under Koranic law. Your property is regulated according to the laws of the Koran. (Moslems think that their own code is superior to the French in some respects: for example, when a Moslem woman marries, she retains control over her own property, as the Frenchwoman does not.)

The Moslems have remained imprisoned behind the ancient social-economic-religious system of Islam. And though they groan and complain of oppression in their medieval prison, they seem to prefer it to the modern way of life. Banking is the mainstay of modern society, but no true Moslem can operate a bank and charge interest. He will, however, place his money in a Christian or Jewish bank and accept the interest paid on it. In North Africa the French have built new towns of striking neo-Moorish architecture. But Moslems do not live in them, although some of the wealthy ones own houses in the new towns. It is not merely that houses in the inaccessible and mysterious native quarters are cheaper; custom also holds the Moslems in their antique setting. Because the Moslem wife, except on special occasions, cannot go outdoors, she practically lives on the roof top. There in the daytime she lolls unveiled and visits with other women across the roofs. During those hours no man may go up to the roof or even look up from the street.

All Jews in North Africa have the status of Europeans. Under the French regime they have been so rapidly Europeanized—the

Cremieux decrees conferred French citizenship on all Algerian Jews as far back as 1870—that their way of life is closer to the European pattern than is that of many Spanish and Portuguese immigrants. Jews throughout North Africa wear only European clothes. Their schooling is so thoroughly European that many of the younger generation do not know the Arabic language. No casual observer can tell them from the Spanish and French.

The French writer Henry de Montherlant said some years ago that Jews were the torch-bearers of European civilization in North Africa. Certainly they are the modern ferment in North African life. As a group they appear to be more in harmony with their environment than other Europeans. No one knows how many Jews there are in Algeria since they have not been counted as such for many generations, but it is known that they outnumber the French and other Europeans, as they do in Tunisia and Morocco.

In competition with Europeans, the Jews have pushed steadily ahead. They have in their favor a close-knit community life and a knowledge of Arabic. Also they have an understanding of the character of the Moslems, which the French apparently lack. And because the Jews know the needs of the Moslems and are familiar with their way of trading, the Moslems prefer to trade with the Jews. The Jews are the middlemen, par excellence, of North Africa. With the desperate crisis of French finance at the beginning of the nineteen thirties, the competition between Frenchmen and Jews became acute.

Since North African production is in the hands of big business using cheap native labor, it undersold on the French market the production of the French peasantry. Governments rose and fell in Paris, but all agreed that Frenchmen must be protected from the threat of cheap African importations. A cartel plan was set up for the French colonies, and North Africa was required to supply commodities to France on the quota system. Goods piled up in the warehouses of Algeria, Tunisia, and Morocco—wheat and barley corn and wine.

In their predicament the North African French vented their wrath on the left parties in the French parliament and on the Jews. Many openly declared that the mass naturalization of Jews in Algeria had been a capital mistake and that a quota system should be applied to Jews in the professions.

In North Africa the French mentality is conservative to the point of reaction. A visitor to the colonies gets the impression that it is there that the powerful rightist tendency in the French nation is most securely entrenched. The spirit of free criticism which used to exert its influence over the press, the theater, and all intellectual life in France has been absent. In extenuation of the French colonists it should be said that as rulers and large-scale exploiters they must constantly consider the native population, whose dominant class has a feudal outlook on life and holds ideas incomprehensible to the modern mind.

During the economic crisis of the nineteen thirties the native North Africans were stirred for the first time by agitation for social reform. This was not an independence movement, but an attempt to get the natives a better deal within the framework of the French administration. Its leaders were mainly young North Africans who had been educated in France. They were aided by their co-religionists in France, thousands of whom had settled there after the First World War. These Moslems in France had joined the Radical Socialist or the Socialist party. Hence the efforts of the French civil and military authorities in North Africa to suppress the movement were nullified by the support given to it by the leftists in France. Though they possessed no organized power in North Africa, the left parties could bring pressure on the French government to compel the North African administrations to permit legal propaganda and a free native press. Simultaneously a movement was started for closer relations between Jewish and Moslem youth; Jewish opinion was always moderate or leftist, because the privileges the Jews had acquired in North Africa were won with the help of liberal elements in France. This faint portent of a political understanding between Moslems and Jews infuriated the French colonists even more than the growing native movement, which the French press was inclined to treat with amused condescension.

Strangely enough, just at this time a wave of unfortunate incidents between Moslems and Jews spread all over North Africa. Arab hoodlums attacked Jews on the street, usually singling out wealthy and prominent men. The attacks were generally attributed to Nazi propaganda, but the Moslem leaders denied this and said they were instigated by members of the Croix de Feu and the Camelots du Roi.[57] In fact, the native press published the sensational news that in some instances French officers were actually discovered inciting the Moslem rabble to riot against the Jews.

In Spanish North Africa, where the Jews and Moslems have remarkably cordial relations, the peace was not disturbed. When news of the violence between Moslems and Jews in French North Africa reached the Spanish Republican administration in Tetuán, it issued a proclamation calling upon both peoples to remember their long association and to respect each other's rights and customs. This proclamation was read in the mosques and synagogues, prominently affixed to walls, and published in the Spanish newspaper. But it was not reported in any French newspaper. It was printed only by the radical native newspaper *l'Action Marocaine*.

Even the reactionary Spanish monarchy was more liberal toward the subject natives than the French Republic. The Spanish regime permitted nationalist publications from Egypt and Syria to enter the country; the French barred them. It allowed the natives some semblance of freedom of speech, which was denied in the French zone. The Spanish permitted circulation of the native Hassani silver money; the French compelled the use of paper money which was often in a state of fluctuation. Even the Spanish Catholic church enjoys more prestige than the French Catholic church among the Moslems. Out of the wisdom of long experience or perhaps because of their Spanish national pride, Spanish priests show no desire to proselytize Moslems.

The French clergy has been accused by the Moslems of exercising religious influence through the administration. Whether this is true or not, the most serious crisis in French–Moslem relations occurred in the nineteen thirties when the French Moroccan administration promulgated the *Dahir Berbère*. For some reason which remains obscure to the neutral observer, the French desired to bring the Berbers living in the Souss and beyond the Atlas Mountains under the French civil code and eventually to make citizens of them. The Berbers are monogamists, their women go unveiled, and their local councils are not strictly based on Koranic law. So the French sought to detach the Berbers from the Arabs by forbidding Moslem teachers and preachers to penetrate into the interior. Not only North Africa but the entire Moslem world protested against the French decree. To demonstrate solidarity with the rude Berbers the young agitators discarded the red fez and silk burnoose for the coarse woolen burnoose and turban of the Berbers. Their organs carried on an incessant campaign against the new law, and they were supported by the publications of their leftist friends in France. The Spaniards too rallied to the side of the Moslems and declared that Morocco possessed a spiritual unity which the nations should respect.

As relations between the conservative North African adminis-

trations and the native leaders drifted from bad to worse, France
itself turned more sharply to the left. When Spain installed a re-
publican government, the natives rejoiced, but the French colonists
were cold to the new turn of events. By the time the Popular Front
government came to power in France, military and colonial opinion
in North Africa was belligerently opposed to it. The North African
militarists not only threatened to march to the aid of General
Franco; they ordered the Popular Front government to cease its
support of the native propagandists and consent to the dissolution of
their organizations in North Africa. Finally, just before the govern-
ment fell, it yielded. The native organizations were proscribed and
their leaders arrested and jailed. Thus the native movements and
their leaders were the first casualties of the reinforced French fascists.

From *Nation*, vol. 156 (May 8, 1943), pp. 663–65.

RACE AND COLOR IN EAST ASIA:
A REVIEW OF "INSIDE ASIA" BY JOHN GUNTHER

For an understanding of the grand drama convulsing the Far East,
the average reader, overwhelmed by one-sided propaganda, should
be equipped with John Gunther's *Inside Asia*. This splendid docu-
ment is a book that should be read and pondered by every intelligent
member of the colored American group. It is pitched to the scale
of a novel in which nations are the leading characters and power
politics the plot. It is a great story with a moral which is obvious;
but like the Bible, whose moral serves differently every religious sect,
the moral of *Inside Asia* may have its special significance for diverse
groups of people.

Evidently the author is sympathetic to the imperialistic mission
of European nations among Asiatic natives, but he is humanitarian
enough to write understandingly of the Japanese as an Asiatic power
and the Chinese and Indians as mercilessly exploited subject peo-
ples. No doubt a Japanese, writing such a book, would be less sym-
pathetic to European nations in Asia and more eloquently apprecia-
tive of Japan's destiny. But as an American observer of the vast,
strange Orient, Mr. Gunther's objective presentation is of greater
value than anything that might have been done by an Englishman or
a Japanese.

The immense mass chorus of this oriental Greek tragedy is the 775,000,000 Chinese, Indians and Malays who are subjected and exploited directly and indirectly by European nations, Britain, France and Holland, with a population of 117,000,000. The Europeans are in Asia to get the greatest profit possible out of their investments. They have no interest in the social welfare of the natives. Probably many of them believe in the need of social welfare for workers—at home in Europe.

The prolific and powerful Japanese nation, checked in its immigration and trade expansion in Europe and America, is striving to control and dominate the already subjected Chinese. And therein is the key to the gigantic struggle of the great powers in East Asia. "Most of Asia is a European colony," Mr. Gunther declares. The imperialist exploitation of the Chinese is colossal, their misery overwhelming.

Exploitation is not always humane, but it is human and universal. The European exploitation of Asia (and of Africa) is viciously inhuman because it is based upon the unscientific and immoral theory of superiority of white persons over black and brown persons. Few modern social thinkers have grappled seriously with the racial roots of the imperialist–capitalist system. Radicals have treated the subject incidentally as if it were not an integral feature of the social system. Socialists and Communists have historically minimized it. So much so that colored American radicals, utterly confused, have denounced the little businessmen of the group as a menace as great as big capitalists. They are chauvinists who stress too much the racial aspect of economic exploitation. Many argue against colored people supporting colored businessmen, who exploit them *just like white businessmen*. The comrades apparently fail to see the vast difference between a man who is exploited as a man and a man who is exploited as less than a man—like an animal. Yet whether in America, Asia or Africa, the imperialists and capitalists possess inexhaustible strength and absolute power mainly because of the special emphasis put upon the difference of race and color among the exploited of the world.

Hitler, dramatically and brutally imposing an inferior status on the Jewish minority, has started a movement that will be rocking the world long after Hitler and Nazism are dead. To fight and defeat Hitlerism, its vile racial theories must also be combated. But how can the so-called democratic nations effectively fight Hitler, when they tacitly endorse him in their attitude towards millions of

brown and white persons exploited in Asia and Africa? How long
can they continue to condemn racial intolerance against Jews and
condone it against Africans and Asiatics, unless all the modern sci-
entific theories and Christian principles regarding humanity are
discarded?

Mr. Gunther shows that the actual condition of China under for-
eign exploitation and native militarists is appalling. Few Americans
have any realistic conception of Chinese life under the foreign con-
cessions: the treaty ports, customs control and extraterritoriality.
Economically and socially the Chinese masses are unimaginably
worse off than the peons of the South or Mexico. Where Europeans
control, Chinese have no social privileges. Educated Chinese, even
the highest officials, cannot enter white clubs, restaurants and hotels.
In Shanghai Park there was placed the insulting sign: "No Dogs
Or Chinese Allowed," Mr. Gunther relates. The present prime min-
ister of China was refused service in a passenger elevator because
it was reserved for whites only. Foreigners control all the wealth
of Shanghai, but they pay no taxes.

The average wage of the semi-skilled Chinese worker is $2.40
a month, and the working day is from 12 to 15 hours. Children start
to work at six. Chinese girls are sold by their parents for $5, for
three years' work in factories under a system of indenture. Two
million people die of starvation every year in China. Twenty-nine
thousand dead bodies were picked up off the streets of Shanghai in
1935. No such horrifying conditions exist in the worst native areas
of South Africa.

Compared to the immense filth-filled cattle-shed of China, Japan
is a neatly cultivated garden. For about 50 years after the Chinese
had their first little taste of the fruit of British exploitation, the
Japanese held their country tightly closed. When, seventy-five years
ago, the white power blasted the little brown men out of their hermit
ways of life, the Japanese immediately and assiduously began to
study the amazing activism of the white invaders who had prodded
them out of their island retreat. Unlike the Chinese, who were con-
tented in considering themselves the favored sons of Heaven, and
the Europeans foreign devils, the Japanese were quickly aware that
they were challengd by a superior type of people. So they went right
out after them to learn their methods. The Japanese copied the
military, industrial, parliamentary and even the social system of the
Europeans, and eventually made themselves a great power among
great powers.

By the American standard, wages are also very low in Japan, but the rate is more than double that paid in China. The general standard and quality of living is on an infinitely higher level than in China. The majority of Japanese live frugally and cleanly. The cost of living is cheap. There is no extreme disparity between the salaries of professional, non-professional and official persons as exists in Europe and America. The Japanese use the most modern equipment in their industrial plants, which are run without graft. They are formidable rivals of the highly industrialized nations in the world's markets.

Mr. Gunther describes all this in detail. He tells us that the Japanese are the only people in Asia who keep abreast of the great Western nations. And that they also have all the "faults" of those high industrialized nations. The Japanese are industrious, efficient and progressive. They are expansionists, determined, self-confident, aggressive. Mr. Gunther clearly shows a preference for the easy-going, charming and inefficient Chinese. The Japanese, too, are aware of the greater and more ancient traditions of the Chinese, to whom they are indebted for their culture. Japanese adore the Chinese cuisine, which is superior to theirs. But they have a mortal fear of becoming Chinafied politically.

The Japanese claim special interests in China. They are jealous of the penetration and influence of other nations in China. All the great nations are naturally jealous of one another and suspicious of each other's motives and moves. But the Japanese have reasons to be jealous. When the Japanese were victorious in the Sino-Japanese war of 1894, China ceded the Manchurian peninsula, which is of utmost strategic urgency to Japan. But the European powers, pretending sympathy for China, compelled Japan to give up the best fruit of her victory. Japan, unable to withstand pressure from the combined European powers, gave back Manchuria to China. Then Russia, despite her almost unlimited territory, seized it. Japan did not regain her prize until she defeated Russia in 1904.

After the American Exclusion Act of 1924, Mr. Gunther says, the Japanese stepped up their expansionist program in China. Japan is the most overcrowded country in the world. The Japanese, facing trade barriers, immigration restrictions and race prejudice, have been compelled to overflow into China. The author points out that Japan is doing in China precisely what other great powers have done. But to a moralist that is no excuse. The inexorable necessity of Japanese expansion seems a more logical one.

The main issue in China is imperialist rivalry. And it is compli-
cated by the problem of race and color. All the great powers in
China are concerned with their own selfish interests. They not only
exploit the Chinese: they discriminate against *all* Chinese in China
because they are not white. The Japanese do not have the goodwill
of the white powers, but they inspire respect. The nationals of the
white nations do not act in Japan as they do in China. As citizens of
a great power, the Japanese in China have equal rights with whites.
They visit hotels, restaurants and cabarets where whites attend. But
I understand that the Japanese are sometimes mistaken for Chinese,
and have to establish their identity.

Aside from the right or wrong of its action in China, the Japa-
nese nation is a barrier against the spread of race and color preju-
dice in Asia. There are large numbers of Chinese in Japan. There
is no case on record of Japanese subjecting Chinese to humiliating
discrimination in Japan as Europeans do in China. Indeed the
Chinese hailed the Japanese as the savior of Asia after they defeated
the Russians in 1905. Sun Yat Sen, the modern Chinese leader, and
General Chiang Kai Shek, the present leader, have both lived as
honored exiles in Japan. Hundreds of Chinese intellectuals, revolu-
tionists and students have found refuge in Japan and received mili-
tary and academic training there.

Today the Chinese revolutionists are arrayed against Japan be-
cause of her invasion of China. But Japan has declared her inten-
tion to institute a new order in China. Japan considers a weak China,
dominated by European powers, a menace to her national growth.
But the white nations opposing Japan are more concerned about
their prestige, which is based upon race and color prejudice and
intolerance. None of these powers has offered to give up the special
concessions by which the Chinese are exploited and degraded.

Human dignity is more precious than prestige, but the Chinese
may believe that white imperialism is more desirable than brown
imperialism. They have had experience with both. A war between
white and brown imperialists for domination in Asia would inevi-
tably develop into a conflict of race. In the interest of all that is fine
in humanity as a whole, and civilization in general, such a conflict
should be averted. For it would be infinitely worse than the present
Japanese adventure in China.

It is better for the cultural interests of all humanity that no one
kind of people should dominate the entire world. Some of us will
understand more who have lived in colonies and seen the agents of

imperialists degrade all of humanity in their treatment of weak subject peoples whose skin is not white. They act as they do because of prestige—that prestige that is thrust forth like a mailed fist in *Inside Asia*—which is sacred to them above elementary human rights.

From *Opportunity*, vol. 17 (August, 1939), pp. 228–30.

7. The Move to Catholicism

LETTERS TO MAX EASTMAN

309 West 112th Street
New York City

July 30, 1942

Dear Max,

It is over a year since we corresponded with each other. Since then I have been knocking around doing various makeshift jobs, was dangerously ill and all the time I have been trying to obtain a place for which I am intellectually equipped. For it seems sheerly silly and wasteful that I should be condemned to doing the things that a thousand ordinary persons can do, when I am capable of performing a more technical and specialized kind of work.

And so this is why I am writing to you. I am trying to get a job with the Office of War Information, especially in handling matters about the natives of Africa and the West Indies and also the American Negro. Besides my intellectual equipment, my travels are a valuable asset, from having given me practical experience. A friend who is helping me has written: "I have a feeling that Max Eastman is on fairly intimate terms with Elmer Davis.[1] . . . Why not put it up to him to put you and Davis in touch?"

Now, if you do know Elmer Davis and feel that you can conscientiously introduce and recommend me to him for a position, I shall be very grateful to you. But I want you to do it only if you feel agreeably disposed. When I started out to try for the job I was informed that it was better not to mention you to recommend me, because you were persona non grata in government circles in Washington. But nobody knows more than you what I am capable of doing in a job of the kind I want to get. And so I shall be glad if a recommendation from you will help instead of hurt.

Yours sincerely,
CLAUDE

309 West 112th Street
New York City

August 13, 1942

Dear Max,

When it was suggested that I should write to you for an introduction to Elmer Davis, I demurred and said you would no doubt seize the opportunity to lecture me like an old country parson preaching against liquor, while holding a flask on his hip: and, besides I was in no mood for a lecture, after the severe illness I went through in which the only hands that ministered to me were those of strangers from the Catholic Mission,* stretched out to snatch me from the Shadow of Death.

Moreover, the point you make is untenable when you say that "the only reason that you have not got one (of high-up jobs) is that you don't like people well enough to handle them and get along with them skillfully. . . ."

Now you have known me in only one administrative capacity in that job which you gave me on the *Liberator* and you are well aware that everybody in that office set-up from Margaret Lane down, besides Crystal, all the girls and even Mylius were fond of me.[2] I got along with all of your collaborators and admirers and even prejudiced visitors from the South. I never once heard of any complaints. Later I couldn't work with Mike Gold, but nobody else could, business manager or girls, for he was an irresponsible and unreliable psychopathic case and the *Liberator* blew up when he took over.

If my former associates criticize me it is purely for intellectual differences—but I have often heard them refer to you as a snob pretending to be a proletarian and as a vain and selfish person.

Apparently, you are deliberately mixing up my private life with my public acts. But you are certainly aware that both things are separate. My parents used to admonish us children always not to mix up our private feelings with public things. I am not an intellectual or a physical prostitute, but I don't think that that is harmful to me. I have managed to get along with people of all races and all walks of life. I went as a green hand to the railroad and after three months' service, I was made 1st. pantryman (corresponding to headwaiter) and held the job for three years. It was no easy assignment, for my associates were tough and conscienceless and I had to

* The Harlem Friendship House; see "Introduction," p. 40. [Ed.]

see that they did not steal all the supplies to take home. I did my job thoroughly and made them respect and like me. Even recently on WPA I was liked by all who had to work with me.

You should be aware that the chief reason why I have not had a job equal to my intellectual attainments is simply because I have no close academic associates nor college degree, and also I am a Negro. My racial group is even more than the white, narrow and hidebound about college qualifications. I know many persons in it who are not very capable, but have had good jobs because they were graduates of Harvard and Yale and Columbia. When white library officials offered Arthur Schomburg the job to become curator of the books which he himself had collected, the Negro academicians, led by Dr. Du Bois, fought against the appointment on the ground that Schomburg did not possess a college degree!

In fact, I don't think that you have ever thought about me as suitable for any administrative job, since we both left the *Liberator*. The stress was placed (rightly of course) on my doing creative work. Even when I returned here in 1934, the only thing you could think of was getting me a job as manservant to some person. But I was not expecting the impossible, for everybody knows that professional jobs are hardest of any to get.

Now, I don't know if I should really send your letter to Elmer Davis, since you hold this idea about my work with others in an administrative capacity. I must first consult with the woman who has been helping me and show her your letter. Even if you don't tell Davis this, you may talk about it to others and it is chiefly by whispering around that reputations are blasted. . . .

I feel bitter, because your statement proves that after 23 years, you know very little about me, your impression is wrong. So far as I have seen, most of the people who succeed in administrative positions are hard and piercing as nails and perhaps those are the qualities which have made them successful. It is easy to try to kick people around, when they are in trouble. . . . A man may be ever so much a son-of-a-bitch, while he is up and in everybody fawns on him—it's when you're down that you learn about your faults.

Yours sincerely,
[Claude McKay]

c/o Charles Page [3]
Squash Hollow
New Milford, Conn.

Sept. 3, 1943

Dear Max,

I want to thank you for responding so generously to Freda Kirchwey and sending a check for $50. I was working at the Federal Shipbuilding Yard at Port Newark, when I had the stroke. It was in my left face just where I had it about twenty years ago in France.

It wasn't that the work was too hard, but it was laborious and I had to be on my feet all the time and peer hard into little rivet holes to do my riveting. I did not wear my glasses, but now I have to wear them to read.

I was taking treatment for high blood pressure, when I sustained the stroke. I had been sent first to the Wright's Aircraft Factory, but they wouldn't take me there, because of the high blood pressure. At Port Newark, I was not examined for that. I was in the Harlem Hospital for over two weeks, but the doctors could do very little and thought it would be best if I came up to this place, which had been offered to me.

It is a summer cottage set deep down in the woods, about five miles from New Milford. And it is very lonely, about half a mile each way from the farmhouses. But I couldn't find anyone to come along, unless I stood expenses and I could not afford that. I have been up here over a month. Selma came up and stayed a week, bringing some friends; she was on her vacation from the Navy Yard and I didn't have to do anything. She would have liked to stay longer, if she did not have to go back to work. And this weekend I expect some other people to come up. I suppose I'll stay here until the end of September or until it starts to get real cold and then I'll have to leave. As it is, it has always been mild since I came up and I use blankets every night. I could stay through the winter, for the friends who own it are out in Chicago, but only a dirt road leads out here and it is very inaccessible in winter. Even now I can get no ice or oil up here, for the trucks will not climb the hill and so I depend on a neighbor to obtain them for me when he drives into town once or twice a week.

I don't know what I'll do when I leave. Just a week after arriving, I received a letter from the city (N.Y.) offering me a clerical job. But it was too late for me to appear at the set time and besides I was required to undergo a medical test!

I have started to write poetry again (very different from my earlier stuff).[4] My best regards to you and Eliena, and thanks again.

> Yours sincerely,
> CLAUDE MCKAY

> Columbus Hospital
> 219 East 19th St.
> New York City

> December 7, 1943

Dear Max,

When you sent Miss Norton * up to New Milford to see me, you gave me a new lease on life, and I want you to forgive me for any stupid thing I ever said with my tongue, for I could do you no harm.

Of course I have had a hectic time, dodging here and there to prevent myself getting caught at this late age. I should like very much to talk to you personally about a few important things. So if you can make yourself available, I shall be very happy.

My love to you and Eliena. I am not so worried by my illness as I am by feeling kind of useless!

> Sincerely,
> CLAUDE

P.S. I look perfectly all right externally so don't be afraid to see me.

> c/o Catholic Youth Organization
> 31 East Congress Street
> Chicago, Ill.

> October 16, 1944

Dear Max,

I must announce to you that on October 11, The Feast of the Maternity of the Blessed Virgin Mary, I was baptized into the Catholic (Roman) Faith.

I have your letter of October 8 and as far as I can remember (I didn't make a carbon copy of my letter), I mentioned to you

---

* Florence Norton, Max Eastman's secretary. [Ed.]

that I was preparing to take the final hurdle and become a Catholic. And in your reply you said, why should I join, why not just work with the Catholics, if they are opposed to the Communists.

But my feelings were more profound than that. I had always wanted to belong to some religion, especially when I was in Europe and Africa,[5] and now that I am back in America, I have chosen the one that meets my needs. After all, Max, what is Truth? It seems to me that to have a religion is very much like falling in love with a woman. You love her for her color and the music and rhythm of her—for her Beauty, which cannot be defined. There is no reason to it, there may be many other women more gorgeously beautiful, but you love one and rejoice in her companionship.

Unlike you, I have never had any religious experience, because my brother educated me without religion,[6] I was pretty well versed in the Bible, but it was like reading any historical or philosophical book, and in my adolescence I came under the influence of the Englishman [Walter Jekyll] who sent me to America to be educated, and who was an agnostic. I used to have great faith in agnosticism, up until World War I, when the German and British agnostics or rationalists lost all sense of reason, became rabid nationalists and began denouncing one another.

So, as far as I am able to see, "truth and mental integrity" are relative human things. The Orient has one standard of "truth and mental integrity" and the Occident another, the Germans have theirs, the English have theirs, the Japanese have theirs, the Americans theirs and each one thinks that his way is the right way. I prefer the Catholic church and its symbolic interpretation of the reality of Christ Crucified.

So, I don't know which is right. Sometimes, I feel as if the Marxists are right when they say that every human thought, emotion and action is determined by dialectical materialism.

Anyway this is a new experience for me and, I suppose, the final stage of my hectic life. I am not the less a fighter. Indeed, one reason for choosing the Catholic church is that besides its religious side, it is the greatest political organization in the world and a bulwark against the menace of Communism. Thank you for *Russian Affairs* and my best to you and Eliena.

Sincerely,
CLAUDE

c/o Catholic Youth Organization
31 East Congress Street
Chicago, Ill.

Nov. 28, 1944

Dear Max,

It was very kind of you to send me Miss Halsey's book,[7] which I found very amusing. I marked the passages about Negroes and Jews and showed them to some of the staff here and some of them were quite confused. Especially about that one which said that Northerners were not much better than Southerners about the race problem.

Well, I am still here and doing my best to be a good Catholic and not allow that to change my attitude of life or my way of life. I saw Dorothy Day [8] about three weeks ago. She has changed a lot, but she appears to me to look much better than when she was around with the *Liberator* crowd. She has a farm out in Easton, Pa., and has invited me to come out there for a retreat around Christmas. She is very religious, of course, something like a saint. I think I will go, for I am booked to speak at West Virginia University on January 3.

Say, do you happen to know of any radical publisher that might take a try at my poems? [9] I tried them on Harper's and Dutton's. The first said they were good writing, but too personal, the second that they were not poetry and too critical of everything, whites, colored and Hollywood and even Washington! And so I have a hunch that I do have something that might make America feel less smug about its fascist-oppressed Negroes, while we are fighting Fascism abroad!

I like your article in the current *New Leader*.[10] Excellent! I think, however, that Roosevelt can get four more years if he wants them. For the Republicans just have no program! And the people, the common people, instinctively know that.

The CIO convention took place here last week. I attended a session and heard Wallace speak.* He said that after the war we must face the fact of having some form of Socialism. [Mayor] La-Guardia came in when Wallace was speaking and there was vociferous applause for him and for General Somerville, who delivered a message from [General] Eisenhower. The Negro delegate among the executives on the platform, one Willard Townshend, grinned

* Henry Wallace, then Vice-President of the United States. [Ed.]

and applauded more than anybody else, when Somerville said, we must not only lick the Japs, but crush them, so that they can never rise again.

Well, Max, it is very cold and I have only my thin topcoat. My best to you and regards to Eliena. If you come to Chicago, please look me up. And if you have any friends out here, who would be friendly, please let me know. Did I inform you that Eddie Welsh was out here? He looks very prosperous.

Sincerely,
CLAUDE

c/o Catholic Youth Organization
31 East Congress Street
Chicago, Ill.

Jan. 26, 1945

Dear Max,

I was in New York for a couple of days during the first week of this month and not having your telephone, I called Miss Norton whose friend informed me that you were out of town for the weekend. I was very much disappointed for I wanted to see you about my poems, which I brought along with me. I was up at Dorothy Day's farm in Easton at a retreat and conference and after I went to Morgantown, where I talked at the West Virginia University.

Now, Max, I should like you to look through these poems for me and make any corrections you think necessary. Harper's had written to me, asking for anything I might have. But, when I sent in these poems they said the writing was fine, but the poems were too bitter and personal! Dutton's thought they were not poems. My [former] publicity agent, Ruth Raphael, who did publicity on *Home to Harlem* and *Banjo,* shouts that they are wonderful, but that a couple of literary friends think they might be worked over.

So, I should like to get your opinion and also see the mark of your blue pencil, for I am aware there is no more excellent judge. Dorothy Day is doing great work and I should like to do an article about her for the *New Leader.* Think they would take it?

Best wishes to you and Eliena and I hope I may get a chance to see you soon again.

Yours sincerely,
CLAUDE McKAY

c/o Catholic Youth Organization
31 East Congress Street
Chicago, Ill.

Feb. 3, 1945

Dear Max,

Thank you for your note and I do wish you would let me know whether or not you received my poems as I did not register them.

I hope too that you and Eliena can get away to Haiti. It has been very cold here and I have been trying hard to protect myself from getting the gripe. But if you do go to Haiti, I shall take a vicarious trip along with you.

Well, things are at last coming to a show-down in Europe and somehow I have a feeling that Stalin is getting ready for one of his great double-crossing acts. It seems I am beginning to admire the genius of His Satanic Majesty and I wait in fear and trembling.

Yours sincerely,
CLAUDE

c/o Catholic Youth Organization
31 East Congress Street
Chicago, Ill.

March 21, 1945

Dear Max,

It was good of you to take time out to give to those poems of mine. One of them, which you liked a little, about our fighting Fascism in Europe while 15 million Negroes were groaning under Fascism here was published in Dorothy Day's *Catholic Worker* for February.[11] And it was liked very much.

Of course, Max, I can understand when you don't like my reference to the word "Fascism," as existent in the United States of America, but I am afraid that you see this thing as a white American. Any Jew from Poland or Nazi Germany would quickly see my meaning. The regime under which Negroes live in the South is more like Nazism than Fascism. There are different kinds you know. I always thought that the Fascism of Primo de Rivera in Spain was the mildest I ever lived under, which certainly must have been due to the innate nobility of all the Spanish people. Certainly what Hitler was trying to do to the Jews in Europe, denying them political and social rights, taking their money, etc., is just what has been done to the Negro in the South.

Once I said that to Levitas [12] and he had to agree that I was right. Any movement to help the Negro in the South is merely trying to restore what was taken away from him. I don't like the word, Fascism, myself; but it is the currently used word. Dictatorship, also, is nothing new. We have had military dictatorships in Central and South America for decades! Yet today, Americans like to think of these as democracies, because they are allied to the U.S.A. How funny! There are different forms of dictatorship as there are different forms of Fascism. Mussolini used the castor-oil bottle; Hitler preferred the axe!

Up until 1912, when the French took over Morocco, Jews there lived under a form of Fascism in their ghettos, quite as Negroes in the South. And since then, the Moors have, under the French, lived under a form of Colonial Fascism. The names change, but I guess there is nothing new under the sun.

However, I was happy to hear from you again. And the poems! They are wonderful to look at after you chop them up! That makes me think of the old days. Oh, I wish I had the old style! But today, I feel more like Pope and Swift or even Catullus than like Shelley and Keats and the Elizabethans.

However, I thank you a lot for what you are doing to the poems. For I do want to do a book of them. When you point out two good lines that gives me an indication of what is wrong with the rest!

Oh, and won't you please seal the envelope when you write again. This is a pretty big organization and people are nosey and I don't want everybody to know what we are writing about. My best to you and Eliena,

Sincerely,
CLAUDE

c/o Mon. Jose Garcia, V.G.
P.O. Box 327
Albuquerque, New Mexico

August 7, 1946

Dear Max,

Your letter, when you were on your way to Cuba, found me quite ill again and I just couldn't write. Besides, I'm so easily tired out. They have given me all the new drugs: Penicillin, Soluble B, Salyrgan. But nothing seems to reach this dropsical swelling up of the stomach, from which my mother died.

I nearly died in Chicago and came down here in May. The doctors thought I would be dead by now, but I am still alive. This is a health resort and I have met a few old women and men who know you, and don't like your recent works, especially the articles in the Scripps-Howard—thought they didn't really say anything. I myself thought you could take what Lenin said and what Stalin said and show more conclusively that both Stalin and Lenin had exactly the same aim, but that Stalin's way of working the thing out was more devious, perhaps more correct from the Bolshevik point of view. I really think that for carrying Russia to its present state Stalin, ruthless as he is, was an infinitely better man than Trotsky. By the way I read part of Trotsky's latest on Stalin and I think it stinks. It really seems to me not to be written for American readers but for Russian readers in the years to come when the dictatorship may have ended. It seems that Trotsky wants above everything else to prove that Stalin was an S.O.B. and a Menshevik, just as he was.

Well, I cannot write any more, for I get so easily tired out, but I am trying to do another book. I feel like hell inside of me but everybody says that outwardly I look so well. But I am weak as a rat and constantly wasting away.

The *Catholic Register* of Denver had a long summary of your articles. I did not see it but the nuns at St. Joseph's Sanitarium told me so.

Well, my best to you and Eliena, and God bless you both.

Sincerely,
CLAUDE

c/o Msgr. Jose Garcia, V.G.
Box 327
Albuquerque, New Mexico

August 28, 1946

Dear Max,

I was more glad than you can imagine to hear from you. I am back in the hospital again after having a setback. I should like to see your article in the September *Mercury*.[13]

Of course I am not very political especially since I became a

Catholic, but I try to see things from the standpoint of right and wrong and when Soviet Russia is wrong I will say so. When the U.S. and Great Britain are wrong I will say so too, and the two latter in my mind are more often wrong than the Soviet nation. I am certainly never going to carry the torch for British colonialism or American imperialism abroad.

Please thank Miss Norton for her nice note, for when I wrote that thing about you in my *Long Way from Home* I did myself think that it was a good tribute. And I had hoped that some day I might write a short biography of you; something like what Gorky wrote about Tolstoy and in which Tolstoy stands head and shoulders above Gorky.[14] But you were so angry when the book came out even to semi-denounce what I had written at the party that the publishers gave for me that I was crestfallen. And you may remember Walter White and how he too so foolishly reacted when I had merely said about him what Lady Astor so generously repeated in London during World War II. So I thought I would write no more about my contemporaries since they are such over-sensitive people.

My new book is about my childhood in Jamaica which is a source of rich and inexhaustible material.[15] I have such a rich field to write about that I don't have to mess myself up about contemporary personalities and events. I have had a hard time but I have also had some superb moments and in spite of my chronic illness I don't want to go sour on humanity, even after living in this awful land of the U.S.A. I still like to think of people with wonder and love as I did as a boy in Jamaica and the Catholic Church with its discipline and traditions and understanding of human nature is helping me a lot. Please let Miss Norton read this letter and tell her I shall write to her when I feel a little stronger, but writing to you now is taking everything out of me. Tell Eliena I should like to see her and hear her laugh. By the way you might try to get me a publisher for my new book. It is very short and Bishop Sheil has promised to write a preface. But my agent in Chicago has not made any headway in New York and last I heard from him he had contacted Dutton who said they would want to see the entire book. But although it is brief I think it is very good, rich and lush and smelling of the soil of Jamaica. When I told some people in New York what I was writing they wrote back to say that I was a coward to turn my back on politics. But really it is silly for I have never been a political writer; I never claimed to be one.

What you say about me is very pleasant but I wish you would

put it in print. Why don't you write an article on Negro writers and Negro literature? I am sure you could easily get it placed in the *Reader's Digest* or in the *American Mercury* or in a periodical like the *Catholic Worker* or *America*. The Denver *Catholic Register* always features you and it is the largest Catholic weekly in the West, with about four million circulation.

I think the Lenin-Trotsky-Stalin controversy is definitely dated and that people are more interested in the Soviet Union as threatening the so-called democracies of the U.S.A. and Britain.

It was good of you to write to me. You know how much I appreciate your letters. Life in the hospital is very tiresome but I hope I shall get well again and meet you and Eliena in New York. Say hello to any of the old friends. I hear from Dorothy Day pretty often. She is doing fine work down there near Chinatown [16] and I came here to Albuquerque at the suggestion of one of her devoted followers, a Mr. Hennacy,[17] who however is not a Catholic, but a Christian Anarchist.

With my love to you all,

Sincerely,
CLAUDE MCKAY

St. Joseph's Hospital
Albuquerque, New Mexico

September 16, 1946

Dear Max,

You ought to be ashamed to mention Dorothy Day in the way you did because she is not ignorant-minded and she is not neurotic. You are also aware that at no time did you ever do my thinking for me even when people might have thought so. You know that intellectually I do my thinking for myself and I don't know if you remember when you were living in Marcel Cachin's house at Antibes and had written the book *Science and Revolution* in which you declared to the world that you were a Marxist and I read the manuscript and told you that I did not believe that Marxism was a science.[18] And that I believed John Stuart Mill was a greater social economist than Marx whose first and second books on socialism I had seriously read in London back in 1920.

Therefore I am not mouthing any Stalinist propaganda slogans. I am not a Marxist or Communist and never was one, but if Communists sometimes say the truth in spite of all their lies I am not going to say the truth is not the truth. [The] United States giving of independence to the Philippines has been given with a string to it. We all know that it was the beet sugar growers' organization in this country which objected to the coming in of free cane sugar from the Philippines, which gave impetus to the drive to free the Philippines. And as for India you have pulled a big boner there. If the British Labor Government were sincere it would first remove the British army in India. Have you forgotten how just a few months ago the native Indian army which was struggling for freedom was shot down and put in bondage by the white British Navy and Army? Equality of white and brown people: bosh! You all ought to try to bring that about in America before going abroad to Asia, and even Africa, to try your experiments.

Whatever the Soviet nation has done is not worse than what the British Empire has done in its 300 years more or less of world domination. Have you forgotten the revolt in Lucknow when Indians were shot like balls through the mouths of British cannon? Have you forgotten the degrading conditions of Amritsar at the end of the last World War, when the Governor had Indian natives crawl on their bellies before white troops? I have always thought that every Englishman and American is a dyed-in-the-wool hypocrite when it comes to seeing and facing other people's problems. In all my life I have never been a reactionary and I won't be one now, mouthing occasional pieces for the capitalist press, because I know one thing, the capitalists do not want me and I don't want anything of them; whatever the Soviets are bringing into the world it is something new, just as the Mohammedan regime which swept through Asia and Africa and Spain in the seventh century. It wasn't that Mohammedanism was better than Christianity but it happened that Christianity then was rotten to the core. I am a Catholic because I believe that the Catholic church has a spiritual message for mankind's spiritual nature which we can get from no heads of state.

I subscribe wholeheartedly to Sec. Wallace's speech of Sept. 12.[19] I would prefer my name in history should stand beside his instead of the neo-reactionaries of the *New Leader*. In my opinion no state is perfect because mankind is far from perfection. I do not fear that the Russian system will ever conquer America, but I do not care if it conquers the people of Asia or Africa. I do not think that mouthing goodwill the democracies have anything to offer such people. I should say to the so-called democracies of the United States and

Great Britain: set your own house in order and do not try to scare up a war against Soviet Russia.

I am not a partisan of Communism, nevertheless, I have nothing but contempt for people who accepted Lenin's dictum about the bourgeoisie and now are opposed to the Russian Government for trying to bring it about in devious ways. I joined the Catholic church because structurally, traditionally and fundamentally it is the foe of Communism, and please remember that there is a formidable left wing within the Catholic church because it can accommodate all, even you.

Yours sincerely,
CLAUDE McKAY

Epilogue

McKay spent the last two years of his life in and out of hospitals in Albuquerque, San Diego, and Chicago. Suffering for years from high blood pressure, after 1940 he had developed a serious heart disease that was complicated by dropsy, a condition that he maintained had proved fatal to his mother and grandmother.[1] From Albuquerque where he had been sent by friends to recuperate, he traveled in the late fall of 1946 to San Diego, and there he passed the winter. In the summer of 1947 he returned to Chicago and remained there until his death the following year.

Since his first arrival in Chicago in the spring of 1944, McKay had served Bishop Bernard Sheil as a special consultant on racial problems and radical politics. He also worked in the headquarters of Chicago's Catholic Youth Organization, and from time to time lectured and taught in that center's educational program.

Despite his illness and the variety of his Church-related activities, McKay also continued to write. Between 1944 and 1948, he completed a memoir of his childhood in Jamaica, "My Green Hills of Jamaica" (see p. 311), his "cycle manuscript" (see pp. 324–25, n.88), several additional sonnets that appeared in Dorothy Day's *Catholic Worker*,[2] and a number of magazine articles.[3] Finally, in the last months of his life he prepared his *Selected Poems* for publication. As it turned out, this last volume did not appear until 1953, five years after his death. In spite of the best efforts of Carl Cowl, his literary agent in New York, McKay could not find a publisher for either his new or his old works, which by 1948 were all out of print.

Despite the consolation offered by the Church, McKay could not suppress the bitterness (and occasional outbursts of rage) he experienced as a writer who had seen better days. To Cowl he wrote, "You must understand that there is much opposition to my getting published! From Communists, . . . from literary cut-throats who were in high places in the New Deal . . . from Negro leaders of the NAACP [and] the Urban League, . . . and even from certain groups of Catholics."[4] Reading only his letters to Cowl, it would be easy to assume that in his last years McKay succumbed completely to bitterness. But he was never a simple person, and such a conclusion would be unwarranted and quite misleading.

As his letters to Max Eastman reveal, McKay remained to the end a passionate advocate of honesty and justice in both life and literature. Cedric Dover came close to the truth when he wrote of McKay that he was "a man who was bitter because he loved, who was both right and wrong because he hated the things that destroyed love, who tried to give back to others a little of what he had got from them and the continuous adventure of being a black man in a white society." [5]

Notes

INTRODUCTION

1. For summary analyses of McKay's poetry and prose, see Jean Wagner, *Les poètes nègres des Etats-Unis: Le sentiment racial et religieux dans le poesie de P. L. Dunbar à L. Hughes (1890–1940)* (Paris: Libraire Istra, 1963), pp. 211–81; and Robert Bone, *The Negro Novel in America* (New Haven: Yale University Press, 1956), pp. 67–75. A recent assessment of McKay's continuing significance can be found in George E. Kent, "The Soulful Way of Claude McKay," *Black World*, vol. 20 (November 1970), pp. 37–51.

2. See Charles Glicksburg, "The Negro Cult of the Primitive," *Antioch Review*, vol. 4 (March 1944), pp. 47–55; and Rayford Logan, E. C. Holmes, and G. F. Edwards, eds., *The New Negro Thirty Years Afterward, Papers Contributed to the Sixteenth Annual Conference of the Division of the Social Sciences* (Washington, D.C.: Howard University Press, 1955), p. 62. Most standard literary histories of the period do not even mention the Negro Renaissance. On this point, see Abraham Chapman, "The Harlem Renaissance in Literary History," *College Language Association Journal*, vol. 11 (September 1967), pp. 35–38. The terms "New Negro," "Negro Renaissance," and "Harlem Renaissance," have all at various times and in various contexts been used in referring to the black literary scene as a whole in the 1920s. The first book-length study of this period is Nathan Irvin Huggins' *Harlem Renaissance* (New York: Oxford University Press, 1971). See also the collection of essays in Arna Bontemps, ed., *The Harlem Renaissance Remembered* (New York: Dodd, Mead, 1972).

3. Until quite recently critics have found it difficult to take any black writer seriously, not only because of racial prejudices, but also because black writing did not fit neatly into the traditional literary categories of the academic critics. As recently as 1966 one respectable critic could seriously maintain that "we wait, still, for a Negro writer who can tell us, truly, what it is like to be a Negro." (David Littlejohn, *Black on White: A Critical Survey of Writing by American Negroes* [New York: Grossman Publishers, 1966], p. 170). Littlejohn's condescension toward all black literature represents an older, white approach that is now changing, but his views are probably still shared by many academic critics.

4. The McKay family's middle-class orientation is reflected in their letters to Claude McKay in the McKay Papers, James Weldon Johnson Collection, Yale University Library.

5. Max Eastman, "Biographical Note," in *Selected Poems of Claude McKay* (New York: Bookman Associates, 1953), p. 110. U'Theo (1872–1950), subsequently rose to prominence as an agricultural leader in Clarendon Parish. His obituary was featured in the Kingston *Daily Gleaner* (undated clipping in the possession of Hope McKay Virtue).

6. Claude McKay, "Boyhood in Jamaica," *Phylon*, vol. 13 (2nd Quarter, 1953), p. 141; an article excerpted by Cedric Dover from Claude McKay's "My Green Hills of Jamaica," an unpublished memoir of his youth written in 1946. See the typescript in the Schomburg Collection of Negro Literature and History, New York Public Library. After his mother's death he dedicated several poems to her memory (see, for example, "My Mother," on p. 119 of this volume).

7. See especially the poem "The Heart of a Constab," in Claude McKay, *Constab Ballads* (London: Watts, 1912), pp. 62–63.

8. Walter Jekyll (1849–1929) was one of those hardy, independent Englishmen who were found sprinkled throughout Britain's Victorian Empire. He could, in fact, be easily mistaken today for a character lifted from the Empire fiction of a writer such as Joseph Conrad or Somerset Maugham. Jekyll had originally come from an old, upper-class family in Surrey, but he had long resided in Jamaica and apparently possessed moderate wealth. When McKay met him he was in his late fifties and lived simply in the Blue Mountains just north of Kingston. Educated at Harrow and Trinity College, Cambridge, where he graduated with honors in 1872, Jekyll was deeply learned in music, literature, language, and philosophy. After receiving an M.A., he had entered the ministry, but in the great debate between religion and science, he had decided against the faith and had renounced his orders. In "My Green Hills of Jamaica," McKay described Jekyll as a man "disillusioned with British liberalism, yet he did not believe in socialism or any of the radical parties of the day. . . . He was . . . something of a Buddhist and did not think that the world could be reformed." Among Jekyll's scholarly interests Jamaican folklore stood high. In 1907 he had published *Jamaican Song and Story*, a collection of Annancy tales, field songs, and dance tunes. According to McKay, Jekyll was generally considered mildly eccentric, but his independence, integrity, and humanity had won him the respect of all classes in Jamaica; he moved with equal ease among both the island's elite and the peasantry. See Walter Jekyll, ed., *Jamaican Song and Story: Annancy Stories, Digging Sings, Dancing Tunes, and Ring Tunes* (New York: Dover Publications, 1966), a new edition with introductory material by Philip Sher-

lock, Louise Bennett, and Rex Nettleford. See also Jekyll's obituary in the *Daily Gleaner* (August 19, 1929); and in the *Handbook of Jamaica, 1930* (Kingston, 1930), p. 557. Squire Gensir, in Claude McKay's last novel, *Banana Bottom* (New York: Harper and Bros., 1933), is a fictionalized version of Jekyll.

9. Claude McKay, *Songs of Jamaica* (Kingston: Aston W. Gardner, 1912). Also in 1912, Jekyll and McKay set six of McKay's dialect poems to music and published them as *Songs from Jamaica* (London: Augener, 1912). For collectors, this is probably the rarest of McKay items.

10. Jean Wagner, *Les poètes nègres des Etats-Unis,* op. cit., p. 219 (editor's translation).

11. Claude McKay, *Songs of Jamaica,* op. cit., pp. 63–65.

12. Paul Bohannan, *Africa and Africans* (Garden City: Natural History Press, 1964), pp. 11–13.

13. Claude McKay, *Constab Ballads,* op. cit., pp. 7–8.

14. Claude McKay, "My Green Hills of Jamaica," op. cit., p. 82.

15. A good study of Jamaican life, which agrees in its details with the portrait drawn by McKay in his dialect poetry, is Madeline Kerr's *Personality and Conflict in Jamaica,* 2nd ed. (London: Collins, 1963).

16. McKay never identified his "English" benefactor. It may have been Walter Jekyll.

17. His daughter, Hope McKay Virtue, now resides in California. A graduate of Columbia Teacher's College, she teaches in the California public school system.

18. Claude McKay, "Travail," in the *Workers' Dreadnought* (London, January 10, 1920), p. 1601.

19. Richard Hofstadter, *Social Darwinism in American Life,* 2nd ed. rev. (Boston: Beacon Press, 1955).

20. Claude McKay, "Exhortation: Summer, 1919," in *Harlem Shadows* (New York: Harcourt, Brace, 1922), pp. 49–50.

21. *Seven Arts,* vol. 2 (October, 1917), pp. 741–42. These early poems appeared under the pseudonym "Eli Edwards" because McKay did not wish his employers to discover he was a poet. See Claude McKay, *A Long Way from Home* (New York: Lee Furman, 1937), p. 26.

22. Claude McKay, *A Long Way from Home,* op. cit., pp. 28–29.

23. Letter from Claude McKay to Max Eastman, July 28, 1919. The Eastman–McKay letters were loaned to the editor by Max Eastman. These letters have since been deposited by the Eastman family in the Indiana University Library, Bloomington, Indiana. For details concerning Eastman's life and career, see his two autobiographies, *The Enjoyment of Living* (New York: Harper and Brothers, 1948) and *Love and*

Revolution: My Journey Through an Epoch (New York: Random House, 1965). For a recent critical study of Eastman, see Milton Cantor, *Max Eastman* (New York: Twayne Publishers, 1970).

24. For an almost complete listing of those artists and writers who appeared in the *Masses* and the *Liberator,* see Daniel Aaron, *Writers on the Left: Episodes in American Literary Communism* (New York: Harcourt, Brace and World, 1961), pp. 403–4.

25. Ibid., p. 92.

26. *Liberator,* vol. 2 (July 1919), p. 7.

27. Joseph Freeman, *An American Testament: A Narrative of Rebels and Romantics* (New York: Farrar and Rhinehart, 1936), pp. 243, 245–46, 254.

28. John Hope Franklin, *From Slavery to Freedom: A History of American Negroes,* 2nd ed. rev. (New York: Knopf, 1961), pp. 471–73.

29. Claude McKay, *A Long Way from Home,* op. cit., pp. 38–44. McKay identified his English admirers only as "the Grays," a brother and sister who had admired his dialect poetry.

30. I. A. Richards in his "Preface" to Claude McKay's *Spring in New Hampshire* (London: Grant Richards, 1920), p. i. The book's title is from a poem of the same name which McKay wrote while working as a waiter in a Dartmouth, New Hampshire, resort hotel in 1916.

31. Letter from I. A. Richards to Dr. Robert C. Reinders, May 19, 1966, quoted in Wayne Cooper and Robert C. Reinders, "A Black Briton Comes Home: Claude McKay in England, 1920," *Race,* vol. 9 (1967), p. 76.

32. Claude McKay, *A Long Way from Home,* op. cit., pp. 73–91.

33. Ibid., p. 69.

34. Wayne Cooper and Robert C. Reinders, "A Black Briton Comes Home," op. cit., pp. 79–81.

35. Daniel Aaron, *Writers on the Left,* op. cit., p. 82.

36. Aside from the *Messenger,* only scattered copies survive of the journals produced by these early black socialists. Most of the early issues of Garvey's *Negro World,* for example, have been lost. See Theodore Draper, *American Communism and Soviet Russia* (New York: Viking Press, 1960), pp. 315–35; see also James Weldon Johnson, *Black Manhattan* (New York: Knopf, 1930), pp. 246–51. Two important sources of information concerning Negro radicals in postwar New York are the government publications that resulted from the Red Scare of 1919: Investigative Activities of the Department of Justice, Exhibit No. 10, "Radicalism and Sedition Among Negroes as Reflected in Their Publications," 66th Congress, 1st Sess., Sen. Ex. Doc. 153, vol. 12 (serial no. 7607), pp. 161–87; and New York State Legislature

Joint Committee Investigating Seditious Activities, *Revolutionary Radicalism: Its History, Purpose, and Tactics, with an Exposition and Discussion of the Steps Being Taken and Required to Curb It, Being the Report of the Joint Legislative Committee Investigating Seditious Activities, Filed April 24, 1920, in the Senate of the State of New York,* 4 vols. (Albany: J. B. Lyon, 1920), vol. 2, pp. 1476–1520.

37. Claude McKay, *A Long Way from Home,* op. cit., p. 67. The editor was unable to locate those issues of the *Negro World* which contained McKay's articles. Apparently only a few scattered issues of the early *Negro World* have survived.

38. Marcus Garvey, quoted in Edmund David Cronon, *Black Moses: The Story of Marcus Garvey and the Universal Negro Improvement Association* (Madison, Wisc.: University of Wisconsin Press, 1955), p. 152.

39. Claude McKay, *A Long Way from Home,* op. cit., pp. 108–15.

40. Ibid., pp. 130–46.

41. Claude McKay, "Review of *Harlem Shadows,*" *New York Times Book Review* (May 14, 1922), p. 17.

42. Robert Littel, "Review of *Harlem Shadows* and *The Book of American Negro Poetry,*" *New Republic* (July 12, 1922), p. 196.

43. Walter White, "Review of *Harlem Shadows* and *The Book of American Negro Poetry,*" Bookman, vol. 5 (July 1922), p. 531.

44. James Weldon Johnson in the *New York Age,* quoted in R. G. Johnson, "The Poetry of Dunbar and McKay: A Study" (Unpublished M.A. thesis, University of Pittsburgh, 1950), p. 29.

45. Alain Locke, ed., *The New Negro: An Interpretation* (New York: Albert and Charles Boni, 1925).

46. Joseph Freeman, *An American Testament,* op. cit., p. 256. See Michael Gold's *Jews Without Money* (New York: Horace Liveright, 1930); an autobiographical novel of his childhood which has become a minor American classic.

47. Claude McKay, *A Long Way from Home,* op. cit., p. 103.

48. Ibid., p. 139.

49. Joseph Freeman, *An American Testament,* op. cit., p. 257. This was a position McKay maintained aggressively throughout his life.

50. Daniel Aaron, *Writers on the Left,* op. cit., p. 95.

51. Claude McKay, *A Long Way from Home,* op. cit., p. 150. As this quote would suggest, McKay and his wife never reconciled their differences. McKay never developed a permanent sexual relationship with anyone. In fact, many of his love poems were written in celebration of fugitive, one-night affairs (see "A Memory of June," in *Selected Poems,* op. cit., p. 99). As in other areas of his life, McKay was in truth profoundly ambivalent regarding his sexual preferences. Some of

his friends remember him as primarily, if not totally, homosexual; others knew nothing of his homosexuality and regarded him as heterosexual, while some who knew him best maintain he was bisexual. Whatever his orientation, he had difficulty maintaining an intimate relationship with anyone over a long period. To Max Eastman, he wrote: "I ought to be closely attached to somebody, woman or even man, instead of being off at loose ends living lone-wolfishly. But I never can feel a sentimental attachment for the persons that attract me intellectually. And the types that stir up passion in me are no good for intimate attachment. . . . I can't get my mind and my emotions in harmony together and con-centrated on someone. That's my whole tragedy. I need somebody to look after me. But generally I appear so strong to people, as if I don't need looking after. Last time I was in Paris Fanny Rappaport [Dr. F. Vogein-Rappaport, who became the wife of the late Pierre Vogein, McKay's best friend in France] told me that I looked in every way as if I were sufficient unto myself. So there I am. And whenever I try to get away from myself I choose the wrong person. . . ." (Letter from McKay to Max Eastman, June 28, 1933; in the Max Eastman–Claude McKay Letters; see note 23 above.)

52. Ibid., pp. 153–55.

53. Ibid., pp. 155–66.

54. Theodore Draper, *American Communism and Soviet Russia,* op. cit., p. 327.

55. "Resolutions on the Negro Question," *Resolutions and Theses of the Fourth Congress of the Communist International* (London: Communist Party of Great Britain, 1923), pp. 84–85.

56. Theodore Draper, *American Communism and Soviet Russia,* op. cit., pp. 328–29.

57. Claude McKay, *A Long Way from Home,* op. cit., p. 168.

58. Ibid., p. 223.

59. Ibid., p. 225.

60. In *A Long Way from Home,* McKay mentions that he had come down with pneumonia while working as an artist's model in a Paris studio. He also mentions that he had earlier entered a Paris hos-pital, without, however, specifically naming the illness that put him there (*A Long Way from Home,* pp. 230–31, 253). Shortly after his arrival in Paris he was hospitalized for the treatment of syphilis, which he had in its early, infectious stage. His hospital treatment was successful, and he was discharged as cured. But he was understandably worried, and from time to time he apparently felt it necessary to treat himself with the poisonous, arsenic-based medicines then used for the control of syphilis. Finally, in 1930, after suffering for months from severe headaches and fits of nervousness, he journeyed to Berlin, where he was thoroughly examined by leading specialists in the disease. They

found him completely free of all venereal diseases and concluded he had probably been "over-medicined" (McKay to Eastman, December 1, 1930, Eastman–McKay Letters). Information concerning McKay's hospitalization in Paris was obtained from Dr. F. Vogein-Rappaport and from the *Liberator* artist John Barber, who was in Paris at the time and helped McKay financially during his hospitalization. He later got McKay his modeling job in the studio of André Lothé.

61. Letter from Claude McKay to Arthur A. Schomburg, undated [1925]; in the McKay folder of the A. A. Schomburg Papers, the Schomburg Collection, New York Public Library. In 1927 McKay stated that he burned "Color Scheme" after failing to find a publisher. See letter from Claude McKay to William Aspenwall Bradley, April 15, 1927; McKay–Bradley correspondence in the possession of Mrs. W. A. Bradley, Paris, France.

62. Claude McKay, *A Long Way from Home*, op. cit., pp. 281–83; letter from McKay to W. A. Bradley, June 4, 1927, McKay–Bradley correspondence.

63. Alain Locke, ed., *The New Negro*, op. cit., pp. 3–4.

64. Robert Bone, *The Negro Novel*, op. cit., p. 62.

65. For a more extended discussion of Claude McKay's relation to the Negro Renaissance, see Wayne Cooper, "Claude McKay and the New Negro of the 1920s," in C. W. E. Bigsby, ed., *The Black American Writer, Volume II: Poetry and Drama* (Baltimore: Penguin Books, 1971), pp. 53–65.

66. W. E. B. Du Bois, "The Browsing Reader: Review of *Home to Harlem*," *Crisis*, vol. 35 (June 1928), p. 202.

67. Clipping from the *Chicago Defender*, March 17, 1928; in the McKay folder, of the Schomburg Papers, Schomburg Collection, New York Public Library.

68. John R. Chamberlain, "Review of *Home to Harlem*," *New York Times*, March 11, 1928, p. 5.

69. Carl Van Doren, "Review of *Home to Harlem*," *Nation*, vol. 126 (March 28, 1928), p. 35.

70. Claude McKay, *Banjo: A Story Without a Plot* (New York: Harper and Brothers, 1929), p. 319.

71. Ibid., p. 319.

72. Ibid., pp. 320–24.

73. Claude McKay, *A Long Way from Home*, op. cit., p. 319.

74. Letter from Langston Hughes to Claude McKay, March 5, 1928; Hughes Papers, James Weldon Johnson Collection, Yale University Library.

75. Letter from Claude McKay to W. A. Bradley, February 10, 1928; McKay–Bradley correspondence. The surviving manuscript of "Romance in Marseille" belongs to Mrs. Hope McKay Virtue. A copy

of it is also on deposit at the Schomburg Collection, New York Public Library.

76. Letter from Claude McKay to Max Eastman, December 1, 1930; Eastman Papers, Indiana University Library.

77. McKay's expectations regarding *Banana Bottom* and the difficulties he encountered as a result of its failure are fully revealed in his letters to Max Eastman; Eastman Papers, Indiana University Library.

78. Claude McKay, "Note on Harlem," in Jean Wagner, *Les poètes nègres des Etats-Unis,* op. cit., pp. 582–83.

79. Interview with Miss Selma Burke. McKay's correspondence from various officials in the Federal Writers' Project form part of the McKay Papers in the James Weldon Johnson Collection at Yale. See also Jerre Mangione, *The Dream and the Deal: The Federal Writers' Project* (Boston: Little, Brown, 1972), p. 245.

80. The most forceful critique of *A Long Way from Home* was Alain Locke's review in the *New Challenge,* vol. 2 (Fall, 1937), pp. 81–85. In building his case against McKay's aggressive individualism, however, Locke failed to mention that McKay had criticized him at length in the book under review. See McKay, *A Long Way from Home,* op. cit. pp. 312–14.

81. See W. E. B. Du Bois, "Segregation in the North," *Crisis,* vol. 41 (April, 1934), pp. 115–17. See also "On Black Separatism: 'Organize Our Economic and Social Power No Matter How Much Segregation It Involves,'" in John H. Bracey, Jr., August Meier, and Elliott Rudwick, eds., *Black Nationalism in America* (Indianapolis and New York: Bobbs-Merrill Company, 1970), pp. 288–98.

82. Interviews with Romare Bearden, Jacob Lawrence, and Mrs. Countee Cullen Cooper.

83. Claude McKay, *Harlem: Negro Metropolis* (New York: E. P. Dutton and Co., 1940); Jerre Mangione, *The Dream and the Deal,* op. cit., pp. 257, 262.

84. Claude McKay, *Harlem: Negro Metropolis,* op. cit., pp. 183–84.

85. Roi Ottley, "Review of *Harlem: Negro Metropolis,*" *New York Times* (November 24, 1940), p. 5; Ted Poston, "Review of *Harlem: Negro Metropolis,*" *New Republic,* vol. 103 (November 25, 1940), p. 732.

86. Ellen Terry, *The Third Door: The Autobiography of an American Negro Woman* (New York: David McKay, 1955), p. 187. Interview with Ellen Terry.

87. Ibid., p. 187.

88. Claude McKay, "Tiger," *Selected Poems* (New York: Twayne Publishers, 1953), p. 47. In his last years McKay began once again to

write poetry and before his death produced a sonnet cycle of fifty-four poems, some of which appeared in Dorothy Day's socialist-pacifist weekly, the *Catholic Worker*. McKay's *Selected Poems* also contains a few of these later poems, but the majority are unpublished and form part of the McKay Papers in the James Weldon Johnson Collection. As a whole they do not measure up to his earlier poetry. His magazine articles cover the same ground as the poems in a much more forceful and effective way.

89. At the time of his death, McKay's daughter was in New York City studying at Columbia University. They had been planning to see each other in New York. As it turned out, she saw her father for the first time at his Harlem funeral service.

1. EARLY ARTICLES, 1918–1922

1. Accompanying this essay were five poems—"To the White Fiends," "The Conqueror," "The Park in Spring," "Is It Worthwhile," and "Harlem Shadows." It seems that "Harlem Shadows" was written after McKay moved to New York in 1914. As editor of *Pearson's Magazine,* Frank Harris probably included "Harlem Shadows" with the others, which do seem to have been written at an earlier date. "Is It Worthwhile" and "The Conqueror" in particular reflect the same pessimism and disillusionment that pervaded his Jamaican dialect poetry. Neither contains any reference to racial problems, but only indications of a general recognition of human depravity. They were not very well written and were never included in his published volumes.

2. For a more detailed account of McKay's childhood, see his unpublished memoir, "My Green Hills of Jamaica," in the Schomburg Collection, New York Public Library.

3. Edward Carpenter (1844–1929) was a British author whose studies and commentaries on human sexuality were much discussed in the 1920s. His most popular book in America was *Love's Coming of Age* (1896), but he also wrote on the nature of democracy and other social questions. Carpenter was a great admirer of Whitman, whom he visited in America.

4. *Songs of Jamaica* and *Constab Ballads* were both published in 1912.

5. McKay never identified the friend mentioned here. He was always reluctant to write in any detail about his unsuccessful restaurant business, which must have ended disastrously. In 1928 he advised

James Weldon Johnson not to reveal the location of his former business or otherwise discuss it at any length in writing about McKay's forthcoming book, *Home to Harlem.* Letter from McKay to James Weldon Johnson, March 10, 1928; Johnson Papers, James Weldon Johnson Collection, Yale University Library.

6. McKay was employed at the time with the Pennsylvania Railroad.

7. Thomas Carlyle (1795–1881), Scottish essayist and historian, criticized industrialism, extolled the virtues of the vanishing craftsman, and preached the redemptive value of common labor for the masses. At Tuskegee Booker T. Washington emphasized the training of skilled craftsmen and farmers. In *The Souls of Black Folk* (Chicago: A. C. McClurg, 1903), W. E. B. Du Bois acknowledged the necessity of vocational training, but he criticized Washington's failure to promote higher academic education for the Negro race's "talented tenth." Du Bois also attacked Washington's willingness to compromise the black man's human rights in order to strengthen his own immediate influence among whites. McKay first read *The Souls of Black Folk* in Kansas. "The book," he later reported, "shook me like an earthquake," *A Long Way from Home,* op. cit., p. 110.

8. Oswald Garrison Villard (1872–1949) owned and edited the *Nation* from 1918 until 1932. Other whites prominent in the founding of the NAACP included Mary White Ovington (1865–1951), Joel Spingarn (1875–1939), William English Walling (1877–1936), Charles E. Russell (1860–1941), and Dr. Henry Moskowitz (1879–1936). Ovington, Walling, and Russell were all socialists at the time of the NAACP's founding in 1909–1910.

9. For a summary of American socialist attitudes toward Negroes during this period, see James Weinstein, *The Decline of Socialism in America, 1912–1925* (New York: Monthly Review Press, 1967), pp. 63–74.

10. A. Philip Randolph (1889–   ) and Chandler Owen (1889–1967). See Introduction, page 14.

11. Samuel Gompers (1850–1924) was the chief founder and president of the American Federation of Labor.

12. The National Brotherhood Workers of America during its brief existence from 1919 until 1921 attempted to federate all the existing black unions and to "serve as an agency for organizing those Negroes who did not belong to a union," in a manner similar to the United Hebrew Trades. See Sterling D. Spero and Abram L. Harris, *The Black Worker* (New York: Columbia University Press, 1931), pp. 117–19.

13. W. E. B. Du Bois joined the American Socialist Party in 1911 and resigned in 1912.

14. For the full story of Morel's campaign against the French and

their use of black troops on the Rhine, see Robert C. Reinders, "Racialism on the Left: E. D. Morel and the 'Black Horror on the Rhine,' " *International Review of Social History*, vol. 13 (First Quarter, 1968), pp. 1–28.

15. Countess Constance Georgine de Markiewicz, nee Gore-Booth (1876–1927), was an Irish Nationalist who in 1900 married the Polish Count Casimir Dunin de Markiewicz. After the establishment of Ireland's independence, she served as the minister of labor under Eamon de Valera and also as a member of the Irish parliament.

16. Robert Erskine Childers (1870–1922), was of Anglo-Irish descent. He favored the complete independence of all Ireland and opposed the Irish Free State established by the Anglo-Irish treaty of 1922. In the civil strife which followed the treaty, he was captured by Free State soldiers and executed as a traitor.

17. For an account of nineteenth century Irish-American antipathy toward blacks, see Carl Wittke, *The Irish in America* (New York: Russell and Russell, 1970), pp. 125–49.

18. C. T. Cramp was president of the National Union of Railwaymen.

19. McKay is most likely referring to a speech Shaw delivered to the Fabian Society in London, November 28, 1919. It later appeared as a supplement to *The New Commonwealth,* December 12, 1919. This speech was reprinted under the title "Socialism and Ireland" in Bernard Shaw, *The Matter with Ireland,* David H. Greene and Dan H. Laurence, eds. (London: Rupert Hart-Davis, 1962), pp. 214–32.

20. Henry Mayers Hyndman (1842–1921) was an English socialist writer and politician of upper-class origin. Shaw was most probably referring to Hyndman's flowing beard and his dignified manner and bearing. The *Dictionary of National Biography* describes him as having "remained always something of an aristocrat among socialists, in temper as well as in manner, impatient with differences, but always ready to make any sacrifice for the cause."

21. *Shuffle Along* was not a burlesque in the modern American sense of the term, but a pioneering musical comedy with a definite story line. Most probably McKay is here characterizing it as "burlesque" because of its broadly comic aspects. See McKay's later comments on *Shuffle Along* in *A Long Way from Home,* op. cit., pp. 141–43.

22. The American Southern Orchestra was an American Negro band organized and led by the black composer and musician Will Marion Cook.

23. St. Phillip's is a predominately black Episcopal Church in upper Manhattan. There is also a black St. Phillip's Episcopal Church in Brooklyn.

24. Samuel Coleridge-Taylor (1875–1912) was an English composer of African ancestry on his father's side.

25. Harry T. Burleigh (1866–1949) was perhaps America's best known black singer and composer in the early decades of the twentieth century. He served for over fifty years as the baritone soloist for St. George's Episcopal Church in Manhattan and counted the American financier J. P. Morgan among his friends.

26. Henry Ossawa Tanner (1859–1937) was an American Negro painter of considerable accomplishment who spent all his productive years in Europe.

27. William S. Braithwaite (1878–1962) was an American Negro poet, critic, and anthologist of magazine verse who served for years as the poetry editor of the *Boston Evening Transcript*. A man of generally conservative nature, he tended to minimize specifically racial themes in his poetry and criticism.

28. The Lafayette Players began as the Anita Bush Stock Company in 1915 at the Lincoln Theater. In 1916 they moved to the Lafayette Theater and were thereafter known as the Lafayette Players. See Sister Mary Francesca Thompson, "The Lafayette Players, 1915–1932," (Unpublished Ph.D. dissertation, University of Michigan, 1972).

29. Florence Mills (1895–1927) enjoyed stardom for only six more years. A ruptured appendix resulted in her premature death in 1927.

30. Eubie Blake (1883–   ) and Noble Sissle (1889–   ), besides writing the music and lyrics, also appeared in *Shuffle Along*, Blake as musical conductor and pianist and Sissle as a vocalist and actor.

31. The Harmony Kings were a quartet consisting of Harold Browning, E. E. Drayton, W. H. Berry, and W. H. Hann.

32. Sam Peck and Steve Jenkins, two main characters in *Shuffle Along* were played by the famous black comedy team of Flournoy Miller and Aubrey Lyles. Miller and Lyles also wrote the book for *Shuffle Along*.

33. "Onion" Jeffrey was a black comedian, well known in his day, who appeared under his own name in *Shuffle Along*.

34. William Monroe Trotter (1872–1934) was for many years the militant black editor of the *Boston Guardian* and an early opponent of Booker T. Washington. For awhile, he seemed destined to share the influential leadership role that passed to W. E. B. Du Bois, but Trotter's contentiousness eventually alienated most of his friends and followers. See Stephan R. Fox, *The Guardian of Boston, William Monroe Trotter* (New York: Atheneum, 1970).

35. Alexander Bedward believed himself to be Christ reincarnate. His ascent into heaven was to be accompanied by the destruction of the white race. In 1920 his scheduled ascension was repeatedly post-

poned, and he was ultimately committed to an asylum where he died. For more on Bedward, see Donald William Hogg, "Jamaican Religions: A Study in Variations" (unpublished Ph.D. dissertation, Yale University, 1964).

36. In 1922 Garvey was arrested and indicted by the Federal government on charges that he had "knowingly used 'fraudulent representations' and 'deceptive artifices' " in the sale of his Black Star stocks through the mails. Although the evidence against him was weak, he was tried and convicted in 1923. After the failure of all legal appeals, he was jailed in 1925 and deported in 1927.

37. McKay is here referring to white Ku Klux Klansmen, whom Garvey at one point considered his natural allies; they too wished to see all blacks return to Africa. See Edmund Cronon, *Black Moses*, op. cit. pp. 103, 188–90.

38. Charles W. Wood (1880–1954) had a long career as a journalist for the *New York World, Forbes Magazine,* and *Collier's*. While serving as a drama critic for the *Masses* and *Liberator,* he regularly interviewed leaders of the American "establishment" for the Sunday editorial section of the *World*. See Charles W. Wood, *The Great Change: New America as Seen by Leaders in American Government, Industry, and Education, Who Are Remaking Our Civilization* (New York: Boni and Liveright, 1918). In the spring of 1922, Wood also reported upon the breakup of a *Liberator* fund-raising ball by the city police, who objected to McKay and other blacks dancing with white women. See "An Open Letter from Charles W. Wood to Hon. Richard Enright [Police Commissioner] and Hon. John F. Hylan [Mayor] on the breakup of the *Liberator* Ball," *Liberator,* vol. 5 (June 1922), pp. 9–10.

39. William Gropper (1897–   ) is an American painter and illustrator whose works hang in the Museum of Modern Art in New York City and in other museums around the country. His cartoons and drawings appeared regularly in the *Liberator* and later in the *New Masses*. Gropper has confirmed the details of this incident, and he also remembers that he went several times with McKay to dances in Harlem, where they once encountered American black prejudice against McKay as a West Indian. Letter from William Gropper to Wayne Cooper, May 14, 1964.

40. *Chauve Souris* was a musical review that featured Russian entertainers, musicians, and themes. See McKay's review, "What Is Lacking in the Theatre?," *Liberator,* vol. 5 (March 1922), pp. 20–21.

41. Thomas Dixon (1864–1946) was a Southern Baptist minister whose popular racist novels extolling Southern Civilization included *The Clansman* (1905), which in 1915 was made into the film *The Birth of a Nation*.

42. McKay is probably referring to the publication *John Bull*, a generally heavy-handed and humorless magazine of political and social commentary founded in 1903 in London by the English editor and politician Horatio Bottomley (1860–1933).

43. George S. Viereck (1884–1962) was born in Germany and came to the United States as a child with his parents. In 1914 he founded the *Fatherland* (later called the *American Monthly*) in which he ardently defended German national interests, both during and after World War I. In 1920–21, Viereck joined E. D. Morel's racist crusade against the French use of African troops in the German Rhineland. See Ray Beveridge, "The Black Terror in Germany," *American Monthly*, vol. 12 (December 1920), pp. 301–2.

2. THE RUSSIAN EXPERIENCE, 1922–1923

1. In the fall of 1922 the remaining *Liberator* staff members decided to convert the magazine into an organ of the Communist party, and in November 1924 the *Liberator* merged wtih the *Soviet Russia Pictorial* and the *Labor-Herald*. See Daniel Aaron, *Writers on the Left*, op. cit., pp. 91–96.

2. Boardman Robinson (1876–1952), American artist and illustrator, was a member of the editorial staff of the *Liberator*.

3. The "race story" McKay refers to was an account of a "legal lynching" in Texas. See Lucy Maverick, "Out of Texas," *Liberator*, vol. 5 (June 1922), pp. 28–30.

4. Eastman's "brilliant joke" consisted of an attack upon the hypocrisy of those generals and ministers of state who were at the time "pinning medals on the coffins" of Unknown Soldiers, while living ex-soldiers were being forced into bread lines. "And if this [unknown] soldier should by some mysterious accident suddenly become known—become, that is, a real individual—they would have no such impulse or emotion toward him. Suppose he should poke a wooly head up over the side of the coffin and murmur, 'Why for you-all reckon you's makin' dis big fuss ovah me?' The bubble would be pricked . . ." (Max Eastman, "Editorial," *Liberator*, vol. 4 [December, 1921], p. 5). Interestingly enough, in 1930 this idea became the topic of a poem by James Weldon Johnson. His poem "Saint Peter Relates an Incident of the Resurrection Day" was inspired by events of a later date and was not directly related to Eastman's editorial comment. See James Weldon Johnson, *Saint Peter Relates an Incident: Selected Poems* (New York: Viking Press, 1935), pp. ix, 13–21.

5. For McKay's account of his activities at the Colored Soldiers' and Sailors' Club in London, see Claude McKay, *A Long Way from Home,* op. cit., pp. 67–68.

6. From "Address of the International Working Men's Association to President Lincoln [November 1864]." The full text of this address, together with the reply of Charles Francis Adams, U.S. Ambassador to Great Britain, on behalf of President Lincoln can be found in Karl Marx, *The Karl Marx Library, Vol. 2: On America and the Civil War,* ed. and trans. by Saul K. Padover (New York: McGraw-Hill, 1972), pp. 236–40.

7. John Bright (1811–1889) and Richard Cobden (1804–1865) were British advocates of free trade and nonintervention in foreign wars. In the 1830s and 1840s, they had led a successful campaign to repeal the British Corn Laws. Charles Bradlaugh (1833–1891) in his day was a famous advocate of free thought and a successful English parliamentarian.

8. George Bernard Shaw, the author of the plays *Arms and the Man* and *John Bull's Other Island,* was decidedly more political and polemical in all his writings than was Oscar Wilde, the author of *The Picture of Dorian Gray.*

9. The U.S. Marines occupied Haiti in 1915, following a period of internal political strife that threatened the Haitian government's ability to pay its foreign debts. The U.S. occupation of Haiti lasted until 1934.

10. John Reed (1887–1920), radical American journalist and poet, described the Bolshevik seizure of power in October 1917 in his book, *Ten Days That Shook the World* (New York: Boni and Liveright, 1919). Reed discussed the racial problem in America with Russian Communist leaders in 1920. A former editor of the *Masses,* Reed, on behalf of the Communist International, invited McKay to Moscow in 1920. See Theodore Draper, *American Communism and Soviet Russia,* op. cit., pp. 319–22.

11. McKay first met Sen Katayama (1858–1933) in New York. See Claude McKay, *A Long Way from Home,* pp. 164–66. McKay states that Katayama had attended Fisk University, but Hyman Kublin states that Katayama attended Maryville College in Maryville, Tennessee. Kublin does not mention Fisk and tends to minimize Katayama's interest in the American race problem. See Hyman Kublin, *Asian Revolutionary: The Life of Sen Katayama* (Princeton, N.J.: Princeton University Press, 1964), pp. 55–59.

12. Boris Pilnyak (1894–1937) was a well-known Russian novelist. "Okonoff" and "Feodor" were lesser-known figures whose names McKay may have mistransliterated. It has not proven possible to identify them.

13. McKay is referring here to Korney Chukovsky, a well-known

Russian man of letters whom McKay discusses at length later in this essay; "Zamiatan," was Yevgeny Zamyatin (1884–1937), the novelist; and "Maishack" was Daniel Marshak, a minor poet of the early Soviet period.

3. POETRY, 1912–1925

1. See, for example, the poems "To E. M. E." and "Heart Stirrings," in Claude McKay, *Songs of Jamaica,* pp. 51–52, 69–71. Walter Jekyll's philosophic pessimism can be inferred from McKay's sympathetic portrayals of him in the novel *Banana Bottom* and in "My Green Hills of Jamaica," as well as from the subject matter of Jekyll's own published works. In addition to compiling *Jamaican Song and Story,* Jekyll also wrote and edited several other books. These included *The Wisdom of Schopenhauer as Revealed in Some of His Principal Writings,* selected and translated by Walter Jekyll (London: Watts, 1911); and *The Bible Untrustworthy: A Critical Comparison of Contradictory Passages in the Scriptures, With a View To Testing Their Accuracy* (London: Watts, 1904).

2. In *Songs of Jamaica* and *Constab Ballads,* the influence of several British poets can be seen—Burns, Shelley, Wordsworth, Tennyson, and Kipling—all of whom McKay at times more or less unconsciously imitated in his various moods. In the three poems included here, however, he employs the dramatic monologue in a manner reminiscent of Robert Browning.

3. On Sept. 27, 1971, *Time* magazine reported that the rebellious prisoners at Attica State Prison in New York had "passed around clandestine writings of their own: among them was a poem written by an unknown prisoner, crude but touching in its would-be heroic style . . . 'If We Must Die.' "

4. AN ARTICLE AND LETTERS, 1925–1932

1. McKay discussed his relationship with the American expatriate caravan in *A Long Way from Home,* pp. 243–46. Although he sympathized with the white American writers and artists in Europe and understood their reasons for leaving the United States, he concluded that his motives for remaining so long abroad were different: "Color-

consciousness was the fundamental of my restlessness. And it was something with which my fellow-expatriates could sympathize but which they could not altogether understand. For they were not black like me. Not being black and unable to see deep into the profundity of blackness, some even thought that I might have preferred to be white like them. They couldn't imagine that I had no desire merely to exchange my black problem for their white problem. For all their knowledge and sophistication, they couldn't understand the instinctive and animal and purely physical pride of a black person resolute in being himself and yet living a simple civilized life like themselves" (Claude McKay, *A Long Way from Home*, p. 245).

McKay also mentions in *A Long Way from Home* that Sinclair Lewis and Frank Harris, both of whom he saw in France, advised him regarding the stylistic and technical problems he encountered as a beginning novelist (pp. 259, 268). In 1926, McKay stayed for several weeks with Max Eastman and his wife at Antibes in the south of France, where he completed the original, short-story version of *Home to Harlem*. While there he met F. Scott Fitzgerald, who (much to everyone's merriment) at first mistook McKay for a house servant. See Max Eastman, *Love and Revolution*, op. cit., p. 468. After the publication of *Home to Harlem*, Fitzgerald sent McKay a congratulatory card in which he wrote, "[I] can't tell you how I enjoyed your book. . . . For me it was one of the two most worthy novels of the spring." Postcard from F. Scott Fitzgerald to Claude McKay, May 25, 1928, in the McKay Papers, James Weldon Johnson Collection, Yale University Library. In the same card Fitzgerald further noted a "Zola–Lewis" influence in the railroad scenes of *Home to Harlem*, which stood in contrast to "the emotion of the purely Harlem scenes." McKay mentions Fitzgerald's comments in *A Long Way from Home*, op. cit., p. 259.

2. From William S. Braithwaite, "The Negro in Literature," *Crisis*, vol. 28 (September 1924), p. 208.

3. McKay did begin this novel or one with a similar theme, but he never finished it. See letter from Claude McKay to Arthur A. Schomburg, August 1, 1926, in the McKay folder of the Schomburg Papers, the Schomburg Collection, New York.

4. McKay is referring to a Garland Fund grant he received in 1924. The Fund provided McKay with a check for fifty dollars a month from April 1924 through July 1925. Roger Baldwin, one of the administrators of the Fund, wrote Sinclair Lewis enquiring about McKay's use of the money, and he asked whether or not McKay shouldn't return "home." In his reply to Baldwin, Lewis conceded that some American writers had been "enfeebled" by remaining abroad too long, but he did not think that would be true of McKay. "As he is a Negro," Lewis

wrote, "he has here an ease, a chance to forget social problems and consider the vast material he has already accumulated, which he would never have in America. Tolstoy would have presumably never have written *War and Peace* without some experience of war but certainly also he would never have written it while serving as an artillery officer. . . . This whole matter of writers abroad is complicated, and I fancy that only the writer himself can decide it . . . and decide it not so much from rational grounds as from his feeling about it. I'd leave it up to Claude himself." Copy of letter from Sinclair Lewis to Roger Baldwin, January 19, 1925, in the McKay Papers, James Weldon Johnson Collection, Yale University Library.

5. Jessie Fauset (1882–1961), the literary editor of the *Crisis,* wrote in 1924 a novel of Negro middle class life entitled *There Is Confusion* (New York: Boni and Liveright). In the next ten years she wrote three other novels. Robert Bone has characterized her "as an authentic old Philadelphian (known as "OP's" in the colored society of that day), [who] was never able to transcend the narrow limits" of her background in the novels she wrote. Bone points out, however, that she nevertheless often championed in the *Crisis* "the young rebels of the Harlem school," and he quotes McKay's remark in *A Long Way from Home* that "all the radicals liked her, although in her social viewpoint she was away over on the other side of the fence" (p. 112). See Robert Bone, *The Negro Novel in America,* op. cit., pp. 101–2.

6. In *A Long Way from Home,* McKay implied that there was a contradiction between Mary White Ovington's apparently "gracious, almost sweet" manners and the severity of her judgment against Booker T. Washington. He seems to have felt that beneath her charm she lacked a certain generosity of spirit. Regarding Joel Spingarn, McKay's objections were less precise. He appreciated Spingarn's interest in his poetry but not what he felt was Spingarn's bourgeois depreciation of his political radicalism. See McKay's ambivalent comments on both Spingarn and Ovington in *A Long Way from Home,* op. cit., pp. 113, 147–48.

7. Joel Spingarn established the Spingarn medal in 1914. It is defined as "a gold medal to be awarded for the highest or noblest achievement by an American Negro during the preceding year or years." The first recipient of the medal was Professor Ernest E. Just, the Howard University biologist, in 1915. See Langston Hughes, *Fight for Freedom: The Story of the NAACP* (New York: W. W. Norton, 1962), p. 67.

8. The citation accompanying each Spingarn medal varies, of course, according to the achievement of the individual awarded. McKay was probably referring to the full, general statement of the award's purpose,

which reads as follows: "The purpose of the award is twofold—first to call the attention of the American people to the existence of distinguished merit and achievement among American Negroes, and secondly, to serve as a reward for such achievement, and as a stimulant to the ambition of colored youth." This statement is from a descriptive brochure of the Spingarn medal published by the NAACP.

9. Walter White (1893–1955), who was at the time Field Secretary of the NAACP, was also corresponding with McKay during this period. See Charles F. Cooney, "Walter White and the Harlem Renaissance," *Journal of Negro History,* vol. 57 (July 1972), pp. 231–40.

10. McKay owed Spingarn more than one favor. It was Spingarn who arranged for McKay's poems to appear in *Seven Arts* in 1917 and who found him a publisher for *Harlem Shadows* in 1922 (*A Long Way from Home,* pp. 147–48). Besides serving the NAACP from its inception until his death in 1939, Spingarn also had a distinguished career as a professor of English at Columbia University. In American literary history Spingarn is best remembered for having introduced to America the aesthetic ideas of Benedetto Croce, the Italian philosopher and historian.

11. The *New Negro* was published by Charles (1894–1969) and Albert Boni (1892–   ). Ironically it was the Bonis who organized in 1914 the Washington Square Players, which developed into the Theater Guild, the theater that sent McKay to the balcony to view *He Who Gets Slapped.*

12. Locke had first presented most of the material in the *New Negro* in a special Harlem number of the *Survey Graphic,* vol. 6 (March 1924). The "White House" had originally appeared in the *Liberator,* vol. 5 (May 1922), p. 16.

13. "Negro Dancers" first appeared as a three-part sonnet sequence in the *Liberator,* vol. 2 (July 1919), p. 20.

14. The novel to which McKay refers was never published. He began it after his failure to find a publisher for "Color Scheme" in 1925. At the suggestion of Harper and Bros., the publication of McKay's short stories was postponed, and he instead expanded one of them, *Home to Harlem,* into a novel (see Introduction, p. 27).

15. See George W. Jacobs, "New Yorker Flays McKay's *Home to Harlem,*" *Pittsburgh Courier,* April 7, 1928.

16. Eric Walrond (1898–1966) was a black writer from British Guiana. After World War I, he wrote for Garvey's *Negro World* and later for other journals. In 1926, he published a volume of short stories, *Tropic Death* (New York: Boni and Liveright). He eventually settled in London.

17. Harold Jackman (1901–1961) taught in the New York public

schools. A handsome and affable man, he was a friend and confidant of Countee Cullen and other writers and artists of the Negro Renaissance.

18. McKay described Grace Campbell as "one of the pioneer Negro members of the Socialist party," in *A Long Way from Home,* p. 109. Hubert Harrison (1883–1927) was also a pioneering black socialist and one of the first black intellectuals McKay met after coming to New York in 1914. Born in the Virgin Islands and educated in the New York public schools, Harrison became one of the first and greatest in a long line of Harlem street-corner orators. He also contributed articles and book reviews to a number of newspapers and magazines through the years. In 1917 he established a short-lived publication, *The Voice,* and after its demise founded another in 1919, which he called the *New Negro.* In 1920–21, he edited Garvey's *Negro World* and published a collection of essays and articles (see Hubert Harrison, *When Africa Awakes* [New York: Porro Press, 1920]). In the 1920s, Harrison lectured for the New York City Board of Education and shortly before his death attempted to launch another journal, *The Voice of the Negro* (1927). A man of imposing physique, encyclopedic knowledge, and rare oratorical ability, Harrison became something of a legend in his lifetime, although he has since been largely forgotten. Henry Miller has described him as a soapbox orator without peer: ". . . I was in the midst of a long-drawn-out rhapsody about another Negro, my quondam idol, Hubert Harrison. I was telling them of all I had learned standing at the foot of his soapbox in Madison Square. . . . There was no one in those days, I told them candidly, who could hold a candle to Hubert Harrison. With a few well-directed words he had the ability to demolish any opponent. He did it neatly and smoothly too, 'with kid gloves,' so to speak. I described the wonderful way he smiled, his easy assurance, the great sculptured head which he carried on his shoulders like a lion. I wondered aloud if he had not come of royal blood, if he had not been the descendant of some great African monarch. Yes, he was a man who electrified one by his mere presence. Beside him the other speakers, the white ones, looked like pygmies, not only physically but culturally, spiritually. Some of them . . . carried on like epileptics, always wrapped in the Stars and Stripes, to be sure. Hubert Harrison, on the other hand, no matter what the provocation, always retained his self-possession, his dignity. He had a way of placing the back of his hand on his hip, his trunk tilted, his ears cocked to catch every last word the questioner, or the heckler put to him. Well he knew how to bide his time! When the tumult had subsided there would come that broad smile of his, a broad, good-natured grin, and he would answer his man—always fair and square, always full on, like a broadside. Soon everyone would be laughing, everyone but the poor imbecile

who had dared to put the question . . ." (from Henry Miller, *The Rosy Crucifixion, Book Two: Plexus,* Evergreen Black Cat edition [New York: Grove Press, 1965], pp. 560–61).

20. William H. Ferris (1874–1941), black journalist and author, attacked McKay and *Home to Harlem* in the *Pittsburgh Courier* (March 31, 1928). For a time Ferris helped edit Garvey's *Negro World.* Before World War I, he wrote a two-volume work entitled *The African Abroad: On His Evolution in Western Civilization, Tracing His Development Under the Caucasian Milieu* (New Haven, Conn.: Tuttle, Morehouse, and Taylor, 1913).

21. *Blackbirds* was a musical review that had a considerable success on Broadway before its European tour in 1929. It had an all-black cast but had not been conceived and written by blacks as had *Shuffle Along.* See McKay's comparison of the two shows in *A Long Way from Home,* op. cit., pp. 142–43.

22. McKay was working on the novel "Romance in Marseille," which he finished and later revised but never published (see Introduction, pp. 33). McKay's unhappiness in Paris was caused by the presence there of his wife, whom he had not seen since he left the United States in 1922. He had invited her to Paris after learning from his relatives in Jamaica that she was planning divorce proceedings in New York that were likely to prove very costly to him. After her arrival in Paris he spent a great deal of time persuading her to settle for a divorce that would not, as he expressed it, "take the little I have made out of my pocket." Letter from Claude McKay to William A. Bradley, June 17, 1929, in the Bradley–McKay correspondence, Paris. From time to time, McKay did send money for his daughter's support to his relatives in Jamaica. His daughter, Ruth Hope, whom he had never seen, grew up in Jamaica and lived with both her mother's and father's relatives. Letter from Rachel K. Cooper (Claude's sister) to Claude McKay, December 26, 1929, in the McKay Papers, James Weldon Johnson Collection, Yale University Library.

23. Frank Harris (1854–1931), who was Irish by birth, had been among the first to publish McKay's poetry in *Pearson's Magazine* in 1918. Although remembered today chiefly for his multivolume, semi-pornographic *Life and Loves* (1923), he had earlier had a great career in London as editor of the London *Evening News,* the *Fortnightly Review,* and the *Saturday Review.* George Bernard Shaw, Oscar Wilde, and H. G. Wells were among Harris' early discoveries as an editor, and all had appeared in his journals at the start of their careers. McKay thus knew him only in his declining years, when Harris was struggling hard (and sometimes unscrupulously) to keep himself financially afloat. McKay nevertheless loved Harris for his brilliant conversation, his courage in adversity, and for his unabated zest for life. In 1926

McKay met Harris in Nice and in *A Long Way from Home,* he recorded with sadness Harris' evident physical deterioration: ". . . Harris invited me to drink champagne with him. We went to the terrace of a cafe on the Promenade. Harris was not a steady free drinker as he was when I had known him seven years before in New York. His skillful hands trembled under the weight and accumulated cares of three-score years. His hair was dyed, and from the heat of the Midi and of alcohol some of the color had dissolved and mixed with the perspiration oozing from the deep lines of his face, which resembled an antique many-grooved panel with some of the paint peeled off" (p. 126). See also McKay's other descriptions of Harris in *A Long Way from Home,* op. cit., pp. 9–25, 97–99, 127–29, 265–71.

24. Ernest Dowson (1867–1900) was an English poet whose poem "Cynara" includes the often quoted refrain, "I have been faithful to thee, Cynara! in my fashion."

25. McKay made his first trip to Morocco in the fall of 1928. See his account in *A Long Way from Home,* op. cit., pp. 295–309.

26. The French critic Andre Levinson reviewed McKay's work in a series of three articles in *Les nouvelles litteraires* in the summer of 1929. A summary of his views on McKay can be found in Andre Levinson, *Figures americaines: dix-huit études sur des écrivains de ce temps* (Paris: Editions Victor Attinger, 1929), pp. 177–95.

27. The following poems by McKay appeared in the *Crisis* between 1924 and 1928: "The Skeleton" and "The Void," vol. 27 (June 1924), p. 67; "A Daughter of the American Revolution to Her Son," vol. 30 (March 1926), p. 228; "In the Hospital," vol. 33 (February 1927), p. 202; and "The International Spirit," vol. 34 (June 1928), p. 196.

28. Max Eastman, *The Enjoyment of Poetry* (New York: Charles Scribner's Sons, 1913).

29. Edgar Guest (1881–1959), was for many years on the staff of the *Detroit Free Press.* He wrote many volumes of popular verse.

30. Martin Tupper (1810–1889) was an English versifying moralizer whose *Proverbial Philosophy* (1838) has the distinction of being didactic prose written in verse form.

31. For McKay's views on Joyce, see *A Long Way from Home,* op. cit., p. 246.

32. For a summary discussion of the ideas of the New Humanism as it was presented by the conservative American critics Irving Babbitt (1865–1933) and Paul Elmer More (1864–1937), see Alfred Kazin, *On Native Grounds: An Interpretation of Modern American Prose Literature,* Anchor Books edition (New York: Doubleday, 1956), pp. 197–238.

33. McKay is apparently referring here to the Cubists, or more likely the lesser imitators of such Cubist masters as Picasso and Braque.

34. V. E. Meyerhold (1874–1942) was a Russian actor and director who established an experimental revolutionary theater in Moscow following the Russian Revolution.

35. Eastman cited as belonging to "the realm of literary truth," the following quote from Pascal: "I lay down as fact that, if all men knew what others say of them, there would not be four friends in the world." Quoted in *The Literary Mind*, op. cit., p. 244.

36. Julien Benda (1867–1956), the French philosophical and critical writer whose best-known work in English is *The Betrayal of the Intellectuals*, Beacon paperback edition (Boston: Beacon Press, 1955), which warns against the retreat from civilized values. The book was originally published in Paris in 1927.

37. At the time, McKay was writing his last novel, *Banana Bottom*.

5. EXPERIMENTS IN FICTION, 1928–1941

1. Claude McKay, *Banjo*, op. cit., p. 314.
2. Ibid., p. 314.
3. Letter from Claude McKay to Claire Lennard, January 31, 1947, in the McKay Papers, James Weldon Johnson Collection, Yale University Library.

6. LETTERS AND ESSAYS, 1934–1948

1. Maxim Lieber, author's representative and editor, served for a brief period as McKay's literary agent.

2. Max Eastman, *Artists in Uniform* (New York: Knopf, 1934).

3. Emma Goldman (1869–1940) was a Russian-born feminist and political anarchist who spent most of her adult life in the United States. On December 21, 1919, she was deported along with 248 other foreign-born radicals to the Soviet Union. She soon became disillusioned with the Bolshevik regime and left Russia in December 1921. In 1925 she published a full critique of the new Soviet state entitled *My Disillusionment in Russia*, Apollo paperback edition (New York: Thomas Y. Crowell, 1970). She spent the remainder of her life in Western Europe and Canada.

4. Louis Fischer, "The Tragedy of Trotsky," *Nation*, vol. 138 (May 2, 1934), pp. 498–99.

5. In *A Long Way from Home* (p. 140), McKay identified Marguerite Tucker as a friend from the *Liberator* period.

6. In his letters to Eastman, McKay never named the eccentric old professor, and his identity remains uncertain.

7. McKay is referring to Hanem Salem, a woman whom he met in Morocco. Her letters to him, some of which have had paragraphs deleted, are in the McKay Papers, James Weldon Johnson Collection, Yale University Library.

8. Glenway Wescott (1901–   ) is an American short-story writer, novelist, poet, and critic. His best-known work is perhaps his early volume of short stories, *Good-Bye Wisconsin* (1929). McKay first met him in France. See Claude McKay, *A Long Way from Home*, op. cit., p. 267.

9. Camp Greycourt (now called Camp LaGuardia) is still maintained by the City of New York as a refuge for destitute men. Today it houses homeless alcoholics and other derelicts, who use it as a place of "retirement." Mr. Hudson, Commander Howe, and Mr. Hale were all government officials responsible for the administration of relief in the New York City area.

10. A few of McKay's sonnets on the various cities he had visited were included in his *Selected Poems*, notably "Moscow," "Barcelona," and "Tetuán." Most, however, were never published. They are included among the McKay Papers in the James Weldon Johnson Collection, Yale University Library.

11. Heywood Broun (1888–1939) was an American journalist who in the 1930s wrote for the Scripps-Howard newspapers.

12. Freda Kirchwey edited the *Nation*. McKay is referring to his article "There Goes God! The Story of Father Divine and His Angels," *Nation*, vol. 138 (February 6, 1935), pp. 151–53.

13. Eric Posselt (1892–   ), American author and editor, was a friend of McKay's. During World War II, Posselt edited *Give Out! Songs of, by and for the Men in Service* (New York: Arrowhead Press, 1943).

14. Max Eastman, *Art and the Life of Action* (New York: Knopf, 1934).

15. This is a reference to Max Eastman's legal troubles over the distribution and film rights to the motion-picture documentary of the Russian Revolution *Tzar to Lenin*, which he made and produced in collaboration with Herman Axelbank. See Max Eastman, *Love and Revolution*, op. cit., pp. 527–32, 615–17.

16. Claude McKay, "Note of Harlem," *Modern Monthly*, vol. 8 (July 1934), p. 368. This poem was reprinted in Jean Wagner's *Les poètes nègres des Etats-Unis*, op. cit., p. 582.

17. The article appeared in the *Nation* (February 6, 1935). See

Claude McKay, "There Goes God! The Story of Father Divine and His Angels," op. cit., pp. 151–53.

18. Russell Blackwell, a cartographer, was a friend of McKay's. A man of strong democratic-socialist convictions, he eventually fought on the Republican side during the Spanish Civil War.

19. In the 1930s, Eastman's anti-Soviet views brought him into often bitter conflict with Michael Gold, Robert Minor, and other former members of the *Liberator* staff who joined the Communist party. Eastman's quarrel with Frank Harris occurred much earlier when the *Liberator* and *Pearson's Magazine* were both housed in the same Greenwich Village building. Bad feelings had developed between the two men when Harris published an erroneous, derogatory article about Lenin in *Pearson's,* which Eastman promptly exposed in the *Liberator* as factually incorrect.

20. Floyd Dell (1887–1969), the novelist; Crystal Eastman (1881–1928), Max Eastman's sister and a dedicated feminist and social reformer in her own right; and Robert Minor (1884–1952), the cartoonist, artist, and illustrator—were all at various times members of the *Liberator* editorial staff during McKay's association with the magazine.

21. The League of American Writers was a communist-inspired and controlled organization of writers, most of whom were not themselves members of the Communist party. Created in 1935 as part of the worldwide Popular Front of communist and western democratic forces against Fascism, the League ceased to exist in 1942. It never achieved the influence over American writers that McKay had feared and warned against in this and other articles.

22. These were all noncommunist writers during the 1930s.

23. Earl Browder (1891–   ), was the general secretary of the American Communist party throughout most of the 1930s.

24. Waldo Frank (1889–1967), American novelist and social critic, served as the chairman of the League from 1935 until 1937. Before the Second Congress convened, however, Frank published an open letter "asking for an international commission of Socialists and Communists 'to study the evidence of the Moscow trials [wherein Stalin condemned to death many top Bolsheviks for their alleged treason to the new Soviet state] and of Trotsky's counter charges.'" This proposal led Browder to attack Frank on the opening night of the Second Congress. See Daniel Aaron, *Writers on the Left,* op. cit., pp. 359–60.

25. Rorty's article appeared in the *Socialist Call* (June 5, 1937), p. 8.

26. Like the League of American Writers, the National Negro Congress was a united-front organization created in 1936. At first the Congress enjoyed wide noncommunist support among interested blacks

of all political persuasion. With A. Philip Randolph as its first titular president, it emphasized a general program of broad racial advancement. After 1940, however, Randolph and other noncommunists were forced out of their positions of leadership within the Congress, and it became almost exclusively a communist-dominated organization.

27. John Chamberlain (1903–   ), writer and editor, was the book editor of *Harper's Magazine* during this period; Frances Winwar (1900–   ) is the pen name of the novelist Frances Grebanier, nee Vinciguerra; Babette Deutsch (1895–   ) is a poet and critic.

28. Vladimir Mayakovsky (1893–1930) and Sergei Esenin (1895–1925) were prominent Russian poets of the early Soviet period who committed suicide.

29. McKay is probably referring to those few writers on the New York Federal Writers' Project who were allowed "to work at home on their own material with the sole stipulation that they report to the Project office once a week with evidence of their work." McKay and another black writer, the young Richard Wright, were two of ten writers who participated in this arrangement (Jerre Mangione, *The Dream and the Deal,* op. cit., p. 245).

30. Philip La Follette (1897–1965) was elected Governor of Wisconsin in 1934 on a Progressive party platform that called for extensive reforms on both the state and national levels.

31. The *Tagebuch* was a radical Berlin journal of the Weimar period. McKay had traveled to Berlin in 1930 for medical treatment (see note 60, pp. 322–23).

32. After some initial success with an earlier writers' group in the spring and summer of 1937, McKay's opposition to the admittance of whites had led to the group's disruption. This letter was, therefore, an effort to reconstitute a Negro Writers Guild along the lines he had originally envisioned. See his letter to the white liberal writer Helen Boardman in the McKay Papers, James Weldon Johnson Collection, Yale University Library.

33. The Young Liberators was a youth group associated with the procommunist Harlem magazine *The Liberator,* which was published in the mid-1930s.

34. McKay had more to say regarding Father Divine's united front with the Communists in *Harlem: Negro Metropolis,* op. cit., pp. 47–49.

35. Ira Kemp began his career in Harlem politics as an independent soapbox orator, one of many in Harlem during the Depression years.

36. Frank Crosswaith (1892–1965) black socialist and labor organizer, devoted his life to the problems of black workers in the United States.

37. Adam Clayton Powell, Jr., "Soapbox," *New York Amsterdam News* (October 30, 1937), p. 13.

38. During the 1930s the Communist party advocated self-determination for Negroes in the southern Black Belt, where Negroes composed the majority of the population. For a summary discussion of the Communist position regarding black nationalism during this period, see Theodore Draper, *American Communism and Soviet Russia,* op. cit., pp. 315–56.

39. Alain Locke, "Review of *A Long Way from Home,*" *New Challenge,* op. cit., pp. 81–85.

40. George S. Schuyler (1895–   ), black American journalist and novelist, had a regular column in the *Pittsburgh Courier* during this period. Noted for his caustic humor and satire, his work was often reprinted in other black newspapers.

41. George S. Schuyler, *Black No More* (New York: Macaulay, 1931).

42. McKay was fond of referring to the Urban League as a "welfare organization," but it has always had the broader function of working to open wider career opportunities for Negroes in American business and industry, in addition to maintaining a variety of social services through the years. The Urban League was established in 1911.

43. Sufi Abdul Hamid died in a plane crash, July 30, 1938.

44. Ted Poston, *"Harlem:* Claude McKay's Book Sees Negroes' 'Way Out' in Economic Segregation," *New Leader* (November 23, 1940), p. 5. Ted Poston (1906–   ) is a black American journalist who writes for the *New York Post.*

45. Although chosen as an alternate selection by the Book-of-the-Month Club, *Harlem: Negro Metropolis* sold only slightly over 1300 copies.

46. Edward K. Welsh (1902–   ) had a long career as an international labor-union organizer for the American Federation of Labor–Congress of Industrial Organizations (the AFL–CIO).

47. Planning for the March on Washington began in January 1941, and the March was eventually set for July 1. It was called off when on June 25, 1941, President Franklin D. Roosevelt issued his Executive Order 8802, which forbade discrimination in the employment of Negro workers in defense industries or government. Although hailed as a significant victory by many black leaders the Order was in fact often ignored by employers, especially in the South.

48. After the fall of France to Germany in 1940, a pro-Nazi French government was established in the south of France at Vichy.

49. W. A. Domingo (1889–1968) was not released from British detention until early in 1943. A native of Jamaica, Domingo had long been involved in black radical activities. He was the first editor of Marcus Garvey's *Negro World,* and in 1920 he established his own journal, the *Emancipator,* which ran for several weeks. He also wrote

for Randolph and Owen's *Messenger*. After the publication of Mc-Kay's poem "If We Must Die" in 1919, Domingo seized upon the theme and commented: "New Negroes are determined to make their dying a costly investment for all concerned. If they must die, they are determined that they shall not travel the valley of the shadow of death alone, but that some of their oppressors shall be their companions.

"This spirit is but a reflex of the Great War. . . . The demand is uncompromisingly made for either liberty or death, and since death is likely to be a two-edged sword, it will be to the advantage of those in a position to do so to give the race its long denied liberty.

"The New Negro has arrived with stiffened backbone, dauntless manhood, defiant eye, steady hand, and a will of iron. His creed is admirably summed up in the poem of Claude McKay" (from the *Messenger*, September 1919).

Although Domingo lived in New York, where he ran a successful West Indian import business in the years after World War II, he worked for Jamaican national independence and retained his Jamaican citizenship until his death.

50. The riot to which McKay refers took place in Houston, Texas, in September 1917. Convinced their lives were endangered, the Negro soldiers in Houston armed themselves and killed seventeen whites.

51. In 1938, McKay offered the following thoughts concerning a possible direction for American Negro group organization:

"These are amazingly epochal times, with the world passing through profound changes. Fifteen millions of colored Americans constitute the largest minority in this country. Are we organized as a group to promote our interests under the changing world order? . . .

"The colored minority should have an organization adequate to the needs of these times. The National Association for the Advancement of Colored People is to our group what the Civil Liberties Union is to the nation. The Urban League, which has broken new ground under the New Deal, is essentially a social service agency. Our group needs a new organization with the force and drive of the Jewish Congress. . . .

"The colored group should organize along the lines laid down in the late James Weldon Johnson's little book, *Negro Americans, What Next?* But as . . . Johnson suggested, I believe the new organization should be an outgrowth of existing organizations. It should be controlled by an executive of responsible colored leaders. Perhaps the first step towards such a new organization should be the formation of a real unity group, which would seek to bring the elder statesmen of the colored minority, such as W. E. B. Du Bois, Robert Russa Moton, Eugene Kinckle Jones, and others to join a round table discussion with younger men such as Philip Randolph, Walter White, Charles S. Johnson, and Professor Abram Harris.

"Certainly our group should be as much interested in the rich experience of living leaders . . . as it is in the achievements of Frederick Douglass, and others of his period. The group should guard against those elements, which while pretending to work in the interests of Negro unity are actually sabotaging it.

"This is an historic period of profound social and economic changes and adjustments on a world scale. And the color problem today is radically different from what it was twenty-five years ago. Then it was a problem of color prejudice, peculiar to our group, with the issues more or less highly individualized. Today it is the intricate problem of minority adjustment and survival under highly centralized systems.

"Other minorities are interested in the colored minority, the largest in the country. If it is effectively organized, it could be in the vanguard of progressive forces. . . .

"The colored minority faces the issue of deciding whether it will organize itself, so that it can stand on an equal footing with other minorities, such as Jews and Catholics and command their respect and cooperation, or whether it prefers fine-sounding, but unreal organizations, which have no more influence and authority than the bombastic and poetic periods of the old-fashioned Negro preacher." (From Claude McKay, "Author Assails [National] Negro Congress for Message Sent to Washington on Jews," *New York Amsterdam News* [November 26, 1938], p. 11.)

52. Abdel-Krim (1882–1963) was the leader of the Moors in the Rif region of Morocco. His war against Spanish and French domination of the area lasted, with brief interludes of peace, from 1921 until his defeat in 1926. See Rupert Forneaux, *Abdel-Krim: Emir of the Rif* (London: Secker and Warburg, 1967); and David S. Woolman, *Rebels in the Rif: Abd El Krim and the Rif Rebellion* (Stanford, Calif.: Stanford University Press, 1968) for two recent accounts of Abdel-Krim.

53. Dorothy Thompson (1894–1961) was an American journalist whose column was syndicated by the *New York Herald-Tribune* between 1936 and 1941.

54. Anne O'Hare McCormick (d. 1954) was a free-lance foreign correspondent for the *New York Times* during the interwar years.

55. Zaghlul Pasha (d. 1927), was the leader of Egyptian nationalist forces after World War I; he demanded the complete independence of Egypt from British domination.

56. Kemal Ataturk (1881–1938) was the first president of the Turkish Republic (from 1923). Under Ataturk's leadership, Turkey largely abandoned its feudal institutions and entered upon a period of revolutionary reforms designed to modernize and to strengthen its position as a contemporary European state. Shorn of its ancient Middle Eastern Empire as a result of defeat in World War I, Turkey thus

sought to revitalize itself under Kemal Ataturk's vigorous leadership during the 1920s and 1930s.

57. The Croix de Feu and the Camelots du Roi were extreme right-wing, Fascist-type organizations in France during the interwar period.

7. THE MOVE TO CATHOLICISM

1. Elmer Davis (1890–1958), the writer and distinguished radio news commentator, headed the Office of War Information during World War II.

2. Margaret Lane was the business manager of the *Liberator*. Edward F. Mylius was a bookkeeper who worked for the *Liberator* for a while in 1921. When he left the magazine in October 1921, he took with him $4500 in operating funds, a theft that almost led to the *Liberator*'s immediate demise. See Max Eastman, *Love and Revolution*, op. cit., pp. 265–72.

3. McKay was given the use of a cottage in Squash Hollow by Tom and Mary Keating (formerly Mary Jerdo), two Catholic friends he had met at the Harlem Friendship House. Charles Page was a resident of Squash Hollow who allowed McKay the use of his mailbox.

4. These are the poems of McKay's unpublished "Cycle Manuscript," in the McKay Papers, James Weldon Johnson Collection, Yale University Library (see note 88 on pp. 324–25).

5. McKay's religious feelings had been most strongly awakened in Spain and Morocco, and not simply by their respective religions but perhaps more importantly by the distinctive quality of their people. In 1929 he wrote to William A. Bradley that "French life is too nervous and sharp for my temperament. It may be that I exaggerate but as soon as I crossed the border (into Spain) I felt as if I had escaped from a swarm of wasps to find myself among a people who can appreciate simple dignity when they meet with it, because dignity is a fundamental of their social life. This is my fourth visit to Spain and each time my liking increases. I am afraid I shall at last grow romantic about *some* country" (Claude McKay to William A. Bradley, October 2, 1929, Bradley–McKay Correspondence, Bradley Papers, Paris).

Morocco affected McKay in similar ways. To Max Eastman he wrote that "no place has satisfied me since I left home as much as Morocco. There are many things in the life of the natives, their customs and superstitions, reminiscent of Jamaica" (Claude McKay to Max Eastman, December 1, 1930, Eastman–McKay Correspondence, Eastman Papers). Again, in 1931 McKay wrote to Bradley that "The 'best seller' will be the Jamaica book—dealing with the religious customs and social [life] of the peasants. I am ripe for it as I am also feeling very religious now among the Moslems" (Claude McKay to William A. Bradley, January 25, 1931, Bradley–McKay Correspondence, Bradley Papers, Paris).

6. This is not quite correct. McKay was educated to agnosticism by his brother, U'Theo, who had rejected their father's Protestant orthodoxy.

7. Margaret Halsey, *Color Blind: A White Woman Looks at the Negro* (New York: Simon and Schuster, 1946).

8. Dorothy Day (1897–   ) is the cofounder with Peter Maurin of the Catholic Worker Movement and editor of the *Catholic Worker*. McKay had first met her in Greenwich Village during the *Liberator* period before she had converted to Catholicism. Her movement and paper have been consistently Christian, socialist, and pacifist.

9. McKay is referring to the unpublished poems of his "Cycle Manuscript," op. cit.

10. Max Eastman, "A Case of Campaign Oratory? *New Leader* Ignores Vital Election Issue, Eastman Contends," *New Leader* (November 25, 1944), p. 4. Eastman claimed that the *New Leader* had not answered "fairly and squarely" many of the questions Governor Thomas E. Dewey of New York had raised concerning American foreign and domestic policies during his unsuccessful campaign for the presidency in 1944.

11. The poem actually appeared in January. See Claude McKay, "Look Within," *Catholic Worker,* vol. 11 (January 1945), p. 8.

12. Samuel M. ("Sol") Levitas (1894–1961) was the editor of the *New Leader* during the period McKay contributed to it.

13. Max Eastman, "Behind Soviet Foreign Policy," *American Mercury,* vol. 7 (September 1946), pp. 261–69.

14. Maxim Gorky, *Reminiscences of Nikolaevich Tolstoy,* authorized translation by S. S. Koteliansky and Leonard Woolf (New York: B. W. Huebsch, 1920).

15. McKay is referring to his unpublished memoir, "My Green Hills of Jamaica," op. cit. In *A Long Way from Home* (p. 111), McKay stated that Walter White was "whiter than many Europeans—even biologically," and that he was "Negroid simply because he closely identifies himself with the Negro group." In his book, *A Rising Wind* (Garden City, N.Y.: Doubleday, Doran and Co., 1945), pp. 54–55, White reported that Lady Astor said much the same thing.

16. McKay is referring to the Catholic Worker mission house, which ministers to the needs of the down and out on New York's Bowery.

17. Ammon Hennacy (1893–1970), the Catholic anarchist, was a long-time crusader for peace.

18. Eastman's book was published in England as *Marx, Lenin and the Science of Revolution* (London: George Allen & Unwin, 1926).

19. In a speech in Madison Square Garden on September 12, 1946, ex-Vice President Henry Wallace warned that the United States "could not handle the forces in the world by a 'get tough' policy with Russia. . . ." Wallace cautioned against the United States trying to pick up the broken pieces of British imperialism in the Middle East and elsewhere in the world.

EPILOGUE

1. Letter from Claude McKay to Carl Cowl, March 1, 1947, McKay Papers, James Weldon Johnson Collection, Yale University Library.

2. McKay published twelve poems in the *Catholic Worker* between 1945 and 1947 (see Bibliography).

3. See Claude McKay, "On Becoming a Roman Catholic," *The Epistle,* vol. 7 (Spring 1945), pp. 43–45; "Why I Became a Catholic," *Ebony,* vol. 1 (March 1946), p. 32; and "This Race Problem," *March of Progress,* vol. 9 (1945), pp. 264–67. Perhaps the best statement regarding McKay's progress toward Catholicism and his life within the Church is Eddie Doherty's report of his interview with McKay, entitled "Poet's Progress," *Extension,* vol. 41 (September 1946), pp. 5, 46.

4. Letter from Claude McKay to Carl Cowl, February 13, 1948, McKay Papers, James Weldon Johnson Collection, Yale University Library.

5. Claude McKay, "Boyhood in Jamaica," *Phylon,* op. cit., p. 146. Although these words were attributed to McKay himself by Cedric Dover, who edited this article from McKay's memoir, "My Green Hills of Jamaica," this sentence does not appear anywhere in McKay's original manuscript, but seems to have been added by Dover as an unacknowledged tribute to his late friend. Cedric Dover, the author of *American Negro Art* (Greenwich, Conn.: New York Graphic Society, 1960), was an Anglo-Indian. He and McKay both wrote memoirs of their respective colonial childhoods and at one time planned to publish them together in a volume that was to have been entitled "East Indian —West Indian."

Bibliography

I. WORKS NOT CITED IN NOTES

In the last ten years there has been a slow but steady growth of interest in Claude McKay by critics and scholars. Opinion concerning the quality and significance of his work is far from unanimous, but there seems to be a dawning awareness that despite the uneven artistry of his work, the whole of it nevertheless surpasses the sum of its parts. The following is not a comprehensive list of everything that has been written about McKay; it is instead a partial list of the critical commentary about him that has appeared since his death in 1948 and is intended to supplement the works already cited in the Notes.

1. Unpublished Thesis and Dissertations

Conroy, Sister M. James. "Claude McKay: Negro Poet and Novelist." Unpublished Ph.D. dissertation, English Department, Notre Dame University, 1968.

Cooper, Wayne. "Claude McKay: The Evolution of a Negro Radical, 1889–1923." Unpublished M.A. Thesis, History Department, Tulane University, 1965.

Lang, Phyllis Martin. "Claude McKay: The Later Years, 1934–1948." Unpublished Ph.D. dissertation, English Department, University of Illinois at Urbana–Champaign, 1972.

2. Articles and Books

Barksdale, Richard K. "Symbolism and Irony in McKay's *Home to Harlem.*" *CLA Journal,* vol. 15 (March 1972), pp. 338–44.

Barton, Rebecca Chalmers. *Witnesses for Freedom: Negro Americans in Autobiography.* New York: Harper and Brothers, 1948.

Bronz, Stephen. *Roots of Negro Racial Consciousness: The 1920s, Three Harlem Renaissance Authors.* New York: Libra, 1964.

Cartey, Wilfred. "Four Shadows of Harlem." *Negro Digest,* vol. 18 (August 1969), pp. 22–25, 83–92.

Collier, Eugenia. "The Four-Way Dilemma of Claude McKay." *CLA Journal,* vol. 15 (March 1972), pp. 345–53.

Conroy, Sister M. James. "The Vagabond Motif in the Writings of Claude McKay." *Negro American Literature Forum,* vol. 5 (Spring 1971), pp. 15–23.

Cruse, Harold. *The Crisis of the Negro Intellectual: From Its Origin to the Present.* Apollo paperback ed. New York: William Morrow, 1967.

Cooper, Wayne. "Claude McKay." *Encyclopaedia Britannica,* 1969 edn.

Dover, Cedric. "These Things We Shared: An Appendix." *Phylon,* vol. 14 (2nd Quarter, 1953), pp. 143–44.

Drayton, Arthur. "McKay's Human Pity: A Note on His Protest Poetry." *Black Orpheus,* No. 17 (June 1965), pp. 39–48.

Gayle, Addison. *Claude McKay, the Black Poet at War.* Detroit: Broadside Press, 1972.

Jackson, Blyden. "The Essential McKay." *Phylon,* vol. 14 (1953), pp. 216–17.

Kaye, Jacqueline. "Claude McKay's *Banjo.*" *Présence Africaine,* vol. 73 (1970), pp. 165–69.

Margolies, Edward. *Native Sons: A Critical Study of Twentieth-Century Negro American Authors.* New York: J. P. Lippincott, 1968.

Ramchand, Kenneth. "The Road to *Banana Bottom.*" In *Modern Black Novelists: A Collection of Critical Essays.* M. G. Cook, ed. Englewood Cliffs, N.J.: Prentice-Hall, 1971.

Ramchand, Kenneth. *The West Indian Novel and Its Background.* New York: Barnes and Noble, 1970.

Smith, Robert A. "Claude McKay: An Essay in Criticism." *Phylon,* vol. 9 (1948), pp. 270–73.

Stoff, Michael B. "Claude McKay and the Cult of the Primitive." In *The Harlem Renaissance Remembered: Essays.* Arna Bontemps, ed. New York: Dodd, Mead, 1972, pp. 126–46.

Tolson, Melvin B. "Claude McKay's Art." *Poetry,* vol. 83 (1954), pp. 287–90.

II. WORKS BY CLAUDE McKAY

In addition to McKay's published works, there is a substantial amount of unpublished material in private collections and research libraries in the United States and abroad. The McKay Papers in the James Weldon Johnson Collection at Yale consists of the personal papers, manuscript material, and letters McKay had in his possession at the time of his death. The remainder of his letters are widely scattered. There are a significant number of letters by McKay, however, in the following collections: the Schomburg Collection and the H. L. Mencken Papers at the New York Public Library, the William Stanley Braithwaite Papers at the Harvard University Library; the Alain Locke Papers at the Howard University Library in Washington, D.C.; the NAACP Papers in the Library of Congress; the Eastman Papers in the University of Indiana Library at Bloomington; and the Rosenwald Fund Papers at the Fisk University Library in Nashville, Tennessee.

Of all McKay's unpublished material, his letters are by far the most important, from both a literary and historical point of view. He was an excellent letter writer, and necessity forced him to write many. A complete edition of his letters should someday reveal one of the great stories in Negro American literary history.

The bibliography below lists McKay's published books and also most of his articles, book reviews, poems, and short stories, which are arranged in alphabetical order according to the magazines in which they originally appeared. Except for those books which were originally published in a foreign language, the foreign editions of McKay's books are not included in this bibliography.

1. Published Books

AUTOBIOGRAPHY

A Long Way from Home. New York: Lee Furman, 1937.

A Long Way from Home. New York: Arno Press, 1969.

A Long Way from Home. Harvest paperback ed., Introduction by St. Clair Drake. New York: Harcourt Brace Jovanovich, 1970.

NOVELS

Banana Bottom. New York: Harper and Bros., 1933.

Banana Bottom. Chatham, N.J.: Chatham Book Seller, 1970.

Banjo: A Story Without a Plot. New York: Harper and Bros., 1929.

Banjo: A Story Without a Plot. Harvest paperback ed. New York: Harcourt Brace Jovanovich, 1970.

Home to Harlem. New York: Harper and Bros., 1928.

Home to Harlem. Avon paperback ed. New York: Avon, 1951.

Home to Harlem. Cardinal paperback ed. New York: Pocket Books, 1965.

COLLECTED POETRY

Constab Ballads. London: Watts, 1912.

The Dialect Poetry of Claude McKay: Two Volumes in One.

Vol. 1: *Songs of Jamaica;* vol. 2: *Constab Ballads.* Preface by Wayne Cooper. Freeport, N.Y.: Books for Libraries, 1972.
   Harlem Shadows. New York: Harcourt, Brace, 1922.
   Selected Poems of Claude McKay. New York: Bookman Associates, 1953.
   Selected Poems of Claude McKay. Harvest paperback ed. New York: Harcourt, Brace and World, 1969.
   Songs from Jamaica. London: Augener, 1912. (Six songs set to music. Lyrics by Claude McKay; music by Walter Jekyll. Eleven pages.)
   Songs of Jamaica. Kingston, Jamaica: Aston W. Gardner, 1912.
   Spring in New Hampshire and Other Poems. London: Grant Richards, 1920.

SHORT STORIES
   Gingertown. New York: Harper and Bros., 1932.
   Gingertown. Freeport, N.Y.: Books for Libraries, 1972.
   Sudom Lincha ("Under lynch law"—original English title not determined). Moscow, 1925.

OTHER PUBLISHED BOOKS
   Harlem: Negro Metropolis. New York: E. P. Dutton, 1940.
   Harlem: Negro Metropolis. Harvest paperback ed. New York: Harcourt Brace Jovanovich, 1972.
   Negry v Amerike ("The Negroes in America"). Translated from English into Russian by P. Okhrimenko. Moscow, Petrograd, 1923.

2. Articles and Book Reviews

The African
   "A Little Lamb to Lead Them: A True Narrative," vol. 1 (March–April 1938), pp. 107–8, 112.
American Mercury
   "Father Divine's Rebel Angel," vol. 51 (September 1940), pp. 73–80.
   "Mystic Happiness in Harlem," vol. 47 (August 1939), pp. 444–50.
Common Sense
   "Dynamite in Africa: Are the Popular Fronts Suppressing Colonial Independence?," vol. 7 (March 1938), pp. 8–11.
Crisis
   "Letter to the Editor," vol. 33 (July 1921), p. 102.
   "A Moscow Lady," vol. 28 (September 1924), pp. 225–28.

"Soviet Russia and the Negro," vol. 27 (December 1923–January 1924), pp. 61–65, 114–18.

"What Is and What Isn't," vol. 18 (April 1924), pp. 259–62.

Ebony

"Why I Became a Catholic," vol. 1 (March 1946), p. 32.

The Epistle

"On Becoming a Roman Catholic," vol. 2 (Spring 1945), pp. 43–45.

Jewish Frontier

"For Group Survival," vol. 4 (October 1937), pp. 19–26.

"Lest We Forget," vol. 8 (January 1940), pp. 9–11.

The Liberator

"The American Type [a review of *Three Soldiers* by John Dos Passos]," vol. 5 (January 1922), pp. 8–9.

"Birthright [review of *Birthright* by T. S. Stribling]," vol. 5 (August 1922), pp. 15–16.

"A Black Star [review of *Emperor Jones* by Eugene O'Neill]," vol. 4 (August 1921), p. 25.

"Garvey as a Negro Moses," vol. 5 (April 1922), pp. 8–9.

"He Who Gets Slapped [review of *He Who Gets Slapped* by Leonid Andreyev]," vol. 5 (May 1922), pp. 24–25.

"How Black Sees Green and Red," vol. 4 (June 1921), pp. 17, 20–21.

"A Negro Extravaganza [review of *Shuffle Along,* a musical review by Noble Sissle and Eubie Blake]," vol. 4 (December 1921), pp. 24–26.

"What Is Lacking in the Theatre?," vol. 5 (March 1922), pp. 20–21.

March of Progress

"This Race Problem," vol. 9 (1945), pp. 264–67.

McClure's

"Review of *Home to Harlem,*" in James Clarke, ed., "Significant Books Reviewed by Their Own Authors," vol. 40 (June 1928), p. 81.

Messenger

"Letter to Editor," vol. 4 (October 1920), p. 7.

Nation

"Harlem Runs Wild," vol. 140 (April 3, 1935), pp. 382–83.

"Labor Steps out in Harlem," vol. 145 (October 16, 1937), pp. 399–402.

"North African Triangle," vol. 156 (May 8, 1943), pp. 663–65.

"There Goes God! The Story of Father Divine and His Angels," vol. 140 (February 6, 1935), pp. 151–53.

Negro History Bulletin

"An Unpublished Letter from Claude McKay, Poet and Literateur," vol. 13 (April 1968), pp. 10–11.

New Leader

"Anti-Semite Propaganda Fails to Attract Negroes," May 20, 1939, pp. 5–6.

"Claude McKay Replies to Poston on Solution of Negro Problems," December 7, 1940, p. 6.

"Fear of Segregation Furthers Negro Disunity," November 15, 1941, p. 4.

"Heard on the Left," August 30, 1941, p. 3.

"Moroccan African Colonies, Graveyard of Spanish Government, Threatens French Liberties," February 18, 1939, pp. 2, 5.

"Morocco: Duce Uses Anti-Semitism to Win Moslems to Fascism," November 18, 1939, pp. 4, 6.

"Morocco: Nerve Center of Nations' Colonial Power Politics," November 11, 1939, p. 4.

"Nazi Control of France Threatens Liberty of French Colonials," September 27, 1941, p. 5.

"Negro Author Sees Disaster If the Communist Party Gains Control of Negro Workers," September 10, 1938, p. 5.

"Negroes Are Anti-Nazi But Will Fight Anglo-Saxon Discrimination," October 25, 1941, p. 4.

" 'New' Crime Wave Old Story to Harlemites: Poverty Brings Prostitution, 'Mugging,' Robberies," November 29, 1941, p. 5.

"Out of the War Years: Lincoln, Apostle of a New America," February 13, 1943, p. 4.

"Pact Exploded Communist Propaganda Among Negroes," September 23, 1939, pp. 4, 7.

"Where the News Ends," June 10, 1939, p. 8.

New York Amsterdam News

"Author Assails Negro Congress for Message Sent to Washington on Jews: Calls Body Organization of Leaders; No Followers," November 26, 1938, p. 11.

"Claude McKay Versus Powell," April 15, 1939, p. 11.

"Claude McKay Says," November 6, 1937, p. 4.

"Letter to Editor," July 23, 1938, p. 8.

"Looking Forward," April 22, 1939, p. 11.

"Looking Forward," May 13, 1939, p. 13.

"Looking Forward," May 20, 1939, p. 13.

"Looking Forward," May 27, 1939, p. 12.

"McKay on Spain," February 25, 1939, p. 7.

"McKay Says Schuyler Is Writing 'Nonsense,' " November 20, 1937.

Opportunity

"A Job in London," vol. 15 (March 1937), pp. 72–75.

"Once More the Germans Face Black Troops," vol. 17 (November 1939), pp. 324–28.

"Race and Color in East Asia [review of *Inside Asia* by John Gunther]," vol. 17 (August 1939), pp. 228–30.

Pearson's Magazine

"A Negro Poet Writes," vol. 39 (September 1918), pp. 275–76.

Phylon

"Boyhood in Jamaica," vol. 13 (2nd Quarter, 1953), pp. 134–46.

Workers' Dreadnought

"A Black Man Replies," April 24, 1920, p. 2.

"The Capitalist Way: Lettow-Vorbeck," February 7, 1920, p. 6.

"Communism and the Local Councils of Action," September 25, 1920, p. 6 [pseud. Hugh Hope].

"An International Money Crisis," February 14, 1920, p. 8.

"The Leader of the Bristol Revolutionaries," August 7, 1920, p. 7 [pseud. Hugh Hope].

"Letter to the Editor," October 2, 1920, p. 2 [pseud. Hugh Hope].

"Review of *Poems* by L. A. Motler," August 21, 1920, p. 2.

"Review of *Reminiscences of Leo Tolstoy* by Maxim Gorky," August 21, 1920, p. 2.

"Socialism and the Negro," January 31, 1920, pp. 1–2.

3. Poems

Bookman

"Mulatto," vol. 42 (September 1925), p. 67.

Cambridge Magazine

"After the Winter," "Alfonso, Dressing to Wait at Table, Sings," "The Barrier," "The Castaways," "Flowers of Passion," "I Shall Return," "Love Song," "The Lynching," "A Memory of June," "Morning Joy," "North and South," "On Broadway," "Reminiscences," "Rest in Peace," "The Spanish Needle," "Spring in New Hampshire," "To O. E. A.," "To Winter," "To Work," "The Tropics in New York," "When Dawn Comes to the City," "Winter in the Country," vol. 10 (Summer 1920), pp. 55–59.

Catholic Worker

"And No White Liberal Is the Negro's Friend," vol. 12 (October 1945), pp. 4–5.

"Around Me Roar and Crash the Pagan Isms," vol. 12 (July 1945), p. 4.

"Christ Among the Dictators," vol. 12 (October 1945), pp. 4–5.

"Faith," vol. 11 (January 1946), p. 3.

"I Turn to God," vol. 12 (July 1945), p. 4.

"It Is the Negro's Tragedy I Feel," vol. 12 (July 1945), p. 4.

"Look Within," vol. 11 (January 1945), p. 8.

"Middle Ages," vol. 13 (May 1946), p. 5.

"Tiger," vol. 12 (January 1946), p. 3.

"Truth," vol. 12 (January 1946), p. 3.

"The Wise Men of the East," vol. 12 (October 1945), pp. 4–5.

"The Word," vol. 14 (July 1947), p. 2.

Challenge

"For a Leader," vol. 1 (September 1934), p. 5.

Crisis

"A Daughter of the American Revolution to Her Son," vol. 30 (March 1926), p. 228.

"In the Hospital," vol. 33 (February 1927), p. 202.

"The International Spirit," vol. 34 (June 1928), p. 196.

"The Skeleton" and "The Void," vol. 27 (June 1924), p. 67.

Interracial Review

"The New Day," vol. 19 (March 1946), p. 37.

Liberator

"Absence," vol. 5 (March 1922), p. 22.

"Africa," vol. 4 (August 1921), p. 10.

"After the Winter," vol. 2 (July 1919), p. 20.

"Alone," vol. 5 (July 1922), p. 14.

"America," vol. 4 (December 1921), p. 9.

"Baptism," vol. 4 (October 1921), p. 7.

"The Barriers," vol. 2 (July 1919), p. 20.

"A Capitalist at Dinner," vol. 2 (July 1919), p. 20.

"The Dominant White," vol. 2 (April 1919), p. 14.

"The Easter Flower," vol. 4 (March 1921), p. 6.

"Enslaved," vol. 4 (July 1921), p. 6.

"Flirtation," vol. 4 (August 1921), p. 10.

"French Leave," vol. 5 (April 1922), p. 27.

"Futility," vol. 5 (January 1922), p. 23.

"Home Thoughts," vol. 3 (February 1920), p. 19.

"If We Must Die," vol. 2 (July 1919), p. 21.

"In Bondage," vol. 4 (August 1921), p. 10.

"Jasmines," vol. 4 (August 1921), p. 11.

"The Little Peoples," vol. 2 (July 1919), p. 21.

"A Memory of June," vol. 4 (August 1921), p. 10.

"Morning Joy," vol. 4 (August 1921), p. 11.

"Mother," vol. 3 (March 1920), p. 24.

"The Negro Dancers," vol. 2 (July 1919), p. 20.

"Negro Spirituals," vol. 5 (May 1922), p. 16.

"The New Forces," vol. 5 (July 1922), p. 14.

"Night Fire," vol. 5 (May 1922), p. 16.

"On the Road," vol. 5 (March 1922), p. 22.

"La Paloma in London," vol. 5 (January 1922), p. 23.

"Petrograd: May Day, 1923," vol. 6 (August 1923), p. 15.

"A Roman Holiday," vol. 2 (July 1919), p. 21.

"Spring in New Hampshire," vol. 2 (August 1919), p. 46.

"Subway Wind," vol. 2 (August 1921), p. 10.

"Thirst," vol. 4 (December 1921), p. 9.

"Through Agony," vol. 4 (December 1921), p. 9.

"The Tired Worker," vol. 2 (August 1919), p. 46.

"To the Entrenched Classes," vol. 5 (May 1922), p. 16.

"To Ethiopia," vol. 3 (February 1920), p. 7.

"To One Coming North," vol. 4 (August 1921), p. 11.

"To the White Fiends," vol. 2 (September 1919), p. 25.

"The Tropics in New York," vol. 3 (May 1920), p. 48.

"The White City," vol. 4 (October 1921), p. 7.

"The White House," vol. 5 (May 1922), p. 16.

Literary Digest

"America"; "Home Thoughts"; "Outcast," vol. 75 (October 28, 1922), p. 33.

Messenger

"J'accuse," vol. 3 (October 1919), p. 24.

"Labor's Day," vol. 3 (September 1919), p. 31.

Milwaukee Arts Monthly

"Honeymoon" and "Moon Song," vol. 1 (October 1922), p. 8.

Modern Monthly

"Note of Harlem," vol. 8 (July 1934), p. 368.

Nation

"Home Song," vol. 122 (March 24, 1926), p. 318.

New Masses

"Song of New York, vol. 1 (May 1926), p. 15.

Opportunity

"America," vol. 2 (May 1924), p. 142.

"America in Retrospect," vol. 4 (November 1926), p. 342.

"America in Retrospect," vol. 27 (January 1949), p. 9.

"Desolate," vol. 4 (November 1926), p. 338.

"My House," vol. 4 (November 1926), p. 342.

Pearson's Magazine

"The Conqueror"; "Harlem Shadows"; "Is It Worthwhile?," vol. 39 (September, 1918), p. 276.

"My Love," vol. 48 (March 1922), p. 33.

"Soul and Body," vol. 45 (December 1919), p. 664.

"To the White Fiends," vol. 39 (September 1918), p. 276.

Workers' Dreadnought
    "Battle," October 9, 1920, p. 5 [pseud. Hugh Hope].
    "The Beast," July 10, 1920, p. 8 [pseud. Hugh Hope].
    "Birds of Prey," October 9, 1920, p. 5 [pseud. Hugh Hope].
    "A Hero of the Wars," April 17, 1920, p. 2 [pseud. Hugh Hope].
    "Joy in the Woods," April 10, 1920, p. 3.
    "Re-Affirmation," July 3, 1920, p. 7 [pseud. Hugh Hope].
    "Reality," April 24, 1920, p. 1 [pseud. Hugh Hope].
    "Samson," January 10, 1920, p. 1601.
    "Song of the New Soldier and Worker," April 3, 1920, p. 4 [pseud.
Hugh Hope].
    "Summer Morn in New Hampshire," July 31, 1920, p. 6.
    "Travail," January 10, 1920, p. 1601.
    "To 'Holy' Russia," February 28, 1920, p. 7.
    "Verse [two poems]," October 9, 1920, p. 5 [pseud. Hugh Hope].

4. Short Stories (All of the following except "The Little Lincoln" were included in "Gingertown.")

    "High Ball," *Opportunity,* vol. 5 (May–June 1927), pp. 141–44,
169–72.
    "The Little Lincoln," *The Liberator,* vol. 5 (February 1922), pp.
24–25.
    "Mattie and Her Sweetman," *This Quarter,* vol. 2 (October–
November–December 1929), pp. 119–210.
    "Mauvaise tête [Truant]," translated from the English by Georgette
Camille, *Europe* (Paris), vol. 26 (June 15, 1931), pp. 207–26.

Index of Names